The Guide to

SUCCESSFUL SHORT-TERM
PROGRAMS ABROAD Second Edition

D1418294

Edited by Sarah E. Spencer + Kathy Tuma

NAFSA

**Association of
International Educators**

NAFSA: Association of International Educators is an association of individuals worldwide advancing international education and exchange. NAFSA serves its members, their institutions and organizations, and others engaged in international education and exchange and global workforce development. NAFSA sets and upholds standards of good practice; provides training, professional development, and networking opportunities; and advocates for international education.

Library of Congress Cataloging-in-Publication Data

The guide to successful short-term programs abroad / edited by Sarah E. Spencer & Kathy Tuma. -- 2nd ed.
    p. cm.
 Includes bibliographical references and index.
 ISBN 978-0-912207-91-9
 1. Foreign study--Administration--Handbooks, manuals, etc. 2. American students--Travel--Handbooks, manuals, etc. 3. College students--Travel--Handbooks, manuals, etc. 4. Faculty advisors--Handbooks, manuals, etc. 5. College administrators--Handbooks, manuals, etc. I. Spencer, Sarah E. II. Tuma, Kathy. III. NAFSA: Association of International Educators (Washington, D.C.)

 LB2376.G75 2007
 370.116--dc22

                    2007029075

TABLE OF CONTENTS

C

PART II
PRINCIPLES OF ACADEMIC COURSE DESIGN

PART III
PROGRAM DEVELOPMENT AND EVALUATION

PART IV
PREPARING TO TRAVEL

PART V
REFLECTIONS FROM THE FIELD

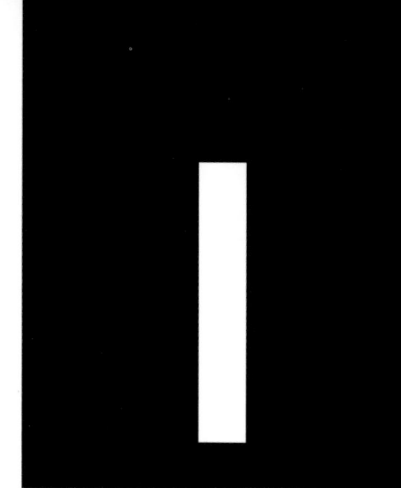

INTRODUCTION

Sarah E. Spencer and Kathy Tuma

For students who are older, of minority background, employed (46 percent of full-time students under age 25 are employed at least part-time), disabled, or have limited funds, study abroad is not perceived to be an option. The more typical study abroad models and structures mostly ignore the needs of such students.

— *1990 National Task Force on Undergraduate Education Abroad[1]*

Amazingly, a mere 17 years ago, most students, especially those who could not take advantage of a full term or year overseas, did not study abroad as part of their academic degree. Since we first published this book in 2002, the ground continues to shift annually in terms of numbers, destinations, curricular models, and the impact short-term, off-campus programs make on education and the world. These programs—credit-granting, service-learning, internship, international, domestic, summer, January, embedded in a semester—create opportunities for a far greater range of students to leave their homes to access other cultures and explore alternate ways of learning. In many ways, the evolution and availability of short-term programs have democratized study abroad for U.S. higher education students.

The impact of short-term program development shapes education's landscape beyond its participants. Because most academic programs are faculty-directed, short-term programs have literally 'internationalized' many professors, beyond standard campus internationalization initiatives. Faculty find that their teaching and traveling in other countries enables them to bring back new knowledge and cultural experiences to their home campus. Likewise, a traditional catalog course based in the Western canon finds itself reimagined into the cross-cultural context when taught overseas. Short-term programs allow educational institutions, such as community colleges, which may never have considered study abroad, the opportunity to internationalize with strategic intention.

Our primary goal in publishing this book is to enable anyone—education abroad professionals, teachers in higher or secondary education, volunteer, or church group leaders—to obtain a baseline for developing and safely administering short-term off-campus programs. This new volume updates the 2002 publication. While the original content remains intact, we wanted to research and add topics that had emerged in the last four years. Based on a review of SECUSS-L postings, our colleagues consistently inquired about nonstudents accompanying programs as well as leadership issues; we therefore have added new information in Chapter 3: Administrative Processes, as well as updating Chapter 13: Roles and Preparation of Program Directors. Many of you also asked about budgets and financial issues, resulting in a brand new chapter on Financial Matters. We also added a new chapter on Service Learning, Internships, and Independent Study, all of which carry significant intercultural opportunity.

Because short-term programs differ from one another in location, length, topic and goals, time of year, and audience, we hope you will use this book as a guide. We provide the tools to build successful and quality short-term programs, but it is up to you to decide what is the best structure and fit for your participants and your organization. This guide remains written from the perspective of U.S. higher education, although we welcome international partners and organizations to use this book for their own programs.

How Short is Short-term?

Within higher education, the definition of short-term programs abroad has changed significantly over the last 50 years. First considered as year-long, and then as a semester, they are now considered one- to eight-week programs (less than a term), usually faculty-directed and sponsored by a home institution or a consortium. Short-term program models are in abundance, taking place during the January or May term, in the form of two weeks off campus embedded in a regular term or semester-length class, or as a six-week summer program. Programs can be based in one city, one country, or travel to multiple sites or countries. And, in increasing numbers, institutions are offering domestic short-term programs that require similar logistical and pedagogical considerations.

Positioning Short-Term Programs Abroad

Most of us agree that the longer the encounter a student has with another country and culture, the better. As participation continues to significantly increase annually, student populations new to study abroad will likely choose a semester or short-term program because they are more accessible. The reasons students seek short-term opportunities are numerous, and as participation and programs grow, so do the motivations. Examples of students seeking short-term programs abroad include:

- ☐ Nontraditional undergraduate students with home, job, and family responsibilities.
- ☐ Undergraduate students who are double or triple majors with very structured and tightly scheduled degree plans.
- ☐ Students who cannot afford the loss of income from an on- or off-campus job for a semester, but who can take three to four weeks off to participate in a short-term program.
- ☐ Working graduate students seeking study and professional opportunities who cannot be released from job and family responsibilities.
- ☐ Students who are simply not willing to take the leap to study abroad for a longer period of time without first having some exposure of a shorter duration.
- ☐ Semester or academic year returnees who convince themselves (and sometimes their parents) that they can go abroad (again) during their senior year.
- ☐ Students with increased curricular restrictions in their major/minor field and core areas.

Whatever the reason, two things are clear. First, the market for short-term programs has dramatically increased in the last decade, and there are no indications that it is or will be decreasing. Recent data from *Open Doors: Statistics on International Student Mobility* show that just over 50 percent of all students studying abroad participated in short-term programs.[2] And second, for students who cannot spend a longer time overseas, it is imperative to provide quality academic and intercultural experiences of shorter duration.

A Departure from the Ideal?

The international education community has moved toward short-term programs abroad in a big way. As a community, we recognized that if the goal of giving vastly more students an overseas experience was to be realized, short-term programs were key to that vision. Short-term study abroad has always had its critics, and at times, deservingly so. Schools have used these programs to increase their numbers without any deliberate attention to quality, including intercultural growth and an active learning environment that is reflective and integrative. Initially, many short-term programs were designed with a 'tour' pedagogy, with focus only on seeing and doing. Students were expected to experience, without the academic underpinnings considered fundamental to coursework. Most importantly, it was the lack of cross-cultural engagement that supported this tour mentality. 'Island' semester programs—those that replicate the home campus environment, where students take home campus courses, live together in residence halls, and travel together—often suffer similar criticism.

As short-term programs continue to develop and outpace others, educational institutions must maintain a balance between short-term and longer-term educational and cultural opportunities. Deliberate attention to semester and year-long study through curricular integration, work with academic departments and faculty, as well as administrative support, must be advocated and planned for in collaboration with short-term program growth. As professionals, we need to be well versed in the different outcomes of program models, balancing and acknowledging the limitations of short-term programs, such as sustained cultural immersion, with the contributions of such programs, especially access to diverse student populations.

Starting Out—How to Use This Guide

Although we assume the readers of this book will primarily work in higher education, the tools found in specific sections can be used by a variety of groups. All of the audiences noted below have two things in common beyond creating short-term programs: they need logistical and group support and they need to function in the cross-cultural context. This guide provides the information needed to succeed in both areas.

All Short-Term Programs

All readers should start with the backbone of successful program management, feasibility, logistics, and financial management, covered in Chapters 7, 8, and 9.

Part IV: Preparing to Travel, is also essential reading as it covers liability, safety, security, and health, as well as program directors and participants' intercultural and logistics preparation. Attention to all these areas not only can ensure a safe experience for all, but can make the difference between a 'been there, seen that attitude,' and a truly cross-cultural experience.

Higher Education (education abroad or international programs offices, senior administrators, and faculty)

Because this volume was inspired, developed, and authored by higher education professionals, each chapter addresses a need, issue, or solution in designing and administering short-term programs. Part I: Working Within Higher Education will be an invaluable resource for identifying your allies, creating efficient administrative processes, and recruiting a community of colleagues.

For both undergraduate and graduate credit-granting programs, Part II: Principles of Academic Course Design is indispensable, as it not only covers a diversity of program model ideas, but design issues for off-campus curriculum and considerations for teaching on the road. Chapter 10: Marketing and Promotion, Chapter 11: Student Selection and Enrollment, and Chapter 12: "It Changed My Life: Strategies for Assessing Student Learning" are key to program management.

While a majority of U.S. study abroad participants are undergraduates, graduate programs are dramatically increasing their offerings too, and short-term courses are an ideal model. While this book reflects an undergraduate predisposition, it can and should also be actively used by faculty and administrators who focus on graduate students. Although program development logistics and academic structure are similar, working with graduate students may differ in a number of ways including:

o Group Dynamics: Many graduate courses do not include the same kind of group experience as undergraduate courses—they may not utilize group airline tickets, and students may be located in different cities, desiring to combine business travel or to extend their stay for personal travel.

o Travel-Savvy Students: Graduate students tend to be more travel savvy than their younger colleagues. Many have traveled before and may have higher expectations of hotel and bus quality.

o Flexibility: Graduate students may need more flexibility built into a study abroad program (e.g., can they skip a group dinner to deal with a work or family situation).

o Communication rarely occurs in person, with students relying heavily on e-mail and phone contact. For this reason, it is important that your printed and electronic information is accurate and very detailed.

Faculty/Program Directors

All faculty and program directors, with or without administrative support of an international office, should read the following relevant chapters: Chapter 5: Designing the Academic Course, Chapter 12: "It Changed My Life": Strategies for Assessing Student Learning, Chapter 13: Roles and Preparation of Program Directors, Chapter 14: If You Cross the Sea... Program Leadership for Intercultural Development, Chapter 15: Orientation and Reentry, and Chapter 16: Safeguards for Short-Term Programs. Don't miss the conclusion, Part V: Reflections from the Field, written by a well-experienced short-term faculty director.

Service Learning and Volunteer Programs

These programs may be academic or purely experiential. A new chapter on these opportunities has been included in this updated volume. Also focus on Parts III and IV.

High School Students

These groups may also be credit-granting or experiential. Parts III and IV provide resources for program development and orientation, but also consider using Tips on Guiding Students to Cultural and Intellectual Mileposts, found in Part II, Chapter 5.

College Alumni

Short-term programs catering to alumni groups are increasingly popular. Most are experiential, but may use a seasoned faculty director who has taught academic courses overseas. See Parts II, III, and IV as well as the comments about graduate students mentioned above. There are similar issues for both groups.

Nonacademic Groups (e.g., musical organizations, sports groups, and religious groups): Depending on the program objectives, focus on Parts III and IV, because logistics, financial matters, and orientation are important for all group travel.

We are pleased to have the opportunity to share the knowledge we have gained in our many years of administering short-term programs. We sincerely hope this guide proves useful to the many people directing and administering such programs.

Good luck and good planning!

Endnotes

1 *A National Mandate for Education Abroad: Getting on With the Task.* Report of the National Task Force on Undergraduate Education Abroad (ERIC Document Reproduction Service No. ED 331 340)[t], May 1990.

2 See *Open Doors online, Report on International Educational Exchange,* http://www.opendoors.iienetwork.org (January 2007)

ACKNOWLEDGMENTS

For initial inspiration: Mickey Slind, Scott Lomas, Janis Perkins

For additional review and contribution: Nik Wilson, Adrienne Kaufmann, Anne King, Sommer Leonard, Ruth Mason, Sue Moro, Pam Nice, Ana Scofield, Catherine Spaeth, Susan Verdi Webster, Dawn White

For listening and ideas: Maynard Tuma, Nik Wilson, Martha Johnson, Mary McGuinness, George Dordoni

Our past and current team members: Peter Hovde, Allison Keith, Susan MacNally, Anders Uhrskov, Tim Pauly, Lisa Chieffo, and Mark Lund

Our past presenter colleagues, the countless participants at NAFSA national and regional conferences, and the faculty directors with whom we have worked.

For the support of our offices: International and Off-Campus Studies, St. Olaf College, Northfield, MN (Eric Lund, Helen Stellmaker, Karen Engler, Roseanne Galegher, Jodi Moen, Pat VanWylen), and International Education, University of St. Thomas, St. Paul, MN (Ann Hubbard, Eric Delacruz, Rachael Herkenhoff, Sarah Huesing, Sommer Leonard, Ruth Mason, Catherine Spaeth, Sarah Stevenson)

Drew Banks, Chris Murphy, and Lisa Schock of NAFSA's Publications Department

Barry Stinson, regional director, AustraLearn: North American Center for Australian and New Zealand Universities

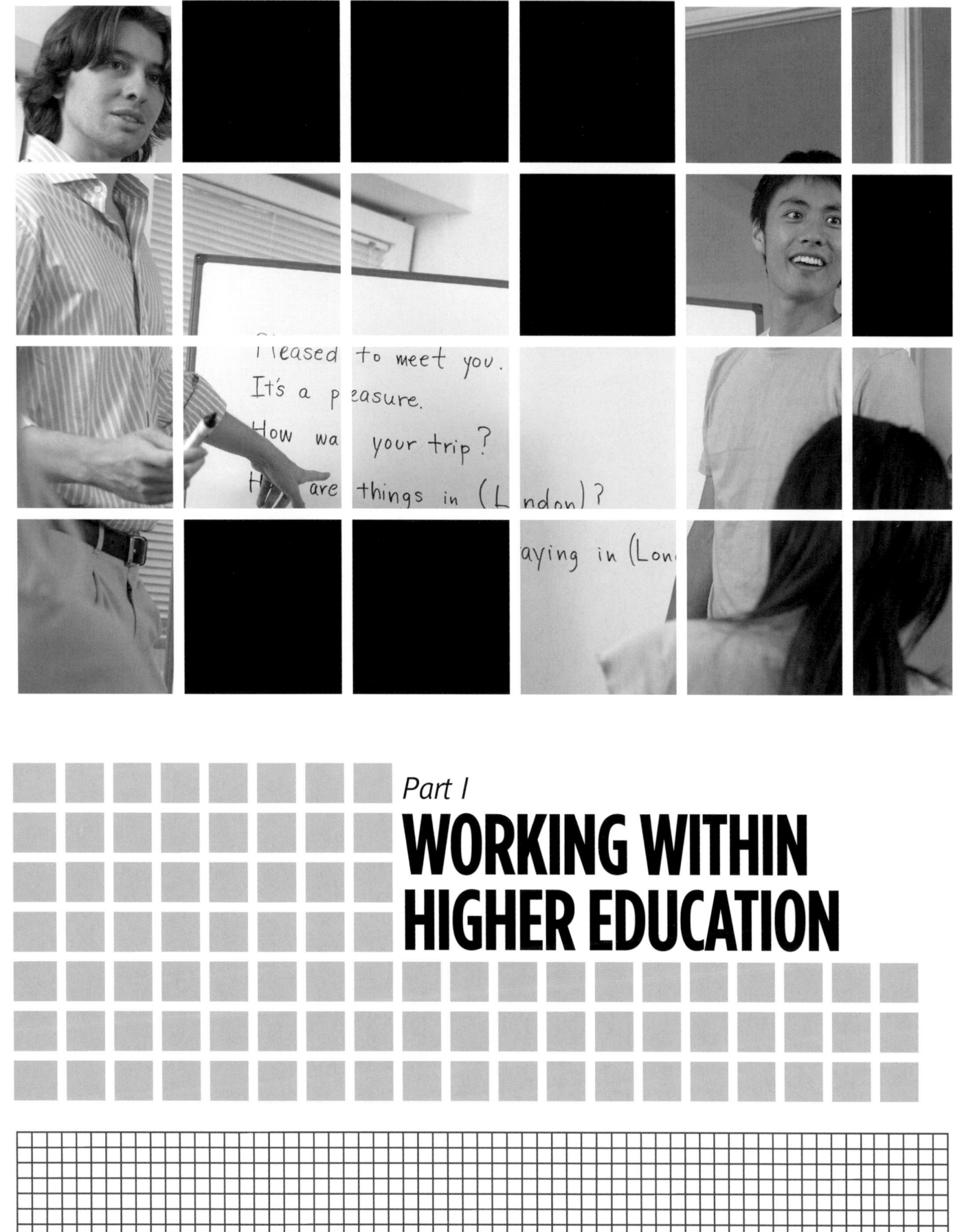

Part 1

WORKING WITHIN HIGHER EDUCATION

BUILDING INSTITUTIONAL SUPPORT

Peter Hovde and Kathy Tuma

Just five years ago, when the first edition of this book was published, this chapter on building institutional support was designed to give advice on how to convince the naysayers of the value of short-term study abroad programs. Since that time, more and more institutions have joined the short-term bandwagon and come to realize the potential value of these programs in helping to internationalize their campuses, to give unique opportunities to students and faculty, to do it in a fiscally conservative way and—let's face it—to increase their numbers.

As I talk with those attending the short-term workshop at NAFSA conferences, more and more of them are coming with a mandate from their institutions to build the numbers of short-term study abroad programs. Oftentimes, however, these same institutions do not put the money where their mandate is. This chapter is designed to provide advice on convincing any remaining naysayers and on how to capitalize on the current enthusiasm for short-term study abroad programs to build a solid, academically strong, culturally rich program for your institution.

This chapter in the first edition of this publication was written by Peter Hovde, a political scientist and former director of an international office at a small, private institution. Much of Peter's message is still relevant—despite the changes in campus climate mentioned above—and much of that original chapter follows.

Your situation is probably unlike mine. Your institution may be public, whereas mine is private. Your university may be vastly larger than my college, or your college smaller.[1] Your institutional culture may be more attuned to globalization than mine, or less so.

I do not think those differences in institutional context matter very much. Each of us has the same task: to make it possible for as many students as possible to have the best overseas learning experience possible. To attain that end, we each have to get a large number of people with their diverse institutional interests to do what they otherwise would not do. That process—of getting others to do what they should have the good sense to do anyway, as Harry Truman would say—is politics. To accomplish that end by remaking your institution in important ways, as James MacGregor Burns would say, is leadership.[2]

Two things to remember before we set off. First, as a political scientist, I see the world through a set of political lenses, which give me insights others do not see. Remember that your training and your experience—be it as economist or educator, partner or parent—have given you lenses and insights that you can bring to this task. Your unique combination of lenses and insights will serve you well if you hark back to them. Second, remember that those who stand in your way on the road to success—indecisive dean, irascible faculty, inflexible bureaucrat—are (probably) not the malicious louts they may appear to be. They are nearly always well-intentioned, committed people possessed of the responsibilities and agendas of the offices they occupy. To build institutional support for your program, it is your task to expand those sets of responsibilities and to place study abroad high on their agendas. Or, put more simply, to change their institutional outlook, and to modify their motivations. That's all ...

1

THE GOAL IS TO BUILD A WINNING COALITION

In politics, the side with the most votes wins. The trick in politics is to get more people, and more committed people, on your side than any other side. Bringing diverse people with different perspectives, motives, and incentives into a coalition under one banner or behind a candidate is a real trick. In short, coalition building is the essence of politics. And so it is with building institutional support for a study abroad program.

The trick is finding allies to build a winning coalition out of all that diversity and difference, a coalition whose members—your allies—will help you get what you need to run a successful study abroad program.

YOUR ALLIES

Program Providers and Vendors

Services needed from program providers and vendors can range from the purchase of group airline tickets to contracting all logistics. Most published advice and some university regulations would keep the relationships with these support organizations distant and competitive, always looking for the lowest bid.

A minority of directors take a different approach, looking for agencies and agents who are consistently cost-effective and reliable, and bringing them into the fold as coalition partners. When things go wrong at the worst possible time—which they do with stimulating regularity in this business—the cost of a service does not seem like such an important criterion after all. Far better to have an agent whom one can contact day or night, and on whose ability and judgment one can rely.

Administrative Offices

Sending students abroad requires the active participation of many of the college's administrative offices, the business office, the financial aid office, and the registrar's office chief among them. Unfortunately, short-term programs abroad place new sets of demands on these offices that may not fit well in either time frame or task with their standard operating procedures. In short, the international office represents more work for these offices, work that is seen as an overload (more students to deal with) and is more labor intensive (often requiring individual attention to a student or problem). In short, other administrative offices see the study abroad office as a big pain. That is, unless these offices (their directors and staffs) are brought into your coalition.

Bringing these offices on board requires a three-pronged strategy. First, assign a liaison from your office staff to work with these offices. He or she will unavoidably get to know, on a personal basis, the staff who work in the trenches of those other offices that are key to your program success. Your liaison will get to know the needs of both the people and the processes of those offices, which is key to

the second step in bringing these partners into the coalition. The second prong of the strategy is to "ease their pain." That is, design your office procedures to conform to theirs, and do your work in such a way that it does a lot of the work for them. For example, simply designing and modifying a financial worksheet for international office use that exactly meets the informational needs of the financial aid office can warm and strengthen the bond between the two offices. Third, these people who labor in the administrative trenches of universities are its unsung heroes. In my view, our colleges would fall apart without them. Singing their praises at every opportunity—both to their faces and to those higher up (and to the faculty)—is not only the effective thing to do, it is the right thing to do.

Students (and Parents)

The direct targets of your activities are the students themselves, and for undergraduates, their parents. Convincing students to go abroad is the obvious task, but convincing parents that their child going abroad is a good idea may be even more important. And it is easy to overlook the parents in the flurry of your recruiting efforts. Talking to groups of parents during summer about the importance of study abroad in a global age is very well received. Sending mass mailings to parents either promoting programs or reassuring them in troubled times is both the effective and the right thing to do. Calling each parent to inform them that their child's group has arrived safely at its destination, and that everything is fine, will pay big dividends. That a few parents will contact the university's president to express their appreciation for the thoughtfulness of your office for that phone call will not hurt your institutional support one bit.

The strategy to build institutional support among students is pretty simple. It is a principle contained in the motto of our program: "Your experience of a lifetime." Do whatever you can to insure that outcome for each and every student, and then ask them to help you convince the next generation of students to follow in their footsteps.

Prospective Students and Parents

Whether they intend to participate during their matriculation or not, many students use the existence of a study abroad program as a marker of the quality of the institution. This is even more true of parents, who are quite receptive to the idea that students need to be prepared to succeed in the global culture, and who are quite willing to believe that study abroad is the best way for their children to prepare for the future. The same is true for most college and university ranking systems, even those ranking systems that use a rather short list of evaluative criteria.

It does not seem to matter much to students whether the college operates its own programs or farms them out to providers, nor does the extent of study abroad offerings seem to matter all that much. That students have easy access to study abroad options is what matters most. However, colleges and universities without a study abroad program place themselves at a competitive disadvantage, content to be considered second rate by many prospective students and parents.

On the other hand, requiring one's students to study abroad—except for some schools with exceptional constituencies—can dampen the enthusiasm of prospective students and parents for the college. U.S. students often bridle at "having" to do something, even something they otherwise might like to do, and requiring students to go abroad will give more cautious parents pause. For some students and their parents, just going off to college is a step big enough. Simultaneously signing up for both higher education and education overseas is a step too far.

Some middle ground would offer the best approach—a program of either encouraging or inducing students to study abroad, rather than requiring it. That way, more hesitant students and students for whom study abroad is a low priority when they enter the university will get a chance to discover why study abroad is so important and beneficial as they rub shoulders with older students who have already studied overseas. A college that either encourages or induces study abroad is likely to have better success in retaining its students as well, for the prospect of overseas experience can tie students to the institution, overcoming other factors that might push them toward another university.

Alumni and Friends

Alumni can lend powerful support to your study abroad efforts. Those graduates who were program participants are not hesitant about singing the praises of study abroad to important constituencies, both on campus and beyond its confines. Alumni can sell your program to prospective participants and their parents, either face-to-face (during a family weekend, for example) or in your promotions and advertisements (either printed or electronic). More persuasively than anyone, alumni can explain how the study abroad experience affected the trajectory of their lives—how it made them much more confident in such a very short time, how it altered their perspective on the world, and how it changed their career path. And nothing sells better to students and parents these days than careers—that a student is more likely to find the right one, or a better one, because of study abroad. Even those alumni who did not go abroad and regret missing out on the experience do not mind telling others that they made a mistake.

It is never too late to create alumni. Short-term programs abroad for "alumni" and "friends" can be especially popular with graduates of your college, as well as its friends (even if that friendship just got started with the deposit for a program abroad). Such programs can stand on their own, or they might tag along with a university musical ensemble on its overseas tour. Such experiences can build close relationships among alumni, friends, and faculty members, and current students on the performance tours.

It might be too much to expect older alumni and friends to have the kinds of transforming experiences that younger students often take away from study abroad. However, if alumni tours are made sufficiently and engagingly academic, the experience can open the minds, the hearts, and even the wallets of those old dogs who have learned new tricks. Development directors will sometimes send along an officer, ever ready to help those opening processes along, although this tactic might seem a bit transparent.

Especially powerful alumni can be especially powerful allies of study abroad when they are asked to participate in curricular reform or strategic planning for your university. These alumni did not attain their success by being hesitant or timid, so they are likely to have either studied or traveled abroad and are convinced of the merits of such experience for all students. It is difficult to overestimate the value of the support of powerful alumni, both for your programs and for your college.

Senior Administrators

The important directions of any college or university are generally set by a rather small group of people, the senior administrators (presidents and provosts, deans and directors). Their support is essential for the maintenance and defense of your programs. Their support is absolutely crucial for the expansion of your programs.

The numbers game. "How many students do you send abroad?" Reporting a large number in response to that question is the measure of success these days. That question is asked in either absolute terms or percentage terms, and answered in the way that makes the school look best.

Large universities can support a wide array of programs of their own, and send large numbers of students overseas. Smaller colleges have the advantage of being able to send larger percentages of their students overseas on fewer programs. Success in either numbers or percentages can go nearly as far as the photographs, the prose, and the poetry of students' experiences abroad in building solid support for your program.

A director at a small college would have the advantage of having greater access to top-level decisionmakers. That kind of personal relationship with the top administrators is an advantage that builds institutional support all on its own. The darker side of that advantage, however, is that the director will be directly involved and responsible when something goes wrong.

Crisis Management

An old U.S. State Department hand once said that crisis comes at you "like a tiger out of the night." In more technical terms, a crisis is generally a surprise, is a direct threat to major institutional values, and normally demands quick decisions made in the absence of complete information. Crises seem most often to start with a phone call in the middle of the night. They threaten our highest values—the safety of our students and staff, and secondarily our college's legal liability and reputation—and force us to try to predict the future with precise clarity while groping around in a fog of inadequate information.

Crisis management for study abroad could fill its own volume. Our topic here is building institutional support. Crises do contain great danger, but they also contain great opportunities to build institutional support, if you are a good crisis manager. And if you are lucky.

The least bad kind of crisis to have is the anticipatory crisis. In such a case, something has happened overseas in a place where you are planning to send students, but the students are not there yet. This gives you a chance to get a briefing on the desks of the president and other top-level crisis decisionmakers first thing in the morning. Examples would be a terrorist group announcing they would begin including tourists on their list of terrorist targets just as you are about to send your students to Turkey, or the Luxor massacre occurring just as your students are about to depart for Egypt. The briefing would include the nature of the situation, alternative courses of action, your recommended course of action, and a few supporting documents from the media or the Web with important information highlighted.

In the examples just described, your office and your crisis team[3] had an opportunity to show how professionally it handled a major problem. This kind of organizational performance is highly valued by the top administrators, and will build organizational support for your programs and office like few other accomplishments. With each successive crisis, your reputation will build and your institutional support will increase. The dark side, however, is that you will be expected to perform just as effectively in any future crisis and a failure will not be quickly forgiven. Welcome to the world of 24-hour on-call.

Faculty

In their attitudes toward the study abroad enterprise, faculty come in four stripes: hostile, indifferent, supporting, and active. Think of faculty as forming four concentric rings around the international office, with hostile faculty on the periphery, and active faculty forming the protective inner ring.

Faculty who are *hostile* to international education and question its legitimacy and its drain on university resources usually prefer subversion to public expression of their antagonism toward study abroad. Hostile faculty seem to have a way of worming their way onto curriculum committees where they can use their votes to obstruct study abroad initiatives. Efforts to persuade hostile faculty of the folly of their ways pretty much fall on deaf ears, and are usually a waste of time. Isolating and marginalizing hostile faculty by the statements of your important allies showing how out of

step they are with trends in higher education is the most effective strategy.

Indifferent faculty members are not a major problem, unless they compose the vast majority of the faculty. There is potential in this ring, however. Indifferent faculty can be roused from their lethargy by the realization that their discipline has gone global, or that their focus of professional passion is threatened by some international issue or has some important contribution to make to the global human condition. Such realizations can be engendered by, for example, dangling grant money in front of this faculty to explore the international implications and contributions of what they do, or more effectively (but more haphazardly) by some serendipitous self-realization.

Supporting faculty are those who recognize the importance of study abroad, yet are not actively involved in taking students overseas. Supporting faculty are crucial to any initiative in study abroad, from helping to get the program passed by the faculty senate to assisting in recruiting students whom others will take overseas. All that is required to arouse their support is information about programs and initiatives, and simply being asked to help.

Active faculty are those who direct programs abroad. They are the backbone of the international office. Their efforts determine not only the existence of a short-term program, but its quality as well. Spare no effort in support of your active faculty.

So, the strategic approach to faculty is really quite simple: narrow the widths of the outer rings and broaden the widths of the inner rings. A simple strategy, but not so easy to accomplish. Tactically, that means isolating and marginalizing the hostile faculty, ignoring or arousing the indifferent, engaging the supporting faculty, and doing everything you can for the active faculty. That last task—doing everything you can for the active faculty—is of such importance that its discussion takes up most of the rest of this chapter.

There are two key principles that will bring about the faculty support and participation a successful program requires.

1. Make your study abroad program unassailably academic. In contrast to the numbers game needed for outside recognition, the road to success with faculty is paved with academic quality. Faculty bred to respect the classroom as the only place where true learning can occur are initially suspicious that real learning can occur residentially immersed in a culture or on the road. They must be shown otherwise.

At the beginning, it takes masses of documentary evidence to convince skeptics. Learning assessment surveys and reentry interviews, logs of contact hours, examples of papers and exams, syllabi, texts, and so on, all will be examined with the skeptics looking for chinks in the case for short-term study abroad. But when the best of the faculty come on board your program as directors, as they inevitably seem to, their leadership ensures the academic quality of the program offerings. With their arrival, the evaluation game changes. Acceptable evidence of learning moves from the quantitative to the qualitative, even to the anecdotal. In our own case, logs of contact hours faded before the realization that something memorable happened to almost every student almost every day of the program, whether it was planned in the itinerary or not. With institutional experience, the realization dawns that study abroad is the most effective means of engendering the higher-end outcomes—the "education of the whole person" kinds of goals—many of our colleges claim to produce.[4] These shifts occur because of the reputations of the finest faculty, and because of the creative ways they design learning experiences abroad for your students, and simply because of the way learning outside the comfort of our own culture affects us all. But skeptics will continue to be hired as faculty, so we all must continue to collect evidence of the obvious.

2. Focus on faculty first (last, and always). That principle simply means to get faculty what they need to do the job of giving students an experience of a lifetime. You cannot have a good program without good faculty. No matter what directors and other administrators do, your short-term programs are only as good as the faculty who direct them. The best way to improve a program is to make good faculty even better and more numerous. Faculty development is the best investment a college or program can make in its future.

Faculty need to become more skilled and better at directing students abroad. Faculty also need to be able to overcome their understandable fear of taking students abroad.

Summer workshops, monthly briefing sessions on various leadership topics during the academic year, and one-on-one meetings with staff can all assist faculty in gaining the skills and the confidence required to take students overseas. Veteran faculty directors are your key resource here. They are the human capital of your program, the repository of the wealth of experience and insight about delivering the benefits of short-term study abroad to students.

However, on-campus learning can only go so far. As with students and staff, the best international education for faculty can only occur overseas, for the gains in learning skills and gaining confidence are far greater abroad than at home. This approach to faculty development costs money, however. There are two potential sources for this faculty development money—external and internal.[5] There are few external funding agencies that will fund faculty leadership training overseas. It just looks too much like a boondoggle. Internal funding is more flexible, but far more limited in supply. Beyond that, there is the issue of what skill or quality the faculty need to develop. Is it familiarity with the site to be visited, or is it learning how to direct short-term programs in a succession of sites? Our faculty prefer the latter. The most

efficient method we have found to develop future faculty directors is to bring them on existing courses abroad as assistant directors so they can learn the ropes on site. There is no mechanism that produces greater support for the program among faculty than a "free trip" abroad.[6]

Make faculty full partners in all stages of the study abroad process, from planning and costing through assessment and evaluation. Such partnership will shrink the faculty/administrative divide, and reduce the conflict between the international office and the faculty, who always want all the extras on their seminar at less than actual cost.

Provide the most incentive possible for faculty to participate in short-term study abroad. Gaining these incentives for faculty is not easily done, however. Our summer program directors get a greater salary than faculty who teach summer school on campus, reflecting the greater contact time and added responsibilities of directors abroad. However, the college did not always find that case compelling, and it took more than 20 years for that policy change to be made. Nonfinancial incentives to faculty—such as specific credit toward promotion and tenure for study abroad leadership—seem even more difficult to obtain.

In summary, development of both the faculty and curriculum are the most important accomplishments to building institutional support for short-term programs abroad. How one does those jobs is far less important than that the jobs themselves get done. Make sure that all your efforts to develop faculty and curriculum are visible to faculty and administration alike.

ERODING INSTITUTIONAL SUPPORT

There are many ways and means to dissipate the institutional support for international education that has accumulated. Circumstances can do it, your adversaries can do it, and you can do it.

Circumstances

Global events such as September 11 will temporarily decrease enrollments and erode psychological support for study abroad. None of the many types of allies noted above is immune. Trends, both global (e.g., inflation abroad) and national (e.g., consumer confidence), can diminish support as prices of programs and costs to the college increase. Conflicts among senior administrators can put you between a rock and a hard place. Most of these circumstances are outside your control, but their impact can be lessened. Imposing cost-containment measures on program budgets can help, as will building safety measures into your programs, but only if you are seen to be doing these things. Notice has to be given via various media to the college at large (ranging from mass mailings to parents to memos to the top administrators) describing what you are doing and why your actions are going to solve the problem.

Adversaries

Resistance to your study abroad administration often comes from within the campus international education community itself. Foremost is the faculty member who wants to run his or her program free of any interference from your office, and above and apart from the university rules that govern all study abroad programs. A secondary source of resistance can be the directors and coaches of musical organizations and sports teams, who often do not want their concertizing or game schedule cluttered by cross-cultural experience and learning. All such resistance is difficult to fight directly, because it seldom is done in the open. A better approach is to get the top administrators to do the job for you by policy edict. The issue of centralization is discussed in Chapter 2, Administrative Processes.

Conclusion

As a brief summary, the basic principles that have structured this essay are printed below. They are guidelines that I have found valuable in building institutional support for study abroad programs.

o Build and nurture webs of affection among your allies.

o Make your programs and activities visible.

o Make your programs unassailably academic.

o Focus on faculty first (last, and always).

o Give students an experience of a lifetime.

Endnotes

[1] The terms "college" and "university" are used interchangeably in this essay.

[2] Burns, J. McGregor (1978) *Leadership*. New York: Harper & Row.

[3] If you do not have a crisis team, form one comprising people with cool heads and clear-eyed judgment who are willing to drop everything, including their personal lives if need be, until some resolution of a crisis has been attained.

[4] Koester, J. (1985). *A Profile of the U.S. Student Abroad*. New York: Council on International Education Exchange. Nicely summarized research concerning the effects of study abroad.

Other examples are as follows:

Carlson, J. S. and Widaman, K. F. (1988). The effects of study abroad during college on attitudes toward other cultures. *International Journal of Intercultural Relations, 12, 1-17.*

Carsello, C. and Greiser, J. (1975). How college students change during study abroad. *College Student Journal*, 10, 276-278.

Hansel, B., and Grove, N. (1986). International student exchange programs: Are the educational benefits real? *NASP Bulletin*, 70, 84-90.

Juhasz, A. M., and Walker, A. M. (1988). The impact of study abroad on university student's self-esteem and self-efficacy. *College Student Journal*, 22(4), 329-341.

Kauffman, N. L. (1983). The impact of study abroad on personal development of college students. (Doctoral dissertation, Indiana University, 1983). Dissertation Abstracts International, 44, 1350A.

Nash, D. (1976). The personal consequences of a year of study abroad. *Journal of Higher Education,* 47, 191-203.

Sell, D.K. (1983). Attitude change in foreign study participants. *International Journal of Intercultural Relations*, 7, 131-147.

Stitsworth, M. H. (1988). Personality changes associated with sojourn in Japan. *The Journal of Social Psychology*, 129, 213-224.

[5] For a comparative discussion of the impact of three models of international faculty development, see Hovde P., Ellig N., Krejci M., Rice M., and Sandgren D. (1997). An evaluation of faculty study abroad: a response to Lambert's strategic questions. International Education Forum 17, 23-31.

[6] "Free" in a very qualified sense. Our faculty go abroad with a clear expectation that they will be directing their own seminar in the near future.

ADMINISTRATIVE PROCESSES

2

Lisa Chieffo and Julie Johnson

Once the need for short-term programs abroad has been established at an institution, how does one begin developing a program? What critical questions should be asked, and of whom? The purpose of this chapter is to examine the administrative processes necessary to plan, implement, and sustain a short-term program and to highlight policy issues that should be considered when initiating such a program.

Developing and administering quality short-term programs abroad requires no fewer resources, and as much attention to detail, as required by study abroad programs or exchanges of a longer duration. In order to create a sustainable short-term program, careful consideration must be given to administrative and academic processes, policies, and resources. Here is a sample of responsibilities that a program administrator may carry:

- ☐ Build support on campus for short-term programs.
- ☐ Determine program model and design; establish criteria for successful programs.
- ☐ Determine timing for proposal review and development.
- ☐ Recruit faculty.
- ☐ Create committee to review proposals.
- ☐ Market the program: design flyers, brochures, electronic media; conduct promotional activities, including fairs and classroom presentations.
- ☐ Make logistical arrangements abroad, including arranging for transportation, lodging, activities, classroom, research, computer facilities.
- ☐ Assess risk factors of location and program activities; inform students and faculty on health, safety, responsibility, and insurance issues.
- ☐ If working with consortia: recruit for, accept, and process applications from outside institutions.
- ☐ Review applications; notify students of acceptance decisions.
- ☐ Maintain student records.

- ☐ Arrange payment to vendors, including travel agents, tour guides, program providers, or organizations contracted for lodging, classroom space, and so on.
- ☐ Confirm that students have registered for courses.
- ☐ Collect program fees, including deposits; process withdrawals and issue refunds.
- ☐ Pay the bills.
- ☐ Prepare budgets for program, faculty, and students.
- ☐ Prepare passenger lists for travel agents; check and distribute airline documents.
- ☐ Provide training for faculty directors and other leaders, such as staff or teaching assistants.
- ☐ Provide predeparture orientation for students and faculty.
- ☐ Prepare program handbooks for students and faculty.
- ☐ Respond to emergencies or problems during program.
- ☐ Conduct program evaluations.
- ☐ Respond to the questions and concerns of faculty, students, parents, administrators, and other staff.
- ☐ Close budget at end of program; manage excess funds or budget deficits, reimburse faculty expenses.
- ☐ Provide reentry support to students and faculty.
- ☐ Maintain contact with service providers in anticipation of future programs.

The introduction of short-term programs abroad may flow easily into the current structure and calendar of administration for longer-term academic study abroad and exchange programs. It may, on the other hand, require the creation of new or different administrative structures such as separate application deadlines, an additional application review process, and different timelines for students to pay deposits or withdraw from the program.

Applications may be received from students outside of the institution or from noncredit participants (if this is permitted). These applications may necessitate a different approach to fee collection, course registration, financial aid, and even group travel as students depart from various areas of the country.

Keeping these issues and responsibilities in mind while developing an administrative structure will help determine which tasks the international office or faculty director can manage, which are best handled by another office on campus, and which tasks will require an outside service provider.

LAYING THE GROUNDWORK FOR ADMINISTRATIVE STRUCTURE

Building Support on Campus for Short-Term Programs Abroad

The previous chapter examined different constituencies on campus that may assist in endorsing short-term programs as another avenue of meeting the institution's international mission; this section briefly considers which offices on campus should be consulted when establishing administrative procedures. Most international educators realize that it does indeed take a campus to run a study abroad program. Chapter 3 thoroughly examines how many departments—from the registrar's office to campus publications—can support these programs.

It is crucial to know one's campus before establishing an administrative structure for short-term programs abroad. Who are the key decisionmakers within each academic or administrative department? Who will have a say or has a vested interest in how these programs are organized and managed? Taking the time to identify and meet with these individuals and working to establish supportive relationships increases the likelihood of a successful program.

Working Within Existing Administrative Structures

It is essential to determine whether short-term study abroad academic and administrative models are already in place elsewhere on campus. For example, the continuing education or summer session office may be involved in administering short-term programs for academic credit and may have experience working with off-campus participants. These offices could be a source of collaboration and may be able to absorb some of the administrative and fiscal responsibilities that the international office cannot manage.

At the same time, one must be sensitive to turf issues and to departments and faculty that are already involved with existing programs. Individuals who have been organizing what they view as successful programs for years or decades may not appreciate another office "appropriating" their forms or procedures, or—even worse—modifying or attempting to improve upon them. Such issues are less likely to emerge at an institution with a centralized model of study abroad administration.

Models of Administration

Until the last quarter of the 20th century, individual faculty and departments facilitated most study abroad activity. With the large increases in student participation, the number of programs available, and the heightened awareness of risk and liability issues, many institutions have created and staffed international or study abroad offices. (For the purpose of this chapter, the terms "international office" and "study abroad office" will be used interchangeably.) Since most administrative processes focus on the role of the study abroad office, the institution must determine the services and level of administration for which this office is responsible. This is often a balancing act between what the resources will allow and the expectations of faculty directors and their academic units. In order to describe various institutional scenarios, this section presents and discusses three models of program administration: decentralized, centralized, and hybrid.

Institutional Organization

The location of the international office within the organizational structure of the institution will largely determine the administrative model used in creating and managing short-term programs abroad. An office under the umbrella of academic affairs will generally have greater credibility and visibility than an office under student affairs. This is significant when reaching out to academic units for assistance in program development. An office within academic affairs is usually under the leadership of a dean, or under a director who reports to the senior academic leadership. Some international offices report directly to a dean or vice president of international programs, who report directly to the provost.

If the international office is within a college (typically, the college of liberal arts) or within a department (e.g., foreign languages, area studies center) of a larger university, the administration of short-term programs abroad may be restricted to the departments or schools within that college. For small colleges, a staffed office may not exist, in which case faculty in each department must manage programs without support. An office that is located within student affairs may have a broader reach throughout the institution, but is less likely to have a credible voice in program development, as such offices are often limited to general study abroad and travel advising.

Decentralized Model

In a decentralized model of administration, an individual faculty member, department, or college will manage its own short-term programs abroad, with little or no input or assistance from the international office. An example is a program operated by the foreign language department, perhaps a longstanding summer program with a solid relationship at a language institute abroad and with a regular rotation of faculty directors. An attempt by the international office to draw such programs into a centralized process may be seen as interference and unwanted treading on academic and political turf.

On the other hand, established programs can serve as resources when one is seeking to develop a program model and administrative processes. The department may have established procedures for working with program providers, designing predeparture orientation for students and faculty, and managing program budgets, and there may be precedents for using financial aid and granting credit. Preexisting short-term programs may also have useful contacts, such as host institutions, service providers, and travel agencies, all of which can be valuable to the international office for future program development.

There may be situations in which a faculty member or academic unit proceeds to develop a program without requesting or after rejecting the assistance and input of the international office. In such instances, knowing the role and standing of the study abroad office within one's institution is crucial. Some institutions require, via the mandate of senior administration, that all off-campus academic programs be monitored to some extent by the international office. That office's relationships with key academic decisionmakers may allow some degree of influence over the assessment of risk factors at the program location, and over other areas where the institution may be liable.

An additional decentralized model is that in which another administrative unit on campus provides services and support to the academic department. An office of continuing education or summer sessions may be responsible for the management of student records, including course registration, marketing, and making logistical arrangements for a group of students in a particular major led by a faculty member from their department. In this case, the international office is still an important voice in assessing health and safety factors and in providing preparation, reentry support, and program promotion.

If the international office is small, resources are limited, or the primary function of the office is general study abroad advising, a decentralized approach to short-term programs may be the most feasible, as long as the office maintains some level of oversight in matters of liability and student health and safety.

Centralized Model

In a centralized model, the international office plays the primary role in developing and administering short-term programs abroad. These responsibilities may include:

☐ Program design and development;

☐ Requesting that a faculty committee is established;

☐ Recruiting faculty directors;

☐ Reviewing proposals;

☐ Making all logistical arrangements and arranging payments to service providers;

☐ Promoting the program;

☐ Reviewing applications;

☐ Managing student records;

☐ Advising students;

☐ Providing training to faculty and staff directors and predeparture orientation to students;

☐ Responding to on-site problems and emergencies;

☐ Conducting and responding to program evaluations; and

☐ Providing reentry support to students and faculty.

If several short-term programs are proposed and approved for the same term, a centralized office will need substantial resources of time and personnel.

The faculty director of the short-term program should assist in the development of the program by contributing his or her knowledge of the region and any academic and logistical contacts at the program site; determining the program's academic content, itinerary, and activities; creating or contributing to a program handbook; and participating in orientation.

In this model, most institutions require that programs be proposed, reviewed, and approved by a standing committee of faculty members (which may or may not have administrative staff or student representation), or at least by the chairperson and dean of the faculty director. This specific process is outlined later in this chapter.

Advantages of a centralized model. The distinct advantage of a centralized model is the standardization of policies and procedures across programs, no matter which academic unit or department is granting credit for a program. A centralized model ensures that:

☐ Faculty are aware of and operate under policies established by the administration and the international office;

☐ Participants have been appropriately screened;

☐ Procedures for the application and use of student financial aid have been clearly communicated and adhered to;

☐ Pricing of short-term programs abroad follows a standard formula;

☐ Billing and collection of fees are standardized;

☐ Orientation for both students and faculty is conducted; and

☐ Issues of liability, responsibility, risk management, insurance, and crisis management are addressed.

A centralized model means that the international office is aware of all program development and management issues as they occur.

Managing growth in a centralized model. The international office may find itself a victim of its own success as short-term programs grow, with greater numbers of students participating and more faculty expressing interest in directing programs. It is therefore imperative to have a plan for managing the growth of these programs. A division of responsibilities among staff and faculty should be clearly spelled out from the beginning of the program development process, and there must be support from the senior administration to either control growth or add additional resources.

Hybrid Model

Short-term program abroad administration may also fall into the hybrid model category. The international office may be too small to handle the responsibilities of a centralized model, or there may be long-standing programs in academic units that resist being brought under the management of the international office or that are well-managed under the current system. Some units may be eager to have the international office handle all of the administrative details, whereas others may need assistance in certain areas but are able and willing to develop and manage their own programs. Another office, such as continuing education, may already be administering summer programs but will turn to the international office for assistance in orientation, preparing faculty, assessing health and safety risk factors, and finding contacts at potential program sites. International office staff may find themselves juggling several or all of these scenarios if several short-term programs are in the works.

A hybrid model may promote successful collaboration with several different academic units, each of which may have a different history, program model, and administrative needs.

Moving Toward a Centralized Model

A degree of centralization and standardization is recommended, and in fact, is *essential* if short-term study abroad is to develop and become a sustainable international option at an institution. If efforts to centralize are met with resistance by those already administering short-term programs abroad, it may be time call upon one's support structure of key decisionmakers.

First, it is important to create a credible argument for the standardization of policies and procedures for short-term program management, such as the one found at the end of this chapter. Areas of concern that will likely capture the attention of the senior administration are institutional liability, academic integrity, selection of participants, standardized processes, and collection of program fees.

Institutional liability. Faculty directors who have not had training or experience in supervising groups of students overseas, and/or who are not aware of health and safety issues or of procedures for responding to emergencies, put the institution at greater risk of liability. Students who have not received an orientation at which issues of health, safety, responsibility, insurance, cultural adaptation, and academic expectations are addressed are also a potential liability for the institution. In making one's case, it is most persuasive to present areas of concern and to offer ways to prepare both faculty and students for the overseas experience, rather than to suggest that the international office make the decision about who is qualified to direct a short-term program.

Academic integrity. Courses that are held overseas for institutional credit should not simply replicate the on-campus experience in an off-campus setting. Without a standard approach to approving and evaluating short-term programs abroad, there is no guarantee that a course makes use of its locale or enhances the academic unit's existing curriculum. A faculty committee reviewing all proposals for short-term programs abroad, or a committee within each college organized by or with the participation of the international office, will ensure that these courses fulfill the academic mission of the institution. Similarly, a standardized evaluation form for all short-term programs will demonstrate through reliable measures that the courses met defined criteria for academic and intercultural effectiveness. See Chapter 12, "It Changed My Life": Strategies for Assessing Student Learning, for examples.

Selection of participants. Policies for participation in study abroad may already exist at your institution. Such policies may prohibit participation in an off-campus program by students who are on academic or conduct probation. A faculty member or academic unit independently organizing a short-term program may not review student records to verify that students are in good academic and conduct standing. Disregard for or ignorance of admissions policies puts the institution at risk by encouraging unqualified students to participate, and will ultimately cast a spotlight on disparate standards of acceptance. See Chapter 11, Student Selection and Enrollment.

Standardized and transparent processes. Having different application and payment deadlines or varying requirements for students may not be problematic when an institution sponsors only a small number of programs. However, once enrollments begin to grow, and the number of programs increases, it becomes very difficult for staff to keep track of what is due when for each program. Students will not always receive quick or accurate replies from the program's faculty director about procedural matters and will most likely contact the study abroad office for answers to their questions. From the students' point of view, the institution will appear increasingly unprofessional and the staff incompetent if these answers are not instantly available in the central office assigned to oversee international programs. It is only a matter of time before complaints make their way to the president's office.

Collection of program fees. A faculty member or academic unit independently administering a short-term program may collect program fees in a way that does not comply with institutional policy. For example, students may submit payment directly to a faculty director or to a program provider not properly sought out and bid for by the institution.

If credit is granted for the course, the faculty director is essentially acting on behalf of the institution, and indirect payment for services makes the institution liable for any negligent behavior or policies of the third-party provider. Any direct collection of program fees by the faculty director or academic unit also means it is unlikely that the student will have access to financial aid monies to offset the cost of the program and may not receive an official transcript reflecting the course or study abroad experience. By not participating in a standardized billing system, the academic unit will have difficulty collecting delinquent fees or processing refunds.

The "Proposal for Standardizing Policies and Procedures for Short-Term Study Abroad Programs" at the end of this chapter can be partially or wholly adapted to suit any institution; simply insert institutional data under "list student participation numbers" and "list courses offered."

Once credible arguments for the standardization and/or centralization of policies and procedures have been established, one must determine which services the education abroad office will provide to academic units developing programs. The document "Program Development and Administration Responsibilities for Short-Term Off-Campus Programs" shows different models of the division of responsibilities among faculty directors, the administrator for study abroad programs, and program providers.

COURSE AND PROGRAM APPROVAL PROCESS

Once you have determined an administrative structure (assuming that it is a centralized or hybrid model), and clarified the responsibilities of the international office and faculty directors vis-à-vis the management of the short-term programs, it is time to consider the course and program approval process.

Depending upon the institution's administrative structure for short-term programs, proposals can be solicited campus-wide or from certain academic units (e.g., the college of liberal arts, area studies centers). If the structure is more decentralized, the academic units may take the full responsibility of selecting courses to be offered on study abroad programs, while the international office may be asked to consider the administrative feasibility of a program, but not its academic content. See the flowchart, "Review of International Education Programs," at the end of this chapter for an example of a centralized review process for a private university.

Why a Course and Program Approval Process Is Needed

As discussed above, the course and program approval process is an area to focus on when making an argument for a centralized approach to the development and management of short-term programs. A standard method of reviewing and evaluating proposals ensures the following:

☐ The integrity of the academic work across units. It also asserts the value of international education to the institution as a whole, rather than belonging to one college, school, or department.

☐ The ability to review and the authority to reject courses based on factors such as assessment of risk in area or region, sound academic objectives, and the maintenance or assurance of academic quality.

☐ A process to manage the number of programs in one discipline or country in order to avoid direct competition for students.

☐ A method to manage growth. There may be more proposals than resources can support.

The approval process will require forming a review committee, developing criteria for selection, determining a timeline for submission and review, creating standardized proposal forms, and disseminating information about short-term programs to the faculty.

Proposal Review Committees

A committee that reviews short-term proposals can serve many different functions, including the following:

☐ Review and approve academic content.

☐ Set unit or campus-wide policy for study abroad and exchange programs.

☐ Establish guidelines for program development.

☐ Create standards for admissions and for program budgets.

☐ Approve affiliation and exchange agreements.

☐ Review student program and scholarship applications.

☐ Evaluate existing programs.

The committee's charge may be identified as academic review, setting administrative policy, or both. Most members discover that this kind of committee work has a very high learning curve and unpredictable complexities, so it is important that the committee has sufficient time to carry out its responsibilities. Members should have international experience, especially as faculty directors, and the committee must have strong leadership. See the "International and Domestic Off-Campus Studies Committee" outline at the end of this chapter.

Working with existing committees. If a study abroad committee already exists, the review of short-term program proposals may simply be added to its responsibilities. If the short-term programs are developed through one academic unit, the committee may consist only of faculty and senior administrators from that unit, as well as a representative from the international office. The proposal process could be a two-step process, whereby the academic unit has the responsibility of determining the academic appropriateness of the course and the study abroad review committee has the task of examining the cultural integrity and administrative feasibility of the program. In the latter model, the program proposal would come to the study abroad committee after receiving approval from the department chair or school director and the academic or college dean.

The course or courses being proposed for a short-term program may be existing courses or first-time offerings from the academic unit. If a course is new, faculty should complete the departmental process for proposing a new course well in advance of submitting the course for inclusion in a study abroad program. There may be a way to have the course approved on a trial basis for one program cycle, before going through a formal review to be added to the department's permanent roster of courses. As short-term programs abroad grow, an academic unit may form a subcommittee from an existing curriculum committee to review the courses to be offered abroad.

Standing committee of the faculty. Regardless of the size of the institution, most international programs administrators discover that a standing committee of the faculty or university is required to reinforce the authority to approve or reject proposals, and to make policy for these programs.

A standing committee focusing on off-campus programs can be a strong ally in advocating for a standardized, centralized approach to short-term program development. In addition, presenting key decisionmakers with sample criteria, proposal and budget forms with suggested guidelines, and a timeline will demonstrate that input from the study abroad office is necessary.

Course and Program Proposals

Again, depending on administrative structure, short-term program proposals may be an appendix to the standard on-campus proposal for new courses, or a separate, detailed document.

These proposals fulfill several functions:
- ☐ Present detailed information about the program (for future use in program publicity);
- ☐ Compel the faculty director to articulate the academic or learning objectives of the program;
- ☐ Demonstrate how the site and learning objectives are integrated;
- ☐ Prompt the faculty director to think through various aspects of the program (academic, financial, logistical, etc.) as he or she responds to proposal questions;

- ☐ Provide a written record of commitment should a discrepancy or disagreement arise later on.

See the course proposal samples at the end of Chapter 5, Designing the Academic Course: Principles and Practicalities.

The deadline for review of course proposals must take into consideration the amount of time needed to develop and recruit for the program. Generally, at least 12 months lead time is required before the program is to take place. A detailed timeline for developing a short-term program can be found in Chapter 7, Feasibility Studies.

Criteria for Reviewing Proposals

The review committee will be charged with either approving or rejecting short-term program proposals, or making recommendations to a senior academic official who will make the final decision. A negative decision should be related directly to the program criteria established, with suggestions to improve the program for future consideration.

The academic, intercultural, and logistical standards for short-term programs abroad should be no less exacting than those for programs of greater duration. In fact, the program's objectives and the stated pedagogical methods of reaching the objectives must be even more specific, clearly articulated, and demonstrable, given the brevity and intensity of these programs.

General Criteria for Short-Term Programs[1]

Academic/Cultural

- ☐ Is the academic rigor comparable to courses offered on campus? Are the prerequisites clearly stated and appropriate? Do the courses enhance or supplement, rather than duplicate, on-campus curriculum? If a new course is being offered, has it been approved by the academic unit's curriculum committee and/or chairperson?
- ☐ What are the intended academic goals of the program? Are these feasible goals given the program duration and the resources and facilities available to students?
- ☐ Who is the intended audience for the program? Do courses offered have a broad enough appeal (are they general education courses or required courses for majors or minors) to attract a sufficient number of applicants?
- ☐ What are the academic advantages to offering these courses abroad? What are the advantages to the specific location proposed?
- ☐ What are the qualifications of the faculty? Does the faculty director have prior experience in this country or region? Does the faculty director have prior experience taking students abroad? How were the host country faculty selected? What are their qualifications? Will a graduate teaching assistant be necessary? If so, how will that/those graduate assistant(s) be selected?

- □ What are the admissions requirements for the program? At a minimum, do they match admissions requirements for other institutional short-term programs?
- □ Is the projected program size conducive to an effective learning environment, given the location, facilities, and proposed activities?
- □ How will this program integrate students into the local academic and community lives?
- □ What is the nature and degree of exposure to the host culture and language?

Logistical
- □ How do the materials and session(s) prepare students for the academic and intercultural experience?
- □ Will international air travel be done as a group, or will students be expected to make their own arrangements?
- □ What is the nature of support services available to students? Have health clinics, a hospital, the nearest consulate or embassy been identified in case there is an emergency?
- □ What library, computer, and research facilities are available at the program site? Are these sufficient for students to complete assigned work?
- □ How will students be counseled to spend their free time? Will on-site safety issues require the faculty director to spend much free time with the students, or will the students be able to engage in independent activities?

General
- □ What evidence is there of student interest for this program (including its location and content)?
- □ How will this program be marketed? What student populations will be targeted for promotional activities?
- □ Is this program sustainable (i.e., are faculty members interested in directing it in future years, are there other faculty who can take leadership on a rotating basis, are the facilities abroad able to host future groups)?
- □ How does the projected cost of this program compare with the cost of the institution's other short-term programs abroad? How does it compare with the cost of other programs at the same site offered by peer institutions?
- □ By what method will the participants evaluate the course and the program, and when?
- □ How does this program fit into the range of programs already offered by the institution? Are there other programs in this geographic area or with this academic content? Does this program compete with or complement those existing programs?

Proposals will often fall into a gray category, and with some tinkering—revising expectations, perhaps adding an on-site program provider—would be approved to operate. The committee must determine if there is enough time for the faculty member to resubmit the proposal to be considered for the same term. It may also happen that a well-composed, feasible proposal is submitted, but the evidence of student interest is not apparent or is in doubt. The committee can approve the program, with the caveat that if a certain quota is not met by the application deadline, either the faculty director will have to make some concessions in his or her compensation, or the program will be canceled and applicants will receive a refund of any deposit monies.

Screening/Approving Faculty Directors
Much has been said about how an institution might ensure the academic quality of short-term programs abroad, but no mention has been made of the selection process for the faculty who will direct the programs. Education abroad professionals know that directing a study abroad program requires skills different than those necessary to be a good classroom instructor. Unfortunately, not all faculty who propose such a program possess the necessary skills and disposition to be a good faculty director. Sometimes this does not become apparent until the faculty member has directed his or her first program, and the participants have provided feedback on their evaluations. But sometimes it becomes obvious, even as early as the proposal process, that a particular faculty member is not the best choice to lead a study abroad program.

No matter the type or size of institution, such situations are tricky and must be handled carefully. Rather than reject a program due to its proposed director, in some cases the director can be persuaded to withdraw the program from consideration when he or she is presented with a realistic picture of the demands placed on faculty directors. An established list of director responsibilities will prove invaluable in such an instance (see Chapter 13). This is also the point at which having a trusted circle of well-respected faculty and senior administrators comes in handy, as these individuals can suggest the least offensive course of action. While it may be possible on some campuses for a faculty committee to reject a proposal due to the identity of the director, at other institutions this would be an invitation for a lawsuit, and therefore the unfortunate outcome of such a dilemma may be to allow the unsuitable faculty member to lead a program, perhaps with extra staff support, with future decisions based on the person's performance as director.

POLICY ISSUES
It is best to base policies for off-campus programs on existing on-campus policies if possible, and to modify them as necessary.

The Academic Calendar

The question may arise as to whether a program abroad should be permitted to take place outside the regular starting and ending dates of an on-campus semester or session, or whether a program may be fully embedded within a regular term, such as spring break. Such issues are best addressed in consultation with relevant units on campus who may have experience with similar special domestic programs. For example, the graduate office or education department may regularly offer intensive, Saturday summer courses that span more than one regular summer session, and therefore they may already have a model for handling grade reporting and other logistical issues that arise when courses are scheduled at unusual times.

An additional issue that is likely to arise when programs are not in accordance with the institution's academic calendar is that of missed classes. Will the institution allow a January-term program to return to campus after spring semester has begun? What about embedded, spring break programs that depart before the break has officially begun? In most instances these are questions that cannot be answered by a faculty committee, though such a committee may make a recommendation to the provost or other senior administrator for a top-down decision.

Credit

If the program falls within a regular academic term (e.g., summer session, January term, intersession), standards for the number of academic credits offered are probably already in place, with the credit hours determined by the academic unit offering the course. The courses offered abroad should be granted the same amount of credit as comparable courses on campus. If graduate credit is available on an undergraduate short-term program, the sponsoring academic department will need to determine if and how much extra work is required in order for students to earn graduate-level credit.

Evaluation methods will need to be adjusted to fit the nature of a course conducted off-campus. If students are to produce research papers, will they have access to libraries or other research facilities, or computer labs? Will handwritten papers be acceptable? If the participants are to submit artwork, do they have adequate and appropriate studio space? Will final papers or projects be due before the end of the program, or will students have an opportunity to submit a final draft upon return to the United States? If final assignments are submitted late (i.e., after the end of the regular session on campus), can provisions be made with the registrar's office for faculty to submit final grades late as well? The chapter on academic course design (Chapter 5) will examine in detail various approaches to teaching tactics, guided free time, and evaluation methods for short-term programs.

Nondegree Students

A policy should be set regarding whether nondegree-seeking students may participate in off-campus programs. Most institutions will allow such students to participate, based on the permission of the faculty director and on a space-available basis. If these students are allowed to participate, it is important to define the expectations for their inclusion and the payment process. The range of grading (letter grade, pass/fail, audit) and their different student status may affect the group dynamics. Generally speaking, it's best to handle all program participants in the same manner, namely that they all pay the same amount and take the same number of courses for credit and a grade. Such a policy not only strengthens the integrity of the program (keeping away from the "study tour" stereotype), but also helps to maintain a sense of egalitarianism among the students.

Faculty Load and Salary

The effect of a short-term program on a faculty member's teaching load is of critical importance to the academic unit sponsoring the course. At issue is the possibility that the faculty member will request or be entitled to a decrease in the teaching load during the regular academic year in order to direct an off-campus course. This may decrease the department's on-campus course offerings during a given semester, or require the department to pay an overload stipend or hire an adjunct instructor to teach the course.

Instructor compensation must be determined before the budget is finalized. Possible salary models may include:

☐ The short-term course is counted into a regular teaching load and there is no change in the faculty member's normal salary;

☐ The short-term course constitutes a teaching overload, so the faculty director receives a supplement;

☐ The short-term course is part of a summer or intersession term, with the department maintaining a separate budget for those terms;

☐ The faculty director's salary is covered on a per student basis by program fees; or

☐ The salary is covered by separate funding from within the department of record or study abroad office.

Again, one should first refer to normal on-campus policy to begin clarifying this issue. It may be that faculty teaching a course abroad are compensated in the same way as their colleagues who teach on campus during the same term, with the salary amount already determined in a collective bargaining agreement or other document. The issue of faculty salary is also examined in the section in Chapter 9, Financial Matters.

Program Size

Careful consideration must be given to the number of participants admitted to the short-term program abroad. The student/faculty ratio should ideally be smaller than that of an on-campus course, as the role of the faculty director extends far beyond the classroom. His or her time on-site will be spent not only on instruction and evaluation, but on arranging logistics, dispensing travel advice, counseling students struggling with the demands of cultural adaptation, resolving housing and budget issues, and responding to problems.

Considerations in determining the program size include:

- ☐ Confirm the on-campus minimum class size. Try to keep to that policy, unless there are field or research reasons to take fewer students.
- ☐ Program budget. A minimum number of students may be required for the program to be fiscally feasible. (An agreed upon minimum set by the academic unit and the international office.)
- ☐ The maximum number of students may be determined by the facilities available at the program site (e.g., housing, transportation, access to cultural sites, excursion arrangements).
- ☐ The faculty director may also have a preferred maximum number that he or she is willing to take, based on activities planned, coursework required, and evaluation methods. Typically, a course with one faculty director will have between eight and 20 participants, but some faculty have reported that two directors should not take more than 25 students.
- ☐ Additional staff, as discussed below, will affect how many students can participate.

Ultimately, the specific discipline and course requirements, and perhaps also the budget, will determine the program size. A geology field course may have a lower student/faculty ratio, based on intense supervision needs, than a more traditional, classroom-based course, for example. Make sure that a consistent policy is established, and that if deviations occur, they are well documented and understood by all. In most cases, faculty are well-prepared with arguments as to why they must keep their program small, so any exceptions to the established program minimum must be transparently clear. Finally, if study abroad course enrollment falls below the institutional minimum, it is important to check with the appropriate campus office to find out whether faculty salaries are then automatically reduced and prorated.

STAFFING

The participation of a second faculty member, staff member, or graduate-level teaching assistant can be of tremendous help to the faculty director—most importantly in providing a second set of eyes and ears, and additional leadership support. This additional staff can be available to make logistical arrangements, lead excursions, conduct lectures, or provide backup in the event the faculty director is called away to respond to a problem. Ultimately, the decision regarding whether or not a program can support an additional leader must be made within the framework of an established policy based on logical and transparent factors, such as program location, group size, faculty director experience, and perhaps even financial factors.

Defining Roles of Additional Staff

The faculty director and/or the study abroad office will need to clearly define the role of additional, nonteaching staff. It is best to have a job description or set of responsibilities and expectations available to possible candidates and the department, and to interview potential assistants. The leadership team should also spend time before departure discussing their interaction with students—the level of formality, use of titles or first names, engaging in free time activities with students (including potentially high-risk activities such as bungee jumping), and if staff will drink alcohol with students. (The issue of alcohol should also be discussed with the institution's risk manager and dean of students.) Because these programs have such academic, intercultural, and social intensity, it is imperative that the leadership team understand each other's expectations and roles vis-à-vis the participants.

The expenses for additional staff, including salary, travel costs, and meal allowances, may fall upon the academic unit of record or the study abroad office, or be factored into the program budget to be charged to the participants on a per-student basis.

Participation of Family Members/Friends

The faculty director may desire to bring along family members, a partner, or a friend for part or all of the program. A policy regarding travel companions must be clearly stated in the program proposal guidelines. Some institutions may prohibit any participation of family members or any party not directly contributing to the academic or administrative content of the program; other institutions may have a more generous policy that allows nonfaculty and family members to accompany and even participate, as long as doing so does not interfere with the teaching of the courses or the availability of the director to the students. At a minimum, faculty guests who participate in the program in any way should be asked to complete a liability waiver similar to that of the students.

Similar to additional staff, the role of a travel companion must be carefully defined. They may have specific skills to contribute to the program such as proficiency in the language or knowledge of the host country. In these situations, there may be a role for them in the program, with some of their expenses supported by the program budget. If, on the other hand, the program budget will not support any expenses for faculty guests, it is important to communicate this to faculty directors early in the program development process.

Guest status and risk management. If family or non-faculty members are allowed to participate in the program, consideration must be given to their academic and financial status: will they be required to register for the courses and pay the tuition? If it is a family member, will he or she be required to pay the program fee, including a portion of the accommodation and board? Or does the person pay only for items that cause additional expense (for example the difference between a single room and a double room, presuming that the program would pay for a single room for the faculty director)? If group reservations are made and perhaps even paid in advance for hotel rooms, airline tickets, or theatre tickets, can faculty guests be included? If so, how and when is the study abroad office to be reimbursed? In addition, it is necessary to consult with institutional counsel and/or the office of risk management to determine if any policies exist regarding the participation of family members and if there is any risk to the institution by allowing them to accompany the group.

Children. Policies and practice differ from institution to institution with regard to faculty bringing children on short-term programs abroad. Some colleges allow and encourage family participation, whereas others prohibit children under age 16 from accompanying the group. Not allowing children may limit the number of faculty who are willing to direct programs, and sometimes children can even bring an added benefit to the group, not to mention the growth experience for the children themselves.

If faculty are allowed to bring their children, consider that short-term programs based at one site work better than programs that include more travel, and that children must be accompanied by another adult who is responsible for their supervision. When planning a short-term program with faculty who intend to travel with their children, it is wise to ask them how they envision child care and emergencies while they are otherwise engaged with the responsibilities of their courses and students. This allows one to express concern for the children's well-being while at the same time emphasizing that the faculty members' main responsibility during the program is to the students, and it is for this that the faculty member is being compensated.

PLANNING FOR ROUND TWO!

It is not likely that *all* of the policies and procedures for short-term programs abroad can be determined and an administrative structure established before the first program proposal is ready to be reviewed by the committee, or even before the first group of students is about to board the plane. There will be many unforeseen challenges that require education abroad professionals to frequently revise expectations, the administrative model, and policies and procedures as the programs develop and grow.

By maintaining a working document of how well procedures are functioning, and by meeting regularly with key decisionmakers, one ensures that all voices are heard in the planning process and that problems can be resolved as they occur. Even before the first program concludes, it is wise to have a strategy for how to spread the word of its success, how to recruit faculty for the following program cycle, and how to recruit other academic units to sponsor short-term programs abroad. "Entrepreneurial" faculty, schools, and departments make the best partners as one begins to expand short-term abroad programs and to standardize policies and procedures.

Endnotes:
[1] Based in part on criteria suggested in Hoffa, W. and Pearson, J., editors (1997), *NAFSA's Guide to Education Abroad for Advisers and Administrators*, Second Edition, NAFSA: Association of International Educators, Washington, D.C.

KEY OFFICES	IMPORTANT POLICY QUESTIONS
Academic deans	Is there support at the highest levels for short-term programs abroad? Can the dean secure funding for faculty salaries?
Department chair/ school directors	Are there faculty with study abroad leadership experience or others with similar experience who can be recommended? Are there suggested majors to target for faculty recruiting? How will short-term programs abroad affect faculty load, salaries, and full-time enrollments for the department? Is there an ideal time for short-term programs? Will chairs and directors be committed and enthusiastic advocates among their faculty?
Registrar	Will the short-term course require a special registration code? How will students register for the course? How can late grade reporting be accommodated? Will the transcript reflect study abroad? If students from other institutions are participating, which office will prepare and distribute a transcript?
Business office	Which office will manage the budget for the short-term program abroad? Who will negotiate contracts for goods and services and approve vendors? Who will conduct financial wire transfers? Which office will issue deposits to service providers, and provide faculty with meal allowances and discretionary funds? What is the refund policy for study abroad program fees? For tuition? Which office will issue refunds of program deposits for students who withdraw? Who will reconcile accounts at the end of the program? Where will excess program funds be placed, and how will deficits be managed?
Financial aid	Can participants in short-term programs abroad apply for financial aid? Is there a separate application, a different process, or time frame? If eligible, will students receive financial aid monies prior to the start of the program?
Risk management	Is emergency medical and/or health insurance required of all participants? Does a contract with an insurance provider need to be negotiated? Will the risk management office need to assess the health and safety conditions of a program location?
Legal counsel	Do program-specific releases and/or an acknowledgment of risks need to be drafted? Do contracts with service providers need to be reviewed and approved by legal counsel? Can legal counsel clarify the responsibilities of the faculty director and the relationship of the program to the service providers and guest lecturers?
Continuing education/ existing departmental programs?	Are there short-term programs abroad in existence at your institution? How are they administered? Can you collaborate? How do you avoid duplicating effort? Are there turf issues of which you should be aware?

Proposal for Standardizing Policies and Procedures for Short-Term Study Abroad Programs

The goal of international education is to provide all qualified students, graduate and undergraduate, with the opportunity to participate and succeed in a study abroad experience. One method to meet the needs of a diverse group of students is through short-term study abroad, which is defined as a 2- to 6-week, faculty-led program. Our short-term programs abroad have experienced tremendous growth over the past 4 years, including an increase in participation from 144 to 345 students and an expansion of programs from 20 to 28, with 35 programs in place for the 1997–98 academic year. This growth also translates into a sharp increase in administrative responsibilities for the international education staff. To meet our stated goals, we need consistent policies and procedures for all short-term programs abroad. Standardization means that we can better represent and protect the university, improve each student's experience, and facilitate the process for faculty. We propose the following policies and procedures:

1. Course Proposals

✓ All faculty will submit a *Course Proposal for a Short-Term Study Abroad Program*, outlining the course description, syllabus integrating how site visits enhance learning objectives, previous site experience, role in the teaching load, and approval by the department chair or program director.

✓ Guidelines for developing such proposals will be provided to faculty and chairs or directors by the international education office. These guidelines are not meant to be either prescriptive or binding. However, considering them will assist in the development of solid programs that are academically strong and feasible abroad.

✓ Department chairs or program directors will verify the academic rigor of the proposal and its place within department plans and staffing needs.

✓ Proposals must be accompanied by a tentative budget.

✓ The January term proposal deadline is December 1.

✓ The summer program deadline is May 1.

2. Review of Proposals

✓ The Academic Review Committee for International Education (ARCIE)—a standing committee of the faculty—will review and approve proposals as well as assessment programs. The committee's purpose in reviewing proposals is to examine logistics, preparation of the faculty, the viability of geographic areas, how site visits enhance the learning objectives of the course, and to approve courses.

✓ Budgets will be reviewed and approved to ensure that salary, stipends, and benefits are included, as well as emergency funds and other expenses.

✓ Curricular and academic issues, such as credit substitutions, prerequisites, and general education requirements must be resolved in the department *before* the proposal is submitted.

✓ A maximum of 35 (including all consortium) courses will be offered each year. If course proposals exceed this maximum, ARCIE will select courses or recommend additional resources.

3. Administration of Courses

✓ Courses will be administered by the staff of the international education office.

✓ Administrative responsibilities will include: coordinating program development, establishment and adherence to timelines, final budget approval, coordinating with faculty on marketing and promotion, facilitating the application and approval process, financial billing and disbursement of all funds, registration of students, organizing a general orientation session and providing orientation materials, preparation and facilitation of application, and evaluation and final report forms. As well, the international education office will provide mandatory faculty training.

✓ Faculty not working with a program provider will be responsible for presenting students with a full syllabus and detailed itinerary before departure.

4. Student Orientation

All short-term programs abroad will have a mandatory student orientation, with a general session coordinated by the international education office.

5. Evaluations

✓ Faculty will ask students to evaluate the academic component of the course by using the appropriate institutional or department forms. Students will also complete a questionnaire about the organizational and logistical aspects of the course.

✓ In addition, the international education office will ask faculty to convene a meeting upon their return, to document travel, accommodations, and unforeseen problems, and to provide a detailed financial accounting.

6. Policies for Short-Term Programs

Policies and procedures will be the responsibility of the international education office. Revisions and additions to the policy will be reviewed by the Study Abroad Advisory Committee or ARCIE, which will make appropriate recommendations to the appropriate committee.

Background for Proposal

Development

Short-term study abroad has been offered since the early 1970s and most student participation has occurred through consortia relationships. Our relationship with the consortium has been very satisfactory to date, as it has allowed faculty to teach courses abroad with substantial support regarding travel details.

On an annual or biannual basis, faculty have offered their own programs outside the consortium, which we refer to as "institutional courses," including courses sponsored by the Spanish, French, and Biology departments.

Enrollment

The last 3 years have seen an "explosion" in student participation.
List student participation numbers.
The increase continues for the following term. *List statistics.*

Proposal for Standardizing Policies and Procedures for Short-Term Study Abroad Programs (contd.)

Course Offerings

There has also been a notable increase in the number of courses offered in the last 3 years. *List courses offered.*

Problem Areas

The following areas have proven to be areas of concern for the international education office's staff:

Course Selection/Approval: Currently, there is no policy for the proposal, review, and administration of short-term programs abroad. This situation allows any faculty member to propose a course at any time and take a group of students abroad independent of any involvement from the international education office. Faculty has been operating under the general policies for the January term or summer courses, which require approval by the department chair. The international education office has offered administrative services and guidance on a resource basis, when it was requested, or we offer and encourage faculty to use our services. As a result, many faculty choose to work with our office, and when numbers were modest, we were able to respond on an ad hoc basis. However, as numbers have grown, so have the expectations for services. Given the current and increasing demand for international education office services, if we are to be efficient and effective we need to establish standard operating procedures.

Standard Rules of Participation: Study abroad policy states that students are not allowed to study abroad if they are on academic or disciplinary probation. Faculty who take students abroad do not necessarily request or verify academic and/or disciplinary records, and on most application forms, do not seek the authorization necessary from each student to verify their status.

Standard Approach to Pricing: At present, pricing is the decision of the faculty director. All short-term study abroad courses should have a stated program cost, which includes academic fees, travel expenses, and the university off-campus study fee. The registrar's office and the office of business affairs seek the international education office's direction in defining proper course and fee coding.

Facilitation of Financial Aid: If students wish to apply for or use current financial aid, they must work with student financial services. The international education office has developed a system to provide the registrar's office and student financial services staff with specific budget figures, official documentation from each student going abroad, and confirmation that student accounts have been cleared for additional billing. If faculty work independently, students will not benefit from the clear, seamless procedures that are in place for other study abroad programs, and this places undue, last-minute burden on staff from many different departments.

Standardized Billing: A system has been created to allow participants to be billed through their student accounts for programs. The many advantages to this system include the following: no individual or office functions as a bank or a collection agency; the designated individual (parent or student) receives the bill; financial aid matters can be considered by trained personnel, and students receive institutional credit for the course, paying the institution that transcripts the credit rather than an external vendor.

Collection of Fees by Proper Sources: Some faculty who work independently have collected monies directly from students and thus do not comply with the university policy that all funds collected on behalf of the university be administrated by a department of the institution, not by individual faculty members.

Liability for the University: Because there are no standardized procedures, there is no guarantee that faculty who take students abroad independently but on the behalf of the university, are aware of risk management and insurance issues. Faculty must also take the proper steps to advise and educate students about their responsibilities as study abroad participants. Further, faculty need to be well informed so that they do not make decisions that could increase the risk of liability for the institution.

Coordinated Orientation Programs: Currently, there is no coordinated orientation program for students or faculty. As an institution, we want to ensure that students receive a *thorough* predeparture orientation and information on academic expectations, cultural issues, health and safety, travel and logistics, and behavioral expectations. In addition, there is no policy ensuring that faculty should be informed about issues of institutional liability.

[Source: Adapted from the University of St. Thomas]

Program Development and Administration Responsibilities
Short-term Off-Campus Programs

Program/Faculty Directors	International Education (IEC)	Program Provider
GENERAL		
▪ Finalize itinerary. Notify IEC.		

▪ Provide IEC with:
  ○ Program dates
  ○ Final course title
  ○ Number of credits
  ○ If non-UST students are welcome to apply
  ○ If family or guests will accompany program.		

▪ Identify program provider. If program provider is not selected, faculty take responsibility of all logistical and academic arrangements, except IEC will coordinate airfare.	▪ Advise on selection of program provider. ▪ Assist with Request for Proposal, if required.	▪ Provide UST with contract.
▪ Obtain written contract from program provider.	▪ Review and sign all contracts.	
▪ Identify special health considerations.	▪ Advise on special health considerations. ▪ Schedule Travel Clinic with Health Services.	▪ Identify special health considerations.
▪ Notify IEC of any links to your own Web site, department, etc.	▪ Manage all Web site content.	
BUDGET/TRAVEL/LOGISTICS		
Budget	**IEC manages all financial issues**	
▪ Submit budget figures to IEC (see example).	▪ Review and create final budget.	▪ Provide budget numbers to faculty or IEC.
	▪ Approve program cost.	
	▪ Provide budget information to Student Financial Services.	

Program/Faculty Directors	International Education (IEC)	Program Provider
BUDGET/TRAVEL/LOGISTICS (con't)		
	▪ Create student billing sheets for Student Financial Services and Business Office.	
▪ Provide payment information, e.g. invoices. Provide receipts and the *UST Employee Travel and Reimbursement* form for any program expenses that must be reimbursed to faculty director.		▪ Provide payment information and timeline to IEC (wire, draft, credit card).
		▪ Submit final payment invoice to IEC.
Airfare		
▪ Identify airline departure and arrival dates and flight requests. Notify IEC.	▪ Notify airfare provider of required airline tickets.	▪ Process flight deviations.
	▪ Pay all deposits on travel.	
	▪ Submit full names to airline or program providers.	
▪ Obtain or renew personal passport, if required. Submit copy to IEC.	▪ Obtain visa information and request visa forms. Coordinate all visas.	
Meals		
▪ How many group meals? What meals will be provided?	▪ Complete Student Financial Services database with expenses and number of meals provided.	
MARKETING/RECRUITMENT		
▪ Recruit students for program.	▪ Marketing of curriculum through Web site, *Bulletin Today*, and a printed list of all short-term programs available.	
▪ Advise students.		
▪ Create brief short course description for Web (see example)		
▪ Create full Course Description (see example).	▪ Edit course description.	
	▪ Post on Web site.	

ENROLLMENT

Program/Faculty Directors	International Education (IEC)	Program Provider
• Decide on enrollment criteria.	• Establish all enrollment materials, including forms required by faculty and/or program provider as well as the number of photos required from students.	• Notify IEC if additional forms are necessary (including liability waivers, etc.).
• Review application dossiers.	• Place enrollment procedures and materials on Study Abroad Web site	
• Set up and conduct interviews (per procedures established by IEC).	• Create and mail *Notification of Status* letters to students (accept, deny).	
• Make final selection of students. Notify IEC of those students selected or denied.	• Refund deposits.	
	• Manage student data for reporting.	
	• Communicate with faculty regarding all enrollment changes, issues, etc.	
	• Provide enrollment updates, etc. to program providers.	• Request enrollment updates as required.

ACADEMIC/REGISTRATION

Program/Faculty Directors	International Education (IEC)	Program Provider
• Syllabus	• Advise on course content.	
• Organize on-site classrooms, class schedule and "processing" sessions.		• On-site classrooms and class schedule, if required.
• Order books.		
• If part of course is taught at UST, request classrooms. Notify students and IEC.	• IEC notified of UST classroom, if used.	
• Submit course for major/minor and/or general requirement approval.	• IEC notified of M/M/G requirement proposals and status. Assist faculty if necessary.	
• Notify IEC of status and/or approval.		

Program/Faculty Directors	International Education (IEC)	Program Provider
Registration		
▪ Identify course number/section number. ▪ Notify IEC of course number NOTE: Because of the irregularities of setting up study abroad courses, the Registrar's Office will set up all undergraduate courses and review graduate course set up.	▪ Provide course number/section number to Registrar. ▪ Provide student information for registration. ▪ Provider transcript "footer" information to Registrar.	
ORIENTATION		
▪ Notify IEC of audiovisual needs for orientation (slide projector, vcr)	▪ Schedule General Orientation session and breakout sessions following.	
▪ Schedule course orientation if not held after General Orientation session. Notify IEC and students.	▪ Create and distribute student handbook.	
▪ Hold additional individual group meetings.	▪ Provide *Culturegrams* for all locations available.	
▪ Provide course-specific information.	▪ Provide Passport Information to students (via Policies & Procedures and Web site).	
▪ Provide airline and itinerary information and enough copies for students and their emergency contacts.		
▪ Attend faculty directors' dinner.	▪ Organize faculty director's dinner. Notify all faculty directors.	
▪ Attend other faculty director training events.		
PRE-DEPARTURE		
▪ Correspond with students.	▪ Create and distribute International Student ID cards.	▪ Continue to communicate details and planning with faculty and IEC.
▪ Provide IEC with photo and birth date for International Teacher ID card (form enclosed).	▪ Create student evaluations and give to faculty for distribution at end of course.	
▪ Provide IEC with final syllabus and travel itinerary.	▪ Order UST credit card (if required).	

Program/Faculty Directors	International Education (IEC)	Program Provider
BUDGET/TRAVEL/LOGISTICS (con't)		
	▪ Create student billing sheets for Student Financial Services and Business Office.	
▪ Provide payment information, e.g. invoices. Provide receipts and the *UST Employee Travel and Reimbursement* form for any program expenses that must be reimbursed to faculty director.		▪ Provide payment information and timeline to IEC (wire, draft, credit card).
		▪ Submit final payment invoice to IEC.
Airfare		
▪ Identify airline departure and arrival dates and flight requests. Notify IEC.	▪ Notify airfare provider of required airline tickets.	▪ Process flight deviations.
	▪ Pay all deposits on travel.	
	▪ Submit full names to airline or program providers.	
▪ Obtain or renew personal passport, if required. Submit copy to IEC.	▪ Obtain visa information and request visa forms. Coordinate all visas.	
Meals		
▪ How many group meals? What meals will be provided?	▪ Complete Student Financial Services database with expenses and number of meals provided.	
MARKETING/RECRUITMENT		
▪ Recruit students for program.	▪ Marketing of curriculum through Web site, *Bulletin Today*, and a printed list of all short-term programs available.	
▪ Advise students.		
▪ Create brief short course description for Web (see example)	▪ Edit course description.	
▪ Create full Course Description (see example).	▪ Post on Web site.	

International and Domestic Off-Campus Studies (IDOCS) Committee

A. The general purpose of the IDOCS committee is to consider, review, and promote courses, plans, and policies relating to international and domestic off-campus academic programs.

B. Responsibilities include

1. Granting probationary approval for first-time offerings, off-campus courses, and programs (both domestic and international). Approval of these courses will signify approval of all relevant additional requirements prior to the committee's approval:

   a) Department or program major credit

   b) General education credit

   c) Cross-cultural credit

   d) Area studies credit

2. Reviewing, evaluating, and recommending off-campus, noninterim courses and programs (both domestic and international) to the faculty for final approval during the second year of operation.

3. Reviewing, evaluating, and recommending off-campus field supervisor courses to the faculty for approval.

4. Acting on behalf of the faculty in approving as ongoing interim courses (both domestic and international) those courses offered for the second time (within 3 years of the first offering).

5. Advising on administrative policies and procedures for courses and programs administered by the international and off-campus studies office.

6. Promoting a global perspective through:

   a) encouraging scholarship and expertise supporting international and off-campus study;

   b) nurturing effective relationships between on-campus and off-campus study;

   c) fostering ties with other academic institutions that support international and off-campus study;

   d) advising on continuing education and alumni programs that further the aims of international and off-campus study;

   e) aiding the promotion of international career opportunities; and

   f) supporting recruitment, admissions, and integration of international students and scholars on campus.

C. Personnel

1. One elected faculty member from each of the five faculties of the college, two students elected by the student body, and the director of international and off-campus studies.

2. Term of office:

   The term of office for the elected faculty members is 3 years. One of the elected students will be a junior and one a senior. Both students should have had an off-campus experience.

[Source: Adapted from St. Olaf College]

Review of International Education Programs

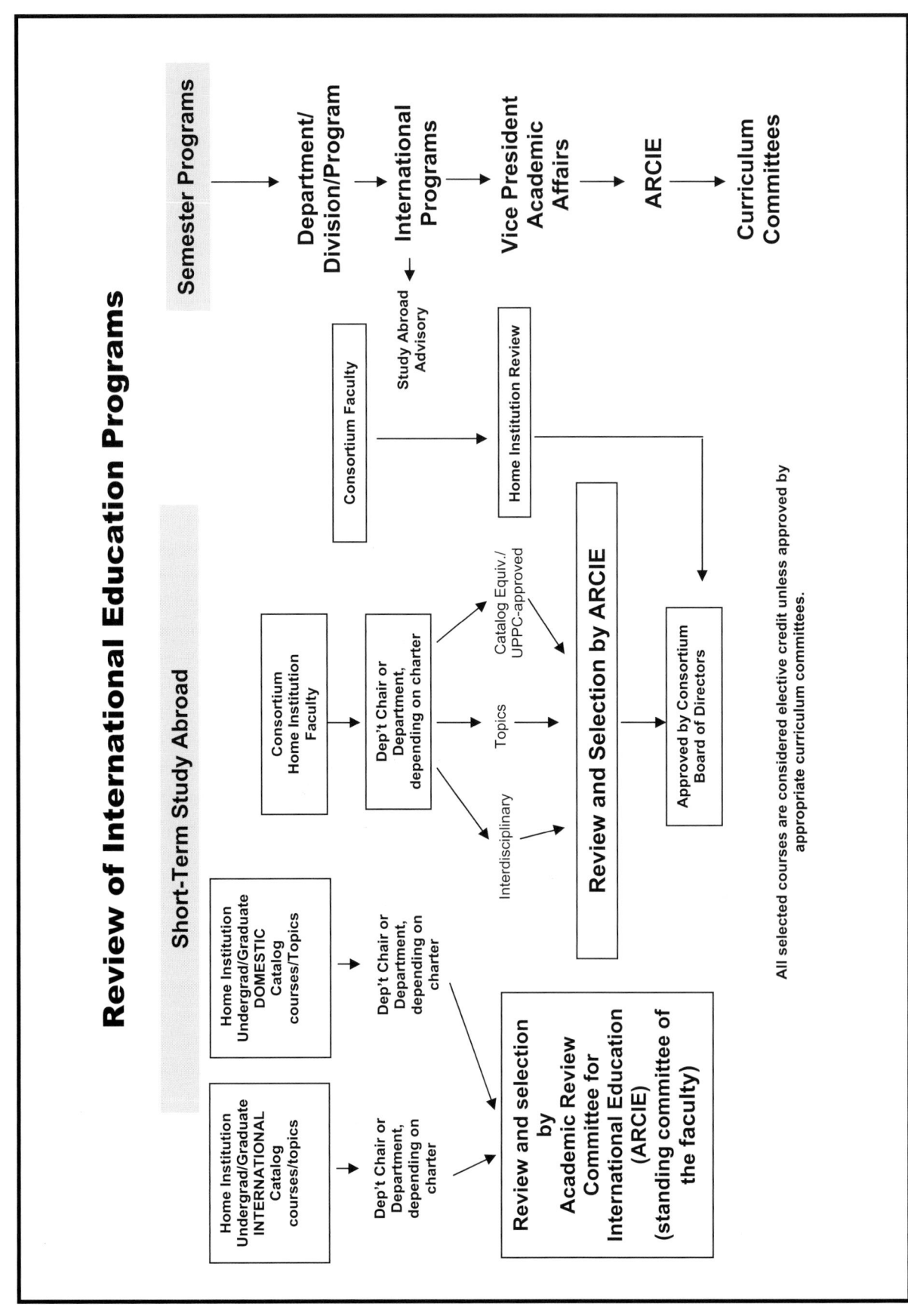

[Source: Adapted from the University of St. Thomas]

INTERNAL SUPPORT SYSTEMS:
IT TAKES A CAMPUS TO RUN
A STUDY ABROAD PROGRAM

Dawn White

By their very nature, short-term programs abroad intensify the relationship between the international office and administrative and academic units on campus. In most cases, these programs require modifications to policies and procedures already in place for longer-term study abroad programs as well as on-campus courses. Two elements that have a great impact on the extent to which policies and procedures need to be modified on your campus are (1) the degree to which study abroad is accepted by your institution as an integral part of a student's university experience, and (2) the amount of administrative flexibility inherent in or built into your institution's internal systems.

This chapter examines the relationship between the international office and the other departments on campus that are essential to the successful administration of short-term programs abroad.

Academic Affairs

As the office ultimately responsible for all academic programs on your campus, academic affairs is likely to take more than a passing interest in the shape and content of short-term programs abroad. Indeed, most international offices are regularly tapped for information on their programs as part of the institution's annual update to its regional accrediting body.

Information routinely requested includes the following:

☐ Where in the world programs are offered.

☐ Whether the programs carry graduate or undergraduate credit.

☐ The number of students enrolled.

☐ Whether there is an on-site administrator.

☐ Whether there is a cosponsoring organization.

Accrediting agencies are also interested in the existence of contractual relationships with nonaccredited organizations, which include most institutions and program providers abroad, and whether or not any substan-tive changes were implemented in existing programs or are planned for the coming year.

If your office is asked to provide this information, consider it an opportunity to promote awareness of your programs instead of a reporting burden. Use the information request as an opportunity to highlight the innovative opportunities your office is creating for students and faculty to gain international experience and expertise. If the university's mission is already geared toward a greater international profile, you have the perfect opportunity to promote short-term programs abroad as a way of enhancing that mission and positioning the international office as central to that effort. If the university does not focus on its international profile, you have yet another opportunity to make a case in favor of including study abroad in the university's mission.

Institutional Priorities

Keeping institutional priorities in mind as you work with faculty to develop short-term programs abroad or identify program providers will further enhance your relationship with the academic leaders on your campus. If service learning is a priority, seek to incorporate a service-learning element in some of your short-term programs. If student retention is a priority, assess how many of your short-term program participants have come back to graduate from your institution. If the percentage is high, which is likely, make sure your president and provost know that study abroad is a powerful retention tool. If diversity is a priority, show how international opportunities can be attractive to participants from underrepresented groups. Make it a point to link short-term study abroad with other campus initiatives, and keep campus leaders informed of those links.

Academic Deans

You will be recruiting faculty from individual colleges and may be asking the departments to fund faculty salaries for the programs. Deans are one of the most important sources of support. Not only do they have the ear of the president or provost, they have budgetary oversight of their units and help set the mission for and tone of those units. Deans can assist in recruiting faculty and in helping you navigate the sometimes murky waters of college politics, turf, and faculty relations.

ACADEMIC DEPARTMENTS

Once you have sold the idea of short-term study abroad to an academic dean, the chair of a department or the director of a school can help determine which faculty will be enthusiastic and capable program directors and administrators; who has prior experience directing or teaching in a program abroad; what areas of the department curriculum could be enhanced by a short-term program; what potential for participation exists within the majors offered at the school; the appropriate timing of such a program; and how a short-term program could fit into a faculty teaching load and existing salary.

Working with faculty in the creation and administration of short-term programs abroad can be one of the most enjoyable parts of your job. Faculty in academic departments support international offices in a number of ways: they review course proposals, advise students about programs abroad, publicize program opportunities in their classrooms, and often evaluate coursework students bring back from abroad. If they also happen to be developing and directing programs abroad, their contributions are even greater.

Study abroad professionals tend to focus so much on the student experience of education abroad that it is easy to overlook the personal and professional gains that departments and faculty members can realize. A faculty member's experience directing a short-term program can:

- ☐ Culminate in the design of new courses, adding currency to a department's roster of course offerings and enriching its curriculum.
- ☐ Lead to the development of research interests or enhance existing ones. Although the work involved in directing most short-term programs usually precludes faculty from engaging in independent research opportunities while the program is underway, some faculty can extend their stays abroad to make the very best professional use of their time.

- ☐ Result in scholarly publications, an outcome highly valued in the promotion and tenure process.
- ☐ Contribute to an increase in student credit hours for the department. A charismatic teacher with a loyal following will attract program participants. In the same vein, students who have a truly positive experience abroad under the guidance of an excellent faculty member may take more courses from that professor once they are back on campus. Either way, the increase in student credit hours is a boon to the department.
- ☐ Spark innovative approaches in methods of teaching and evaluation that are suitable for transfer to the home campus setting. The experiential nature of short-term programs abroad—a feature that sets them apart from programs of longer duration—often serves as the driving force behind the development of new approaches to student learning and assessment.

All of these outcomes have the potential to enhance a faculty member's portfolio. This is especially true on campuses that have gone through the process of internationalization: teaching abroad is more likely to be valued, incorporated as one criterion of faculty scholarship, and reflected in the institution's promotion and tenure guidelines.

There is potential for a mutually beneficial relationship between academic departments and international offices. Faculty members appreciate the expertise of study abroad professionals in preparing budgets, orienting students, and providing logistical support. Study abroad professionals appreciate the fact that the academic content of a faculty-directed program is the province of the department. Because each unit understands what it can offer the other, a complementary relationship is established that feeds the development of short-term opportunities abroad for students and faculty.

Yet the relationship between international offices and academic departments is not without its challenges. As discussed in the previous chapter, a challenge surfaces in the form of the faculty member who for years has run a proprietary program abroad without the involvement of any campus office and who wants the situation to stay that way, even if policies and procedures established on campus in the interim warrant a change. Campus politics will usually determine how such a situation is addressed.

Relations with academic departments can also be tested when a short-term program takes place during a term or semester, requiring students to miss regularly scheduled courses. This puts a burden on faculty members to make special arrangements for the students missing class, but the argument can reasonably be put forth that this is the same kind of accommodation that is made for athletes and band members who are out of the classroom for brief periods of time. Faculty members who know of these situations well in advance are more likely to be accommodating.

An additional challenge comes from faculty members who think that the only place students can learn is in their own classrooms. Such faculty are not likely to be supportive of any type of study abroad program, even short-term, if it takes students off campus. Fortunately, such faculty are exceptions to the rule. Most people engaged in the business of educating students understand and appreciate that study abroad professionals are dedicated to creating opportunities for students and faculty to gain overseas experience.

Academic Advising

Academic advisers often form long-lasting relationships with students, guiding them through the entire course of their academic programs. These advisers are likely to know a great deal about the personal lives of their advisees. If they are made aware of the reasons students have for not participating in traditional study abroad programs (e.g., financial obligations or family commitments), the advisers are in a powerful position to recommend a short-term program abroad as a feasible and attractive alternative.

A strong selling point for students participating in short-term programs abroad is that their progress toward graduation is unlikely to be interrupted by a brief sojourn abroad. Indeed, this is one of the reasons short-term study is so attractive to today's university students. A pressing issue for students is how the credit earned abroad will apply toward graduation requirements. Will it fulfill a general education requirement, a distribution requirement, a major or minor requirement? Will it qualify for internship or service-learning credit? Or will it fall into that general category of "elective credit?"

A student's academic adviser, who might also be a faculty member in the student's major department or an administrator assigned to a larger unit, can be instrumental in influencing or even determining how credit will be applied.

Because one of the goals of academic advisers is to guide students toward timely completion of their degree programs, it is in their best interests to facilitate the process of program participants getting useful academic credit applied toward their graduation requirements. Inviting suggestions from academic advisers about the possibilities for credit earned on short-term programs during the program development stage may even yield more student participants: the advisers are more likely to be invested in the success of the program if they helped shape it.

THE REGISTRAR'S OFFICE

The sheer number of administrative tasks that directly affect students on programs abroad, ranging from the way courses are coded internally to the way grades earned abroad are recorded on student transcripts, makes the registrar's office a key player.

Building Courses into the System

A given course is "built" by the registrar's office when certain elements—including but not limited to the title, level, beginning and ending dates, instructor of record, and grading options—are entered into a computer program using information supplied by the appropriate academic unit. Departures from the norm usually require special handling, and short-term courses abroad often fit this category.

Timelines

As the short-term courses abroad are built, information is added that distinguishes them from on-campus courses. For example, a special mechanism may be developed to override regular tuition and fee charges if tuition for a program abroad is included in the program fee. And because the timeline for developing and administering short-term programs abroad is often completely independent of regular university processes, the timeline for building them in the registrar's office may be different as well, creating an additional reason for special handling. Also, the timeline for registering students, processing grade reports, and generating transcripts varies greatly according to the actual dates of the short-term program.

Blocked Registration

The registration process must be controlled so that only program participants are able to register. There are probably as many ways to do this as there are institutions. If the course is listed in the school's schedule of classes or available online, certain information such as the course registration number can be withheld, or the consent of the instructor can be required to complete the registration process. On many campuses, registration is completed not by the student but by the program administrator, because students must be approved to participate in the course. This is especially effective if registration is tied to payment of program fees or other administrative processes, such as allocation of financial aid. On the other hand, registration is a good double check for the international office—if a student fails to register, it may mean that his or her plans have changed but he or she neglected to notify your office.

Temporary or "Dummy" Courses

Several course registration issues need to be considered. Temporary or "dummy" courses—to be replaced later by courses reflecting the student's actual enrollment—are often used in situations where course registrations are not finalized until students are well into the program or where the registration triggers a program charge on the student's university account. Due to their limited duration and the fact that fewer courses may be involved, short-term programs abroad are more likely to have discrete course names and numbers assigned, but there may be valid reasons to use temporary registrations, such as when a course's credit comes from another institution. If this is the case, the registrar's office then relies on the international office to submit paperwork to replace the temporary registration with a student's "real" courses and credits. Often this happens at the time grades are ready to be recorded on the student's permanent academic record, which may be sometime after the program has ended.

THE BUSINESS OFFICE

Especially for institutions that administer their own short-term programs, creating and maintaining a partnership with the business office is key. Why? The management of budgets for short-term programs is often very complicated.

As discussed in Chapter 8, Logistics, it is likely that your office will need to place deposits for accommodations, group flights, and arranged activities, or conduct site visits long before any program revenue is generated to allay these costs. Where will these monies come from?

If wire transfers need to be made to overseas accounts, which office will conduct the transactions? There may be rules about signing contracts and negotiating fees and payments, particularly if the service provider is overseas. You may be able to make arrangements up to a certain dollar limit (e.g., arranging group travel with your preferred travel agent); above that amount, services must be sent out for bid and your office may not be able to use its preferred provider. What about "corporate" credit cards? Can your faculty director get one in the institution's name?

If there is more than one program, will the fees be placed into separate program accounts or one general fund? Who will process refunds for students? Which office will provide the faculty director with a per diem advance and monies needed during the program? Which office will reconcile the accounts upon completion of the program?

Be sure to check out Chapter 9, Financial Matters, for a discussion on reporting systems for faculty directors.

Whenever possible, use the existing account system to bill students for their short-term programs abroad. In the past, short-term programs were billed separately from the standard on-campus billing system, with an invoice sent directly to the student studying abroad, and the student then making payment to the international office or the faculty director's personal checking account to cover travel logistics.

It is obvious that this independent system does not work for many reasons, including the increased liability of handling students' money outside of the normal institutional channels.

Student Accounts

If students are not billed through their student accounts at your institution, consider advocating to the business office for the following reasons:

- ☐ The international office does not function as a bank or collection agency.
- ☐ There is increased time to collect final payments.

- ☐ The designate person(s) receives the bill, including parents.
- ☐ Financial aid matters can be considered by trained personnel, by working directly with the financial aid office.
- ☐ Students are receiving institutional credit for the course and therefore should be paying the institution that grants the credit.
- ☐ By billing students through their on-campus accounts, the process parallels the usual billing procedures for longer-term study abroad.

The Financial Aid Office

When it comes to financial aid, many students do not leave home without it. Increasingly, students rely on federal, state, and institutional grants and loans to help finance their study abroad programs. The compressed nature of short-term programs abroad and their unique organizational characteristics create a need for the financial aid office and the office or individual responsible for the short-term program to work closely together to make sure the financial aid process encourages rather than hinders study abroad. This is especially important if an off-campus course is offered through a program provider, which mixes a third party into the equation.

Program Budgets for Financial Aid Counselors

The financial aid office determines the amount of financial aid a student is eligible to receive based on the cost of tuition and estimated living expenses in the local community. A short-term program abroad necessitates the creation of a separate budget, not only because living expenses abroad can vary dramatically from those on the home campus but also because instructional costs are not the same. These budgets, typically prepared in the international office or by the faculty director and sent to financial aid, break down the program fee into student, instructional, and administrative expenses. Students often have the opportunity to apply for additional aid, usually in the form of loans.

Maintaining Student Eligibility

Since the financial aid office must also receive documentation that students passed a requisite number of credits before their aid for the next term is released, the administrator needs to develop procedures that allow students to maintain their eligibility for aid. Say, for example, that one of your students is on a short-term program involving intense field work on site but also requiring a written report to be submitted when the student is back on campus for the next term. Failing to receive a grade for the study abroad course may prevent that student from getting aid for the following term, since the student will technically be seen as not having completed a full academic load.

One creative way to address such an issue is to assign the student an "in progress" or temporary passing grade, based on successful work on site and the presumption of a final project to be turned in. This kind of creative solution requires trust and a partnership between the financial aid office, the registrar's office, and the international office, and depends on careful record keeping and appropriate follow-up in all three offices.

How to Modify On-Campus Procedures

What is clear from the descriptions above is that someone is going to extra effort on behalf of the study abroad participant—and it is usually more than one person in more than one office at various times in the short life cycle of a program abroad. If you find that policies and procedures on your campus impede short-term study abroad, it may be time to overhaul them. These may be the legacy of a previous generation of administrators who were resistant to change, or they may simply be outdated. If the answer to every question regarding a given procedure is "because it's always been done that way," it is clearly time to reevaluate the procedure. Advances in technology can serve as a springboard to innovation. Advances in mindsets can do the same.

To start building these important relationships, propose a meeting with the registrar, the business office, and the financial aid officer. After first expressing gratitude for the assistance and cooperation these key people provide in making study abroad possible for so many deserving students, you can suggest a review of procedures with the goal of streamlining the process. Busy administrators embrace timesaving measures. Encouraging innovations leads to outcomes that everyone can support. It is important for you to remain flexible throughout this process and to be willing to listen. Your ideas for streamlining the system may need to be adjusted.

Do not overlook the power of anecdotal evidence to assist your cause. Point out other campuses whose offices have endorsed streamlining measures. Suggest that the administrators talk to their colleagues on other campuses who can provide reassurance that they are not going out on a limb while at the same time providing models worthy of emulation. The bottom line: if your campus administrative officers equate streamlining a process with reducing the effort they have to expend—without relinquishing control—you may find them extremely receptive allies.

You may even be able to convince your colleagues in those other essential offices to give you the ability to build courses, register students, process program payments, apply financial aid, and/or record grades. Some campuses have gradually assumed more and more of the tasks that were once the exclusive province of specialized offices. By granting certain people in the international office the authority to perform designated tasks—virtually all of them done electronically—directors of the other offices maintain oversight of their own systems while essentially reducing the work load of their staff. The result? A much more efficient process, and a fine example of interoffice trust and collegiality.

DEAN OF STUDENTS/DIVISION OF STUDENT AFFAIRS

The dean of students and your student affairs colleagues can provide invaluable support to off-campus programs.

Because of the group structure and the larger pool of students going abroad, conduct or behavioral issues may become a problem while overseas. A process to send students home is described in Chapter 16, Safeguards. You should work with your dean of students office to write student conduct procedures, such as those also found in the Sample Disciplinary Rights and Procedures for Study Abroad Programs, Academic and Nonacademic, at the end of Chapter 16. Behavioral expectations should be an integral part of any general student policy handbook.

Most institutions do not allow students to apply for or participate in study abroad programs if they are on conduct probation. You may have a student who is put on probation after being accepted and approved to study abroad. Work with the dean of students office to negotiate the case. Sometimes students are placed in the conduct system at the end of the term, right before departure. Depending on the situation, a student may be allowed to depart for the off-campus program after signing a behavior contract and discussing the case with the faculty director and the dean of students.

As discussed in Chapter 11, Student Selection and Enrollment, the dean of students office may provide student disciplinary records (with permission from the student) for past infractions, or provide an endorsement to study off campus. See sample Consent to Release at the end of this chapter.

New Student Orientation/Residence Halls

Recruit your student affairs professionals to help promote study abroad opportunities at new student orientations, especially short-term programs abroad aimed at first-or second-year students. Also make sure that resident hall personnel, such as resident assistants, know what opportunities are available, and ask them to promote study abroad.

HEALTH AND WELLNESS

Fortunately, many services offered to students on campus can be extended to participants of short-term programs abroad. Professionals in the health center and the counseling center possess knowledge that is valuable in preparing students for aspects of their brief sojourns abroad that they had not considered. They may welcome opportunities to share their expertise and to develop country-specific or program-specific plans for students to stay healthy while abroad. These colleagues can also be useful in faculty director orientations and training, so faculty can ask questions and work through situations before going abroad with students.

Health Services

Health service professionals (i.e., nurses and doctors) can play a key role in preparing students to study abroad. Work with the health services department to identify required immunizations for region-specific areas (see the Peru example in Chapter 16, Safeguards: Health Issues), and propose that they offer these prescriptions or inoculations at the health center. Also ask them to participate in orientations and review written materials such as handbooks and Web sites.

Your health services colleagues may also work with students after they return, when symptoms may appear and need to be diagnosed.

Counseling Center

Counseling professionals also play a role in preparing both faculty and students to go abroad, as well as assisting with situations while the group is overseas.

Be sure a representative from the counseling center is available to talk to faculty directors and other staff responsible for short-term programs abroad. The counselor can discuss how to deal with certain situations, such as a student going off prescription medication or refusing to eat. If circumstances that warrant counseling develop abroad, make sure a counselor and the program's on-site personnel talk to each other. Confirm that some members of the counseling staff have current passports, in case one of them needs to bring a student home.

HUMAN RESOURCES

Your human resources department can provide information on the benefits available to faculty directors and other leaders such as staff or teaching assistants while they are out of the country. Remember to discuss appropriate levels of medical evacuation for all international sites. Like students, faculty and staff should understand their health insurance and how it travels abroad.

GENERAL COUNSEL/RISK MANAGEMENT

Great strides have been made in the last decade in establishing guidelines and best practices with health, safety, and risk management. With short-term programs abroad, where so many aspects of these issues are condensed, there is less time to deal with emergencies of any kind.

As documented in Chapter 16, Safeguards, your institution's legal counsel and risk management personnel can help you prepare contingency plans to deal with the unexpected: medically evacuating a student or faculty director, notifying a student of a family emergency at home, dealing with a natural disaster in the field, or coping with a political crisis at home or abroad.

Legal Services

The legal affairs or services office should be made aware of the short-term programs abroad and their locations. Program-specific waivers of responsibility and acknowledgment of risks forms may need to be drafted; any new waiver should be reviewed and approved by the general counsel of your institution. In addition, any contracts for goods and services provided by third party agencies or organizations (e.g., travel agencies, host institutions, local transportation companies) may need to be reviewed and approved by institutional counsel.

Risk Management

The risk management office can play an important role in supporting a decision to reject a program proposal that presents too great a health or safety risk, based on its location or proposed activities. This office can also negotiate emergency medical and/or health insurance coverage for students and faculty. It can also assist in creating a budget line for emergency contingency funds for a single program or a set of short-term programs abroad.

PUBLICATIONS/COMMUNICATIONS

International offices are well versed in publicity strategies for their programs, but often they do not think about publicity beyond the immediate need of using it to recruit students. Tapping into the vast network of communication lines across campus is an extremely effective way not only to promote a particular short-term program abroad but also to advocate for study abroad in general. Ask your publications department to create materials and brochures that will carry the institution's "image" and highlight your programs.

Contributing to Internationalization

The success of a program is determined not just by what happens to the students on site but also by the educational value placed by the institution on the students' experiences. Campus leaders and colleagues need to know about these students' experiences in order to value them. The more the institution and its members value these experiences, the more they will promote them, especially if short-term study abroad is viewed as a significant contributing factor in the process of internationalization. Keeping the campus informed also draws attention to international offices as leading agents in facilitating opportunities for students to have meaningful intercultural experiences.

When the latest statistics on short-term study abroad are published in the annual Institute of International Education's *Open Doors* report, send notes to your campus media office and your government relations officer, indicating your institution's role in participating in significant study abroad trends.

Staff/faculty newsletters and daily bulletins are obvious places to advertise opportunities for faculty to direct programs abroad as well as to call for proposals. They are also excellent venues to carry follow-up stories on program participants and faculty directors.

Student newspapers can serve the same function for students and faculty. Invite the campus editor to visit your office at least once a year. Ask the editor to assign a reporter to check in on a regular basis. Invite a campus reporter to orientations and reentry sessions. (Be prepared to get a phone call if a student is sent home from the program, a political situation arises, or complaints about your enrollment process surface.)

If your students are in programs that include service-learning components, facilitate opportunities for students to share their experiences with the campus community on return. Ask your campus media office for assistance in developing public service announcements to publicize student presentations of their experiences abroad.

If your campus has its own radio station, suggest that the station interview students and faculty before they go and after they come back.

Alumni Magazine

Editors of alumni magazines are always on the lookout for story ideas that reflect well on the university, even if they do not specifically feature alumni, so suggestions are likely to be well received. The unique features of short-term programs abroad make good copy.

On-Campus News Services

Occasionally, media sources will contact your institution wanting an interview either of general interest or pertaining to some global crisis. Have a plan for dealing with these requests. Especially if the interview is dealing with a particular crisis issue, it may be better for the communications director to deal with the media since your office will be busy dealing with the crisis.

ADMISSIONS

Admissions counselors routinely visit local high schools and community colleges. Ask your admissions staff to highlight short-term study abroad as an exciting option for new and transfer students.

CAREER CENTER

Ask the career center advisers on your campus to talk to students about how study abroad can enhance employment prospects and how short-term study, with its frequent emphasis on field work and experiential learning, can help them develop skills beyond the academic framework. Invite alumni who participated in short-term programs abroad to talk about how their experiences abroad shaped their career paths.

INSTRUCTIONAL TECHNOLOGY

Computers are so much a part of campus life now that students are forced to make major adjustments when they go abroad on programs where computer access is limited. Unless students have the comparative luxury of ready access to laptops, the opportunity to use computers is even more limited on short-term programs abroad.

Laptops Abroad

You might consider making it an institutional policy that the faculty director be equipped with a laptop to take along lecture notes, to keep a running report throughout the program, or to facilitate e-mail access for emergency communication. A faculty director's department might be a resource for portable computer equipment. Program providers are often one step ahead of universities in offering this level of support. Check with your university's instructional technology office to assess institutional policies regarding borrowing computer equipment to take abroad.

Program Web Site

Often a Web-savvy student member of the study abroad group will be willing to build a program Web site. The site can contain both academic and logistical information. Access to a laptop (and digital camera) allows the site to be updated regularly for the home campus, family, and friends.

Digital Cameras

Many faculty directors find it useful to take a digital camera along to visually document students on site. These photos can assist in the recruitment process for the next program and be used for publicity materials and creative academic journals. Check with your university's instructional technology or communication department to see if a digital camera is available to take abroad, or advocate to have one purchased specifically for the program abroad by the academic department, the international office, or the institution.

The welfare of students and faculty abroad, couched in phrases about liability concerns, can bolster arguments for institutional investment in instructional technology equipment for short-term programs.

CONCLUSION

This chapter has looked primarily at the offices on campus that can and do provide essential support for short-term programs abroad. Your institution's internal organization, including whether it is largely centralized or decentralized, will also have an impact on how your programs are run. Nothing will influence the success of your programs and the level of collaboration you can expect as much as campus attitudes about the intrinsic value of short-term study abroad programs and their place in a student's academic experience.

A short-term program is characterized by the brevity of the actual time spent abroad, but an enormous amount of time still goes into its planning, and the academic and cultural impact it has on students is long term and far reaching. Keeping offices across campus in the communication loop and actively pursuing every avenue of publicity that draws positive attention to the uniqueness of short-term programs will reap rewards for the international office and reflect favorably on the university. That is why it is important to think "long range" and "big picture" when it comes to incorporating these programs into the system.

CONSENT TO RELEASE OF GENERAL INFORMATION

I approve and consent to the dean of students' office staff's contact with the off-campus study program adviser, program director, field supervisor, interim instructor, and/or interim course adviser regarding any academic, emotional, medical, or behavioral problem that I may be experiencing at St. Olaf College. I understand that this information will be shared confidentially only with the faculty member responsible for the program for which I have applied, for the purpose of evaluating my qualifications for study on the program specified on this application.

_____

Signature of applicant   Date

_____

Print name   Program

If you have any concerns about this release form, please discuss them with the appropriate dean in the dean of students' office.

PROCEDURAL NOTE ON ABOVE:

When the international and off-campus studies office receives the completed applications:

1. If the above consent form is signed, the student's name will be included in a list sent to the dean of students' office. The appropriate assistant/associate dean will place a check mark after the name of any student about whom there are concerns. The names of those students so checked will be shared with the off-campus study program adviser, program director, field supervisor, interim instructor, and/or interim course adviser. The faculty member will contact the appropriate assistant/associate dean to discuss the concerns.

2. If the above consent form is not signed, the unsigned form will be sent to the dean of students' office. That office will consult with the student to discuss the reasons for a lack of signature. After this discussion, a student may sign the form, in which case the procedure listed in item 1 above is followed. If the student does not sign the form, the off-campus study program adviser, program director, field supervisor, interim course instructor, and/or interim course adviser will be informed that the consent form was unsigned and the faculty member will make the decision whether or not to consider the student's application.

[Source: Adapted from St. Olaf College]

Part II
PRINCIPLES OF ACADEMIC COURSE DESIGN

PROGRAM MODELS

Kathy Tuma

More than 2,000 short-term programs abroad are described in the annual reference guide, *Short-Term Study Abroad*, published by the Institute of International Education. Approximately 60 percent of the programs are sponsored by U.S. accredited colleges and universities. The remaining 40 percent are sponsored by providers (e.g., institutions without U.S. accreditation such as foreign universities and institutes and adult education centers, as well as other U.S.-based and foreign organizations).

Short-term programs are offered year round: during the regular academic calendar, break times, and the summer. Although many programs are developed and administered by the home institution, others are predesigned programs that enroll students from a number of U.S. colleges and universities.

The type of program that best suits your institution can be determined by a careful review of resources, including the following:
- ☐ Faculty willing and able to teach off-campus courses.
- ☐ An administration that is supportive of faculty proposing off-campus programs.
- ☐ Sufficient staff resources to administer the programs.
- ☐ A student body willing to take advantage of the program offerings.
- ☐ The financial ability of the students and the institution to undertake a specific program.

If you have willing faculty but limited staff resources, consider using a program provider to assist with the planning. If you have students anxious to participate in short-term programs but you lack administrative support, think about sending your students on already existing programs.

At the end of this chapter, you will find a Venn Diagram. Use it as an exercise that may help you decide how to best operate short-term programs on your campus.

The following pages will give you information on various program models. As you will see, there are many ways to design and administer successful short-term programs abroad.

FACULTY-DIRECTED PROGRAMS

One of the most common short-term models is to offer a course directed by a faculty member from the home institution. Individual faculty and/or academic departments typically propose off-campus courses that expand existing curricular offerings.

In many cases, the idea for such a course comes from the faculty member's own experience. For example, a theater professor returning from sabbatical in London is inspired to develop a course to introduce students to the multitude of theater experiences available there. Or a French department faculty member who recently completed dissertation research in Francophone Africa proposes to take students to this less-traditional region for language study.

In other cases, the faculty member or department recognizes the value of offering a course in a particular location, but does not have contacts in the region. The political science department may wish to offer students the opportunity to study the European Union, but does not have any contacts in Belgium and Luxembourg. The religion department may want to develop a Buddhism course in Thailand, taking advantage of that country's numerous temples and the chance to experience monastic life, but no faculty have been to Asia.

Often, the potential faculty director or international office will have sufficient contacts in the area to arrange the academics and the logistics internally. However, there may be other cases where it will be necessary to employ a program provider for academic resources, logistical needs, or both.

The benefits of a course developed and directed by a member of your own faculty are many:

☐ The course can be designed to specifically fit the existing curriculum or to fill a gap in the department's offerings.

☐ The faculty member accompanying the group abroad fully understands the academic expectations of the institution.

☐ Students have the opportunity to get to know a faculty member in a setting very different from the classroom, and vice versa.

☐ Increasing the international experience of your students and your faculty leads to an enhanced internationalization of your campus and curriculum.

PARTNERSHIPS: CUSTOMIZED PROGRAMS AND PROGRAM PROVIDERS

Many U.S. institutions wish to host their own short-term programs abroad, but do not have the resources or the long-term commitment necessary to set up the on-site facilities. A great option for short-term programs is to work with a program provider to create a customized program for the institution.

As fully explained in Chapter 8, Logistics, program provider organizations work with universities to develop programs tailor-made for the needs of that U.S. institution, both and on-site. Services of program providers can include travel and logistics, on-site support staff, academic support, student services, publicity, enrollment services, orientations, insurance, payment processing, and other services, depending on the organization. Universities are able to select the services they desire when they are designing a program.

A program provider generally has offices in both the United States and overseas. One of the most important elements to remember about the customized program model is that the U.S. institution always retains the identity of its own program. Although there may be other U.S. institutions using a particular program provider overseas, each university designs and administers its program in a way that best suits its students and faculty.

A program provider is useful for universities who may only want assistance with certain sections of a short-term program abroad, to free up the faculty director to focus on teaching, or to coordinate certain aspects of the on-site administration of the program. In any case, it is important to work with a provider that is flexible, in order to provide assistance where it is needed and not be forced into a "package deal."

DIRECT ENROLLMENT IN PREDESIGNED PROGRAMS

Universities and colleges are increasingly offering students the opportunity to enroll directly in programs operated by other U.S. or foreign institutions. By encouraging participation in predesigned short-term programs abroad, institutions increase the number of academic fields and geographical locations available to students.

Advantages of this model include the expansion of study abroad opportunities in more countries and academic fields, with differing program lengths and a variety of cost options. Predesigned programs also require a minimum of resources from the sending institution. However, the home institution has little or no influence on the course design and curriculum.

It is important to research the academic credibility of predesigned programs and to advise students when they are selecting a program. Most institutions have policies for students participating in predesigned courses sponsored by a program provider, including a process to approve short-term programs for credit. The transfer of credit, grades, and various forms of financial aid must be considered before the student studies abroad.

A HYBRID MODEL: PREDESIGNED AND CUSTOMIZED PROGRAMS

A hybrid model combines a predesigned program with the opportunity for the home institution to influence the program content, course offerings, and curriculum.

Hybrid models offer an option to allow some elements of a short-term program abroad to be modified according to the requirements of the home institution. An academic department may ask that adjustments be made to an existing program to better serve the department's academic and logistical needs. The ideal situation is when the program provider and the institution become partners in developing a customized, hybrid model.

Hybrid models can include several types of cooperation between the program provider and the home institution, such as the following:

☐ The program provider is responsible for the infrastructure but also plays a significant role in the academic program. This includes hiring foreign (local) faculty and making arrangements for the integrated site visits. The home institution provides the students and sometimes may provide a faculty director.

☐ A joint venture where some elements of an existing program are negotiated and adapted to meet the needs of the home institution (e.g., adding specific lectures or site visits). In addition, some courses may be taught jointly by foreign and U.S. faculty.

Like the predesigned model, a hybrid program allows the home institution to save resources—especially staff—but still provides the flexibility to customize a program to take advantage of the academic and cultural resources of a program provider while meeting the academic needs of the sending institution.

Although these kinds of partnerships have few disadvantages, they do take more time than predesigned programs. The direct cost of the hybrid program paid to the provider may appear higher than the cost of independent faculty-directed programs, where the cost is absorbed by the faculty mentor or the international office because they are providing the staffing resources.

When well organized, the hybrid program can combine the advantages of the faculty-directed program (e.g., faculty involvement and faculty development) with the advantages of a predesigned program (e.g., a greater opportunity for cultural immersion, and a reduced responsibility for the home institution to provide a minimum number of students).

EXCHANGE MODELS

It is possible to develop a short-term program abroad from an exchange agreement. The U.S. institution typically earns one to two credits for each student they have enrolled in a short-term program at a foreign institution, and as a result, credits build to support tuition for incoming semester-long or year-long exchange students.

This type of program is developed to accommodate:

☐ U.S. students who are unprepared linguistically to enroll in the host institution for a semester or year.

☐ U.S. students who are willing and able to participate in a short-term program, but not in a long-term program due to curricular constraints.

☐ A steady supply of international students willing and able to attend the U.S. institution.

The intercultural component of such a program is potentially much richer than with other short-term programs. The bilateral institutional involvement allows students and faculty from both institutions to extend their experiences. Intercultural exchange is not limited to the time that the students are on the host campus, but expands to include time that they may interact with exchange partners on their own campus as well.

In developing a budget for this type of program, you need to consider exchange policies that may already exist, including the following:

☐ Do you need to build in administrative costs for the incoming exchange student?

☐ If the exchange is for tuition only, will this be a problem for incoming students?

☐ How will exchange imbalances be handled?

☐ What will be the cost considerations of slow credit accrual or of not having a regular supply of qualified exchange candidates?

In any type of exchange program it is important to have a written agreement that spells out the obligations of each institution. Such an agreement is particularly important if an exchange arrangement includes a considerable difference in the services provided by each institution.

Ideally, each year the number of outgoing students will balance with the number of incoming students. Try not to build credits too slowly (over more than one year) or you will lose the buying power of the tuition collected.

Although this model offers great benefits to the students and faculty of the participating institutions, it also requires strong faculty and administrative support from both sides. Be sure that such support exists before proceeding.

CONSORTIUM PROGRAMS

When a number of institutions offer short-term programs abroad, they may want to consider forming a consortium in order to share students and faculty directors and increase the number of short-term opportunities.

The structure of the consortium will vary, depending on the culture and involvement of the home institutions. It is important to have a board of directors comprising representatives from each institution. The representatives can be deans, faculty, international directors, and/or administrators. Significant faculty representation will ensure academic quality.

Most successful consortia have a lead institution or organization to facilitate student enrollment and orientation, while each home institution is responsible for faculty recruitment and support, student advising, and other defined details. Most consortia also retain a program provider to organize all logistics and travel and to coordinate marketing.

A consortium model can bring a significant increase in student enrollment with limited use of institutional resources. Like most synchronized efforts, the role of each institution must be clearly defined and formal documentation and contracts must be created and approved by each institution.

EMBEDDED PROGRAMS

An embedded program is one where a short-term international experience is included as part of a regular term course. The international component of a course may come during fall or spring break, during interterm break, or in the summer immediately following the end of the regular term. The key is that the international experience is part of the academic requirement of the course.

Ideally, the embedded experience comes at a point during the term that allows the faculty director the opportunity to provide extensive preprogram preparation and postprogram follow-up.

Although an embedded program works in many circumstances, it is particularly well suited to graduate programs and "weekend" colleges whose student bodies are often unable to be away for more than a week or two.

SAMPLE PROGRAMS

The following are examples of real short-term programs abroad currently offered by U.S. organizations.

MBA Immersion Seminars: Multiple Locations

The Global Immersion Electives (GIEs) provide students in the MBA and Executive MBA Programs at The Kenan-Flagler Business School with an opportunity to engage in short-term experiential learning abroad for academic credit. There are six different GIEs, each of which combines relevant and timely international business issues with nuts-and-bolts discussions of how to do business in targeted countries or regions. The GIEs highlight some of the most dynamic economies in the world. Depending on the expertise of the lead faculty member, a GIE may place a secondary focus on a specific industry or functional area as well. Currently, the GIE program is scheduled to take Kenan-Flagler MBA and EMBA students to a total of 11 countries on four continents. The GIEs begin with predeparture, interdisciplinary lectures on the Kenan-Flagler campus and culminate in a 10-day to two-week business study tour of the targeted country or region, led by the course professor.

—The Kenan-Flagler Business School,
The University of North Carolina-Chapel Hill

First and Second Year Seminars: Multiple Locations

Global seminars are three-week, three-credit, faculty-directed study abroad programs with no language requirements or prerequisites. These programs are modeled after special on-campus courses developed to help with retention rates among first- and second-year students. The goals of these courses, matching the goals of the global seminars, are to (1) allow the opportunity for personal interactions between students and professors, and (2) create a community classroom culture. Faculty from all disciplines may apply, but they must use the existing on-site partners of the Learning Abroad Center to handle the logistical aspects of the programs. On-site partners also handle emergency issues, cultural orientations, and other supplemental aspects such as survival language classes if they are offered. Global seminars offer students an early option for study abroad and allow them to get their feet wet before making a long-term study abroad commitment.

—University of Minnesota

Service Learning Through Teaching: Nhlangano, Swaziland

Ohio University (OU) partners with the Ngwane Teachers' College in Nhlangano, Swaziland, to offer a program that pairs OU students with Ngwane Teachers' College students to team-teach for the final three weeks of a Swazi student's teaching practice. The program is titled "Service Learning Through Teaching in Swaziland," and runs for approximately five weeks in the summer. Each OU student has one Swazi teaching partner and usually is responsible for teach-ing a section of English or math. OU students live with Swazi students in dormitories (though not with their teaching partners). OU sends a designated person (a graduate student or African studies staff/faculty member; it varies each year) with the group to facilitate group discussions, give journal writing assignments, read journals, etc.

—Ohio University

Predesigned Program: Cambodia

The seven-week summer program in Siem Reap, Cambodia, is designed for students to learn the history of Cambodia—from the ancient times to 1970s—and come to understand it as a case study for geopolitical issues such as nation-building, radicalism, corruption, democracy, and economic development.

Program incudes: Extensive field visits to Angkorean cultural sites, including Angkor Wat, Angkor Thom, Banteay Srei, and Kbal Spean; opportunities to study alongside Cambodian students; and opportunities for volunteering.

—Council for International Educational Exchange

Embedded Program: Cuernavaca, Mexico

Augsburg Weekend College students have the opportunity to register for a course titled "Mexico: The Church and Social Change in Latin America." This course focuses on the relationship of the church to poverty, political oppression, and social justice in Latin America. It examines the ways in which Christian theology has been used to both justify oppression and injustice as well as to support social justice movements. A distinctive aspect of the class is an eight-day study tour to Cuernavaca, Mexico, with two introductory class sessions prior to the study tour and a single follow-up class session after return from Mexico.

—Augsburg College

Combining Study and Service: Romanian Culture Through Experiential Pedagogy and Service-Learning

The on-site portion of the program will span approximately three weeks and will combine an intensive study of experiential pedagogy and adventure education skills with a service-learning project and group wilderness trip. Upon arrival in Romania, the group will receive training from New Horizon's staff in the "hard skills" of adventure education—technical training to include high-ropes, rock climbing, initiative activities and other group-building activities—and then will plan and deliver an adventure program to Romanian youth under the guidance of faculty leader Dave Nonnemacher and New Horizons staff. Participants will end the on-site program with a wilderness trip led by New Horizons staff. Throughout the program, there will be time for writing, discussion and reflection, and at the program's end, students will synthesize their experiences and study in a final paper that addresses their experience and their understanding of Romania, of themselves and of their home culture.

—Northwestern College, Orange City, Iowa

Using Short-Term Study Abroad to Meet an Identified Need: Vocation in Action: Design of a Breadfruit Shredder for Haiti

St. Thomas' engineering and French students helped women's cooperatives in Haiti harvest breadfruit for use as a flour substitute in making breakfast bars for school children. Breadfruit, a naturally occurring food in Haiti, spoils quickly in that highly humid environment. St. Thomas' engineering students designed a manual device to shred fresh breadfruit evenly. The breadfruit is then sun-dried, and the resulting dried shreds have a shelf life of up to a year. St. Thomas' French students then created appropriate visuals for the Haitian users of this breadfruit shredder to understand and maintain that technology. The final design for the "Tommie Shredder" was produced by a graduate student in manufacturing engineering and was delivered along with the culturally appropriate manuals developed by the French students to Haiti.

— *University of St. Thomas*

Combining Academic Study Abroad with Practical Exposure: Medicinal Chemistry in Jamaica

Medicinal chemistry is the application of chemistry in the context of human medicine. In this course students will gain an appreciation for the drug development process, including how biologically active natural products are isolated, how the structure of a drug relates to its activity, and how basic research into the biochemical mechanism of disease leads to the targeted development of drugs. The course will commence in Chicago visiting Abbot Labs where they will be introduced to the operations of a major pharmaceutical company. Students will then have the opportunity to attend an international conference on medicinal and natural product chemistry. The Mona Symposium, held at the University of the West Indies (UWI) in Kingston, Jamaica, will provide an opportunity for students to meet professional medicinal chemists and graduate students from around the world in a casual environment focused on science. Besides the Mona Symposium, Chemistry 260 will provide extensive opportunities for cross-cultural learning, including working with undergraduates at UWI to carry out the isolation and characterization of a biologically active natural product from an indigenous Jamaican plant, field trips and guest lectures related to Jamaican history, culture, and economy.

— *St. Olaf College*

VENN DIAGRAM

Look carefully at the list of program needs below. Knowing the situation on your campus, assign each of these responsibilities to one of the circles. This should not be the ideal or the preferred but the reality of who is willing and able to accomplish each of the tasks. Overlap the responsibilities where appropriate. For example, Logistics will likely overlap between International Office and Program Provider. Course schedule may overlap between Program Provider and Faculty. Orientation should fall into all three categories.

Hopefully this exercise will assist you in determining the best means for administering short-term programs at your institution.

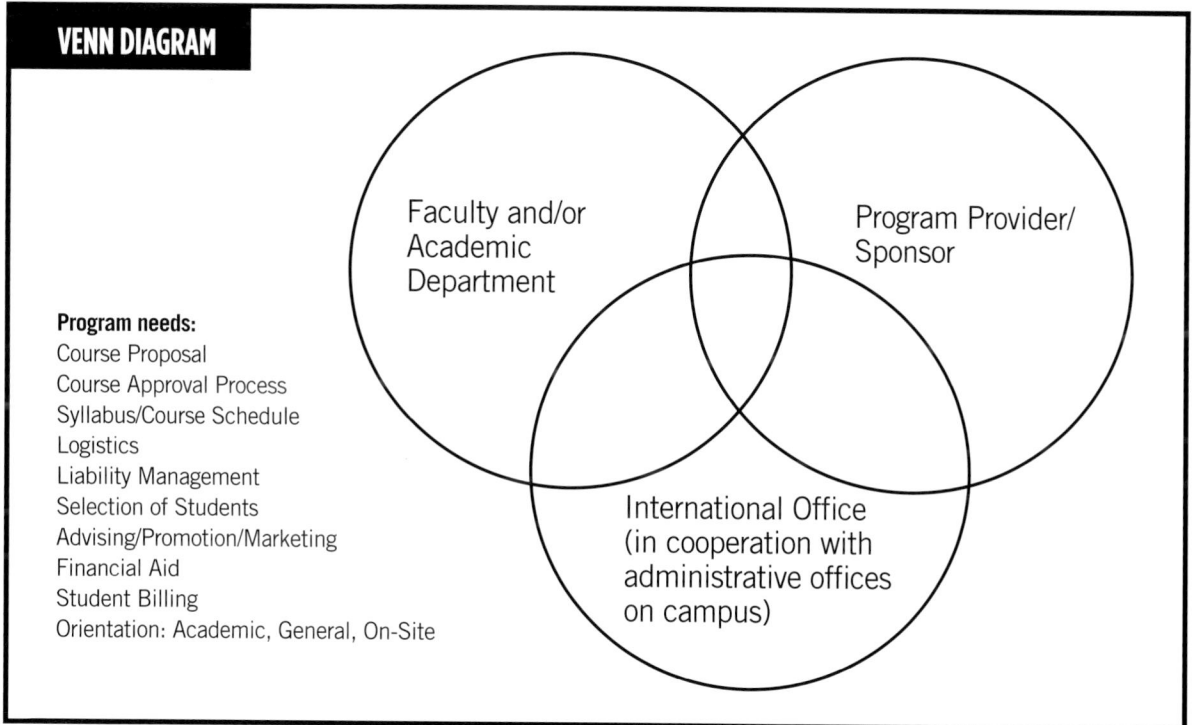

VENN DIAGRAM

Faculty and/or Academic Department

Program Provider/ Sponsor

Program needs:
Course Proposal
Course Approval Process
Syllabus/Course Schedule
Logistics
Liability Management
Selection of Students
Advising/Promotion/Marketing
Financial Aid
Student Billing
Orientation: Academic, General, On-Site

International Office (in cooperation with administrative offices on campus)

[Source: Adapted from St. Olaf College]

DESIGNING THE ACADEMIC COURSE: PRINCIPLES AND PRACTICALITIES

Elise Amel and Anders Uhrskov

Because short-term programs abroad differ from the on-campus teaching experience, this chapter focuses on the components of an academically successful short-term course off-campus. Chapter 14 concentrates on the educator becoming an international educator.

For faculty who are used to meeting students in their classes three times a week and during office hours and are comfortable with the rhythm this brings, it is a challenge to shift gears to short-term programs that are by nature quite intense academically, personally, and physically. The professor moves from having ready access to a variety of resources and tools to being the primary resource person who guides students using strategies and capacities less familiar.

In order for the academic component of short-term programs abroad to be successful, there are several questions that must be considered. What is the perception of such courses on campus? What does it take to teach on the road; what tools are available to design these courses? What is the landscape of the off-campus classroom, and what are the design issues that are so vastly different from on-campus experiences? There are many possibilities and practical suggestions that have been used successfully to design courses that are academically challenging, personally satisfying, and that promote an awareness of cultural diversity for both faculty and students before, during, and after the time spent abroad.

THE ACADEMIC IMAGE OF SHORT-TERM PROGRAMS

For some parents, administrators, faculty, and students—including academically serious students—short-term study abroad can be perceived as a "term off," a kind of tourism with credit, an experience that is supposed to be not only fun and entertaining, but also academically "lightweight."

It is an unfair reputation, since most short-term programs abroad have a strong academic basis. This

discrepancy can have serious consequences as a mismatch between student expectations and experience can lead to extra strain and greatly reduce satisfaction with the program. Therefore, short-term programs that grant credit, particularly those that travel to more than one site, have an image problem to overcome.

Faculty directors can begin to conquer this image problem by creating a detailed description of the academic curriculum of the program—that is, by articulating the intent and expectations, and then making sure those details are carried out. Remember that nothing is more compelling to other faculty and administrators than an excellent track record.

Proposing a Course

Crafting a solid proposal is the first step in creating a positive experience and image. As described in Chapter 2, Administrative Processes, a faculty member may approach the department chair, dean, or international office with the desire to adapt a catalog course to a foreign environment, or to create a new course that takes advantage of the opportunities of an international setting. Most institutions have a procedure whereby a standing committee reviews study abroad programs proposed by the faculty. If a proposal process is in place, written guidelines and examples should be available. Many committees request more detail than they would for an on-campus course proposal. Although faculty may question the need for such detail, academic quality begins as ideas are articulated in writing and a tentative plan is formulated.

Standard academic content issues must be considered, such as learning objectives, readings, and methods of evaluation. However, faculty must also balance these issues with human limitations (e.g., jet lag) and the practical design concerns addressed in Part III, such as feasibility of site, program development timeline, and cost.

Specific course proposal examples are found at the end of this chapter. A basic proposal should contain the following elements:

☐ A specific description of the short-term program, including:

✓ General and specific learning objectives;

✓ What the students are going to learn (e.g., knowledge, perspectives, skills) in the international environment that they could not learn at home; and

✓ How the program takes advantage of the international environment (e.g., academic and cross-cultural site visits, guest professors, assignments, etc.).

☐ As with traditional syllabi, listings of required reading, assignments, exams or papers, presentations, academic journals, or field observation reports to be used as the basis for the course grading.

☐ A day-to-day syllabus, integrating lectures, site visits, readings, assignments, discussions, reflection periods, and field work. This aids managing student impressions and improves the quality of their work by helping them make connections between activities.

☐ Specific evaluation and grading criteria with explanations.

☐ A predeparture component, preparing students for the academic and cultural experience. Depending on the academic calendar, institutional policy, and the unique structure of each short-term program abroad, this may include seminars, orientation meetings, a required course the previous semester, required readings, or online Web assignments.

☐ A postprogram component, where students are debriefed about their experiences and integrate what they learned abroad into their academic and personal situation back home. Faculty may schedule official seminars that are part of the academic course or more social gatherings such as a photo-swap party or welcome back dinner.

It must be clear to all constituents—colleagues, deans, the registrar, overseas partners, and most importantly, the students—what students will learn and experience, not just what they are going to see or do. By focusing on the academics, these courses can avoid the perception of being a holiday trip or tourist excursion.

DESIGNING SHORT-TERM COURSES: SHAPING THROUGH LEARNING OBJECTIVES
—Pamela Nice

It has been my experience—both as a teacher and as a faculty developer—that defining teaching and learning objectives is the most important factor in course development. When these objectives are clearly and explicitly defined by the instructor, they can help immensely to structure effective assignments and shape the course. Everything is driven by the learning objectives, so the course has a clear focus. This way of approaching course design means that you really need to think deeply about *what you want your students to learn* in your course.

It may be helpful to think of specific knowledge, skills, and attitudes you would like your students to have by the end of your course.[1] The brief duration of most short-term courses is not much time to accomplish your objectives, so you may have to think in terms of introducing and reinforcing them. Or you may find that you have to throw out some of your objectives as being too ambitious for the length of your course. Ideally, you will want to find a way to integrate texts, performances, presentations by guest speakers, visits to local sites and museums, the students' experiences in the locale, field trips, discussions, and written work to help your students wrestle with specific concepts and skills.

I find it easiest to think of three components of a short-term course: the locale, the content area, and the learning objectives. Thinking of the first two, I start developing my teaching/learning objectives. Which objectives should I focus on, given the duration of the course?

It helps to keep in mind that there are factors particular to these courses that challenge the students' focus. Travel may make them tired or lacking in concentration; accommodations and the local population may provide daily challenges; students may get on each other's nerves (and yours) with the 24-hour-a-day contact; class on top of a mountain may sound intriguing until you realize that the goats won't leave you alone.

So it is all the more important to keep focused on your objectives. The cardinal rule is reinforcement. Make your objectives clear and explicit in the orientation, syllabus, class lectures or discussions, reflective assignments, and when giving feedback (either verbally or in writing). Reinforcement is the key to maintaining focus.

AN EXAMPLE FROM "ENCOUNTERING EGYPT THROUGH THE ARTS"

I teach a short-term study course abroad in Egypt: Encountering Egypt Through the Arts. One of my main teaching/learning objectives is to make students aware of their own personal and cultural lenses when perceiving and interpreting another culture. Most of the students have little awareness of their lenses at the beginning of the course. They also tend to have many stereotypes about Arab cultures, combined with an almost total lack of knowledge about such cultures.

MY LEARNING OBJECTIVE:

I want to find a way to increase the students' awareness of their own lenses as they perceive and interpret Egyptian culture through its art and through their experiences in the culture.

INTRODUCING THE CONCEPT: SYLLABUS AND ORIENTATION

At the orientation, I hand out the course syllabus, which mentions my above objective, among others. Students see it in writing. Then I give them an autoethnography assignment (found in Chapter 15), asking them questions about their personal and cultural lenses. They discuss their answers in small groups, and then we have a whole-class discussion on their answers. The word "lens" appears in the exercise and I write it on the board during our discussions. I draw a diagram showing how our lenses work. Some of the questions with this exercise have to do with how the students—at that time—perceive Egyptian, Arab, or Muslim cultures. We also talk about how the students view their own cultures. Usually, there will be differences in the group due to ethnicity, home regions, or personal backgrounds. We talk about how these aspects of our lives help to create our lenses.

PRECOURSE WORKSHEETS

Before the course begins, the students have some background reading to do on Egyptian history and politics, Islam, and some artists. They also read an Egyptian novel. On their worksheets, I ask them at least two questions about their lenses, or the lens of the writer of a text.

EXPERIENTIAL LEARNING AND DEBRIEFING SESSIONS

At last, we arrive in Egypt. Experiential learning begins with a vengeance. The young women receive an obviously unexpected amount of attention from men on the streets. We have a debriefing session near the end of the first day. Why do you think you are getting this attention? Through what kind of lens are the men viewing you, do you think? Why? This leads into a discussion of stereotyping of other cultures—both ours and theirs. Their own emotional reactions give palpable evidence that the way we think can lead to hurtful or embarrassing actions that serve to further alienate us from each other.

CONTENT ANALYSIS

At a class session, we view a contemporary Egyptian documentary. The first question I ask the students is, "What is the lens of the filmmaker? How do we know what the lens is—what elements of the form do we look for? How does this influence the focus of the documentary?"

ASSESSMENT: REFLECTIVE EXERCISE IN ACADEMIC JOURNAL AND/OR FINAL PAPER

During the course, another way I encourage focus is to have the students write an academic journal, some of which is their own reflection, and some of which is in response to questions I give them. At the end of the three weeks, I ask the students to reflect on whether their lenses in relation to Egyptian culture and art have changed, and if so, how. They write their last journal entry on this topic.

In this final exercise, as well as in their final papers, I am able to assess how well the students have learned this concept of lenses. I will see if their lenses have changed through the course, and what kind of self-awareness they bring to this process.

This is just one example of how a teaching/learning objective can focus assignments and shape a short-term course.

COVERING THE MATERIAL

When designing a course from learning objectives, teachers often find that they can't "cover" as much material, and see this as a drawback. However, a large body of research on learning suggests that deep learning seldom happens when the teacher lectures or presents material without having students actively engage with it.[2] Active engagement may include, for instance, writing or discussion assignments in which each student expresses concepts in his or her own words, applies concepts, or relates them to previous knowledge. Such activities take time—more time than merely having the teacher "cover" the material.

Likewise, reinforcement of major principles takes time and requires the teacher to make some tough decisions on which objectives are most important. This sort of intentional course design, however, has real benefits for the students' learning, and is much more fulfilling for the teachers—especially when reading final papers!

Endnotes

[1] This approach to course design came from Tom Creed, who was a faculty development consultant for the University of St. Thomas's faculty development program in the early 1990s.

[2] The pedagogical approaches of writing to learn, problem-based learning, learning through inquiry, and collaborative learning, to name a few, are based on the premise that deeper learning occurs through active student engagement with concepts and through practicing certain skills and attitudes.

TEACHING ON THE ROAD

Although faculty directors may find themselves blissfully removed from the responsibilities of a campus—committee work, administrative duties, and teaching multiple courses—they are likely to experience a loss of the amenities they count on to teach their courses, including:

- ☐ Computer access;
- ☐ Access to copiers;
- ☐ Traditional classrooms, with blackboards and audiovisual equipment;
- ☐ Research facilities, including libraries;
- ☐ Ready access to office materials such as books and a hard drive full of exercises, exam questions, and notes; and
- ☐ Collegial support.
- ☐ On the other hand, the benefits of off-campus teaching are numerous.
- ☐ Because of the relative freedom from campus responsibilities, faculty can take advantage of the organic opportunities that arise in the study locations.
- ☐ There is an enhanced opportunity to get to know the current generation of students.
- ☐ Students are likely to see the human side of faculty directors as they spend more time with each other.
- ☐ The learning experience is based on clear, constant contact with the new cultural milieu, which is visual, auditory, and immediate during every moment of the time spent abroad.
- ☐ Students are free from distractions such as work, family obligations, and a thick social calendar, so faculty can plan meetings throughout the day and evenings without losing the attendance of a substantial number of students.
- ☐ Depending on the course, there is a greater use of independent and service-learning techniques, which benefit students on site and once they return to traditional classroom settings.
- ☐ After teaching abroad, faculty often bring new knowledge, ideas, perspectives, and activities to their on-campus courses.

An effective short-term course abroad draws its design, its resources, its assignments, and its evaluation from the unique opportunities offered by the program site. Teaching techniques and research methodology all have to be rethought and restructured to maintain academic rigor and make the most of each course that is offered. In the next section, we begin to address these issues in greater depth.

TEACHING TECHNIQUES

Generally, methods for engaging with the material as well as the bases for evaluation may be broader than for a course at the home institution. While there may be fewer lectures, lengthy textbook readings, and traditional research papers required, these can be substituted with techniques that integrate cross-cultural elements, including interviews, academic journals, drawings, photos, cultural artifacts, and oral presentations. Even a local "treasure hunt" for images, monuments, and examples of topics under study can open students' eyes to the rich environment surrounding them.

Regardless of the specific techniques implemented, faculty should consider frequent "prepping" and "processing" opportunities. It is critical to prepare students in advance for what they will see, hear, and experience, and what they should be looking for during excursions. Often, discussion can be integrated into local culture and customs such as dining together and afternoon tea or coffee. An evening gathering in a lounge can work as well. Suggested questions for processing can be found at the end of this chapter. Regular debriefing, responding to questions and concerns as they arise, and managing student impressions also enhance the overall academic experience.

Research

Research in the traditional sense rarely works on these courses because access to resources can be limited. One way to circumvent these difficulties is to have students prepare their research before departure or after returning from abroad. Other viable alternatives include field observation reports or presentations and academic journals.

Academic Journals

Opinions differ as to the usefulness of the academic journal: some see the journal as a valuable tool for experiential learning; others believe journaling is a useless exercise that is too difficult to grade. It is true that journaling can be ineffective, containing blow-by-blow details of breakfast and the train ride. However, this type of personal journal is likely to result when the journal is simply assigned at the beginning of the course and collected at the end for evaluation without any regular intervention. When managed effectively, journals can reinforce the relevance of course material, reduce students' feelings of being overwhelmed by providing a theme for student experiences, and provide practice enhancing larger, applied assignments, such as those that integrate site visits with theories from class.

Effective management of academic journaling often begins with its name. Calling it *an academic journal, research log,* or other name emphasizing its scholarly nature can raise student awareness of its purpose. Effective journaling also involves clear discussion with students up front regarding expectations as well as providing specific questions and guiding themes as the course progresses. As is true for any condensed course, timely feedback is imperative to getting and keeping students on the right track.

Entries can be short reflective or integrative essays. For instance, if students are studying workers from different cultures, faculty might direct them to strike up a conversation with a local while riding the train or eating at a pub. Students might ask them about their employer's work policies, or about the individual's job, training, and work experience. Students could summarize their findings, then compare and contrast their findings with their own work experience.

Each course lends itself to some questions that can be prepared in advance of arrival. For example, ask students to apply the components of culture (i.e., values, norms, symbols, etc.) to their experience in a business or with their host family. The questions can also be generated on the spot based on current events and other serendipitous occurrences. Consider the example of having students apply principles of distributive and procedural justice to political decisions and constituent protests they have witnessed in the streets. They could evaluate the leadership qualities of figureheads using readings and research articles to analyze media reports. Or propose identifying the implications of shiftwork and circadian rhythms on the performance of guards seen during a class tour.

Additionally, entries can be creative in nature, including drawings, poetry, and short stories.

If a faculty director chooses to use journals as an evaluative tool, it is imperative that students are provided with clear, understandable criteria regarding how they will be evaluated and graded. Most experienced faculty agree that the more directed you can make the journal assignment, the more reflective and intellectual the work by the student will be. To avoid the "Dear Diary" kind of entry, encourage them to use the journal to:

☐ Describe, interpret, evaluate;
☐ Make observations;
☐ Raise questions;
☐ Note cultural differences;
☐ Transcribe interviews;
☐ Write down information and facts;
☐ Answer questions;
☐ Propose solutions; and
☐ Reach conclusions.

There are several ways to communicate standards and relieve students' uncertainty regarding journal entries. One effective approach is to provide writing samples for students to review. Although time consuming, prompt *feedback* can also help students to improve their integrative writing skills, and if done well, reduce the gap between faculty and student expectations.

ACADEMIC JOURNAL ASSIGNMENT—"IRELAND: UNDERSTANDING CELTIC SPIRITUALITY"

You will be required to keep a daily academic journal of your observations and experiences. This will be subject to periodic review and will be submitted for a grade at the end of the course. It will be returned to you. Your journal does not double as your notebook; you should purchase a separate notebook for class and on-site notes.

Purchase a ruled, 8.5" x 11" spiral-bound notebook to use as your journal, in which you will record your observations, experiences, ideas, reactions, and insights. You may even want to include sketches of the sites we visit. Be prepared to devote at least 30 minutes each day to writing in your journal. Date each entry, and note the location (city or site) in which it was made. Note the name and date, or the chronological placement, of each site you discuss in your entries.

The journal is the place for your descriptions of on-site visits: ancient sites, monasteries, churches, stone crosses, museums, cities, and towns; it is also the place to integrate reflections on readings and lectures, comments on the culture of all dimensions, thoughts about history, and conclusions you may have drawn from conversations. Although our time in Ireland is brief, we will become a small community of shared conversation, and what you write in the journal cannot help but be a result of the interaction with others in the group, with your professors, and with people you meet. A journal is not meant so much to be a solitary endeavor as a personal and reflective one. It should be more than just a record of events, and avoid filling it out with a clutter of unrelated facts. You might choose to write a narrative, first-person approach, thus organizing your thoughts chronologically. The journal is not as confidential as a diary, but it is not a notebook of raw material. Your academic journal is your own thoughtful synthesis of your experience.

Grading: To clarify evaluation of this part of your grade:

C   Average; student shows some evidence of having participated and having read the material.

B   Student who shows a sound and solid grasp of the materials and the variety of experiences, going further in that these are thought out carefully.

A   Students who have done all that is expected of B students and have added a substantial amount of clearly articulated imagination and synthesis of ideas. This means that the A student is the one who has fully integrated and internalized, intellectually and experientially, the variety of what we observe, read, and process on this course.

Journal samples will be available for review during the first week.

[Source: Anne King]

COURSE DESIGN ISSUES

Contact Hours

Since off-campus courses take place in the nontraditional classroom, with diverse and variable schedules, it may be more difficult to define the nature and number of contact hours. As noted in Chapter 2, Administrative Processes, institutional policy must be clear regarding contact hours for study abroad programs.

The common practice is to define as contact hours any activity in which students are engaged with the learning objectives of the course. This includes lectures by the faculty director or in-country experts, site visits, excursions, discussions, and student presentations.

SITE VISITS

Although the bus may stop for the spontaneous monument, bazaar, or even an hour at the beach, it is extremely important to the overall structure and academic quality of the short-term program abroad that students are well prepared for each site visit—the site should be introduced beforehand, summarized, and reflected upon after the actual visit.

One excellent method to involve students is to require one to two students to introduce each site visit to the group, explaining the purpose of the visit, what to expect, and something of the historical or cultural background information. This student group, or another, should be charged with formally thanking the hosts on behalf of the group. Following the visit, the faculty director should process and interpret impressions of the site visit with the students in a formal class or informal discussion period.

Some site visits involve a long bus journey. If the bus has a video player and if videos are available in-country, plan to show a movie that is connected to the site or area. For example, show an historic movie describing Berlin in 1933 or 1945 before the students arrive in the Berlin of today. Students may also use the time to read assignments or write journal entries, if motion sickness does not affect them.

READINGS

Reading assignments should be carefully chosen and apportioned in amounts that permit them to be read in one or two hours in the evening, or during free periods of the day. If possible, distribute reading assignments and specially ordered materials at the orientation, and encourage students to begin reading before they meet at the airport. You can help students stay focused by requiring them to generate discussion questions based on the readings.

Unstructured Time

Unscheduled or "free" time is a complex issue for short-term program design. Too much unscheduled time questions the academic integrity regarding the amount of credit granted, and too little free time compromises the students' ability to learn due to exhaustion and information overload.

Students and faculty need breaks to complete readings and journals, to rest, and to process. How much free time should be built into the program depends on the program model: is it a travel course or is the group based in one place; are students dealing with language barriers; what are the academic objectives of the course?

Faculty may build-in designed or guided free time. Students are required to choose and attend two to three cultural activities during the week, on their own time, and report back to the group. This allows students to build confidence by traveling to the site on their own, doing their own research, and being held accountable for that time.

Not all students will be anxious to spend every moment exploring the culture. Initially, faculty may have to invite the less-adventurous students to accompany them to a theater performance, museum, or meal. Because they lack the tools of experienced travelers, students should be required to bring a guidebook of the city or country. Faculty may have students identify a "Top Ten" list of things to see and do in each major city from the guidebooks in advance of departure.

INDEPENDENT TRAVEL

Some faculty design a course where at least one weekend is free, encouraging students to undertake independent travel. This approach builds confidence, can provide a spontaneous educational occasion, and gives members of the group a break from each other. If faculty schedule more than one day off, proactive steps need to be taken to ensure the students' safety. Students should travel in pairs or larger groups, and should submit information such as their destinations and contact numbers, if available, to faculty before departure. Also, faculty should identify expectations, such as being prepared for Monday morning class, as well as review safety guidelines, especially for travel on overnight trains.

OTHER SUGGESTIONS ON COURSE DESIGN

Faculty Preparation

☐ There is nothing like direct experience with locations, organizations, and culture. Many institutions provide travel grants that faculty can use in advance to help discover opportunities and limitations, and refine teaching objectives.

☐ Initially, novice directors might consider codirecting a program with veteran faculty. Learning the ropes when there is a safety net can provide valuable insights, build confidence, and reduce stress.

Setting and Achieving Academic Goals

☐ If prerequisites are identified, they should be appropriate to the course objectives.

☐ General interest courses are likely to attract higher numbers of students; highly specialized courses may have a much smaller pool of qualified candidates.

☐ The intellectual challenge of the course, its scope, and the work required of students should correspond to the proposed level of the course.

☐ The type and amount of work required of students should be compatible with living and traveling conditions.

☐ Students need to know in advance how they are to procure assigned reading materials (e.g., purchase prior to departure, purchase on site, use local libraries). When students are expected to carry out research projects, faculty should ensure that libraries or other research facilities are available and adequate.

☐ Pedagogically successful programs usually schedule a short presentation or interactive assignment early in the program. Readings and/or assignments get students to start engaging before they leave.

Logistics and Travel Planning

☐ Carefully consider the number of sites visited, their geographical proximity to each other, and the time spent traveling among them.

☐ Consider the mode of travel, and utilize the opportunities it presents for pedagogy.

☐ A good case should be made for the amount of travel proposed. Visiting a large number of sites and/or countries does not necessarily make the best course.

☐ Attempt to balance course lectures, site visits, and unstructured time. Short-term programs abroad can be exhausting, both to faculty and students. Think about jet lag and long bus trips, both of which can add to fatigue.

☐ Balance the different models of site visits: for example, scheduling visits to three museums in one day will produce tuned-out students by the afternoon.

☐ Transit makes for good opportunities for faculty to check in with students, find out how they are doing, learn their progress on journals and readings, discover more about their interests and, in general, stay connected with the group.

☐ Successful courses usually provide frequent opportunities for student groups to process their observations and reactions to the cultures they are experiencing. Specific questions are available at the end of this chapter.

Grading Issues

The most consistent "low mark" on short-term course evaluations is "Were grading criteria clear?"

Faculty across the country who teach courses abroad have grappled with the problem: What is different about grading a course taught off-campus from one taught on campus? The challenge is to figure out how to clearly articulate expectations to students, and evaluate how well they meet those expectations.

While on-campus evaluation tends to be based on traditional methods (e.g., quizzes, research papers, and exams), off-campus courses may rely more on subjective measures due to their experiential nature. Thus, to reduce sense of caprice, students require a precise description of how the experiential components of the course will be assessed. It must be clear that it is not the experiential element itself that is graded, but the process of synthesis. Academic journals are an effective tool for synthesis but are particularly challenging to grade because most students are not accustomed to that form of evaluation.

Grade Distribution

Sometimes the best-prepared and most thoroughly designed course can fall short because students are not sure how they will be graded as the course unfolds. Below are two examples of the basic categories faculty have used to grade a course.

In a science course:

Quiz	5%
Field exercises	40%
Mid-term	20%
Seminar participation	15%
Final	20%

A humanities course:

Attendance	5%
Participation in group discussion	25%
Academic journal	30%
Papers (2 @ 10% each)	20%
Final essay exam	20%

Each of these faculty directors went to great lengths to explain what they meant by "attendance," "participation," and "academic journal."

Grading Standards

In addition to indicating how much credit each component is worth, faculty should clearly articulate expectations regarding the quality of student work. For instance, the following guidelines lay out various levels of sophistication that can be used to define grades:

A	Demonstrates creativity and integration
B	Demonstrates creativity or integration
C	Demonstrates understanding material
D	Demonstrates confusion
F	No show

Although nontraditional evaluation methods are time consuming for faculty directors and may be initially confusing to students, the final intercultural results are well worth the effort.

LEARNING STYLES

Experiential Learning[1]

A lack of understanding about experiential learning can cause an academic image problem. The notion that students can learn anything through travel to another place is grounded in the pedagogical concepts of experiential learning, suggesting "learning is best facilitated in an environment where there is dialectic tension...between immediate concrete experience and analytical detachment."[2] Considered integral to the overall process of educational development, experiential learning is not opposed to traditional notions of learning that emphasize the memorization and recitation of "facts" related to specific topics (book learning), but is more accurately understood as a part of learning that involves grasping the concepts behind those facts within the context of direct experiences with lived relationships with real people and events. In other words, experiential learning does not involve having an experience alone. As an ongoing process, learning through experience requires having a concrete experience followed by some sort of engaged conceptual reflection about that experience, followed by behaviors that utilize those reflections within the context of a new experience, which then generate new ideas about the world, reflection, and so forth.

PEDAGOGY OF PLACE: HOW TO USE RESOURCES ABROAD[3]

All short-term programs abroad should make use of on-site learning resources; if not, why take students at all? However, faculty directors use resources overseas with divergent approaches. Some use the site as a backdrop to enhance their own lectures, creating a situation where they are still considered the "expert." Others use the resources the site has to offer while purposely receding into the background, blending as discussant and student.

It is obvious to most that a course should be planned to take advantage of on-site resources. It takes great effort, however, to discover, contact, and confirm these overseas resources. The following is a sampling of possible ways to get started:

Universities and think tanks. Individual researchers are often willing to discuss their topics of expertise with students, though often at a monetary cost. If your travel schedule finds the group at the right place at the right time, some public lectures at universities can be attended for free. Think tanks are often quite forthcoming though, as their notoriety in the media increases, their interest in public education tends to decline.

Governmental and intergovernmental agencies. Though, again, the quality of presentation varies, governmental and intergovernmental agencies can be quite forthcoming and often have the human and material resources to offer enlightening tours and briefings. Like everyone else, these agencies have political interests and an agenda and will see the world through that set of lenses, but that bias can be turned into an occasion for learning about learning.

Nongovernmental organizations. Nongovernmental organizations (NGOs) are presently the most fertile ground when looking for instructional assistance abroad. Their numbers are expanding daily (exploding, really), and they are usually more than happy to discuss issues on their agenda and other topics of passionate interest to them. They clearly see such public education as serving their organizational goals. Access to NGOs is generally quite easy, as their Web sites usually provide direct e-mail communication.

Media. Success with media outlets is a bit variable, as reporters operate under increasing pressure from deadlines and breaking events can derail long-scheduled meetings. Reporters do have their fingers on many issues of the day at the factual level, although they tend to do less well with causes and consequences of problems, global or local.

Museums. The world contains museums for just about everything, from collections of artifacts and official documents, interview transcripts and diaries, to art and film. Entrance to museums can often be gained at reduced or no cost by student groups, and sometimes student groups enjoy privileged treatment. Students can view the public collections or with some prearrangement can often access the archives.

Artistic expressions. Museums, galleries, and musical and theatrical performances are easily accessible, although sometimes at substantial cost. Nevertheless, the arts have no peer in laying bare the issues and tensions of human experience for our consideration.

Ordinary people. Contact with local people can range from systematic interviews with people in the street to lengthy and open-ended conversations with people about their lives in their homes or places of work. The Center for Global Education at Augsburg College in Minneapolis, MN, has developed a particularly well-considered pedagogy for such interviews with those on the short end of the globalization stick or on the nub of conflict and violence.[4]

Suggestions for Contacting Local Resources

The easiest method of initiating contact with local resources is to write a letter or e-mail stating something to the effect of, "Our group will be in London from Tuesday, May 1, to Friday, May 4. It would best fit our busy schedule if we could meet in the afternoon of Thursday, May 3. We would like to hear about the role and current concerns of the organization and how they relate to [the topic]."

Remember to attach to the letter the (1) description of the school; (2) description of the study abroad program; and (3) description of the class. Follow up with a gift at the visit, kind words of appreciation at the end of a meeting, and thank you letters on return.

COURSE DESIGN AND THE CROSS-CULTURAL LANDSCAPE

Cross-Cultural Enrichment and Encounter

Although it is important to plan specific academic experiences ahead of time, some of the most valuable aspects of short-term programs abroad are the cultural encounters that occur while on site. As previously mentioned, while one purpose is to fulfill academic course expectations, an equally valuable purpose is to take advantage of the unique opportunities in the locality of the site, such as history, culture, society, and nature. A political economics course in Paris will obviously include direct academic components, such as government organizations, but could also include a gathering with local English as a Second Language students, a tour of Notre Dame, and major art museums. Much of this can be planned in advance, but there are always spontaneous opportunities so be prepared to take advantage of these situations when they occur.

Faculty must decide whether cross-cultural enrichment activities, particularly those not directly related to the subject matter, will form a part of the student's evaluation. For instance, a London-based business program may include at least one theater performance. However, it is not only attendance that is counted as part of the student evaluation—participation is also required. The faculty director has a local expert (e.g., a colleague at a university) prepare students before the play and facilitate a discussion following the performance or in the next day's class. Students are expected to include the performance in their academic journal, noting and analyzing any business or cultural themes. This cross-cultural activity, although not directly related to the specific business course objectives, allows students to prepare, experience, and analyze an important characteristic of London culture.

Facilitating the Cross-Cultural Encounter

An important feature of any study abroad program is the cultural encounter between U.S. students and native speakers, guest faculty, or host nationals. Because short-term programs allow less time for cultural immersion, such encounters should be actively incorporated into the course. Careful orientation to cultural differences can make or break the effectiveness of these experiences.

For example, at the North Atlantic Treaty Organization (NATO) headquarters in Brussels, Belgium, an outstanding political scholar from Spain receives a group of U.S. students. She reads from a prepared manuscript and her

fluent English has a very heavy accent. The students, unfamiliar with prepared, read speeches and listening to foreign nationals, stop listening and start daydreaming. Following her presentation, a relaxed, very personable U.S. NATO representative gives the same students a casual, somewhat superficial briefing. Although the Spanish representative's presentation is informative and complex and of far higher academic quality than the NATO representative's, the U.S. students do not like the Spanish presentation but enjoy the American one much more.

This kind of situation can be avoided by advance preparation in discussing alternative communication styles as well as providing guiding questions, thereby enhancing attention. Your role is to challenge the students to adopt and adapt to new forms of listening and understanding that are culturally different from their own. You must impress upon them the importance of this form of understanding.

Cultural Overload: When to Offer a Taste of Home

Most faculty wish for, and indeed expect, students to culturally engage fully while on site, which usually does not include trips to McDonalds, Starbucks, or The Gap. However, especially in short-term programs abroad, students may be less experienced, lack the confidence to try new things, and be inclined to search out the familiar. If you find your students in the local U.S.-owned fast-food chain, use the opportunity to facilitate discussion and set examples.

There may be moments when students must get a "home fix." For example, a month-long course in Barcelona, Spain, included a scheduled group dinner at the end of the second week. When asked what kind of food they wanted, the students requested Pizza Hut. While this initially appalled the faculty director, the experience allowed the group to literally get a taste of home, and then to plunge back into Catalan culture for the final two weeks. In other words, there are moments when it may be appropriate to provide students with the familiar.

Chronic consumption of U.S. fast food, and the attendant and incessant "search" for the recognizable will require you to intervene. One option is to invite the group, or a small group, to come with you to a fabulous local restaurant, allowing you to introduce them to a variety of typical dishes. If they do not speak the local language, spend time with the menu, pointing out familiar foods. Another strategy is to provide students with a list of enticing restaurants.

Not all culture-clash situations involve food. You may have students who insist on nonstop shopping, or who use their free time to sit around the hotel and discuss what they miss at home. In such cases, use these opportunities to assign a compare/contrast entry for the students' academic journals. Depending on the course topic, you may direct them to write about ambiance, architecture, transportation, sport, political activity, business philosophy, social structures, symbols, or customs. Student questions, such as why customers are charged for ketchup in Australia's fast food restaurants, may lead to a fruitful discussion on culture, history, and economics.

TIPS ON GUIDING STUDENTS TO CULTURAL AND INTELLECTUAL MILEPOSTS[5]

Faculty who direct short-term academic programs abroad know full well the challenge of making the most of all their time abroad. We all want students to grow intellectually and personally from the cross-cultural experiences they have. Thus, it is useful to have an idea of what constitutes "best practices" and what has been successful over the years.

The best short-term courses abroad balance experience with processing the experience. Too many experiences without a context in which to study and reflect on them can leave students overwhelmed and unsure of just what they are supposed to be learning.

What follows are ideas from colleagues in the field that may help you in organizing your short-term course by including regular opportunities for group reflection:

- Every two or three days the group should be gathered for a one- or two-hour reflection session. This is a time for the group members to share any insights, concerns, or questions with each other and with the faculty director. Discussion of readings and site visits may also be combined, to give more structure to the session. These regular sessions and the skill with which they are led are key ingredients in determining whether or not the educational experience will be a transformative one.

- Certain rules, accepted by all members of the group, can provide a positive framework for all group reflections. Some helpful ground rules include speaking and behaving respectfully toward and about all members of the group and all resource people; balancing one's desire to speak with the need to allow others time to speak; making one's needs known so that they can properly be addressed.

- There are many different ways the reflection session can be structured but bear in mind one basic principle: Every student should have the opportunity to find a voice within the group. Here are some helpful hints for maximizing the learning of all group members.

  - Speak privately with the more talkative students reminding them to share airtime with others and to cultivate the skill of listening.

  - The quieter students should be specifically invited to speak, but not forced to do so.

  - Although people may disagree with one another, differences should be treated as differing perspectives, not as personal affronts or a contest to see who is right and who is not.

  - When strong feelings emerge it is better to deal with them than to ignore them and let them fester. These feelings may be the result of what students have heard and seen during the day; they may result from intragroup dynamics, or they may be a reaction to some aspect of culture shock.

- If tensions are high in the group, it may be tempting to skip a reflection session. However, an opportunity for reflection can provide a helpful way to redirect the energy of individuals and the group. If a conflict interferes with the group's ability to focus on the program, the conflict needs to be addressed.

Possible Questions to Guide Discussions

Early in the course...
- What do you observe as the key elements of this culture that differ from your own?
- What is in your cultural filter that might prompt you to interpret things differently than the people you are meeting here?
- What in your background seems similar to what we've encountered here? With whom did you resonate most? Why do you think this is so?
- What criteria might you use to decide if someone is telling the truth?
- Can two people who interpret things quite differently both be telling the truth? Why or why not? Have you experienced examples of this?
- What has surprised you most?
- If you could send home a snapshot from the course, what would it be?

In the middle of the course...
- What are your own definitions of democracy, justice, freedom, peace, art, relaxation, spirituality, etc.? How would the mainstream population here define these words? How are your definitions the same? How do they differ?
- What has been a key moment of insight for you?
- What one word would describe your strongest feeling today?
- What did you observe today?
- How is what you are experiencing here different from what you expected?
- What are the main sectors of society from which you are learning? Do their perspectives align well with your own, or are they quite different? How do their goals and values differ?
- What have you learned about the way the United States is perceived in this society? How have this society's perceptions seemingly been shaped?
- How are the social, economic, political, communication, transportation, education, and health systems working in this society? Where does this country seem

strong? Where does it seem weak? Are the same strengths and constraints prevalent in U.S. society?

Near the end of the course...

☐ Who are the key people shaping the field of study you are engaging in here? Are their roles in this society comparable to identifiable people in the United States who have influence in this discipline?

☐ What are the key problems with which this society wrestles? Are these the same problems that are prevalent in the United States?

☐ What signs have you seen of U.S. cooperation with people in this country?

☐ What is the role of the media in this society? Is it similar to the role of the media in the United States?

☐ What is the source of economic power in this society?

☐ What is the role of music, literature, and the arts in this society? How does it compare with the role of these things in the United States?

☐ What is the role of spirituality and faith in this society? How similar is it to the role of these things in the United States?

☐ What connections do you see emerging between your life and the lives of the people here? Will that connection be sustained over time?

☐ What are the strengths of this society as you see it? What do you perceive to be its weaknesses?

☐ If it is true that "the whole world needs the whole world," what do you see as the gift that the people of this society have to contribute to the world?

Closing reflection...

☐ What are the three or four most important images or ideas that you will take from this experience? If you were able to put a photograph on the front cover of a leading U.S. magazine, a photograph that would carry a strong message to the people of the United States about this travel experience, what would that photograph be, and what would the caption be?

☐ What is the main message you want to tell your neighbors, your college peers, and others who may be interested in traveling here?

☐ What questions or disturbing ideas have not been resolved during your time here?

☐ What are you taking back with you from this experience? What are you leaving behind?

☐ What will you do to concretely express your solidarity with the people here when you return home?

Endnotes

1   Special thanks to Joe Kinsella for this material.

2   Kolb, David A. (1984). *Experiential Learning: Experiencing as the Source of Learning and Development.* Englewood Cliffs, NJ: Prentice Hall.

3   Special thanks to Peter Hovde for this material.

4   See Dan Spencer (1989). *"Experiential Education: A Method for Transformation and Liberation."* Global Perspectives 6 (Spring), pp. 1-2, 8-10, and also Dan Spencer (1988). "Models of Learning in Building a Transformative Education." Global Perspectives 6 (Winter), 1-5.

5   Special thanks to Adrienne Kaufmann and Ruth Mason for this material.

PROPOSAL FOR SUMMER/WINTER TRAVEL STUDY PROGRAM

ATTENTION PROSPECTIVE FACULTY DIRECTORS: You may save this form as a draft if you don't finish it all at one sitting by clicking on "save now and submit later" at the bottom of this page. It is essential that you give your program a title and enter the name and e-mail address of the first director in the first department; the form cannot even be saved as a draft without those entries. Please do not use symbols such as apostrophes or the "&" sign in your program's title. The person named as director #1 will be able to edit the draft. When you submit the form, you should receive a "thank-you" message, as well as an e-mail confirming the submission. Upon final submission, the form will be routed for approval to the Chair(s) you specify, and then to the Dean(s), then finally to the Center for International Studies. All directors listed will be notified as the form is sent to each approver. In order to prevent loss of data on those rare occasions when there is a problem with this form, we highly recommend that you save your answers to the questions below in a Word document and cut-and-paste them into the form. If you submit the form prematurely by accident, do not use the BACK button of your browser to re-access the form; this will result in loss of data. Instead, call the Center for International Studies at 831-2852 for assistance.

Academic Term:

Winter 2008: form requested by 12/12/2006 ▼

If Summer, then which Session:

▼

Abroad or USA:

Abroad ▼

Program Name:

REQUIRED

Location:

Approximate Dates: (format MM/DD/YY)

Depart:

Return:

FOR EACH DEPARTMENT THAT PLANS TO SPONSOR THE PROGRAM:

Dept #1 ▼

Chair (or designated authorizer) Name   Email

Director(s) Name   Email   Office Room   Office Phone

Only complete this section if the program is co-sponsored by a second department.

Dept #2 ▼

Chair (or designated authorizer) Name   Email

Director(s) Name   Email   Office Room   Office Phone

Only complete this section if the program is co-sponsored by a third department.

Dept #3 [▼]

Chair (or designated authorizer) Name   Email

Director(s) Name   Email   Office Room   Office Phone

ENROLLMENT DATA:

Enrollment Target: [12 ▼]

Maximum enrollment: [12 ▼] (minimum 12 students per faculty director)

Minimum Credits   [6 ▼] required for participation

Maximum Credits   [6 ▼] allowed each participant

GENEREAL QUESTIONS:

Brief program summary for advertising materials and the web (suggest 100 words), organized in the following manner:

    a) brief overview

    b) academics and excursions

    c) housing / meals

[   ]

In addition to an S-contract for salary, CFIS provides an administrative supplement for the faculty director(s) which lead the program. This includes developing the proposal <u>and budget</u>, recruiting a minimum of 12 students per faculty, accompanying students during travel and serving as academic director. How to you intend to compensate for any budget shortfall if the program does not meet the minimum required enrollment of 12 students per faculty director? Please identify some of the program components (costs) you feel you can cut or reduce in lieu of canceling the program. These may include items that are not part of the student's program fee, or items that do not affect the academic quality of the program such as the administrative supplement. Should reduction or loss of the supplement not make-up the shortfall, other items to consider include extra guest lecturers and faculty per-diem.

[scrollable text box]

COURSE DATA:

Course ID   Course Title (Limit 255 Characters)   Credits   Notes
(XXXX-###)

Would you like to include a service-learning component in
any of the above courses?   [No ▼]

If yes, please describe the service component.
Guidelines for incorporating service-learning on a
course abroad can be found here.   [scrollable text box]

ADDITIONAL QUESTIONS:

If this program has been conducted before, then please just update questions 3, 5, 6 and 7. If it is being offered for the first time, then please complete all items below.

1) Describe program objectives and your rationale for offering this program.

[scrollable text box]

2) Identify site(s) where the program is to take place.

[scrollable text box]

3) What are the advantages of offering this program at each specific location? (response required for all proposals)

```
                                                    ▲
                                                    ▓
                                                    ▓
                                                    ▓
                                                    ▓
                                                    ▓
                                                    ▓
                                                    ▼
```

4) What students does the program target, and how does the program meet their curricular requirements?

```
                                                    ▲
                                                    ▓
                                                    ▓
                                                    ▓
                                                    ▓
                                                    ▓
                                                    ▓
                                                    ▼
```

5) Describe the specific instructional format for each course, including a tentative daily lecture schedule. (In general, a three credit hour course requires about 34 contact hours from the faculty director who will receive the s-contract for each course.) (response required for all proposals)

```
                                                    ▲
                                                    ▓
                                                    ▓
                                                    ▓
                                                    ▓
                                                    ▓
                                                    ▓
                                                    ▼
```

6) Describe the academic requirements (papers, tests, etc.) and methods of evaluating students' performance. (response required for all proposals)

```
                                                    ▲
                                                    ▓
                                                    ▓
                                                    ▓
                                                    ▓
                                                    ▓
                                                    ▓
                                                    ▼
```

7) Does the program require meetings or assignments during the semester prior to the program, or the semester after the students return? If yes, please provide details and justify the need for meetings outside of the winter or summer session schedule. (response required for all proposals)

8) What cultural activities are you considering to be part of the program?

9) How are you qualified to direct this program (eg. research at site, travelled in area)?

10) What are the estimated non-tuition expenses (transportation, lodging, meals, etc.) per student? This estimate forms the basis for a preliminary Program Fee.

11) What Program Expenses do you anticipate other than those covered by the students' Program Fee (eg. Classroom rental, foreign faculty wages, etc.)?

```
[                                    ▲ ]
[                                    ▓ ]
[                                    ▓ ]
[                                    ▓ ]
[                                    ▓ ]
[                                    ▼ ]
```

12) What living accommodations (apartment, homestay, hotel, etc) are planned for students and for the faculty director(s)?

```
[                                    ▲ ]
[                                    ▓ ]
[                                    ▓ ]
[                                    ▓ ]
[                                    ▓ ]
[                                    ▼ ]
```

Additional Comments:

```
[                                    ▲ ]
[                                    ▓ ]
[                                    ▓ ]
[                                    ▓ ]
[                                    ▓ ]
[                                    ▼ ]
```

When you're done, submit!

[SAVE AND SUBMIT LATER]

[SUBMIT NOW]

Thank you for the time an effort you have put into this proposal; we will look forward to working on it with you.

PROPOSAL FOR A SHORT-TERM OFF-CAMPUS PROGRAM

The intent of this proposal is to elicit what you want students to learn from the course, how they will learn it, and how the learning is connected to the sites you will be visiting.

This proposal must be reviewed and approved by the appropriate department chair/program director/dean before it is submitted to the St. Thomas Academic Review Committee for International Education (ARCIE). Therefore, it is important to be as explicit as possible about course goals and teaching methodology, and how these are supported by the off-campus site(s). It is understood that the syllabus may need to be altered as logistical arrangements and academic content are determined over the next several months.

PROPOSED DATE:

I. **PROGRAM DESCRIPTION**

   A. Program title, Primary locations (cities and countries), Faculty director(s) (include department and/or program)

   B. ☐ Graduate course   Number of credit hours _____

       ☐ Undergraduate course   Number of credit hours _____

   C. Have you directed this program before off-campus? If so, how many times?

   D. List any prerequisites? (please explain)

   E. What degree requirements is this program designed to meet?

   F. If English is not the language of the location of the program, will there be a language prerequisite? If not, how will participants carry out their work and interact with the local population, if applicable?

   G. What is the rationale for choice of topics, goals, readings and other elements of the curriculum as they relate to the location(s)?

   H. If the program involves a home stay experience, describe the length of the home stay and the individuals and/or organizations responsible for arranging home stays.

II. **INTEGRATED SYLLABUS**

Short-term programs set themselves apart because they attempt to integrate traditional classroom education with experiential learning and site visits. **It is very important that you demonstrate how the location and local resources enhance the learning objectives of the course.** Faculty directors should formally identify lectures, readings, site visits, group discussions/reflection times and cultural activities that are required parts of the course. As contact hours must be equivalent to those on the home campus, identify the time spent in these activities. Sample proposals are available from International Education.

The syllabus should include the following items:

   A. A course description of 100-200 words. Describe the main theme or focus of the course, its elements (readings, lectures, site visits, independent research) and the itinerary.

   B. A list of the course goals and objectives.

   C. Required and recommended readings.

D. **COURSE EVALUATION.**

Be specific with the % of grade for each requirement such as participation and attendance, assignments, exams or papers, presentations, academic journals, or field observations reports that are used as the basis for the course grade.

E. **DURATION.**

State number of days abroad and the number of contact hours.

F. **THE SYLLABUS MUST CONTAIN THE FOLLOWING ELEMENTS. BE AS SPECIFIC AS POSSIBLE.**

1. **The length of time** in each location
2. The various **educational activities** (lecture titles and topics, readings, site visits, group discussion/reflection time, cultural events, etc.) Clearly demonstrate how these activities are linked to the course objectives and location.
3. Other **culturally orienting activities. Again, identify the link between these activities and the learning objectives of the course.**
4. The length of time spent in these activities. **Contact hours, defined as the time when students are engaged in the objectives of the course,** must be equivalent to or more than those on the home campus.
5. The amount of unstructured time in each day.

III. **ENROLLMENT**

A. What is the minimum and maximum number of students that may enroll in this program?
B. How you plan to recruit students?

IV. **TEACHING METHODS**

A. What teaching methods and other pedagogical approaches are used and how do they facilitate the learning process to ensure that the course objectives are met?
B. Estimate the percentage of the on-site teaching and guiding that you will do yourself. Will you be using guest lecturers? If yes, why and how are they used and how will you integrate them into the course?
C. If there are two faculty directors:
   1. How will they share responsibilities?
   2. What experience do they have working together?
D. If you have directed this program previously, please explain what changes you made based on the experience and student evaluations, and why?

V. **FACULTY DIRECTOR(S) INFORMATION**

PRIMARY FACULTY DIRECTOR: [Name]

Campus address:

Office phone:

Home phone:

Training and experience in subject matter (if the course topic is outside your academic discipline,

describe what training and experience you have to teach this course):

Experience in proposed location(s) and contacts you may have in the host country(ies)

Language(s) and level of proficiency:

Previous experience teaching off-campus programs?

SECONDARY FACULTY DIRECTOR (if any): [Name]

Campus address:

Office phone:

Home phone:

Training and experience in subject matter (if the course topic is outside your academic discipline, describe what training and experience you have to teach this course):

Experience in proposed location(s) and contacts you may have in the host country(ies)

Language(s) and level of proficiency:

Previous experience teaching off-campus programs?

[Source: Adapted from University of St. Thomas]

(Please return to the Registrar's office)

NEW COURSE AND GENERAL EDUCATION PROPOSAL FORM

New course ____   New course plus GE ____   Add/Change GE attribute to existing course [LINK]
Reinstate inactive course ____   Last Taught _____

Dept. No: ____   **Dept. Name:** _____   **Course No:** _____

Catalog Course Title: _____

Class/Lab Course Title: __
(limit of 25 characters)

Draft catalog course description: (limit to 75 words):

Term type: Semester ____   Interim ____   Summer ____
(Interim and Summer school courses cannot be taught during a regular semester without approval as a semester course)

First time course will be offered : Sem I __   Interim __   Sem II __   Summer __   Academic Year _____
or for existing course, has been taught since: _____

Course Location: On Campus ____   Off-Campus - Domestic ____   Off-Campus – Int'l ____

Is this a topics or seminar course? Yes ____ No ____   **If yes:** Topics ____   Seminar ____
(The course number will remain the same each time it is taught, but the course title will include "Top:" or "Sem:" to allow for a change in title)

Does course require a discussion section as a separate registration? Yes ____ No ____

Is this a lab? Yes ____ No ____ **or will this course have a separate lab?** Yes ____ No____

Will course be taught as a half semester course? Yes ____ No ____

Credit Value: .25____ .50____ .75____ 1.00____ other____   **Grading Option:** Graded ____ or P/N ____

Estimate of number of hours of out-of-class student work required for the course per week: _____
(Minimum of 2-3 hours of out-of-class student work required per hour of in-class time for a 1.00 credit course)

Are there fees associated with this course? Yes ____ No ___

If yes, list amount and type $_____   **Type** _____

May a student repeat this course? Yes ____ No ____   **If yes, how many times?** _____

Prerequisite needed for this course? Yes ____ No ____

If yes, list course prerequisites as they should appear in the College catalog:

_____

[Source: Adapted from St. Olaf College]

GUIDELINES FOR OFF-CAMPUS INTERIM COURSES

Off-campus Interim courses are central to the institution's global mission. Such courses are designed to capitalize on opportunities unique to the locations where they are taught and to integrate classroom instruction and experiential learning activities into a well-conceived whole. When appropriate for academic and other reasons, affiliations with local academic institutions are encouraged.

Proposals for off-campus Interim courses shall demonstrate the centrality of the course to the college curriculum. Furthermore, they shall provide a rationale for conducting the course off-campus by explaining the significance of the location(s) to the overall educational experience. The proposal and Off-Campus Supplement together shall provide a clear picture of the careful integration of course content and on-site living and learning opportunities.

When preparing an off-campus Interim proposal, please keep in mind the following guidelines developed by the IOS and IDOCS. By following them closely, you will facilitate IDOCS review of your course. IDOCS may request additional information about your course during the review process or request revisions prior to approval.

The Interim Instructor may teach only the approved course during the program. He/she may not modify the focus or level of the approved course. He/she may not supervise independent study/independent research projects.

New course proposals (including the Off-Campus Supplement) are due in the Office of the Registrar on November 10 of the academic year prior to the year proposed for the course. Letters of intent for offering a repeated interim course are also due in the International and Off-Campus Studies Office by November 10.

A.   GENERAL GUIDELINES

1. An interim course that has not been offered during the last three years is considered to be a new course.

2. Faculty adapting an on-campus course to an off-campus interim must submit a new course proposal with a course number different from that of the on-campus course.

3. Each course shall have a well-defined focus, whether disciplinary or interdisciplinary.

4. Pre-requisites shall be appropriate to course goals.

5. Instructors shall be mindful of how courses fit into departmental or interdisciplinary programs and of how they relate to existing programs in the same geographic area. Faculty members are encouraged to speak to area studies programs and their department chair in advance of submitting a proposal.

6. Instructors shall be mindful also of the intended audience(s), whether majors, non-majors, or both.

7. Instructors who intend their courses to satisfy general education or departmental requirements are encouraged to consult GEC (General Education Committee) and departmental guidelines before submitting proposals and to refer to those guidelines in their proposals.

8. The Interim proposal should provide an accurate and complete summary of all activities associated with the course, including any non-traditional or experiential activities.

B.   ACADEMIC GUIDELINES

1. Courses shall have academic integrity and coherence. The relationship between course content and the course location(s) should be articulated clearly. Instructors should give careful thought to the integration of course readings, lectures, site visits, and independent study and research, and methods of evaluation.

2. Courses shall normally combine experiential learning with more traditional academic learning.

3. The type and amount of work required of students shall be appropriate to the focus and level of the course and compatible with living and traveling conditions. The amount of assigned reading should be similar to what is required in on-campus Interim courses. Students need to know in

advance how they are to procure assigned reading materials (by purchase before departure, purchase on site, or the use of libraries). When students are expected to carry out research projects, faculty should ensure that libraries or other research facilities are available and adequate. If English is not the language of the location of the course, careful thought should be given to how students will carry out their course work and interact with local populations.

4. Courses shall have at least twenty instructional days (not including travel to and from Minneapolis/ St. Paul). The time devoted to classroom or course-related-activities shall be at least as much as for on-campus Interim courses, and normally significantly more. Faculty should submit a preliminary daily schedule for both students and faculty that outlines how mornings, afternoons and evenings will be spent.

5. Means of evaluation shall be clearly stated, realistic, adequate and comparable to those used on campus.

C. ITINERARY

1. In preparing the itinerary, faculty should balance the academic integrity of the course, the logistics and cost of travel. Faculty are encouraged to consider carefully the number of sites they propose to visit, their geographical proximity to each other, and the time that will be spent traveling between them.

2. Instructors must make a good case for the amount of travel they propose.

3. It is expected that the duration of an off-campus Interim will be between 24 days and 28 days, including travel to and from the site(s).

D. COURSE TITLE AND DRAFT CATALOG STATEMENT

1. The course title shall reflect the disciplinary or interdisciplinary focus of the course as well as the place in which it is taught.

2. The draft catalog statement shall describe the main theme or focus of the course, its elements (such as readings, lectures, site visits, independent research), and the itinerary. Information about the student work load and assessment should not be included in the catalog statement. Detailed guidelines are available from IOS.

E. COURSE ENROLLMENT

A suggestion for a minimum and maximum number of participants should be prepared and accompanied with a rationale for those numbers.

F. REVIEW OF NEW COURSE PROPOSALS

To propose a new off-campus Interim course, faculty need to complete a new course proposal packet along with an International & Off-Campus Studies supplement available from the department chair. Proposals (including tentative program budgets) are due at the Dean's office on November 10 of the academic year prior to the year proposed for the course. A new course proposal (first time offered) requires initial approval of IDOCS for one year.

Department chairs are encouraged to arrange 3-1-2 or equivalent teaching loads for all faculty proposing off-campus Interim courses. A member of the faculty will then be able to replace a canceled off-campus Interim course with another course, either during Interim or during Semester II.

G. INTERIM CLASSES PROPOSED FOR A SECOND OFFERING (WITHIN THREE YEARS OF THE ORIGINAL OFFERING):

The second time an interim course is proposed, a letter of intent including signatures of appropriate department chairs and associate deans should be submitted to IOS by November 10, along with the following items:

    ☐ Copy of the original proposal

    ☐ Major, concentration and GEC approvals

    ☐ Copy of the actual syllabus, itinerary and budget used

A report on the first offering of the class, including a detailed plan for the changes in itinerary, budget, course syllabus and any other arrangements. If changes in the course warrant, copies of new GEC applications should be attached.

After an interim course is approved for the second offering, it is considered an "on-going interim" (see Section H).

Department chairs are encouraged to arrange 3-1-2 or equivalent teaching loads for all faculty proposing off-campus Interim courses. A member of the faculty will then be able to replace a canceled off-campus Interim course with another course, either during Interim or during Semester II.

H.   REVIEW OF ON-GOING INTERIMS

Instructors proposing off-campus interim courses already approved by IDOCS as on-going and conducted within the previous three years (by themselves or by someone in the same department) need not submit a new course proposal for review by IDOCS. Instead, they should send a letter of intent including the following items:

1.   Title of the course and course number.

2.   Pre-requisites required for applicants.

3.   Any major, concentration or GE attributes offered in the course. (Please indicate those that have been previously approved and those for which you intend to make a new application.)

4.   An indication of any major changes in the itinerary, activities or course assignments. (If the changes amount to a significantly different course, IDOCS may request more detailed information.)

5.   A tentative syllabus as well as an itinerary.

6.   A preliminary budget.

This letter is to be signed by the instructor and by the department chair. Signature of the department chair confirms approval of the interim by the department. IDOCS will coordinate review of off-campus Interim courses with the Office of the Dean of the College.

Department chairs are encouraged to arrange 3-1-2 or equivalent teaching loads for all faculty proposing off-campus Interim courses. A member of the faculty will then be able to replace a canceled off-campus Interim course with another course, either during Interim or during Semester II.

I.   FACULTY ELIGIBILITY

Any faculty member, with approval of the department chair, may propose an off-campus Interim course to be taught during the second year or a subsequent year on the faculty. Only the person proposing an Interim course shall teach the course. An Interim course instructor shall be familiar with the country(ies) included in the itinerary. Retired faculty members are eligible to serve as off-campus instructors.

J.   TEACHING LOAD

Normally, interim courses are taught by an individual faculty member. A team-taught course may be possible contingent upon:

1.   Approval of department(s) and Associate Dean(s) with regard to teaching loads. Consideration should be given to on-campus guidelines regarding student enrollment for team-taught courses).

2.   Instructional costs not being added to the program costs for either faculty member.

3.   The course proposal should address items 1 and 2.

K.   OFF-CAMPUS MENTORING PROGRAM

To provide opportunities for faculty to gain experience in leading off-campus programs, January interims enrolling 20 or more students may include a second faculty member (mentee) who would accompany the interim group and serve as assistant to the faculty instructor (mentor).

The following guidelines apply:

1. The mentee must not be scheduled to teach during the January interim. Serving as a mentee does not count as teaching a course, so the mentee will normally have a 3-0-3 teaching load.

2. A faculty member who wishes to be considered for a menteeship position must make their request (in writing) to the Director of International and Off-Campus Studies. The faculty member should *not* contact January off-campus interim instructors directly. The Director of the Office of International and Off-Campus Studies will conduct the discussions with the possible mentors.

3. The request should include:

   A list of January off-campus interims that the mentee would prefer

   A proposal for mentee involvement in a future off-campus study program *following* the mentoring program

   The signatures of the mentee's Department Chair and Associate Dean signifying approval of the mentee involvement in the Mentoring Program

4. The faculty instructor (mentor) must have taught at least one off-campus program prior to the start of the mentoring program.

5. All direct program costs (including travel, accommodations, 2 meals per day) for the mentee will be covered by the development fund of International and Off-Campus Studies.

6. A faculty mentee is expected to devote his or her entire effort to the program. Accordingly, family members may not accompany a mentee.

7. Applications should be submitted one year prior to the start of the interim period for which the mentee is applying.

L. **STUDENT ELIGIBILITY**

Students who are sophomores, juniors, or seniors in good academic standing may apply for participation in off-campus Interim courses. First-year students in good academic standing may only apply for participation in foreign language Interim courses (or Education 170). Each course instructor shall establish selection criteria for his/her own off-campus Interim course and describe them in application materials. Applications and acceptance deadlines will be provided by IOS by early April and instructors are asked to make every effort to comply with them.

Regular students must register to take the Off-Campus Interim course for credit. Approved Continuing Education students must register for the course but are allowed to audit.

M. **HEALTH, SAFETY, AND COMMUNICATION**

In the interest of the health and safety of participants in off-campus Interim courses, these conditions shall be observed:

1. Interim courses shall only be offered in countries with which the United States has official relations and for which no Department of State Travel Warning has been issued.

2. Instructors shall arrange for means to contact the home campus either at or near the site(s) of proposed courses, and shall have a clear communication link to the campus. Regardless of the location(s) of an Interim course, instructors are encouraged to be prepared to respond to health and safety problems, whether emergency or routine in nature.

3. All Interim courses must comply with College policies about the rental and use of motor vehicles.

4. All home-stays shall be arranged in accordance with IOS best practice guidelines.

5. All private carriers hired to provide required group transportation scheduled during interim must provide certification of appropriate insurance coverage.

N. BUDGETS, FEES, AND ACCOUNTS

1. Instructors shall develop budgets in cooperation with IOS. Instructor's salary and benefits are met through the operating budget of the college. Participating students pay a fee for all other Interim expenses.

2. Program budgets are to be submitted with the new course proposal or with the letter of intent. Budgets for off-campus Interim courses that have been taught before shall be updated by the faculty, in cooperation with the staff of IOS, during the month of February.

3. It is expected that off-campus interims will operate at the cost stated in the off- campus interims brochure published in April.

4. Pre-course cost adjustments will be made, prior to December 1, if changes in airfare and/or exchange rates result in a difference of greater than 5%. This adjustment can either reduce or increase the cost of an interim.

5. Post-course refunds to students will be processed according to the following policy:

   If the fund balance (amount remaining on campus and the amount returned by the instructor) at the end of an Interim is $100 per student or greater, the full amount will be refunded to the student. If the fund balance (amount remaining on campus and the amount returned by the instructor) at the end of the Interim is less than $100 per student, the full amount will be directed to IOS to cover deficits in other Interim budgets and to support Interim program development. This policy encourages Interim instructors to return unused funds to campus rather than handing them out on site; it reduces the expectation of students of a hand-out at the end of Interim; and it eliminates the need for IOS to process small amounts of money.

O. FINAL REPORT

A final financial report shall be submitted to the Director of IOS by the time interim grades are due, or earlier. A narrative report should contain detailed information about the academics and logistics of the program and should discuss problems, successes, and make recommendations for future programs. This report is due to the Director of IOS and the instructor's Department Chair by March 1. An Interim that is being offered for a second time, as per Section G, must have the narrative report submitted by Interim grades due date with the financial report.

At the conclusion of the Interim, IOS will ask students to complete a returning student questionnaire about organizational and logistical aspects of the course. IDOCS uses the results in reviewing subsequent Interim proposals.

Faculty are strongly encouraged to ask students to evaluate the academic component. This may be done by administering "gold form" course evaluations processed by the ARP (Office of Academic Research and Planning) or by using an instructor-prepared evaluation tailored to the Interim course. Information about course content and the impact of the Interim experience on students' programs of study contributes to the ongoing St. Olaf assessment program.

P. NON-PARTICIPANTS ACCOMPANYING OFF-CAMPUS INTERIMS

Persons who are neither registered for the interim course nor members of the immediate family of faculty leading an off-campus interim, are prohibited from participating unless approval is obtained from the Director of IOS.

Fees payable to the College will be determined by the Director of IOS for all individuals accompanying an off-campus interim who are not registered students, registered through the Office of Continuing Education or participating through prior college arrangements.

[Source: Adapted from St. Olaf College]

OFF-CAMPUS SUPPLEMENT INTERIM PROGRAMS – ST. OLAF COLLEGE

1. Proposals for off-campus Interim courses shall demonstrate the centrality of the course to the college curriculum. Furthermore, they shall provide a rationale for conducting the course off-campus by explaining the significance of the location(s) to the overall educational experience. The proposal and Off-Campus Supplement together shall provide a clear picture of the careful integration of course content and on-site living and learning opportunities.

2. **Itinerary:** Provide an itinerary for the proposed course and include a rationale which relates the itinerary to the academic goals of the course. (See B and C of the Off-Campus Interim Courses section of the IDOCS Academic Policies and Procedures Manual.)

3. **Daily Schedule:** Provide a description of a typical day on site (include daily schedule, description of traditional academic learning and/or experiential learning activities, and student options for free time).

4. **Language Issues:** If English is not the language of the location of the interim course, will there be a language prerequisite for the course? If not, how will participants carry out their course work and interact with the local populations?

5. **Cross Cultural Learning:** Provide a description of how the course will assist students in developing cross cultural competency.

6. **Homestays:** If the Interim involves a homestay experience, describe the length of the homestay, the individuals and/or organizations responsible for arranging homestays, and the criteria used to select host families. (See L of the Off-Campus Interim Courses section of the IDOCS Academic Policies and Procedures Manual.)

7. **Suggested Minimum and Maximum Enrollments:** What are your suggestions for minimum and maximum number of students for this interim? Please provide a rationale for these numbers. (See E of the Off-Campus Interim Courses section of the IDOCS Academic Policies and Procedures Manual.)

8. **Instructor Qualifications:** Provide an account of previous experience in the countries and cultures to be visited (and/or an indication of how you plan to acquire additional knowledge); benefits to your professional development; and previous experience with leading student groups off-campus. Describe your language skills and/or in-country experience if appropriate to the course. (See H of the Off-Campus Interim Courses section of the IDOCS Academic Policies and Procedures Manual.)

Additional Signatures Certifying Approval

_____   _____
Program or Concentration   *Signature*

_____   _____
Program or Concentration   *Signature*

[Source: Adapted from St. Olaf College]

INTERNSHIPS, INDEPENDENT STUDY, AND SERVICE-LEARNING

6

Kathy Tuma

A number of colleagues report increased student interest in international internships, independent study, and service-learning. Many students are seeking out ways to have these types of experiences on a short-term basis. It is important for the International Office to be involved with the operation of these unique learning opportunities.

INTERNSHIPS AND INDEPENDENT STUDY

Both of these areas can lend themselves very nicely to a short-term international experience. Students might find an internship with a banking institution in London or go to Florence to do an independent project on the architecture of the city.

In many cases, these types of experiences are not administered through the international office. They grew up on our campuses as experiences that happened during the regular academic year, usually at a location that enabled the student to easily interact with the internship or independent study site and the faculty supervisor. But with the advent of electronic communication, that proximity is no longer necessary and students are finding opportunities far away from the home campus.

We discovered on our campus that students were participating in these types of international experiences without benefit of any special advice or counseling. Even though they were going off on programs that offered institutional credit, they were not being offered the kinds of basic orientation that study abroad students received. By pointing out the ways in which institutional liability was increased by this omission, we were able to receive agreement that the signature of the director or associate director of the international office was required on any application for international internship or independent study.

Before signing off on an application, we conduct a short interview with each student. During this interview, the students are given a packet of information (see documents at the end of this chapter). They are given institutional waivers and agreement forms that must be signed and submitted with their application. They receive information on the need for the basics—passport, visas, and international student identity card. Students are directed to the U.S. State Department Web site to view the information pertinent to the country they are about to visit; they are directed to the Centers for Disease Control and Prevention (CDC) Web site to see what health precautions are required or recommended. They are invited to attend one of three on-campus orientation sessions held for study abroad students.

We do not provide all of the services that are made available to students on study abroad programs. Those students who have taken the initiative to set up an international internship or independent study tend to prefer to use their own initiative through the entire process. But we provide them with the information needed to be informed travelers. In turn, we also reduce our institution's liability for these students.

INTERNATIONAL SERVICE-LEARNING

I recently had the opportunity to devote time and energy to the development of a Strategic Plan for Service-Learning at my home institution. I came away from this project convinced of just how important it is to the sending institution, the host agency, and the students involved that the service-learning opportunity be well planned, well supervised, and academically rigorous.

In *Academic Service Learning: A Pedagogy of Action and Reflection*, Robert Rhoads and Jeffrey Howard set forth a working definition of service-learning:

Academic Service Learning is a pedagogical model that intentionally integrates academic learning and relevant community service. There are four key components to this definition. First, academic service learning is a pedagogical model, first and foremost it is a teaching methodology, more than a values model, leadership development model, or a social responsibility model. Second, there is an intentional effort made to utilize the community-based learning on behalf of academic learning, and to utilize academic learning to inform the community service. This presupposes that academic service learning will not happen unless a concerted effort is made to harvest community-based learning and strategically bridge it with academic learning. Third, there is an integration of the two kinds of learning, experiential and academic; they work to strengthen one another. Finally, the community service experiences must be relevant to the academic course of study (Howard, 1993). Serving in a soup kitchen is relevant for a course on social issues but probably not for a course on civil engineering. All four components are necessary in the practice of academic service learning.[1]

Campus Compact is a national coalition of more than 950 college and university presidents—representing some 5 million students—dedicated to promoting community service, civic engagement, and service-learning in higher education. Its publication, *Introduction to Service-Learning Toolkit*, offers some simple graphics to illustrate the ways in which service-learning is set apart from other types of learning and other types of service.

RECIPIENT	«	BENEFICIARY	»	PROVIDER
SERVICE	«	FOCUS	»	LEARNING
SERVICE-LEARNING				
COMMUNITY SERVICE		FIELD EDUCATION		
VOLUNTEERISM		INTERNSHIP		

Campus Compact provides these definitions for the five types of programs mentioned above:

Volunteerism is the engagement of students in activities where the primary emphasis is on the service being provided and the primary intended beneficiary is clearly the service recipient.

Community Service is the engagement of students in activities that primarily focus on the service being provided as well as the benefits the service activities have on the recipients (e.g., providing food to the homeless during the holidays). The students receive some benefits by learning more about how their service makes a difference in the lives of the service recipients.

Internship Programs engage students in service activities primarily for the purpose of providing students with hands-on experiences that enhance their learning or understanding of issues relevant to a particular area of study.

Field Education programs provide students with co-curricular service opportunities that are related to, but not fully integrated with their formal academic studies. Students perform the service as part of a program that is designed primarily to enhance student's understanding of a field of study, while also providing substantial emphasis on the service being provided.

Service Learning programs are distinguished from other approaches to experiential education by their intention to benefit the provider and the recipient of the service equally, as well as to ensure equal focus on both the service being provided and the learning that is occurring.[2]

It is not enough to provide the opportunity for students to serve. While there is merit to this, and Habitat for Humanity or spring break relief projects are worthwhile pursuits, true service-learning carries additional responsibilities.

In the March-April 1996 *Journal of Higher Education*, Robert Bringle and Julie Hatcher published an article titled "Implementing Service-Learning in Higher Education." In it, they provide a definition that is still widely used by service-learning practitioners,

We view service-learning as a credit-bearing educational experience in which students participate in an organized service activity that meets identified community needs and reflect on the service activity in such a way as to gain further understanding of the course content, a broader appreciation of the discipline, and an enhanced sense of civic responsibility. Unlike extracurricular voluntary service, service learning is a course-based service experience that produces the best outcomes when meaningful service activities are related to course material through reflection activities such as directed writings, small group discussions, and class presentations.[3]

One thing that is clear from all of my research and interviews is that administering international service-learning programs presents challenges not found in traditional study abroad. For a host of reasons (including but not limited to different cultural concepts of service and ever-changing staff in host agencies), it is crucial for a successful service-learning program to have continuity in leadership. Ideally, this would be a leadership team consisting of a faculty member on the home campus and an on-site coordinator.

The faculty member would be responsible for the development and implementation of a learning plan and the on-site coordinator would be responsible for the arrangement and oversight of the service projects.

Someone on your campus will need to take responsibility for the administration of these programs. Many institutions now have offices that are designed to facilitate service projects. Work with the staff in these offices to see what is already in place and what else needs to be done. Here are several things to consider:

1. Identify faculty members on your campus who have experience with the pedagogy of service-learning. Ask them to be involved in preparing materials to be used by faculty and students.

2. Develop a workshop that faculty members who wish to propose a service-learning program would be required to attend.

3. Develop a course template for faculty supervisors of service-learning internships to use in helping to shape students' learning during the service project. See the sample syllabus at the end of this chapter or visit the Web sites below for additional syllabi. See also "Charting a Hero's Journey" by Linda Chisholm.[4]

Minnesota Studies in International Development Academic Handbook:
http://www.umabroad.umn.edu/programs/ASIA/msidIndia/coursesSemester.pdf

University of Denver International Service Learning:
http://www.du.edu/intl/isl/isl_bosniap.html

4. Develop a series of orientation and reentry exercises for students participating in service-learning programs.

5. Work with your Registrar's Office to implement a special designation on a student's transcript that indicates completion of a service-learning project.

Service-learning programs require a great deal of oversight but, if done well, can provide some of the most rewarding experiences that students and faculty can have on a short-term study abroad program.

Endnotes

1 Rhoads, Robert A. and Howard, J. 1998. *Academic Service-Learning: A Pedagogy of Action and Reflection.* Indianapolis: Jossey-Bass Publishers

2 Campus Compact. *Introduction to Service-Learning Toolkit: Readings and Resources for Faculty (2nd Edition).* 2003. Providence, RI: Brown University.

3 Bringle, Robert G. and Hatcher, J. "Implementing Service Learning in Higher Education." *Journal of Higher Education,* 67, 2 (March/April 1996).

4 Chisholm, Linda. *Charting a Hero's Journey.* New York: International Partnership for Service-Learning. 2005.

"Be the change you wish to see." —Mohandas Ghandi

At its most basic level, study abroad is about observing: walking the Appian Way, strolling the Louvre, or touring Dachau. Service learning abroad is about observing and getting involved: working on a coffee cooperative in Guatemala, teaching math skills in Tanzania, or building homes in Mexico.

Short-term programs abroad that incorporate service learning add a unique pedagogical and contextual dimension to academic courses. Tapping the idealism of both the college student and academe, service learning can address the educational goals of a course and the social needs of a community. However, if service learning is undertaken without a clear articulation of the academic objectives and an understanding of the community partner, it can be disastrous.

Short-term service learning—whether embedded in a course or encompassing the academic term—should be undertaken when the following factors can be addressed by the faculty director:

☐ Academic goals overlap significantly with the goals of the community partner or host site. If the match is not an obvious or easy one, look for other partnerships rather than forcing one. Articulating shared goals will help to ensure a positive first-time experience and, if appropriate, a long-term partnership.

☐ The number of students is easily supported by the work of the community partner. A class of 50 students may overwhelm the community partner and the people they serve; smaller groups of 10 to 20 are generally more manageable. A larger class may be split among several work sites or divided into shifts, alternating classroom time with project time.

☐ Service-learning projects enhance rather then detract from the work of the community partner. Unlike other pedagogical tools, a service-learning component usually involves vulnerable populations and service providers with scarce resources. Care must be taken by the instructor to respect the needs and limitations of both parties.

☐ Service learning addresses your institutional mission (i.e., the social mission of a religious institution or community engagement and citizenship in a public institution). Just as study abroad takes more effort than the home campus classroom, service learning requires as much or more attention and commitment. If service learning can be supported within the context of the institutional mission, there may be a greater likelihood of sustainability over the long term.

If your course meets these criteria, then service learning may be an appropriate pedagogical tool.

Service As Text

One way of conceptualizing service learning is to consider the experience as an additional text, one more means of understanding a topic. As with any text, the faculty member will need to preview it in order to present it well. If visiting the site is not possible prior to the start of the course, you might rely on the knowledge and experience of community partners to guide and familiarize you with the site through correspondence and research.

Faculty who use service learning in their courses may be concerned about grading an unpredictable and subjective component of their class. If treated as a text, then service learning can be seen as a didactic experience that is not graded directly. Just as a text is employed to communicate concepts that are in turn graded through an appropriate assessment, so the learning in service learning can be evaluated. By assigning reflective papers, journals, field observations reports, or presentations, the faculty director can assess the students' comprehension of the academic goals without grading students on the more subjective understanding of the entire experience.

Even Better Than Service Learning at Home?

Service learning abroad can also have several advantages over more traditional service-learning models. As international educators know well, travel can have a unifying effect on a class. Students typically develop deeper relationships with classmates than a traditional classroom setting allows. When guided by the faculty director, this closeness can lead to a more intentional learning community and more intentional reflection on the issues encountered in service work.

These experiences abroad also allow students to immerse themselves in a struggling community rather than just visiting for several hours each week as they might do at home. Students may become more attuned to the complex issues that underlie their direct service and gain exposure to the personal stories that complement and deepen academic concepts. Service learning abroad can also lead students to a more critical evaluation of local issues when they return home.

The most dramatic benefit of service learning may be the in-depth encounter with the host culture. When students are building a home in the highlands of Guatemala side by side with Mayan laborers, they will enter into conversations that are beyond the scope of a classroom interview or presentation. As the indigenous group teaches building techniques to a student in Spanish, the power differential between the "laborer in a developing country" and the "affluent U.S. college student" shifts. Through shared work, the abstractions of global economics, international politics, and intercultural relations are realized—that is, made real—in, for example, the person of Guatemalan farmer Juan Carlos. His lessons in cement block construction may also lead to conversations about scarce resources, differing world views, or Mayan family life. Although the results of such encounters are unpredictable, they offer a cultural exchange rarely found in more structured settings.

Cautionary Notes

Although there are many benefits to service learning abroad, there are pitfalls as well. The following suggestions may help instructors avoid some difficulties associated with service learning:

- ☐ Research the integrity of your community partners just as you would any other teaching resource. Ensure that community partners are truly working in concert with the local community and the people they intend to serve.

- ☐ Confirm with the community partner that the content and scope of the service project is appropriate to the course and reasonable in relation to the skills and abilities of the students.

- ☐ Invest time in preparing students for both the cross-cultural and service aspects of the course. Students will need orientation on working with vulnerable communities or individuals.

- ☐ Spend time examining the motivations behind service. Question "do-gooder" attitudes that may do more harm than good. Your service work will not change the world, but it should advance the mission of the community partner.

- ☐ Guard against students' temptations to demonize one community and canonize the other when injustices are encountered and examined.

Service-Learning Resources

Check first with the resources on your own campus. There may be colleagues in other disciplines or in cocurricular programs who can offer advice, support, and even connections to long-time community partners.

Campus Compact (www.campuscompact.org)

Most states have local chapters of this national service-learning organization. They offer technical assistance when planning service-learning course components and a vast array of written resources on the subject including monographs, sample syllabi, and educational research.

Break Away (www.alternativebreaks.org)

This nonprofit organization assists cocurricular programs in site selection, leadership development, and framing the service experience. Their site bank offers a host of community partners and guidance in selecting an appropriate site.

The Response Directory (www.cnvs.org)

Sponsored by the Catholic Network of Volunteer Service, this directory lists over 180 full-time, religiously affiliated volunteer programs. Many of these programs are familiar with linking college students and recent graduates with social service agencies in their communities. Some welcome short-term classes or volunteer groups as part of their mission.

GUIDELINES FOR IOS REVIEW OF INTERNATIONAL INTERNSHIP/INTERNATIONAL IS/IR APPLICATIONS

1. Director or Associate Director will meet with all students proposing an international experience and sign off on their application. We will take a copy, which will be kept in the file bin in Kathy's office.

2. Director or Associate Director will review the application looking for:

    a. Where and with whom the internship/independent study will be completed (any red flags?)

    b. Make sure that the application contains contact information and dates.

3. We'll give students a packet that contains:

    a. A list of websites that would have helpful information for students traveling abroad.

    b. An International Student ID card application

    c. A copy of the Crisis Management plan designed specifically for students on Internships. (Note that this plan will contain contact information for the Center for Experiential Learning and students will be encouraged to also note information for their faculty internship adviser.)

4. If we have a current immunization sheet for the location to be visited by students, we will print them a copy.

5. We will print them a Culture Gram specific to the country they will visit.

6. If they have not previously attended one of the IOS orientation programs, we will encourage them to attend if one will be held prior to their departure.

7. Center for Experiential Learning or Registrar's office will make sure that students & parents sign the waiver forms, we need not have involvement in that.

[Source: Adapted from St. Olaf College]

INTERNATIONAL INTERNSHIP/INDEPENDENT STUDY APPLICANTS

As you prepare for your international internship or independent study opportunity we strongly suggest that you regularly consult the following websites for information regarding your travel plans.
Since information can change without notice, we encourage you to check these sites out when you first start your planning, two-months prior to your anticipated departure date and more regularly as you get to within one-month prior to departure.

If you already have a passport, check to make sure that it has not expired. If you need to apply for a passport, you can get the information you need at: http://travel.state.gov/passport/passport_1738.html.

NOTE: Many countries required that your passport be valid for at least six months after the date you plan to return to the United States. So, we recommend that you apply for a new passport if yours is about to expire – or at least check the website of the country you plan to visit.

You should check US State Department Consular Information Sheets which provide you with good information about the country to which you'll be traveling and in-country contact information should the need arise. This site will also provide you with country-specific State Department Announcements: http://travel.state.gov/travel/cis_pa_tw/cis/cis_1765.html

It is recommended that you register with the US Embassy or Consulate closest to your place of study. By doing so, you will be notified if there are issues of concern related to United States citizens, specific to the country you are in. You can register online at: http://travel.state.gov/travel/tips/registration/registration_1186.html

This site is the Centers for Disease Control, which has up to the minute information regarding health issues in the country to which you'll be traveling. http://www.cdc.gov/

You should check to see if you need a visa (permission to enter) for the country you plan to visit. You can do that by accessing another State Department website that tells you about foreign entry requirements: http://travel.state.gov/travel/tips/brochures/brochures_1229.html
Regulations about what you can and cannot carry onto an airplane are changing regularly. It is a good idea to check the website of the Transportation Security Administration as you are planning your packing. The website is: www.tsa.gov

The State Department also maintains a website: Tips for Students. It is designed for student advisors and for their students who plan to travel and/or study abroad. http://travel.state.gov/travel/livingabroad_studying.html

The following site contains a great deal of information regarding students studying and traveling abroad. From the home page you can click into a great deal of helpful information regarding your travel plans. http://www.globaled.us/

It's always a good idea to check information from other countries regarding your selected destination. The British Foreign and Commonwealth Office provides information for British citizens similar to the US State Department site. http://www.fco.gov.uk/

Careful planning can make all the difference in the success of your independent study or internship. Please feel free to consult us if you have specific questions.

The Off-Campus Study Office

[Source: Adapted from St. Olaf College]

CULTURAL DIFFERENCE & SOCIAL CHANGE

Anthro 47377 (cross-listed with LAST) Offered in cooperation with the Center for Social Concerns

Instructor: Greg Downey		Office: 619 Flanner Hall	
Class meets: T R 3:30-4:45		Hours: W 3:00-5:00 or by appt.	
Fitzpatrick 356	Phone: 631-3763	http://www.nd.edu/~gdowney	E-mail:gdowney@nd.edu

Course Description

This course is designed for students returning from summer service projects or study abroad programs in impoverished or "developing" countries. In the class, students will conduct research to better understand the sites that they visited. Assigned readings and individually recommended readings will help students to see their individual sites in relation to broader global, regional, and national patterns. The overall goal of the course will be for students to learn how social science analysis might help us to understand and confront problems in cross-cultural contexts.

The syllabus is a work in progress in many senses. First, it is an experiment, offered this semester for the second time. (The first went extremely well, but I hesitate to say too much and establish unreasonably high expectations for you or me.) Second, it is envisioned as part of a larger set of courses to be offered in the future to help students link service experience with academic interests. Third, it is intentionally "incomplete," gaps left in the syllabus that each student will fill in for him- or herself. Finally, it is subject to change — and I hope it will change — over the course of our semester. If "we make the road by walking," we'll do so together, and I reserve the right to modify the syllabus to respond to the path we take.

This class is a space more than a point-to-point route. You have this space, alone and together, to write, read, reflect, and talk about your experience. Your classmates will teach as much as I do, in many senses. I would like you to think about how your service experience might continue to be part of your life and to leave something behind so that what you learn can be shared with those who travel the road behind you. My goal is to help you to understand and, at the same time, to inspire you to think about how things might be different. You will have to read selectively and strategically, and to start early on independent work.

We have been given resources by the Center for Social Concerns and the Helen Kellogg Institute for International Studies to help us, so the outcome of this class is limited only by our imagination and creativity. Last year, the course culminated in a set of public presentations and a poster session — I have scheduled the same but can be persuaded to do otherwise. What makes this course "anthropological" is that we recognize that only through attention to how the people we wish to work with see the world can we cooperate effectively. I assume that every student will participate very actively in class discussions.

Required Texts

David Korten. *When Corporations Rule the World.* Second edition. (Kumarian Press, 2001).
John Isbister. *Promises Not Kept: The Betrayal of Social Change in the Third World.* Sixth edition. (Kumarian Press, 2003).
Norman Uphoff, Milton Esman, and Anirudh Krishna. *Reasons for Success: Learning from Instructive Experiences in Rural Development.* (Kumarian Press, 1998).
Course packet available from the LaFortune copy center (packet #97).

Assignments

Annotated bibliography:

Over the semester, I ask you to keep a running list of the articles and books you read and the Internet pages that you found most helpful in your specific project (class readings not included). Along with each entry, I'd like you to write a sentence or two of notes and reflection:

- □ Why was this piece useful?
- □ What do you take away from it?
- □ How does it relate to what we study?
- □ Would it be helpful to other students?

I expect that this bibliography will include *at least* **twenty items** that are not on our syllabus and some not on the handouts I provide.

Short Essays

You will write a series of short essays, most of them reflective pieces, about your experiences abroad, the class readings, and the relations between them. These essays will be graded S/+/- for content and quality of reflection, and some may serve as the basis of your final projects. You will be asked to turn in at least two double-spaced pages for **eight of the first ten weeks** (most will find it easy to write much more).

Public and Collective Presentation

This assignment is more open-ended and will be negotiated as the class proceeds. The Center for Social Concerns and the other people sponsoring this class would like, if possible, to make students' work publicly available. That way it can be shared with prospective students, alumni, visitors, and others who are interested.

The instructor is open to individual and collective presentations, such as preparing consciousness-raising campaigns, setting up websites, producing a video, or sponsoring an event on campus. This should allow you to get started on senior theses, get directly involved in community action, or explore future careers. Unless we agree on something, you will be involved in **a Conference** at the semester's end. I will review your work individually and do everything in my power to help make your presentations as polished and effective as possible.

Class attendance is mandatory. More than 3 unexcused absences will not be tolerated and will result in reduction in the student's final grade for the course.

SECTION ONE: REORIENTING OURSELVES	
WEEK ONE: INTRODUCTION	
August 23	Get acquainted session
August 25	**Paulo Freire**. 1998. "First Letter: Reading the World/Reading the Word." Pp. 17-26. **Bill Holm**, 1990. "Coming Home Crazy." In *Coming Home Crazy: An Alphabet of China Essays*. Pp. 19-30. Read the Internet articles on Re-entry and Reverse Culture Shock.
WEEK TWO: LASTING IMPRESSIONS	
August 30	**Craig Storti**. 2001. Excerpts from *The Art of Coming Home*. (Intercultural). Pp. 138-160. **(Please skim!)** Visit: http://www.nd.edu/~intlstud/services/returnees/tips.htm — Notre Dame's own "re-entry" resource page.
September 1	Ben Feinberg. 2002. "What Students Don't Learn Abroad." From Chronicle of Higher Education. Bill Donahue. 2001. "My Virtuous Vacation." Pp. 68-74. George Gmelch. 2000. "Lessons from the Field." Pp. 46-57. Ivan Illich. 1968. "Cuernavaca Speech."
WEEK THREE: WHERE WE WERE	
September 6	Readings from small group syllabi on specific regions and independent research. See course webpage for on-line resources.
September 8	*Small group discussion of sites and orientation.* Worksheets and discussion of essays.
WEEK FOUR: MOTIVATIONS AND GOALS (READINGS ARE OPTIONAL)	
September 13	**James Jasper**. 1997. "Culture and Biography: The Pleasures of Protest." Pp. 210-228. **Jeffery L. MacDonald**. 1996. "Crossing the Minefield: Politics of Refugee Research and Service." Pp.255-262

September 15	**Rebecca Anne Allahyari**. 2000. "Introduction: Studying Visions of Charity." Pp. 1-27. **Rev. Martin Luther King, Jr**. 1963. "Letter from a Birmingham Jail." Pp. 83-99.
SECTION TWO: CONFRONTING PROBLEMS	
WEEK FIVE: ECONOMICS AND DEMOCRACY	
September 20	Instructor absent, but part of *Commanding Heights*, a documentary on changes in global governance, will be shown and discussed in class.
September 22	**Class meeting canceled** due to presidential installation at Notre Dame. I would like to schedule a make-up session. **David Korten**, *When Corporations Rule the World*. Read pp. 75-120.
WEEK SIX: BREAKING DOWN COMPLEX PROBLEMS	
September 27	**Peter Taylor**, 2001. "Distributed Agency within Intersecting Ecological, Social, and Scientific Processes." Pp. 315-332. **Daniel Gross**. 1971. "The Great Sisal Scheme." Pp. 255-260.
September 29	**David Korten**, *When Corporations Rule the World*. Read pp. 123-174. Week Seven: Money, poverty, and change
October 4	**David Korten**, *When Corporations Rule the World*. Read pp. 177-185, 205-229 & 265-284.
October 6	**John Isbister**, *Promises Not Kept*. Read pp. 1-29.
WEEK EIGHT: UNDERDEVELOPMENT AND IMPERIALISM	
October 11	**John Isbister**, *Promises Not Kept*. Read pp. 30-101.
October 13	**John Isbister**, *Promises Not Kept*. Read pp. 148-191.
MID-SEMESTER BREAK: OCTOBER 15-23.	
WEEK NINE: FOREIGN POLICY AND JUSTICE	
October 25	**John Isbister**, *Promises Not Kept*. Read pp. 192-241.
October 27	***New Internationalist***, "States of Unrest" and "IMF/World Bank the facts." 2004. Pp. 12-13 & 18-19. *See also course website for additional sources critical of these.* **Kenneth Rogoff**, "The IMF Strikes Back." 2003. *See also the course website for additional sources in support.* ***Please turn in a copy*** of your running bibliography by now if you haven't already!
SECTION THREE: PROPOSING CHANGE	
WEEK TEN: ARE THERE ALTERNATIVES?	
November 1	**John Cavanaugh, Jerry Mander, et al.** "Alternative Operating Systems." 2002. Pp. 151-207.
November 3	**Steven Vago.** 2004. "Strategies of Change." Pp. 357-399. **Mark Langevin and Peter Rosset.** 1997. "Land Reform from Below: The Landless Worker's Movement in Brazil." 323-329. *Instructor will offer each student an individual progress report, broken down into various categories, to help the student anticipate what he or she wants to do to complete the course.*

WEEK ELEVEN: LOCAL PROBLEMS, LOCAL SOLUTIONS	
November 8	**Sally Engle Merry**. "Changing Rights, Changing Culture." 2001. Pp. 31-55. **Richard Flacks**. "Think Globally, Act Politically." 1995. Pp. 251-263. **Norman Uphoff et al**. *Reasons for Success*. Read pp. 1-44.
November 10	**Margaret Casey**. "Development in Madura: An anthropological approach." 1993. Pp. 110-137. **Norman Uphoff et al**. *Reasons for Success*. Read pp. 45-87.
WEEKS TWELVE: FINDING RESOURCES IN THE COMMUNITY	
November 15	Class canceled. Please work on final semester projects! **Stacy Leigh Pigg**. "'Found in Most Traditional Societies': Traditional Medical Practitioners between Culture and Development." 1997. Pp. 259-290. **Norman Uphoff et al**. *Reasons for Success*. Read pp. 88-111.
November 17	Guest speaker: Prof. John Duffy, Department of English "Strategies in speaking and writing for change." *Please note: Prof. Duffy may be a few minutes late. Class will start slightly after the usual start time.*
WEEKS THIRTEEN: LOOKING FOR INSPIRATION	
November 22	**Anirudh Krishna with Roland Bunch**. "Farmer-to-Farmer Experimentation and Extension: Integrated Rural Development for Smallholders in Guatemala." 1997. Pp. 137-152. **Norman Uphoff et al**. *Reasons for Success*. Read pp. 112-156.
NOVEMBER 24: THANKSGIVING HOLIDAY	
WEEK FOURTEEN: NO ALTERNATIVE UNCONSIDERED	
November 29	**Aviva Chomsky**. "'The Threat of a Good Example': Health and Revolution in Cuba." 2000. Pp. 331-357. **Norman Uphoff et al**. *Reasons for Success*. Read pp. 157-195.
December 2	Instructor absent for American Anthropological Association meeting.
WEEK FIFTEEN: CONCLUSION	
December 5	Monday, 7:00 pm. **Semester's end conference**. Hesburgh Center for International Studies, Auditorium and Great Hall. (***Tentative***)
December 6	**Norman Uphoff et al**. *Reasons for Success*. Read pp. 196-217. **Discussion, evaluation & summary**

Note: Because final assignment is public presentation (poster, talk, video, or other project), there will be no final exam in this class.

[Source: Adapted from Greg Downey]

Part III

PROGRAM DEVELOPMENT AND EVALUATION

FEASIBILITY STUDIES

Allison Keith

7

The question of feasibility comes into play in the very earliest of stages of short-term program abroad design. Before the proposal is written, you need to evaluate whether a program can get off the ground. Is there a realistic timeline for developing the program? Has the idea been marketed early enough to get the word out to potential participants? Is the program likely to fit into your students' budgets?

When you look closely at the question of feasibility, all the elements come down to whether the program is marketable. Location, program content, length of program, time of year, and cost all play a part in whether the program will be a success.

FEASIBILITY CONSIDERATIONS

Location

The choice of program site is a key component. Questions to ask include:

- ☐ Does the location match the proposed academic content and learning objectives? Is it popular enough with students to interest them?
- ☐ Does your institution already offer other programs to this location?
- ☐ Are there health or safety concerns related to the site, such as U.S. State Department travel advisories or warnings?
- ☐ Does the program's location allow for only one discipline and group of students, such as learning about agriculture in Argentina, or can the location be used for a general cultural course to open the possibility of participation to a greater number of students?
- ☐ Can the location's infrastructure support your program: safe transportation, access to academic facilities, local support?

A note about site visits. It is expected that a faculty member directing a program be familiar with the program site before arriving. If your faculty member has not yet visited the site, it would be unusual—and in this day and age irresponsible—not to conduct a site visit before bringing students on site. A reconnaissance trip taken by the faculty director can definitively determine if a program's location is feasible. In fact, most institutions require that a faculty director has been on site before developing a new program. Site visits require securing resources through designated program development funds or budgeting the cost into the program fee.

The Academic Calendar

The timing of a program is also crucial to its success. Is the program planned for a time when students can be away from on-campus classes, such as summer break or winter intersession? Does this time of year make the program more expensive due to high travel season rates in specific regions? Have you researched major holidays in the country where the program will be held? If everything will be closed for a three-day national holiday, your group can lose valuable programming time. Are weather conditions favorable to the course's objectives at that time of year? Think about northern and southern hemisphere weather issues: winter or summer, rainy or dry season?

If you are planning an embedded program in the middle of the term, when should it be planned? Are there breaks available so students do not miss other classes? Are part-time graduate students able to travel in the middle of the semester? Planning a program over a school break can allow more students to participate but may also deter some students who are not willing to use special time off (spring break, Christmas/New Year holiday) for academic work.

Duration

What is the program's duration abroad, and will its length fit with the intended audience? Traditional-age undergraduate students may be able to take eight weeks, but working graduate students cannot. Does the length of the program limit the number of participants? Could your program be redesigned to appeal to more students by including some on-campus work in the United States followed by a shorter period of time abroad?

Cost

The program fee may be the final component in deciding if a program is feasible. The idea of a full safari on a Tanzania biology course is attractive, but can the program be made affordable? If the program fee is excessive, you do not have a program. It is worth getting even a rough idea of the program cost during the planning stage to see if you are on the right track. Don't forget to consider current exchange rates and how they might affect the final cost.

Support and Resources

It is essential to make sure that the program has support from the governing bodies (e.g., a senior administrator, department chair, or international office) before it is offered to students, as covered in Chapter 2: Administrative Process. What kinds of resources are required for this program, such as staffing for development and administration?

Likewise it is worth considering the pros and cons of planning the program completely in-house or working with an outside agency for support. Will faculty directors make their own travel arrangements, or will a program provider be hired for support? Are consortial relationships available to share resources? These questions must be answered before a program is planned.

PROGRAM DEVELOPMENT TIMELINE

Timelines vary from institution to institution, but the goal is to plan as far ahead as possible. As you probably already know, launching new projects at academic institutions can take a while. Following is an estimated timeline for program development.

Campus Support and Program Development I (18–12 months)

A year and a half before departure is an excellent timeframe for developing a new program, including determining program feasibility, making a site visit, deciding on academic content and credit issues, detailing the budget and logistics, and confirming program support on campus. During this time, faculty directors are confirmed and program providers secured. A marketing plan based on your audience and objectives should be drafted.

Program Development II (15–6 months)

Program deadlines are established, publicity and recruiting begin, faculty begin training, and itineraries are finalized. Logistical arrangements are confirmed.

Recruiting and Enrollment (8–3 months)

Students are recruited, advised, and selected, and deposits are collected. Coordinate with program providers, travel agencies, and any other organizations so that necessary space is reserved for housing and group flights.

Payment Period (90–60 days)

Collect final payments and begin to pay program providers, airlines, or on-site organizations. At this point, any unused reserved components like airline seats or hotel rooms must be canceled or penalties will apply.

(60–30 days)

Confirm that visas have arrived, if they are required. Orientation, communication from faculty directors, lectures, and registration take place during this time. Contingency funds are finalized and air tickets are issued.

Departure (3 Hours Before Flight)

When possible, it is helpful to have airport assistance for the group, especially if it is a large group. Last-minute problems will need to be addressed and hopefully solved, such as missing passports or airport closures due to weather.

Return

Submit financial paperwork and final reports. Review evaluations. Hold debriefing sessions with faculty directors, administrators, program providers, and students.

WHAT'S NEXT?

Logistics and financial management planning are imperative to successful short-term program abroad planning. Refer to Chapters 8 and 9 to continue with specific program development issues. Remember to think about what you have time to do, and what you are good at. There are many organizations that can support the other areas.

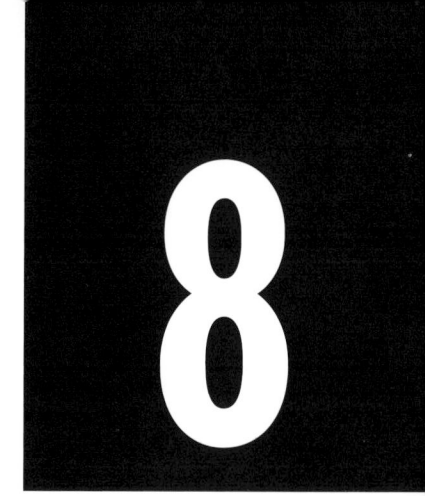

LOGISTICS

Allison Keith and Sue Jackson with Tim Pauly

Once you have settled on a location and academic focus for your program, it is time to consider the practical side of things. Travel arrangements—flights, hotels, site visits, meals—make an international course completely different from the on-campus experience. While it is clear that the academic content will be enhanced by the on-site experience, thorough logistical planning is key to a successful short-term program abroad.

Some program logistics can be planned in their entirety by experienced faculty and staff, while others will benefit from the assistance of an outside agency. This chapter will help you explore the logistical side of program planning and will describe the different forms of outside support that are available to institutions like yours.

In order to plan the logistical components of a short-term program abroad, the following questions must be answered. These answers will also give you the specific information you'll need in setting a budget, as covered in Chapter 9, Financial Matters.

Question 1: How is the group traveling from point of departure to destination, and within country? Which transportation components, if any, are included in the program fee? Some programs offer all-inclusive travel arrangements and others simply require students to show up at the arrival meeting place on the start day.

- ☐ Plane
- ☐ Airport transfer on arrival
- ☐ Train
- ☐ Bus
- ☐ Ferry
- ☐ Public transit
- ☐ Taxi
- ☐ Host families providing transportation
- ☐ Faculty-driven vehicles
- ☐ Other

Question 2: Where does the program originate? This may sound like an odd question, but it is sometimes a good idea for a program to begin from a major hub airport, especially after a holiday or vacation, when students may be at home and not on campus. For example, the institution may be in Colorado Springs, Colorado, which has an airport, but the program may depart from Denver, Colorado. This often reduces the cost and gives students a little more flexibility.

Question 3: Where will the group be staying?
- ☐ Hotel
- ☐ Hostel
- ☐ Host families
- ☐ University residence halls
- ☐ Conference facilities
- ☐ Self-catering apartments
- ☐ Guest farm
- ☐ Bed and breakfast

Question 4: What meals are included?
- ☐ Do accommodations provide meals as part of the cost?
- ☐ Will there be group meals? How many?
- ☐ Where will students take their independent meals?
- ☐ Will a meal allowance be budgeted in the program fee to cover independent meals, or will students be expected to budget their own meals?

Question 5: Is classroom space required?
- ☐ Do the accommodations have meeting space?
- ☐ Will classrooms be needed every day? At special times?
- ☐ What is the charge for renting a classroom?
- ☐ What equipment is needed in the classrooms: white board, PowerPoint projector, etc.?
- ☐ Are special classrooms needed? (i.e., drafting tables, room that can be darkened)

Note: If your group will be staying at a hotel, the bar or lounge may seem to be an easy, laid-back place to hold a class session. However, most groups find it difficult to listen inside a bar, and ultimately find such a location distracting. Check with the owner of the facility before planning any use of common areas for class sessions.

Question 6: Do any special arrangements need to be made to secure local faculty or to enroll students in local institutions?
- ☐ Your faculty's course might be supplemented by a language or culture course taught by local faculty/experts.
- ☐ If you plan to enroll students into local institutions like universities or language schools, you will need to specify the course of study and negotiate the cost.

Question 7: Does the country or countries to be visited require a visa?
If so, you should:
- ☐ Provide extremely detailed information to students about what a visa is and how they should apply for one; or
- ☐ Check with the applicable consulate to see if students can submit their completed documents to your international office, which can in turn deliver the applications all together to the consulate.

Option B gives you the peace of mind of knowing that each student has the necessary documentation. It takes more time up front but can save countless hours later if a student shows up at the airport without the needed visa.

Question 8: Are particular inoculations or medications required or recommended?

- ☐ If so, please refer to the recommendations in Chapter 16, Safeguards for Short-Term Programs.

Question 9: Does the program require a translator or guide?
- ☐ If yes, you will need to secure these services on your own or with an outside agency. Make sure to emphasize to the guides that this is an academic course, not a tour. Send a copy of the syllabus before arrival, and have explicit guidelines articulating that faculty directors will be testing and evaluating students, and your overall expectations for the guide.

Question 10: Are emergency procedures clear?
- ☐ Do the faculty director and students know whom to notify in case of emergency (e.g., home institution and individual family members)?
- ☐ If using a program provider, what procedures do they have in place?

Question 11: Do all participants have adequate health and travel insurance?
- ☐ Will the International Student Identification Card be required to supplement personal insurance?

Passports
- ☐ It is important to encourage students and faculty to apply for their passports as soon as possible—generally a minimum of 8-12 weeks prior to departure.
- ☐ Do not assume that students know the process for applying for a passport—tell them what they need to do.
- ☐ If your campus is not in close proximity to a passport application location, consider inviting an official to your campus to process applications. They are often happy to spend an afternoon processing a large number of applications.
- ☐ For students who already have their passports, are they valid well beyond the dates of the program?

One of the most important decisions to make initially is whether arrangements will be made in-house or by a program provider. The following pages will assist in making that determination.

A NOTE ABOUT INTERNATIONAL STUDENTS

You may have degree-seeking international students applying for a study abroad program. Although they may already be "studying abroad" from their home nations, they provide an invaluable point of view to the academic and cultural experience.

Remember, students who are not U.S. citizens may need to apply for a visa in order to enter the country where the program is to take place.

International students should also be reminded to check with their on-campus advisers to confirm that their paperwork has been completed so they can reenter the United States.

WORKING WITH A PROGRAM PROVIDER OR OTHER OUTSIDE AGENCY

What are Program Providers and What Do They Do?

Program providers are companies that can provide local knowledge and resources to support an institution's program abroad. In addition to managing the logistics of your program, these organizations are also able to assist with the development of a new program, academic planning, and publicity if needed. Each short-term program will have different needs, based on academic and logistical structure, and program providers should offer a lot of flexibility as to what services are included to meet the needs of your particular program.

Does Using a Program Provider Cost More?

Whether using a program provider costs more will vary depending on what services are negotiated and how important the administrator considers the additional support, both off and on site. Many U.S. institutions realize that by sharing the resources of a program provider with other schools, they are actually able to lower the cost of the students' program fee. For example, instead of being forced to rent a classroom for an entire day when it is only needed for a couple of hours, schools can split up the hours through the coordination of a program provider and pay only for what they use. Additionally, institutions sometimes find it much easier to pay one invoice to a program provider in either U.S. dollars or local currency than to worry about making separate foreign payments for student housing, academic needs such as language instruction or classroom space, and guides at museums. Depending on the size and experience of the staff at your institution, having another organization handle financial and logistical arrangements can save time and effort.

A program provider is always willing to put together a proposal detailing the services included and a final cost for the services. This request for proposal must happen in the early phase of program development. With budget figures in hand, it is much easier to decide what is best for students and faculty, as well as the administrator or faculty director.

What Can Be Expected from a Program Provider?

Some institutions opt for a program provider for reasons of liability and financial security. Program providers should have financial stability, good contacts, and references. A program provider should also have clear and established plans to ensure the safety of your students and faculty both during the normal running of the program and during emergencies.

When searching for a program provider, look for one who has a philosophy of education abroad compatible with the philosophy of your institution. They should have solid experience with academic programs and understand the particularities of short-term programs.

Program providers should also have a strong network of on-site resources, including housing and academics facilities/partners. Regular upgrading of facilities and program resources will show that a program provider understands the link between academic quality and the facilities available to students and faculty. Program providers should always be willing to research new program opportunities, and to keep abreast of new locations, museums, or excursions that might add to the academic content of a program. They should be able to offer comprehensive and/or on-site orientations for your group.

Institutions can expect flexibility and accessibility from a program provider. Both parties should collaborate to create a program tailored to their respective needs. Budget flexibility is important, should circumstances arise such as low student enrollment or additional academic needs.

A provider's services should be detailed in an official contract that will eventually be signed by your institution.

Program Provider—Range of Services
- ☐ Program design, including budget
- ☐ Curriculum development
- ☐ Internship placements
- ☐ Orientations
- ☐ Publicity materials

Transportation
- ☐ Airfare for students and faculty
- ☐ Arrival and departure airport transfer
- ☐ City bus/metro passes

Accommodations
- ☐ Accommodations and meal plans
- ☐ Student and faculty housing placement
- ☐ Meal allowances
- ☐ Special meals

Academics/Classrooms
- ☐ Local institution arrangements, classes or classroom space
- ☐ Select local adjunct faculty to be approved by U.S. institution
- ☐ Remuneration of local adjunct faculty
- ☐ Academic support and supervision
- ☐ Faculty office and equipment
- ☐ Classroom scheduling
- ☐ Equipment coordination
- ☐ Guest lecturers
- ☐ Library access
- ☐ Computer and Internet access for students and faculty

Visits/Excursions/Cultural Activities
- ☐ Excursion and activities planning

☐ Museum passes

☐ Buses

☐ Guides

☐ Coordination of cultural activities

Services

☐ Liability insurance

☐ Payment collection (direct payment from students or one invoice to school)

☐ Insurance for students and faculty

On-Site

☐ Student advising

☐ Health and safety implementation

☐ Student handbooks

☐ Access for students to local clubs

☐ Assistance with independent travel

☐ Management of program funds

☐ Facilitation of internships, site visits, etc.

☐ Communication with U.S. institution

☐ Administrative support for faculty and program coordinator

☐ Student evaluations

☐ Evaluation visits from U.S. administrators

What Do Program Providers Expect from Short-Term Program Administrators?

Most importantly, there must be a good spirit of cooperation between the program provider and the U.S. institution. Information must be shared before, during, and after the program. In some cases, this constant communication and support means that the program provider's U.S. office almost becomes an extension of your international office. If your international office is small or understaffed, this connection with the program provider can prove crucial in the school's ability to operate a greater number of programs.

How Can I Find a Reliable Program Provider?

At the time of publication, there is no centralized list of program providers for U.S. institutions. A good method is to ask colleagues for advice and recommendations. Many NAFSA members will use listervs such as the SECUSS-L to get this type of input. References are the best way to find out about a program provider, what type of programs they are experienced in administering, and whether their philosophy fits with the sponsoring institution's goal for its short-term programs abroad.

Other Study Abroad Organizations

Full-service program providers are not the only travel organizations that support short-term programs abroad. The following types of organizations organizations may also be hired to coordinate all or part of your travel logistics:

Travel Agency

You can usually locate a travel agency that is specialized in student travel or group travel to your location. The agency may specialize in a particular area of the world or in a particular theme (e.g., choir performances for a group of musical students). The agencies may or may not be local.

Tour Operator

Tour operators can manage the logistics of a study abroad program. They either have a presence on-site or they use a series of subcontractors to provide travel services such as accommodations, guides, transfers, transportation, special events, meals, etc. Many tour operators have offices in the United States, and they may be headquartered anywhere in the world.

On-Site Program Service Agents

Service agents provide specific services for study abroad programs in a specific area of the world. Examples include home-stay providers, apartment rental agencies, guest lecture providers, internship providers, and classroom rental organizations.

MAKING YOUR OWN ARRANGEMENTS

This section will expand on the checklist from the previous section and will provide some hints on how you and the program faculty can make arrangements without using a program provider. The better the communication and understanding of mutual expectation between the international office and the faculty directing the program, the more smoothly the operation will run, and the fewer cracks there will be into which details can fall.

Air Travel

Most programs require some air travel and airline tickets will often be a substantial part of the program cost. It is imperative that careful research be conducted on the best transaction method for these tickets. Institutional policy or a limited budget may necessitate the purchase of the least-expensive tickets, even if the route is inconvenient with multiple stops and early departure times. However, a program is sometimes better served by a more direct schedule with fewer possibilities of flight delays and missed connections. This can allow the students and faculty director to arrive on site less jet-lagged and ready to begin the program. In all cases, good stewardship of student dollars should be a strong consideration in making arrangements.

Designated Travel Agents

Some institutions have designated travel agents with whom the international office or faculty director must work, even if there are cheaper or more convenient airline tickets elsewhere. In this situation, the administrator should be well acquainted with the practices of the travel agent in terms of how far in advance to make reservations, pay deposits, and purchase the tickets. Benefits of this kind of arrangement include potential flexibility in terms of changing the names of participants, adding or canceling travelers, and an established payment system within the institution.

Finding a Reliable Travel Agent

If your institution allows you to work with any travel agent, consider the following:

- ☐ Confirm that the agency is a member of the American Society of Travel Agents.
- ☐ Confirm that the person you work with has taken Certified Travel Counselor training.
- ☐ Ask for references, particularly from other educational institutions. Call the references. It is important to know that your travel agent is willing and able to accommodate special requests and will be patient with student changes.
- ☐ Make sure that the agent is used to working with groups and will negotiate with the group desks of appropriate airlines. An agent who simply quotes you a rate from the computer is not doing his or her job.
- ☐ If the agent is local, ask if he or she is willing to meet the group at the airport on departure day to do a group check-in.
- ☐ Make sure there is good follow-up once the group has departed—out of sight should not mean out of mind. The agent needs to keep you informed of any changes to the return schedule and should be available to provide assistance in the case of missed flights, etc.

Making Airline Reservations

You may seek multiple quotes for an itinerary—from a local travel agent, a major national student travel company, and a consolidator—and you may want to check with an airline group desk, too. Before asking for quotes, the departure and return dates should be set and the group size defined, as airlines have different criteria for what constitutes a group rate. Some airlines or companies may issue a certain number of free tickets per group.

When making airline arrangements, consider the following:

- ☐ Are there free tickets available with group reservations?
- ☐ What is the service charge per ticket?
- ☐ Is there 24-hour access to change flight arrangements?
- ☐ Will flight deviations be supported?

As when working with program providers, initial contact with a travel agent should be made very early in the program development process. Whenever possible, try to be flexible in program dates to allow the travel agent to research the best fares.

Check to see if there are other services that come packaged with a group booking, such as a night at a hotel.

Be aware of minimum numbers for group bookings; if your group is not likely to reach the needed size, make other arrangements.

Ticket Fees

Many travel agents charge a fee for each ticket issued. If you must use a designated travel agent who charges a fee, there is no option but to pay the fee and build the cost into the program budget. If you have the flexibility to use other travel agents, you will have to decide whether the convenience of working with a particular agency that charges a fee outweighs the savings acquired by finding an agency that does not, but which may not be as convenient in other areas. Try to negotiate a fee waiver or reduction for your group.

Airline Deposits

Airlines require deposits when contracts are finalized. Since this is usually well before student monies are collected, the deposit will have to be covered by bridge funding. Check your institution's policies.

Some airline group desks, in order to offer competitive prices, ask for a significant sum up front, to be refunded once the group has departed. Once again, bridge funding will be necessary for this kind of arrangement. Most airlines will refund the seat deposit after departure.

Electronic Tickets

We've become so accustomed to electronic tickets instead of paper tickets for domestic travel that it is easy to assume there will be no problems with e-tickets for international travel as well. This is usually the case.

However, if your program itinerary requires using more than one airline, ask your travel agent to check to be sure that the computer systems of the two airlines are compatible. If they are not, your group may be stuck at a transit point or forced to purchase new tickets. If there is any question about the airlines systems being compatible, you may wish to request paper tickets.

Cancellations/Refunds

You should consider cancellation and refund policies when reserving tickets. The contract with the airline will outline its policies and important deadlines.

Other Forms of Transportation

Rail

If traveling by train, tickets may be purchased from the agent who facilitated the airline reservations. Consider seat reservations if your group is large or the travel distance is long.

Airport Transfers

It is often most efficient to arrange this transfer from the airport to the accommodation site through an on-site tour operator or bus company. The faculty director or your travel agent may be able to suggest someone to work with. If not, ask someone at the accommodation site to make a recommendation.

Renting Vehicles

Some courses require group travel by rented vehicles, or a faculty director will hire a car for on-site use. Again, the faculty director or your travel agent may be able to suggest someone to work with. Check to see if your institution has an arrangement with a major rental company. Since many rental companies are international, you may be able to take advantage of institutional discounts.

Accommodations

It is important to know the faculty director's expectations in terms of accommodations. Often, when taking a group of students to a familiar place, a faculty director is willing to use his or her host-country contacts to make accommodation arrangements. Deposits are often requested, and, like airline deposits, bridge funds need to be secured until student fees are collected. If there is more than one faculty member with a group, or if there is a teaching assistant assigned to the group, you may wish to plan for one of the group leaders to arrive in the host country a day or two before the rest of the group to get over jet lag, arrange for rentals, and be refreshed when the bedraggled but excited group arrives.

Location Is Important

- ☐ Sometimes a faculty director knows of general areas for accommodations, such as Bloomsbury in London, but does not have specific hotels identified. Consult a travel agent, the Internet, travel books, or personal or professional networks to identify accommodations in a specific area.
- ☐ As with travel arrangements, the least expensive accommodations are not always the best ones. A centrally located hotel may cost more up front but can save in time and travel.
- ☐ Always try to negotiate a group rate. Ask for a free room for group leaders. If the price quoted is too high, ask for a reduced rate. Hotels want to fill their rooms and are often willing to negotiate.
- ☐ Some hotels are reluctant to take student groups. You may have to reassure the hotel that you have carefully screened your students and discussed with them the need for respectful behavior.

Payments for Airline Tickets and Accommodations

Airline and accommodations payments can usually be made by credit card. Be sure to clarify whether a corporate or institutional card is available, or if the faculty director or international office staff must use their personal credit cards and be immediately reimbursed. As covered in Chapter 3, Internal Support Systems: It Takes a Campus to Run a Study Abroad Program, work with the appropriate campus office to obtain a credit card in the institution's name, as it provides another layer of liability between the faculty and on-site organizations. If a deposit is required and it is not possible to use a credit card, funds will have to be sent from your campus.

Again, use your partnership with your business office to do this efficiently.

Meals

Before you can complete your program budget (See Chapter 9, Financial Matters) you need to determine the meal plan for your group.

- ☐ Which meals will be included in the cost of accommodations?
- ☐ Can arrangements be made for special banquets or group meals, either for lunch or dinner? Who will make those arrangements?
- ☐ Is the cost of all other meals built into the budget so the faculty can disburse funds to students to buy their own meals, or must students bring additional funds to buy meals?

Many experienced faculty directors will attest that there is nothing worse than a horde of hungry students. Be sure to take into account arrival times and the number of hours spent on buses, and do whatever is necessary to ensure that food is available at appropriate times. If the group will be arriving in the host country or city too late to get to a restaurant, ask the hotel if a late meal can be arranged. If it will be difficult to exchange money before the next mealtime, arrange for and prepay a group meal.

In some countries, extra precautions need to be made to ensure students do not eat unsafe food. Confirm that the faculty director knows which foods are safe and where such food can be obtained. If the water supply is not drinkable, bottled water should be included in the budget.

In-Country Tour Offices

It is recommended that programs begin with an orientation tour of a city or region, and many cities have offices where such tours can be booked. Tourist offices can also be valuable resources for other information, such as restaurants, local entertainment, reputable vehicle rental agencies, English-speaking doctors, and so on.

Guided Tours

Often faculty directors want to schedule guided tours to specific destinations, the theater, and museums, or plan other excursions that support the academic and cultural learning goals of the course. Advance reservations should be made for tours. Museum entry fees are usually paid on site. Theater tickets may be purchased in advance. Arrangements can usually be made through e-mail or a Web site.

Sensible Things to Do

It is always a good idea to make two copies of all passports and airline tickets or e-ticket confirmation numbers. One set should be sent with the faculty director and the other should remain in the international office. Replacing lost documents is greatly facilitated if copies are available.

FINANCIAL MATTERS

Mark Lund

INSTITUTIONAL POLICIES

Whether your institution is new to offering short-term programs or has been offering them for a long time, it is important to occasionally revisit your institutional budgeting policies. As you might guess, there are many variations on these policies. In an effort to open programs to as many students as possible, your goal should be to promote the policy that offers the best possible financial outcome for your students.

Variety of Tuition Policies

Faculty-directed programs:
- ☐ Home institution collects a reduced tuition fee for short-term study abroad students. Faculty salaries and expenses must be budgeted into the program fee.
- ☐ Home institution collects a reduced tuition fee and pays faculty salary. Faculty expenses must be budgeted into the program fee.
- ☐ Home institution collects and keeps all regular tuition dollars. Faculty salaries and expenses must be budgeted into the program fee.
- ☐ Home institution collects regular tuition and pays faculty salaries. Faculty expenses must be budgeted into the program fee.
- ☐ Home institution collects regular tuition and pays faculty salaries and expenses. These need not be budgeted into the program fee.
- ☐ Home institution collects regular tuition and pays faculty salaries and expenses. Any surplus dollars can be applied to program fee.
- ☐ Home institution does not collect tuition. Faculty salaries and expenses must be budgeted into the program fee.
- ☐ Home institution does not collect tuition and covers faculty salaries and expenses from its general fund.

Consortial or Direct-Enroll Programs:
- ☐ Home institution collects and keeps all regular tuition dollars. Student pays full program fee to program provider.
- ☐ Home institution collects all regular tuition dollars and allows a percentage to be applied to program fee.
- ☐ Home institution collects all regular tuition dollars and allows them all to be applied to program fee.
- ☐ Home institution does not collect tuition. Student pays only the program fee.

Administrative Fees

Many institutions require the international office to build an administrative fee into their budgets to cover the cost of maintaining the international office. This can be a fair compromise if the institution utilizes some of the more liberal tuition policies mentioned above.

If the institution is keeping all tuition dollars AND wants the international office to charge an administrative fee, then it is time for a serious look at the institution's commitment to study abroad. It is easy for treasurers and bursars to see short-term study abroad as a revenue builder for the institution. This would be a time for study abroad professionals and committed faculty to open larger discussions on the importance of study abroad to the overall mission and goals of the institution. Careful consideration needs to be given to the balance between fiscal responsibility and access for students of modest income.

THE PROGRAM BUDGET

As university/college administrators, we understand the importance of budgets. Quality academic programs depend on them. When adequate funds are not allocated, important program components must be omitted. Most university departmental budgets are set within the context of the institution's annual budget. Chief administrators or regents determine the budgets, and directors and staff must work within these budget constraints. Today, given spiraling costs in education, tight budgets plague most programs.

Short-term study abroad budgets are different. They generate their own revenue and tend to be stand-alone budgets outside the university or college's annual budget. This fact makes financial officers generally quite supportive of short-term programs, and study abroad staff build budgets with few external constraints. We are responsible for determining our own constraints and for our own accountability. This is good for our offices, but it can be bad for students if we waste their money or are irresponsible or careless. Setting the budget requires integrity and honesty. We have to earn our students' trust. We must never forget that our goal is education and our office exists to serve our students and faculty leaders. The importance of building budgets should not be underestimated.

Study abroad budgeting is a complicated because task there are so many details. Minor errors can be very costly in terms of money and often lead to failed academic experiences. In an attempt to be clear and comprehensive, yet concise, this chapter is organized into four sections: 1) budget goals; 2) budget checklists; 3) budget spreadsheets; and 4) important lessons learned. Given the diversity of higher education institutions, it is inevitable that some issues will be omitted and some topics will be irrelevant. This chapter is designed to get you started. You will have to do the fine-tuning.

BUDGET GOALS

If our short-term programs are to have integrity, there are several self-imposed goals that should direct all our budget work and serve as constraints. We must:

- ☐ build budgets with sufficient funds to support quality academic programs;
- ☐ keep costs affordable for students without sacrificing academic quality;
- ☐ allocate our students' money, which makes up our budgets, efficiently; and
- ☐ assist faculty directors to ensure all bills are paid in a timely manner.

Finding a balance between the first two goals is difficult. We desire academic quality in all programs, but that can be costly. It is our duty to students to find ways to hold down costs without sacrificing too much academic quality. This requires doing meticulous logistical and program-related research as we explore alternative options. When we lobby on behalf of students to control costs, we must not forget that in healthy business exchanges, both the buyer and the seller should benefit. We need to be tough, yet fair.

BUDGET CHECKLISTS

Increased complexity of programs, legal requirements, safety issues, and rising student expectations have made our work so complicated that it is useful to have checklists to serve as our guides. Two budget checklists are presented in this section to help you get started rather than as procedures for maintaining programs.

When one first encounters the checklists, they could appear overwhelming and even a bit demoralizing. However, study abroad planning and especially budgeting requires detailed work. Be prepared for long hours of minutiae. It is good policy to be thorough—many problems down the road will be avoided.

Budget work requires a team effort. Building a team from offices across the campus is essential. Work closely with them, listen to their advice, and thank them often. The first checklist identifies key budget responsibilities and the personnel assigned to them.

Checklist 1: Identifying Budget Responsibilities and Personnel

- ✓ **Making final budget policy decisions:** Where does the buck stop? You must identify the person who has the final word or budget authority. Personnel involved in final budget policy decisions will most likely involve either the VP for Finance, VP for Academics/Academic Dean/Provost, Controller, Registrar or some combination. Important policy decisions are found in checklist 2 below.
- ✓ **Preparing program budgets:** It is best if a study abroad staff member prepares budgets. This assignment should be given to a person with academic, travel, and international experience who can specialize in this task. Few faculty directors have sufficient experience to prepare their own budget. If faculty insist on this task, work closely with them and require them to get your approval before budgets decisions are finalized and any payments are made.
- ✓ **Administering financial aid and scholarships:** The ideal situation is to identify a person in the financial aid office who can work with all study abroad students. You can then refer students to this particular person. Leave this work to the experts on campus. There are many federal regulations and institutional policies known only to them.
- ✓ **Setting up accounts in the financial services office:** All transactions for each budget must be documented in your institution's financial or business office.

An account will be assigned each program. Your contact in this office is critical. He/she usually monitors all transactions and reviews all financial actions for the controller.

✓ **Charging student accounts:** Most institutions have an office that administers students' accounts. Your office will forward final program prices to this office. They will then bill each student's account. It is this person who ensures that student payments are correctly deposited in each program budget. Your office should not charge students directly. It could cause confusion.

✓ **Collecting deposits and all other payments:** The financial services office collects a variety of student payments. They are in the best position to collect deposits and all other program payments. Keep this task out of the study abroad office. You should not be in the business of handling cash or taking on a collection agency role should students fail to make payments.

✓ **Arranging travel logistics and budget-related academic programming and paying program-related bills before group departure:** This is the critical position. It takes years of experience to understand international travel logistics. This person has the opportunity and responsibility to control program costs. Study abroad staff are best able to make timely deposits and other payments for logistical services. Most money transactions require the study abroad director's approval. Discourage faculty directors from making payments.

✓ **Purchasing foreign currencies and foreign currency bank drafts:** Identify someone in the financial services office. The controller is in a good position to make these purchases. The controller also has information on your institution's cash flow needed to purchase currency in forward markets. Your institution should identify an international bank that provides foreign currency services.

✓ **Setting up and monitoring credit and debit card accounts for on-site payments:** Faculty directors will need to pay for some services on-site. Identify the person in financial services who works with the institution's credit and debit cards. This person will work with you and faculty documenting monthly bills, submitting receipts and preparing monthly credit/debit card reports.

✓ **Preparing final budget report for the controller and external auditors:** While faculty should be responsible for submitting final budget report drafts to your office, the study abroad director should prepare all final reports and sign off on them. If audits raise questions, the director will be asked to justify all payments.

Checklist 2 identifies key budget policy decisions; getting clear answers to each question is critical. You cannot properly prepare a short-term study abroad program budget without these answers.

Checklist 2: Budget Policy Decisions

✓ **What range of target prices does the administration want for its short-term programs?** Study abroad is a privilege, not a right. Families of some students can afford such an experience, but most cannot. Is keeping costs down a priority so study abroad is viable to more students? It is important to identify your institution's general study abroad pricing philosophy. Do you want to encourage as many students to study abroad as possible and therefore keep program costs affordable? Or are high academic and logistical standards for accommodations and travel more important so that cost is not the primary issue?

✓ **Are logistics and planning to be done in-house or by program providers?** Doing in-house planning and logistics often reduces costs and gives you more control over the academic program and all costs. But this takes time, money, and a talented experienced staff. Program providers make planning and budgeting much easier and in some cases may be able to keep costs affordable for students.

✓ **Should you work with specialized vendors such as travel agents?** You may choose to work with travel agents for airfares, ground transportation, and housing rather than make the contacts yourself. An important budget item is the purchase of group airline tickets. Group tickets give you flexibility with final payments, cancellations, and name changes. Group tickets are usually purchased through travel agents. It is best to work with an experienced agent who is an excellent trouble-shooter and reliable rather than automatically accepting the lowest bid.

✓ **How is your study abroad office financed?** Are your staff and office operating expenses covered in your department's budget or does the institution want you to charge study abroad students a fee to help cover program planning expenses?

✓ **Will students be charged tuition?** If tuition is charged, what percent is used to cover program costs and what percent stays on campus? Is tuition money used to pay the faculty salary? The answers can have an enormous impact on the budget.

✓ **Must all participants take the course for academic credit? Can they audit?** For "group chemistry" and fairness reasons, all participants should take the course for credit. If groups are divided between credit and no credit, the different academic requirements may cause dissension and complaints. When no credit is given, student behavior may be affected. If students are allowed to audit, establish the fee and require these students to do all the academic work.

- ✓ **Will scholarships, financial aid, or other institutional money be available?** A majority of university students cannot afford study abroad; without scholarships or financial aid, they will not be able to participate. Acquiring scholarship funds may be desirable—but be forewarned, it is a very difficult challenge and task.

- ✓ **How are faculty directors paid?** Teaching in this program may be part of their regular teaching load and annual salary. If it is not, you will have to cover the salary. In many cases, tuition will be charged and used to cover the salary.

- ✓ **Should health and risk insurance be purchased for participants?** Students must have insurance. They may be able to use their families' insurance. However, getting accurate information about adequate coverage is a difficult task. Most students have no idea how their insurance works overseas. Does your school want you to purchase a good short-term study abroad insurance policy and charge students for short time abroad? The costs tend to be reasonable. Does your institution have its own liability insurance to cover faculty and students?

- ✓ **What is the desired contingency dollar amount for each program?** You will need a contingency policy. It could be a dollar amount per-student or a percent of total program cost. The contingency amount will depend on degree of risk, uncertainties, volatility of the foreign exchange markets and faculty personalities (i. e., big spenders, fiscally tight, nervous about costs, or little fiscal discipline).

- ✓ **Should the college collect self-insurance to cover health cancellations?** One major budget nightmare is a last-minute student cancellation due to health reasons. Its often difficult to get money back from vendors and one less student raises the per-student cost for others. Most difficult of all is having a student forfeit the program money in the midst of a medical problem. Could students be charged a self-insurance fee to cover costs due to last-minute medical cancellations or possibly other unforeseen and uncontrollable expenses?

- ✓ **What unexpected and unforeseen costs will the college cover?** What overrun costs is your institution willing to pay? What costs will be charged students upon return to the United States? For example, who pays the additional costs due to a change of plans related to avian flu, terrorist threats, natural disasters, or bad weather? Make your policy well known to students and family before students apply.

- ✓ **What is the expected minimum and maximum number of days for the program?** To legitimately grant full academic credit, find out the minimum required number of program days. It is common for faculty to request additional days and want to stay longer. Set a policy for the maximum number of days. Remember that each additional day adds about $100 or more to program costs.

- ✓ **What are the minimum and maximum number of students per faculty director?** This is an important academic question with significant budget implications. If the course is taught during the academic year, the registrar and academic dean will want to set a minimum number of students to guarantee that faculty carry a fair share of their department's teaching load. With few students to cover program group costs, per-person costs increase. There is also a fairness issue for students. The maximum number of students will affect the quality of students' experiences. Faculty have less time to work with each student.

- ✓ **What costs are included and excluded in the price charged students?** Identifying which costs are not included is very important. Once these costs are known, you must repeatedly remind both students and faculty of this list. Costs usually not covered include: passports, immunizations, travel to gateway airport.

- ✓ **What faculty director costs are included?** Students usually cover basic costs of the faculty director. They include airfare, accommodations (directors do not share rooms with students), entry fees, and a food per diem. It is important to set fair per diem rates and follow them. Normally, accompanying family member costs are not covered.

- ✓ **What are the deposit, cancellation, and late payment fee policies?** The deposit amount and due date, final payment date, cancellation fees, and late fees for missed deadlines need to be set and enforced. Working with students who have loans may require deadline exceptions. Late fees are a proven method for getting forms in on time. This frees up staff work time to do other tasks.

- ✓ **What are the on-site options for faculty to pay bills?** Can faculty directors be given credit and debit cards? Faculty need options for paying bills on site. Credit and debit cards work best. Purchasing foreign currency bank drafts prior to departure is another option. Travelers' checks are still a viable backup.

- ✓ **What happens if faculty directors spend more money than budgeted?** Aside from unavoidable emergencies, there is always the possibility that leaders, the "loose cannon" types, may spend money on activities not included in the budget. How will these costs be handled? Can you deduct them from faculty paychecks?

- ✓ **What is done with monies left at the end of the program?** If money is left over after the program is completed, what happens to it? Is it returned to students? Is it added to your budget? Is it given to the general fund? Serious thought should be given to returning it to the students. It is their money and brings goodwill.

Once these policy decisions have been made, publicize them and make them well known to the faculty leaders and students. Repeat often and set extremely clear expectations.

BUDGET PREPARATION

Providing quality academic programs is our trade. You must work closely with faculty directors when preparing budgets. Their demands may often be excessive and costly. On the other side, we represent the students who often have limited funds. Because we do not have the typical constraints found in university budgets, it is easy for costs to escalate. We decide if a one-month study program in Europe will cost $2,875 or $4,275.

Controlling costs on behalf of students is one of our major responsibilities. Faculty directors put the greatest pressure on budgets. You need to be able to say no at times. It helps to have seniority, credibility, and administrative backing in order to be successful. Budget work requires long hours of hard work in the trenches. Exploring options leads to cost control. Some cost-reducing actions can increase the academic quality while others can lead to disaster. Hopefully you can find ways to reduce costs that immerse students in the culture. The careful preparation of excel budget spreadsheets enables staff to monitor and control costs by evaluating options. The use of spreadsheets allows us to see the big picture— that is, the final cost with all its details.

One possible approach to budget preparation is to develop two excel spreadsheets for each program. The first excel spreadsheet is prepared to determine the student program cost and provide a record of all logistical arrangements. The second excel spreadsheet is designed for the faculty director. It records all revenues, contingency funds, and payments and lists those payments that faculty are expected to make when on site.

The following analysis of the two spreadsheets identifies different categories of costs, revenue sources, and a method for dealing with unknown variables such as foreign currency exchange rates and the number of student participants. The spreadsheets in this chapter were not designed to include every cost but to be used as teaching tools.

PROGRAM BUDGET AND PER-STUDENT COSTS SPREADSHEET

Please refer to the Program Budget and Per-Student Costs spreadsheet. (p.103) This is the most important budget tool. All vital cost information is recorded in this spreadsheet. A most useful interpretation is to analyze categories of costs from different perspectives.

Category One: Student and Faculty Costs

The first category of cost analysis focuses on the participants. Costs can be separated between **student costs** and **faculty director costs**. All student costs are listed first in the spreadsheet. Faculty directors' costs are recorded at the bottom.

Student costs are divided between **administrative costs** assessed by your institution and **vendor/program provider** costs paid to other institutions and companies. Vendor costs are further divided into three categories: costs paid in dollars before departure; costs invoiced and paid in foreign currencies before departure; and costs paid on site.

The costs to be paid by faculty on site require further clarification. You should estimate the expected costs in dollars and collect the money in dollars. This money is transferred into debit/credit card accounts for faculty use to pay bills abroad. Dollars estimates are used because, while exchange rates are unknown, directors should have some idea of the amount of money they want allocated for group meals, entrance fees, and lectures.

Faculty costs are entered at the bottom of the excel spreadsheet. These costs are straightforward. You will have to decide what faculty costs your institution is willing to cover. Grey areas are immunizations, the exact per diem rate, and any support for accompanying family.

Category Two: Costs Paid in Foreign Currency and Dollars

A second category of cost analysis divides bills between charges in U.S. dollars and foreign currencies. Dollar invoices pose few problems for calculating program costs. However, bills invoiced and paid in foreign currencies cause uncertainties and risks. All foreign currency costs are grouped together in the spreadsheet because the exact dollar costs are not known until the day the transaction is posted. The spreadsheet permits you to experiment with different foreign exchange rates. In the foreign exchange markets, the dollar–foreign currency exchange rates change by the minute. These rates have proven difficult for economists to forecast in the short run. There are no accurate models and far too many variables, making them impossible to predict. To eliminate this uncertainty and risk, it is possible to buy foreign currencies 45, 90, or 180 days before delivery in forward exchange markets at rates guaranteed the day the contract is signed. Typically a 15 percent down payment is required and the balance is due on the delivery date.

Category Three: Individual and Group Costs

There is another important way to analyze costs. Program costs are calculated as either **individual** or **group costs**. Most costs are **individual costs**. In this case, each student is charged a set price for the service. Examples include airfares, entrance fees, and meals.

Group costs are fees charged the entire group independent of the number of students. In these cases, there is a fixed group price for the service and the "per-student cost" depends on the total number of students (i.e., fixed group cost divided by number of students). Examples include a bus price for the day, a classroom charge, or a speaker's honorarium. **All group costs are highlighted in bold italics in the sample excel spreadsheet.** The number of students has also been recorded for each group budget line in the last column for easier reference. All faculty costs are group costs. They include accommodations, airfare, entrance fees, and per diem food costs.

Setting the Final Program Price

Setting the "per-student" program price is a difficult, nerve-racking task. If you unnecessarily set the price too high, some students will be priced out of the program. If the price is mistakenly set too low, you will have to assess a surcharge later. Additional charges after final payments are made should be avoided. It is a public relations nightmare and may invite some hostility. So how are program prices determined when they need to be set months before departure in order to advertise and recruit students?

Excel spreadsheets and formulas make it possible to easily calculate different program costs for changes in the two key unknown variables, the **number of student participants and exchange rates**. The calculated per-student cost in the Program Budget and Per-Student Costs spreadsheet is $4,632. It is based on 16 students and an exchange rate of 6.5 units to one dollar. You might charge students $4,675. But in the six, nine, or even 12 months before the course begins, our world of globalization can bring many changes and some students' plans will change. What can be done to minimize the impact change will have on costs?

Program Costs Sample 1 represents a simplified version of the Program Budget and Per-Student Cost spreadsheet. Tuition and textbook charges are excluded. The per-student cost of the course is $2,981. This cost is based on 16 students and an exchange rate of 8.5 units per dollar. Excel formulas are used to develop the budget. By changing either the number of students and/or exchange rate in line four, all budget lines that depend on the number of students and exchange rates are immediately recalculated to reflect the changes. It takes just a split second to see the effect of a change on the cost per-student. A brief example based on Program Cost Sample 1 follows.

Program Cost Samples 2 and 3 show calculations for four program scenarios. The individual costs calculated in dollars in Program Cost Sample 1 total $1,607. This figure is used for all four cases. The remaining costs fluctuate, as either the number of students or exchange rates change. The examples record extreme cases: 16 to 10 students and 8.5 to 6.5 units per dollar. The "best-case" scenario

(scenario 1: total cost $2,981) reflects 16 students and 8.5 units per dollar. In the" worst-case" scenario (scenario 4: $3,779) there are 10 students and 6.5 units per dollar. In between these extremes are two other cases. Scenario two changes only the dollar exchange rate (8.5 to 6.5) to see its effect and the scenario three changes only the number of students (16 to 10). In this example, the number of students has a bigger impact ($3,417) than exchange rates ($3,282) on per-student course cost.

With this information, programs can be advertised with a range of costs that give a minimum and maximum price. The final program price will depend on exchange rates recorded and the number of students enrolled. One to two months before the course begins you will have to select a final price so student accounts can be charged. After that, you can only hope that no major world events will have a significant impact on costs. It is best to round up the final price for a little protection. For example, if scenario three looks most realistic and the student cost is $3,417, you might consider charging students $3,475.

BUDGET SUMMARY FOR FACULTY DIRECTORS SPREADSHEET

This information is extremely valuable to faculty directors because it gives them an overview of the whole budget, including revenues, and provides guidelines and parameters for their budget responsibilities while on the program.

Please refer to the Budget Summary for Faculty Directors spreadsheet (p. 108). Four major pieces of information are highlighted. First, at the top of the spreadsheet faculty directors can see all sources of revenue and the total amount of money available for their program. Second, all prepaid bills are recorded. It is good policy to send photocopies with faculty, showing proof that the bills were paid, in case there are questions on site. By subtracting prepaid expenses from revenue, you and faculty directors alike know how much money is available for on site expenses.

The third piece of information is quite helpful for faculty. It documents all payments to be paid onsite by the faculty director. In the budget preparation stage, many of these payments are estimates and need to be paid in foreign currencies. Faculty can monitor how their budget is doing by comparing on site bills and payments with earlier estimates. This section also provides faculty with a comprehensive list of payments they are to make and the amounts. An added benefit is the suggested form of payment. Should payment be by credit card or cash from an ATM? Faculty are given a heads up for when they need to get cash from an ATM for future payments.

The final information piece gives faculty some peace of mind. The contingency amount is clearly listed. It is a set amount and is determined when the initial budget is pre-

PROGRAM BUDGET AND PER-STUDENT COSTS

Program Title: 2007	Site: Nation B	Dates: 4 - 27 Jan.	6-Mar-06
Budget Acct #: xxx-000-123	Faculty Director: Dr. Z		

STUDENT COSTS [Students = 16 – Ex. Rate = 8.5]

UNIVERSITY/ADMINISTRATIVE COSTS	Collected in USA DOLLARS		Per-Student Cost		
Tuition - 3 credits	$400 per credit - covers salary)		$1,200		
Administrative Fee	(cover office costs)		$100		
Self-Insurance	(medical cancellations)		$35		
Textbooks	(university bookstore)		$150		
Airfare with Taxes			$875		
Visa			$50		
International Student ID Card	(ISIC)		$22		
Health Insurance	(one-month policy)		$30		

VENDOR COSTS: Paid Predeparture	Paid in USA DOLLARS			Per-Student Cost	Ex. Rate	Students
Airfare In Country		1,200		$185	6.5	
	21 Nights	for cur/pp/pn	$ /pp/pn			
Hotel 1 B&B	5	250	$39	$192	6.5	
Game Park B&B	2	250	$39	$77	6.5	
Hotel 2 half board	4	200	$31	$123	6.5	
Home Stay full board	3					
Hotel 3 B&B	7	250	$39	$269	6.5	
Coach		30,000	$4,615	$289	6.5	16
Van and Insurance		15,000	$2,308	$144	6.5	16

VENDOR COSTS: Paid On Site	Collected in USA DOLLARS for Debit/Credit Cards					
Group Meals				$75		
Entrance Fees				$150		
Metro - Airport Exit Tax				$20		
Contingency/Tips				$250		
Honoraria / Classroom Rental		$3,000		$188		16
Van Petrol		$500		$31		16

FACULTY DIRECTOR COSTS

Airfare			$875	$55		16
Hotel single room			$1,000	$63		16
Per Diem $30/day	22 days		$660	$41		16
Travel to Airport			$100	$6		16
Immunizations/Insurance			$200	$13		16
STUDENT CHARGE	$4,675		Total	$4,632		

PROGRAM COST SAMPLE 1

Program Title: 2007	Site: Nation B	Dates: 4 - 27 Jan.	6-Mar-06
Budget Acct #: xxx-000-123	Faculty Director: Dr. Z		

STUDENT COSTS [Students = 16 – Ex. Rate = 8.5]		Per-Student Cost	Individual Student $ Costs
Administrative Fee	(cover office costs)	$100	**
Self-Insurance	(medical cancellations)	$35	**

VENDOR COSTS: Paid Predeparture	Paid in USA DOLLARS	Per-Student Cost	Individual Student $ Costs
Airfare with Taxes		$875	**
Visa		$50	**
International Student ID Card	(ISIC)	$22	**
Health Insurance	(one-month policy)	$30	**

VENDOR COSTS: Paid On Site	Collected in USA DOLLARS for Debit/Credit Cards	Per-Student Cost	
Group Meals		$75	**
Entrance Fees		$150	**
Metro - Airport Exit Tax		$20	**
Contingency/Tips		$250	**

Costs not affected by exchange rates of number of students			$1,607
Costs affected by exchange rates or number of students			

VENDOR COSTS:	Group Costs Paid in Dollars		Per-Student Cost	Ex. Rate	Students
Honoraria / Classroom Rental	$3,000		$188		16
Van Petrol	$500		$31		16

VENDOR COSTS:	Paid in FOREIGN CURRENCIES			Per-Student Cost	Ex. Rate	Students
Airfare In Country		1,200		$141	8.5	
	21 Nights	for cur/pp/pn	$ /pp/pn			
Hotel 1	B&B	5	250	$29	$147	8.5	
Game Park	B&B	2	250	$29	$59	8.5	
Hotel 2	half board	4	200	$24	$94	8.5	
Home Stay	full board	3				8.5	
Hotel 3	B&B	7	250	$29	$206	8.5	
Coach			30,000	$3,529	$221	8.5	16
Van and Insurance			15,000	$1,765	$110	8.5	16

FACULTY DIRECTOR COSTS

		USA dollars		Per-Student Cost	Ex. Rate	Students
Airfare		$875		$55		16
Hotel	single room	$1,000		$63		16
Per Diem	$30/day	22 days	$660		$41		16
Immunizations/Insurance/Airport		$300		$19		16
STUDENT CHARGE		?????	Total	$2,981		

[Source: Luther College]

PROGRAM COST SAMPLE 2

Program Title: 2007		Site: Nation B		Dates: 4 - 27 Jan.		6-Mar-06
Budget Acct #: xxx-000-123		Faculty Director: Dr. Z				

SCENARIO 1: BEST CASE (many students - 16 and strong dollar - 8.5)

	STUDENT COSTS [Students = 16 – Ex. Rate = 8.5]				Per-Student Cost	Ex. Rate	Students
	ADMIN/VENDOR COSTS: Individual Costs Paid in Dollars				$1,607		
group	Honoraria / Classroom Rental			$3,000	$188		16
group	Van Petrol			$500	$31		16
	VENDOR COSTS:		Paid in Foreign Currency		Per-Student Cost	Ex. Rate	Students
	Airfare In Country		1200		$141	8.5	
	Hotel 1	B&B	5	250	$29	$147	8.5	
	Game Park	B&B	2	250	$29	$59	8.5	
	Hotel 2	half board	4	200	$24	$94	8.5	
	Hotel 3	B&B	7	250	$29	$206	8.5	
group	Coach		30,000	$3,529	$221	8.5	16
group	Van and Insurance		15,000	$1,765	$110	8.5	16

FACULTY DIRECTOR COSTS

group	Airfare			$875	$55		16
group	Hotel	single room		$1,000	$63		16
group	Per Diem	$30/day	22 days	$660	$41		16
group	Immunizations/Insurance			$300	$19		16
	STUDENT CHARGE			Total	$2,981		

SCENARIO 2: CHANGE ONLY EXCHANGE RATE (8.5 to 6.5)

	STUDENT COSTS [Students = 16 – Ex. Rate 6.5]				Per-Student Cost	Ex. Rate	Students
	ADMIN/VENDOR COSTS: Individual Costs Paid in $$				$1,607		
group	Honoraria / Classroom Rental			$3,000	$188		16
group	Van Petrol			$500	$31		16
	VENDOR COSTS:		Paid in Foreign Currency		Per-Student Cost	Ex. Rate	Students
	Airfare In Country		1200		$185	6.5	
	Hotel 1	B&B	5	250	$39	$192	6.5	
	Game Park	B&B	2	250	$39	$77	6.5	
	Hotel 2	half board	4	200	$31	$123	6.5	
	Hotel 3	B&B	7	250	$39	$269	6.5	
group	Coach		30,000	$4,615	$289	6.5	16
group	Van and Insurance		15,000	$2,308	$144	6.5	16

FACULTY DIRECTOR COSTS

group	Airfare			$875	$55		16
group	Hotel	single room		$1,000	$63		16
group	Per Diem	$30/day	22 days	$660	$41		16
group	Immunizations/Insurance			$300	$19		16
	STUDENT CHARGE			Total	$3,282		

[Source: Luther College]

PROGRAM COST SAMPLE 3

Program Title: 2007		Site: Nation B			Dates: 4 - 27 Jan.		6-Mar-06	
Budget Acct #: xxx-000-123		Faculty Director: Dr. I						

SCENARIO 3: CHANGE ONLY NUMBER OF STUDENTS (16 TO 10)

	STUDENT COSTS [Students = 10 – Ex. Rate = 8.5]				Per-Student Cost	Ex. Rate	Students
	ADMIN/VENDOR COSTS: Individual Costs Paid in Dollars				$1,607		
group	Honoraria / Classroom Rental			$3,000	$300		10
group	Van Petrol			$500	$50		10
	VENDOR COSTS:	Paid in Foreign Currency			Per-Student Cost	Ex. Rate	Students
	Airfare In Country			1200	$141	8.5	
	Hotel 1	B&B	5	250	$29	$147	8.5	
	Game Park	B&B	2	250	$29	$59	8.5	
	Hotel 2	half board	4	200	$24	$94	8.5	
	Hotel 3	B&B	7	250	$29	$206	8.5	
group	Coach		30,000	$3,529	$353	8.5	10
group	Van and Insurance		15,000	$1,765	$177	8.5	10

FACULTY DIRECTOR COSTS

group	Airfare			$875	$88		10
group	Hotel	single room		$1,000	$6100		10
group	Per Diem	$30/day	22 days	$660	$66		10
group	Immunizations/Insurance			$300	$30		10
	STUDENT CHARGE		Total	$3, 417		

SCENARIO 4: WORST CASE (few students – 10 and weak dollar – 6.5)

	STUDENT COSTS [Students = 10 – Ex. Rate 6.5]				Per-Student Cost	Ex. Rate	Students
	ADMIN/VENDOR COSTS: Individual Costs Paid in $$				$1,607		
group	Honoraria / Classroom Rental			$3,000	$188		10
group	Van Petrol			$500	$31		10
	VENDOR COSTS:	Paid in Foreign Currency			Per-Student Cost	Ex. Rate	Students
	Airfare In Country			1200	$185	6.5	
	Hotel 1	B&B	5	250	$39	$192	6.5	
	Game Park	B&B	2	250	$39	$77	6.5	
	Hotel 2	half board	4	200	$31	$123	6.5	
	Hotel 3	B&B	7	250	$39	$269	6.5	
group	Coach		30,000	$4,615	$462	6.5	10
group	Van and Insurance		15,000	$2,308	$231	6.5	10

FACULTY DIRECTOR COSTS

group	Airfare			$875	$88		10
group	Hotel	single room		$1,000	$100		10
group	Per Diem	$30/day	22 days	$660	$466		10
group	Immunizations/Insurance			$300	$30		10
	STUDENT CHARGE		Total	$3,799		

[Source: Luther College]

pared. It is unlikely to change. Another key figure is "unallocated funds." This figure, when positive, tells faculty there are additional funds available. In other cases, when negative, it means part of the contingency has been allocated before departure.

Whether the "unallocated funds" budget line is positive or negative depends on the final recorded costs and developments that occur after the students have been given the final program price. In this example, the faculty director received a grant of $1,000 that was not guaranteed when students were given their final cost. There is also a tendency when planning to allocate a few extra dollars to the budget. In the Program Budget and Per-Student Costs spreadsheet, the per-student cost was $4,632, but students were charged $4,675. If any prepaid costs come in lower than estimated, this will also free up some money. In the example, the domestic airfare when prepaid was $10 per ticket less and Hotel 3 was $8 per person per night lower. However, some costs can increase. The visa fee went up unexpectedly by $25.

In the Budget Summary for Faculty Directors spreadsheet, the "expected expenses overseas," including contingency funds, are totaled and subtracted from the "money available for overseas" to calculate "unallocated funds." Hopefully this figure will be in the black rather than the red. The faculty director can then add the unallocated funds to the contingency funds. Conscientious faculty fear overspending or running out of money. These figures can be reassuring. If there are extra funds available, faculty will know they may be able to take advantage of an on-the-spot, unplanned, but once-in–a-lifetime event.

LESSONS LEARNED

The two checklists and two spreadsheets covered the basic "nuts and bolts" of budgets. Additional insights, tips, and lessons have been learned from years of experience. Here are a dozen of the most useful and valuable lessons.

1. Once budget policies and logistical standards have been determined, **publicize** them clearly. Then **enforce your policies with consistency, firmness, and fairness**. It is tempting to make exceptions, cave in to pressure, or grant a special privilege. Do not do this. The news of exceptions spreads rapidly on campus and will come back to haunt you.

2. When faculty directors put pressure on you to raise the price of the program or their per diems, or if vendors attempt to dramatically raise prices the next year, gently but firmly remind them that you are the **caretaker of students' money** and represent students.

3. One key to holding costs down is **airfare prices**. Most institutions buy group airline tickets. This allows them to reserve tickets up to nine months before departure, make small deposits, wait until about 45 days out to report student names, and cancel 10 percent of the tickets with no or minimal penalty. Group tickets

are nonrefundable once written. Internet-purchased tickets may be cheaper, but they have to be purchased in 24 hours, are nonrefundable with no route or name changes, and rarely can you find enough tickets for the whole group at the low price. The option of purchasing airline tickets that are refundable or allow the change of dates tends to be very, very expensive.

4. **Accommodations** are a second large cost. If the program is 25 days long and the average night's lodging is $60, the total bill will be $1,500. If the cost is $25 per night the total cost will be $625. Spending time researching housing costs and options and repeatedly telling students the expected standard of accommodations can save them many dollars. Hotels that have two- or three-star ratings work well. Just make certain they are clean, located in reasonably safe areas, and have good hot water. Students need to know your expectations.

5. Finding a **program provider** that delivers a quality academic course at an affordable cost to students will greatly simplify your budgeting process. In the spreadsheet, most of the budget lines disappear when they are replaced with one line— "provider fee."

6. Prepare clear lists of what **services are included in the advertised price**—and more importantly, what services are not included. Publicize the items not included in the advertised brochures as often as possible. Then ask faculty leaders to reinforce them. The following **services or items are rarely included in the advertised price:** passport, immunizations (they differ from individual to individual), meals that are not part of the program, gifts for home stays, and transportation to the gateway airport.

7. Providing students with **estimates or suggested dollar amounts** for items not included in the advertised price (immunizations, food, and spending money) is an important service rendered to students. Include this information on brochures along with the program price.

8. When you **advertise** the program price, give a **price range** and then very clearly tell students the lower price requires a best-case scenario: a strong dollar, good airfares and taxes, and the maximum number of students. The higher price is worst-case scenario: weak dollar, high airfares and taxes, and minimum number of students. Emphasize that the final price will not be known until student recruitment is done and all prices are known.

9. Faculty have several **options for making payments on site**. The best option will change as banking policies change. Credit card payments (where available) are usually the best. The dollar exchange rate is the best, the transactions are easy, and good records are automatic. Many credit card companies have recently converted foreign currencies to dollars at the time of

BUDGET SUMMARY FOR FACULTY DIRECTORS

Program Title: 2007		Site: Nation B		Dates: 4 - 27 Jan		6-Mar-06	
Budget Acct: # xxx-000-123		Faculty Director: Dr. Z					

REVENUE:		Ex. Rate	6.5	Students	16	Group Total	17
***	$74,800		set price	$4,675	16		
***	$1,000		grant funds	(unexpected funds)			
	$75,800	Total Revenue					

EXPENSES: Prepaid				DOLLARS		FOREIGN CURRENCY	
	$19,200	Tuition		$1,200	16		
	$560	Self Ins.		$35	16		
	$374	ISIC		$22	17		
	$1,600	Admin		$100	16		
	$510	Health Ins.		$30	17		
	$2,400	Textbooks		$150	16		
	$14,875	Airfare		$875	17		
Est. $185	$2,975	Airfare in Country		$175	17		
Est. $50	$1,275	Visas		$75	17		
	$4,615	Transport	Coach/bus			30,000	
	$2,308	Van and Insurance				15,000	
	$3,230	Hotel 1	5	$38	17		
Est. $38	$3,570	Hotel 3	7	$30	17		
	$57,492	Total Prepaid Costs		$18,308	Money Available for Overseas		

EXPENSES OVERSEAS:							
credit card	$2,108	Hotel 2		$31	17	4	nights
debit card	$1,292	Game Park		$38	17	2	nights
credit card	$500	Petrol					
credit card	$2,550	Entrance fees		$150	17		
debit card	$340	Metro/Exit tax		$20	17		
credit card	$1,275	Group Meals		$75	17		
debit card	$3,000	Honoraria					
debit card	$960	Per Diem	$30 x 22	& faculty shots/airport			
	$4,000	Contingency Funds		$250	16		
	$2,283	Unallocated Funds		$16,025			
	$18,308						
					ATM	$8,000	
					VISA	$16,000	

[Source: Luther College]

payment and charged 2 percent to 3 percent. Debit cards provide easy access to foreign currency cash with excellent exchange rates. You do need to find ATMs and hope the card and machine work, avoid the loss or theft of cash, and work with a bank that has minimal charges for withdrawals. Payments can be made in advance by wire. You get lower rates when you buy foreign currency from U.S. banks that specialize in foreign currencies and the wire cost is $15 or more. Foreign currency bank drafts can be purchased for a fee and faculty carry them to pay on site. The dollar rate is lower.

10. Your office and the financial services office **will need receipts for all transactions**. They are required for the external annual audit. They also serve as a constraint or check on your work. The faculty need all the assistance you can give them to ensure all receipts are acquired. The more payments your office makes, the more control you have over records. Remind faculty of the importance of receipts and find methods to help them get and save receipts. This is a big challenge. Also, faculty should be discouraged from becoming bankers for students while on the program. It can be a fiasco when they loan money or help pay for nonprogram meals and then have to collect the money.

11. At the completion of every program there is likely to be **unspent monies**. Do not let the faculty give that money to students on the last day or two of the program so they can go shopping. There is no guarantee that the faculty records are correct; they can only guess the exchange rate on credit cards and ATM withdrawals. Rates are not known until the monthly statements arrive. There are also surprise bills that show up late that faculty or your office have missed. It is best to wait at least two months before you close the books. If there is still money in the account, it is a good policy and brings much goodwill if the money is returned to the students. This is a signal that you have done all you could to spend their money wisely and have no intention of making money on the program.

12. **Treat the faculty directors well.** They have an enormous responsibility for all components of the program. Many rarely work with budgets,m and money matters may not be their strong suit. Meet individually with them and go over the spreadsheets. Provide tips and assure them that you are there to support them. It can make a big difference.

MARKETING AND PROMOTION

10

Kathy Tuma

You cannot have a short-term program without students, and most study abroad courses require some attention to promotion in order to recruit students. The goal may be to create so much anticipation that a marketing plan is not needed. Until then, utilize your faculty director's expertise and enthusiasm to promote the program to students.

STEP 1: KNOW YOUR STUDENTS

The first step in your marketing plan should be an analysis of your student body. There are three types of students:

Type One: The "When Do We Leave?" Student

This student is ready to travel anywhere, anytime. She or he is first in line to receive new brochures and applications and has deposit money in hand.

Type Two: The "I Could Be Convinced" Student

This student may have thought about study abroad but needs a push to make the commitment.

Type Three: The "I've Got All I Can Do To Keep Up On Campus" Student

With this type of student, the challenge is to remove obstacles, whether real or perceived, and show that study abroad (or more specifically, short-term study abroad) is an option.

If you have a campus full of Type One students, you may stop reading and go on to the next chapter. If, like most institutions, many of your students fall into the Type Two and Type Three categories, read on.

There are several reasons students fall into the Type Two or Type Three category.

First generation or at-risk students. For these students, the decision to attend college was a major one. They may have had to struggle with high school guidance counselors, college admissions counselors, or even their own families for the chance to attend college. Simply being on campus is a major achievement.

First-time travelers. Study abroad can seem too adventurous for students who have never had a passport or traveled outside the country. They may be reluctant to take the risk.

Nontraditional students. These are the students with full-time jobs and/or a family. They barely keep their heads above water with all of the responsibilities in their lives and study abroad does not seem like even a remote possibility.

Double/triple majors. These students have a carefully planned schedule and they have ruled out study abroad because a semester- or year-long program would jeopardize their progress toward graduation.

Students with disabilities. Although there are many good opportunities for students with disabilities to study abroad for a longer duration, they may be unwilling to take the chance without first having had the opportunity to prove themselves on a shorter program.

STEP 2: ADVISING

Study abroad advising, in the traditional sense (an adviser and student in discussion regarding goals, type of program, etc.) rarely occurs with students opting for short-term programs abroad. The process of choosing a short-term program is very different from that of choosing to go abroad for a semester or year. Students opt for this type of program because the program goes to a place they have always wanted to see, because it fulfills a needed graduation requirement, or perhaps because their best friend has applied. Students think they do not need to consider the more serious issues that are prevalent in the selection of a semester- or year-long program.

For short-term programs, the quality of the written materials presenting the courses available or specific course descriptions is very important.

Because students often make their choices casually and because we do not have the opportunity to assist them in their program selection, it becomes crucial to provide a careful and thoughtful orientation program. More information about this follows in Chapter 15, Orientation and Reentry.

STEP 3: THE MARKETING APPROACH

The first thing you need to do to promote your courses is to make short-term study abroad **unassailably academic**. That is, nothing about these programs should seem like a trip or a vacation or a junket. They should be marketed as a valuable part of the curriculum, as an opportunity for a student to continue and enhance his or her studies by going beyond the classroom.

Encourage faculty directors to shape the courses in such a way that they will fulfill general and/or major/minor requirements. As much as we wish students would study abroad purely for the joy of learning, we know that they are much more likely to participate in a program that meets an academic requirement.

As long as a course is unassailably academic and developed with an audience in mind, there is nothing wrong with promoting the more exciting aspects of study abroad. The places you can go, the people you can meet, and the things you can learn—these are the essence of short-term programs abroad and they should be promoted shamelessly. Who would not be tempted to leave a Minnesota campus in January to study the literature of the Caribbean? Why not get political science students excited about attending a meeting of the British Parliament?

STEP 4: INFORMING STUDENTS

The mechanisms for getting information to students about your programs will vary depending on your institution. Following are a number of suggestions; it is up to you to determine which will work best for your school. If you are not sure, talk with your campus communication or publication director. She or he should be able to give you good advice about what works well in your situation.

Printed Information

Brochures and Catalogs

If you offer a selection of short-term programs abroad during a specific term, such as summer or January intersession, list these courses in one printed brochure. Include general application, selection, payment, and cancellation information. Arrange the course listings by geographic region or by discipline and include:

☐ Course level/course title
☐ Brief course description
☐ Name of faculty director(s)
☐ Prerequisites
☐ Cost
☐ Maximum enrollment
☐ Requirements that the course fulfills (e.g., "counts toward Art History major/minor," or "fulfills Area A of core curriculum")

Course Descriptions

☐ Consider creating a course description for each short-term program abroad. These one- to two-page narratives give students additional information to help them make appropriate decisions and allow faculty directors to set academic and travel expectations. Include the following topics:

☐ Location(s) and dates, including departure and return dates. Give students an idea of how much travel is required.

☐ Description of academic course: learning objectives, integration of sites, prerequisites, and evaluation methods. What will students learn?

☐ Program structure: what to expect during the program. What will a typical day be like?

☐ Faculty director information: brief biography and previous international experience.

☐ Housing and meals. Where will students live? What will they eat?

☐ Cost. What does the program fee cover?

☐ Information on how to apply.

Place the brochures at various locations around campus, including:

☐ Near the registrar's office;
☐ In appropriate academic department offices;
☐ In residence hall lobbies; and
☐ In other appropriate offices (e.g., the women's center for a course that counts toward Women's Studies majors and minors).

Other methods of getting the word out about your short-term programs abroad include the following:

☐ Student newspaper. Ask the student newspaper to run articles promoting your programs.

☐ Department newsletters. Include information about specific short-term courses abroad in departmental newsletters.

☐ Posters. Put posters on visible bulletin boards around campus.

☐ Tabling. Set up tables in prominent locations and ask past program participants to hand out printed information to interested students.

□ Intercampus mail. Send course descriptions to specific majors and minors, to specific student clubs (e.g., the Pre-Law Club may be very interested in a "Law in London" course), and to academic counselors and faculty academic advisers.

Message Centers

Is there is a place on your campus where students regularly look for announcements—perhaps an electronic message board in the cafeteria? If so, be sure to post information about your short-term programs there.

Electronic Information

□ Put information about courses, application procedures, deadlines, etc., on your office Web site.

□ Ask the faculty director to put information about the course on his or her departmental Web site. Encourage the faculty director to highlight the information, not just list it along with all of the on-campus departmental offerings.

□ Set up and use an office e-mail address to which students can direct inquiries, and make sure that someone in your office checks it regularly and responds to all inquiries.

□ Some office on your campus has the ability to send an e-mail to all matriculated students—most likely it is the registrar's office. Ask a staff member from this office to send an announcement to all students as you approach your application deadline. The following is a sample:

INTERIM 2007 OPEN HOUSE

The Open House for the January 2007 international and domestic off-campus interims will be held in the Black and Gold Ballroom from 4:30 p.m. to 6:30 p.m. on Wednesday, September 13. Faculty instructors for the courses will be available to answer questions about the interims and assist students in completing application forms.

The DEADLINE for applications for the 2007 off-campus interims is October 5. Some interims are already closed based on registrations completed last spring. Please consult the International Office for up-to-date information on open and closed courses.

Call x1234 or stop in at the international office if you have questions.

E-mail Aliases

Find out if your institution creates an e-mail alias for each course. If so, use those aliases to send e-mail messages about programs that may be of interest to students taking certain classes. For example, you could send information about an anthropology program in Guatemala to all of the students currently registered for Intro to Cultural Anthropology.

Open Houses

Arrange at least one Open House at which you promote all of your short-term programs abroad. Ask faculty directors to be present and invite past participants, if they are available. Faculty can bring photos, maps, and souvenirs from the location; play some regional music; or put on a slide show or PowerPoint presentation. Encourage the faculty to be creative.

Ask students to sign lists expressing interest in particular programs. These interest lists can be used to help recruit students later, should the need arise.

Class Visits

Encourage faculty directors to visit classes that would be natural feeders to the short-term course abroad. If the course gives fourth-level French credit, talk with the students currently in the third-level classes.

Miscellaneous Tips for Marketing Your Program

Application Process

Make the application process for your short-term programs abroad as user friendly as possible. The Type One student will be happy to complete an 18-page form; the Type Three student may give up on page 3. Make your instructions clear and concise and ask only for the information you really need; if you want students to print an unofficial transcript from the Web, tell them how to do it. Do not compromise your selection standards but do your best not to put up any roadblocks.

Admissions Office

Encourage your admissions office to include information about your programs in their publicity materials. The programs can be great recruitment tools for the institution and can give you a good head start on marketing.

Language

Choose and use your language carefully. Do not make reference to "trips" or "tours." Emphasize that your programs are academic programs and/or courses.

The Surprise

You may be surprised to find that those reluctant students—the Type Two and Type Three students—come back from their experiences as Type One students. They return with a newfound confidence in themselves and their ability to study in another culture and will often apply for other short-term or even semester- or year-long programs.

Conclusion

One last piece of advice—never get so carried away with your marketing that you promise things you cannot deliver. Nothing will destroy the reputation of a program more quickly than unhappy returned student participants. Market your programs reasonably and honestly and deliver what you promise. This will create a pool of satisfied customers— and they are the best marketing tools of all!

STUDENT SELECTION AND ENROLLMENT

Sarah E. Spencer

The short-term program has been approved and developed, and the budget is in place. Now you are ready to select and enroll students! As the number of short-term programs abroad has increased in the last decade, so have the systems that enroll students in these courses. In the past, "first-come, first-deposit-down" was enough to get a student on a program. Now, many students must submit application dossiers, write essays, and sit for full interviews.

As with most aspects of short-term programming, agreeing on the requirements and systems before marketing to the students and clearly articulating the selection criteria and other enrollment pieces will reduce your organization's liability, limit questions from confused students, and create a better experience for all.

WHY DO YOU NEED A SELECTION PROCESS?

If you are a faculty member without an international office to support your program or an administrator in an understaffed office, you will be tempted to forgo the selection process. You will find, however, that a well-designed selection process is a good use of your time.

- ☐ A selection process ensures seriousness among the students because they cannot take their participation for granted. This reinforces the academic quality of the program.
- ☐ The process articulates the policies and procedures of the program and the institution before the student applies.
- ☐ A selection process creates a system where the best-qualified and best mix of students can be assembled.
- ☐ By following a clear enrollment procedure, students can be treated fairly and uniformly.

The process gives you another opportunity to articulate the academic and intercultural seriousness of the program.

- ☐ If you are administering more than one program abroad, it is important to have an efficient system that is endorsed by your organization and works to manage future program growth.
- ☐ The short-term application and approval timeframe ensures time to enroll enough participants and finalize logistics. For example, if your program departs June 1, and as of April 15 you have four students enrolled, will you be able to make the budget work? Can you maintain your group airline reservations, which require a minimum of 10 seats?

ADMISSIONS PROCESSES

Before designing enrollment materials such as an application, course description, or policies and procedures, you need to determine what kind of admissions process will be in effect.

Admission by Selection

Students submit a full application dossier, which is reviewed by the faculty director or a selection committee. The review occurs after all application dossiers have been submitted and produces the best balance of students, but it is the most time consuming.

Deadlines must be set and adhered to because students will be submitting materials. This system works well if you must select from a large pool of applicants.

Admission by "Rolling" Procedures

Rolling admission, or "first-come, first-money-down," was common for short-term programs when first developed. This process allows the faculty director to immediately accept students and know how many students have been recruited. If you are operating in a consortium, rolling admission is logistically straightforward when distance and different institutions make communication a challenge.

However, rolling admission with minimal eligibility requirements may create a perception of "sign the check; go on the course," without any serious thought from the student. Be aware of this as you develop application and recruiting materials. You can never eliminate the student who chooses a course based solely on geographic locale or weather, but with emphasis on course content and with academic expectations clearly defined before a student applies, you may be able to reduce the number of students who should be going on spring break, not study abroad.

Admission by Seniority

For oversubscribed or popular short-term programs abroad, the least time-consuming process is admission by seniority. By following the official registration list used by your institution, students are enrolled as they would be for an on-campus course.

This process eliminates much of the work, and creates an equitable system exactly like the one used on campus. However, it is a "blind" selection, and faculty directors give up their authority to select students for an overseas experience.

ELIGIBILITY REQUIREMENTS AND SELECTION CRITERIA

Student Eligibility

Eligibility requirements must be outlined and implemented consistently. Most programs set these requirements to ensure that nondeserving students (i.e., those on conduct probation or not academically qualified) are not accepted. The following may be considered:

☐ Institutional/organizational policies (e.g., students currently on academic or disciplinary/conduct probation may not be able to study abroad).

☐ Grade point average (GPA) minimum: your institution may require a minimum GPA to study abroad, or there may be differences in the GPAs required to participate in short-term and longer-term study abroad. Many institutions require students to maintain a minimum GPA of 2.0, with higher GPAs required for upper-level courses.

☐ Course prerequisites.

☐ Other policies set by the administrative office or faculty director.

Criteria for Selection

Increasingly, students want to know how they will be selected, similar to their on-campus course requests to understand details of how they will be evaluated. Selection criteria should be developed, published before students apply, and used consistently during the process. General criteria may include:

☐ Academic preparation and strength;

☐ Sense of maturity, responsibility, and citizenship;

☐ Ability to describe how the study abroad experience will apply to academic and personal goals; and

☐ Knowledge of proposed destination and culture; applicants should be prepared to provide some factual information from both historical and current perspectives.

Program-specific criteria may include first-time study abroad participants, priority given to majors/minors, seniority, etc. Think proactively and publish widely!

Regardless of what process and materials you use, require students to submit complete application dossiers!

THE APPLICATION AND APPROVAL PROCESS

The goal of a defined application and approval process is to collect academic and personal information necessary to screen applications and to administer the program. You want to collect any permissions required to access records, waive Family Eduction Rights and Privacy Act (FERPA) rights, and have students agree to your policies and procedures. If you already have a selection process for your semester and year-long programs, using the same procedures for short-term will help to streamline the process.

Once eligibility and selection criteria and the admissions procedures have been established, application materials must be created and you must determine who will collect the materials. Materials may include the following:

Application/information sheet

☐ Provides necessary student information, emergency contact information, and data required for statistical analysis.

☐ Serves as a contract between the student and the organization. The student's signature allows administrators to access conduct records or bill student accounts for the program fee.

☐ Allows you to check whether the student has a passport, and if the student is a non-U.S. citizen, allows you to take steps to get any necessary visas.

☐ Gives permission to register students, if applicable.

☐ Contains FERPA waiver.

See the sample "Off-Campus Study Application" at the end of this chapter.

Policies and procedures. The policies and procedures document defines what information the student will be responsible for before he or she applies for a program and after the student is accepted. Possible topics include:

- ☐ Philosophy of short-term programs abroad
- ☐ Policies for student participation
- ☐ Academic information
  - Requirements
  - Course credit
  - Grading
  - Program evaluation
  - Taking courses pass/fail
  - Registration information
  - Auditing courses
  - Nondegree students
- ☐ Need for academic or physical accommodation
- ☐ Student responsibility and disciplinary procedures
  - Community expectations
  - Responsible use of alcohol
- ☐ Enrollment information
  - Application dates
  - How to apply
  - Wait-list students
  - Confirmation of courses
  - Transferring between courses
- ☐ Financial matters
  - Program costs
  - Comprehensive program fee
  - Exclusions
  - Administrative fee
  - Payment schedules
  - Cancellation and refunds
  - Financial aid
- ☐ Health and safety information

    Proof of insurance coverage abroad
    Student Identification Card
    Required and recommended immunizations
- ☐ Orientation information
- ☐ Travel information
  - Flight deviations
  - Visas
  - Passports

Consortium application. If you work with other institutions, the consortium should have one form that all students must complete.

Essay or personal statement. Topic suggestions include:

- ☐ Why are you applying for this particular course? Talk about what you hope to learn. Your desire to travel to the destination(s) of the course should not be part of your response.
- ☐ Condensing a four-credit semester course into one month off campus creates a very intense academic experience. What strategies will you use to deal with the intensity?
- ☐ Describe your ideal cross-cultural experience either abroad or in the United States.
- ☐ Part of group travel involves dealing with the unexpected. Give an example of how you have coped with an unexpected situation in the past.

Transcript (unofficial or official). The transcript allows for GPA verification and review of previous coursework. Students may be able to print an unofficial transcript from their institution's Web site.

Budget form. The budget form provides the financial aid office with required information for applying for additional financial aid.

Application fee or deposit. This fee or deposit is required to hold a place in the program, confirm the serious intent of the student, and be used to cover advance logistical payments.

Application checklist. This is helpful in communicating clearly with students regarding the application materials.

FERPA AND STUDY ABROAD

Many administrators ignore the Family Education Rights and Privacy Act (FERPA) of 1974, as amended, which affords students the right to authorize the release of education information to third parties. You will want to make a decision, in consultation with your FERPA expert (registrar, legal counsel) if you will request that students waive their FERPA rights before they study abroad. Such a statement might read:

(Administrator) requests that students authorize the release of education information to third parties by signing the application for "Short-Term Study Abroad." Students sign the following statement and direct questions to the international education office:

I understand that the Family Education Rights and Privacy Act of 1974 (FERPA), as amended, affords students the right to authorize the release of education information to third parties. I also understand that studying abroad may involve circumstances which require (administrator) to release certain information to third parties, but for which it may be difficult to obtain my prior written permission. For these reasons, I herewith authorize university officials to release my education information to parties who, in their judgment, have an interest in the study abroad contemplated by this document provided that those officials, in their judgment, are acting in my interests as well. This authorization is valid from the time I submit this signed document through a period of one semester after my program abroad ends.

SAMPLE APPLICATION CHECKLIST FOR SELECTION

Download application forms using Adobe Acrobat Reader. Print and keep "Short-Term Policies and Procedures," which contains important information such as cancellation fees and passport information.

☐ Submit application materials to (program administrator, faculty director or international office). Incomplete application dossiers will not be accepted.

☐ All courses require the following:

    ☐ Short-Term Application.

    ☐ Study Abroad Agreement. Parent signature required on page 2, if student is considered a dependant for income tax purposes. Submit one copy with your application and keep one for your records.

    ☐ Unofficial Transcript.

    ☐ Receipt for $350 Deposit. Use the attached deposit voucher when making your $350 payment to the business office.

    ☐ Two ID Photos. These photos are not for your passport! You are responsible for applying for your passport.

    ☐ Essay.

    ☐ Course-Specific Materials.

    ☐ Interview. The faculty director will review application materials; not all applicants are guaranteed an interview.

Interview Guidelines

Program directors increasingly look to student interviews as the key determining factor if a student should be selected into a program. Although time consuming, this process allows faculty directors to get to know students and to discuss the motivations and goals for the students' study abroad experience. It also helps to weed out students with potential behavior problems and allows students to ask questions about the program and the process.

If students are interviewed, the following guidelines should be followed:

☐ It is important that interviews are conducted in an unbiased manner, in order to give each student an equal opportunity.

☐ Interviews should be conducted with at least one other person. Possible committee members may include codirectors, other faculty directors, past student participants, or other appropriate faculty or staff.

☐ Students should be initially screened for academic and disciplinary probations and other prerequisites. Other application materials may be used to determine whether a student is selected for an interview.

Preinterview Contracts

Faculty directors may also have students sign a contract before interviewing for their program. This is not a liability release, but focuses on expectations specific to the program (behavior, cultural sensitivity, and/or academic motivation).

Printed Materials Versus the Web

Technology is constantly changing and many organizations are replacing application materials once available solely on paper with the Web as a 24-hour office for students. Web-based applications may require students to submit information electronically by inputting information into Web forms or may provide downloadable application materials such as a Portable Document Format (PDF) file that is printed, filled out, and submitted to the identified office or person.

There are many advantages to using the Web, including:

□ Increased flexibility in updating application materials;

□ Student access to application materials after office hours;

□ Shifting away paper and printing costs from the administrative office;

□ Marketing of related programs via students visiting your Web site;

□ Reduced phone time for staff (when enrollment procedures are clearly documented); and

□ Visibility for your organization's international programs via a Web presence.

The disadvantages, if you see them as disadvantages, are few:

□ If you do not have a Web-dedicated employee, staff will be diverted from other activities.

□ Communication that usually is verbal must be carefully transcribed for Web readership, again requiring staff time.

□ Updating the Web content becomes a daily activity.

□ Updating computer software and hardware is expensive.

□ Ideally, you should have a dedicated Web manager who will devote time to learn and then apply the necessary technology. Minimally, choose someone who is familiar with the processes and programs in your office and provide him/her with quality training.

Approving Students to Study Abroad

After the faculty director has accepted a student, and the student has been approved to study abroad by the administrator, the following steps may occur:

□ Letter of acceptance, covering:

  o Cancellation policy;

  o Reminder of the academic/travel fusion and challenge of this kind of course;

  o Status of passport;

  o Orientation information;

  o Required paperwork;

  o Financial aid information and contact information;

  o Travel logistics, including flight deviations;

  o Billing and final payment information; and

  o Registration and grading (pass/fail).

□ Medical report. Provides personal health and insurance information to be reviewed by the faculty director. This information cannot be collected before a student is accepted to the program. See the sample Short-Term Study Abroad Medical Report at the end of Chapter 16.

□ Study abroad agreement or liability waiver. See samples in Chapter 16, Safeguards for Short-Term Programs.

□ Other forms. These may include the Parental Waiver, host family information (if the program includes a home stay), registration materials, International Student Identity Card application, etc.

Faculty directors receive copies of and travel with emergency contact information, the signed liability waiver or agreement, and the medical report.

UNIVERSITY
of ST.THOMAS
MINNESOTA

Off-Campus Study Application
International Education

UST ID #		Name as it would appear on passport (Last, First, Middle)				

UST E-mail Address	Local Phone # ( )	Mobile Phone # ( )	Mail #	Birthdate (Mo/Day/Year)	Sex ☐ Female ☐ Male

Local Address	City	State	Zip Code

Off-Campus Course/Program Title	City(ies)	Country(ies)

Academic term you plan to participate FA JT SP SU Yr _____	Cum GPA	Present Year in School 1 2 3 4 Grad	Year While Abroad? 1 2 3 4 Grad	Major, Minor or Grad Program

Academic Advisor	Are you currently enrolled at an institution other than St. Thomas? If so, list _____	Do you plan on using any of the following toward program expense? ☐ Grant ☐ Loan ☐ Scholarship

Are you a U.S. Citizen? ☐ Yes ☐ No	U.S. passport number and expiration date: ☐ Do not have one yet ☐ N/A	If you are a holder of a non-U.S. passport, which country is it from?

Emergency Contact Name	Phone Number ( )

Address	City	State	Zip Code

GRADUATE STUDENTS ONLY: Employer, Title	Work Phone

What foreign languages have you studied and for how long? (Please specify high school or college instruction.)

Where did you first hear about Study Abroad at St. Thomas?	What foreign countries have you visited and for how long?

Response to the following is voluntary. Please check one to describe yourself. This information is used for general statistics.
Ethnicity/Race:

☐ American Indian/Alaskan Native	☐ African-American	☐ White, Non-Hispanic	☐ Multiracial
☐ Asian-American or Pacific Islander	☐ Hispanic-American	☐ Do not know	☐ Refused

**If you have a disability and will request on-site accommodations, you must
contact the UST Enhancement Program as soon as possible.**

Your signature verifies the following:

1. I have completed the necessary prerequisites to enroll in this program.
2. International Education programs require that applicants and participants are in good academic and disciplinary standing at the university, and I authorize the staff of International Education at the University of St. Thomas access to my academic and disciplinary records.
3. I authorize International Education to register me, upon acceptance, for the above listed off-campus course or program.
4. I authorize International Education to bill my student account. I understand that all cancellations must be submitted in writing.
5. I have read, understood and will abide to the terms of *Policies & Procedures,* included with this application.
6. I understand that the Family Education Rights and Privacy Act of 1974 (FERPA), as amended, affords students the right to authorize the release of education information to third parties. I also understand that studying off-campus may involve circumstances which require the University of St. Thomas to release certain information to third parties, but for which it may be difficult to obtain my prior written permission. For these reasons, I herewith authorize university officials to release my education information to parties who, in their judgment, have an interest in the program contemplated by this document provided that those officials, in their judgment, are acting in my interests as well. This authorization is valid from the time I submit this signed document to International Education through a period of one semester after my course/program ends abroad.
7. I authorize St. Thomas to make public that I am studying off-campus.   ☐ Yes   ☐ No

Signature of Applicant	Date of Signature

Signature of Faculty Director (only required when noted in application checklist)	Date of Signature

This application must be completed and returned to International Education
On-campus address: 44 N. Cleveland, 1st Floor
Mailing address: Mail #44C-1, 2115 Summit Avenue, St. Paul, MN 55105-1096

IEC USE ONLY
Apply Date _____
Received By _____

INTE 1473 1/06

Attach photos here

[Source: University of St. Thomas]

"It Changed My Life": STRATEGIES FOR ASSESSING STUDENT LEARNING

Patrick Quade

"It changed my life." This conclusion to an off-campus study experience often stands as the total validation of the academic program for students. Students do experience transformations through their immersion in off-campus study programs and we all have witnessed an increase in their intellectual abilities through the structured academic, experiential learning offered on these great programs. However, students, study abroad professionals, and even faculty often find it difficult to quantify or document this growth. Often the distinctions between academic progress and personal growth through experiential learning become blurred.

The character of Tom in Tennessee Williams' play, *The Glass Menagerie,* states early on in the play, "Yes, I have tricks in my pocket, I have things up my sleeve. But I am the opposite of a stage magician. He gives you illusion that has the appearance of truth. I give you truth in the pleasant disguise of illusion."[1] A premise for assessment of any kind should have as its goal the capacity to distinguish truth from illusion, especially in the "It changed my life" statement. All of us want our students to discover the truth, not the illusion. This chapter is intended to provide students, faculty, and off-campus study professionals with a process for developing strategies that will strengthen methods for assessing the various values and documenting the success of short-term programs abroad. The approach is complete with exercises and sample materials to provide the reader with both a theoretical basis and practical implementation suggestions to assist the student, faculty member, and international office in developing a workable strategy for assessing student learning and program quality.

As professionals involved in study abroad, we have an obligation to provide our students and our colleagues with the opportunity and the tools to quantify, reflect, and document all of the possible outcomes from the increasingly popular (and increasingly expensive) off-campus opportunities. We need to develop and employ a comprehensive strategy and efficient methods to assess student learning in all dimensions of the academic and intercultural experience and not be satisfied with superficial and often anecdotal sentiments of student satisfaction with off-campus study programs. The existing research base to begin the development of this task has the capacity to provide a foundation for us today. Institutions are genuinely interested in developing instruments for the assessment of the experiential cultural growth and development that claims to be so transformational for our students. The reader is encouraged to consult the listserv of the Section on U.S. Students Abroad (SECUS-SA-L) and the NAFSA archives for a wide range of documents and current research pertaining to assessment for off-campus study programs.

Four interconnected dimensions for those involved in short-term programs abroad are (1) the academic core, (2) development of intercultural competence, (3) logistics involved in all parts of the program, and (4) assessment of program quality. These four core areas each suggest differing sets of objectives, strategies, instruments, and possible outcomes. For the purposes of this chapter, the writer makes the following assumptions:

- The short-term program is designed around a specific academic course offered by a home-institution faculty member.
- The short-term program is between three and five weeks in duration, although not necessarily all of that time is spent in the off-campus environment.
- The program site is a significant factor for the academic discipline examined by the students and faculty member. The same course could not be offered in an on-campus environment. The site for the program may be international or domestic.
- The students will have substantive and reentry sessions connected with the program.
- Structured experiential learning is among the primary pedagogical styles used in the course.
- In addition to assessing individual learning, the individuals involved in the short-term programs are also interested in overall program quality.

A legitimate element in designing a strategy of assessment is to equip the faculty member with a profile for each student in the group so that the goals and standards used to assess student learning take into account those factors of individual characteristics that will influence assignments and measures needed to reflect individual differences. The following listing indicates those specific details that you may wish to consider when looking at any of the elements in the assessment strategy:

- Gender
- Year in college
- Age
- Previous experience abroad
- Previous experience in this particular country
- Previous academic work related to this off-campus study opportunity
- Internship opportunity
- Course fulfilling major requirement
- Course fulfilling general education requirement
- Elective credit
- Island program
- Immersion program
- Site details
- Home-stay opportunity
- Orientation, reentry
- Language base
- Additional opportunities (field trips, interactive opportunities)

Of course, the faculty member must also determine who will assess the students and whether the students will assess themselves or be assessed. Consider the following options:

- Student self-evaluation
- Faculty (on-site) evaluation
- Faculty on-campus evaluation of student progress
- Student portfolio

Let's begin by looking at a brief essay that appeared on the SECUSS-L electronic sampling results Web site, authored by Donald Rubin and Richard Sutton at the University of Georgia and quoted in the Spring 2001 issue of *International Educator* magazine:

Assessing Student Learning Outcomes from Study Abroad

Study abroad can be one of the most powerful experiences in a student's education. International educators know from observation, example, anecdote, and personal involvement that living and learning in another country can exert profound influence on an individual. Research and evaluation studies over the past three decades have closely examined effects of such international exposure on students. Although the results of those studies are by no means unequivocal, existing research literature warrants the conclusion that studying abroad can enhance many affective or attitudinal outcomes such as students' ethno-relativism, global-mindedness, and sense of self-efficacy.

We are on less firm ground in documenting the effects of study abroad on students' learning outcomes. How have a student's knowledge, thinking skills, and processing abilities improved as a result of studying overseas? Here, the efforts to assess what students have learned face many of the same challenges international educators confront in trying to demonstrate the learning outcomes of general education, the core curriculum, or liberal studies. Those in the field believe intuitively (and in most cases are convinced absolutely) that there are definite learning outcomes associated with successful completion, yet it is difficult to clearly articulate expectations, find ways to measure the achievement by students, and identify factors that influence success or failure.

The centrality of study abroad to undergraduate education will be greatly strengthened when educators can document more effectively its impact on students' academic success, mastery of knowledge, powers of reasoning, critical thinking skills, and intellectual capacity—that is, when educators can show that a veteran of study abroad is not just more well-rounded but also better educated. This evidence can have particular relevance among constituencies who have viewed the overseas experience as, at best, a marginal supplement to academic endeavors. If study abroad can be shown to add meaningful value to the core goals of postsecondary learning, it will cease being a choice that only 1 percent of U.S. students make. Rather, it will become an integral part of college to which every serious student aspires.

Those in the field of international education believe the field will benefit from new research studies that focus on student learning outcomes. Several such studies are underway, incorporating a variety of design elements that can shed light on different aspects of the learning process abroad. For example, the University System of Georgia has recently initiated a multi-year learning outcomes assessment that incorporates analyses of students' transcripts as well as self-reported learning. It compares study abroad participants' knowledge before and after the overseas experiences, and it also compares participants with nonparticipants. Detailed information about academic, logistical, and cocurricular aspects of programs can then be correlated with learning outcomes. Research designs such as this will hopefully yield substantive knowledge about the impact of study abroad on student learning outcomes that will advance debate on, and advocacy for, the value of international education.[2]

The Academic Core

Prior to beginning the task of looking at the first dimension, the core academic experience, it will be helpful to place the learning to be measured in context. One of the most effective tools for this purpose is the Teaching/Learning Goals Inventory developed by Thomas A. Angelo and K. Patricia Cross, and published in *Classroom Assessment Techniques.*[3] The inventory appears at the end of this chapter. The inventory takes a few minutes for the faculty member to complete, but the results enable the faculty member to take a particular course and examine it from the perspective of what he or she truly hopes students will learn. This process gives the faculty member the overarching standards from which to assess student learning.

The faculty member competent in the specific subject area, familiar with the potential to develop that area on site and equipped with a well-defined set of instructional goals along with an accurate profile of students, is prepared to design the short-term study program. This preparation will enable the instructor to structure the course to assist students in developing specific cognitive skills such as creative thinking, comparative models, or systems approaches. Or perhaps the goals will focus more specifically in regard to cross-cultural skills such as cross-cultural communication and awareness of new values and perspectives coupled with critical examination of the host country and the student's own culture. Of course, the professor will detail the specific knowledge and academic skills in his or her field and aid the students in coming to new insights and understanding.

The process of defining instructional goals should not ignore specific knowledge about the host country's human and natural geography, government, societal norms, and value systems.

The following list provides some specific assessment tools to measure instructional goals in addition to specific academic objectives of the course. (Again, with gratitude to Thomas Angelo and Patricia Cross, and used by permission.)

☐ Create an annotated bibliography.
☐ Create a brochure or poster.
☐ Create a budget with full rationale.
☐ Create a case study or analysis.
☐ Create a cognitive map, web, or diagram.
☐ Write a contemplative essay.
☐ Engage in a debate.
☐ Create a diary of a fictional or historical character.
☐ Write an article for publication.
☐ Create a flowchart.
☐ Engage in a group discussion.
☐ Create an instructional manual.
☐ Write a letter to the editor.
☐ Create a lesson plan to teach others.
☐ Create a multimedia presentation.
☐ Prepare a research proposal for a grant agency.
☐ Develop a review of the literature.
☐ Develop a summit conference within the class.
☐ Prepare a term paper.
☐ Create a work of art, architecture, or sculpture.
☐ Use traditional techniques of:

an essay exam, a multiple choice exam,

a series of quizzes, a matching test, or

a term paper.

☐ Deliver an oral report.
☐ Develop a project associated with the learning.

At this point in preparing a short-term course abroad, the academic, cross-cultural, and student learning goals will benefit from a conscientious approach using the pedagogy of the experiential learning model. The reader is referred to Chapter 15, Orientation and Reentry, Academic, for a discussion of Dr. David Kolb's model for developing a quality experiential learning program.

The faculty member armed with theory of experiential learning, their personal, course-specific results from the teaching/learning goals inventory, and a keen awareness of the students enrolled in the course is prepared to design his or her own course goals, assignments, and assessment tools that will make it possible to measure both the capacity for learning and the actual learning that has taken place on an off-campus study program. The end result is to enable the faculty member to assess just what a student knows and is able to do at the end of a course.

Of course, this more elaborate approach can be augmented with the regular course/faculty evaluation forms used on most college and university campuses (see the "Course/Faculty Evaluation Form" at the end of this chapter). The goal, remember, is to determine the academic competency of the student learning in the off-campus environment.

Development of Intercultural Competence

The second major dimension to examine is that of intercultural competency. Janet and Milton Bennett and Mitchell Hammer have produced major studies in this area and the author uses their model of intercultural competence as the standard resource in this area. In addition to the academic skills acquired in a short-term program abroad, another essential core of our efforts is the desire to provide the student with the opportunity to gain intercultural competency, enabling the student to understand other cultures and his or her own. It is in this area more than any other that we need to provide students with accessible tools and assessment techniques to assist them in reaching a clear understanding of their personal growth and development. It is primarily in coming to grips with their own level of intercultural competency that the truth will replace the illusion of how the short-term study experience actually changed their lives.

I quote extensively from the Bennett's work (with permission) first published in 1986, to provide the reader with the background theory and practical aspects of the Developmental Model of Intercultural Sensitivity (DMIS). (See the Bennett Model at the end of this chapter.)

The first reading is from an article titled "Intercultural Communication: A Current Perspective" by Milton Bennett, which appeared in *Basic Concepts of Intercultural Communication* published by Intercultural Press, Inc.

"When people anticipate doing something cultural of an evening, their thoughts turn to art, literature, drama, classical music, or dance. In other words, they plan to participate in one of the institutions of culture-behavior that has become routinized into a particular form. I refer to this aspect of culture as "Culture writ large," with a capital "C." The more academic term that is used by most writers is objective culture. Other examples of objective culture might include social, economic, political, and linguistic systems—the kinds of things that usually are included in area studies or history courses. The study of these institutions constitutes much of the curriculum in both international and multicultural education. For instance, courses in Japanese culture or African American culture are likely to focus on the history, political structure, and arts of the groups. While this is valuable information, it is limited in its utility to the face-to-face concerns of intercultural communication. One can know a lot about the history of a culture and still not be able to communicate with an actual person from that culture. Understanding objective culture may create knowledge, but it doesn't necessarily generate competence.

The less obvious aspect of culture is its subjective side—what we can call "culture writ small." Subjective culture refers to the psychological features that define a group of people—their everyday thinking and behavior—rather than to the institutions they have created. A good working definition of subjective culture is the learned and shared patterns of beliefs, behaviors, and values of groups of interacting people. Understanding subjective cultures—one's own and others'—is more likely to lead to intercultural competence.

Of course, social reality is constructed of both large and small "c," aspects of culture; people learn how to behave through socialization into the institutions of the culture, which leads them to behave in ways that perpetuate those same institutions. As noted above, traditional international and multicultural education tends to focus only on the objective mode of this process; in contrast, intercultural communication focuses almost exclusively on the subjective mode. For instance, interculturalists are concerned with language use in cross-cultural relationships, rather than in linguistic structure. They study how language is modified or supplanted by culturally defined nonverbal behavior, how cultural patterns of thinking are expressed in particular communication styles, and how reality is defined and judged through cultural assumptions and values. In the following pages, examples in each of these areas will illustrate how understanding subjective culture can aid in the development of skills in cultural adaptation and intercultural communication.

Levels of Culture

The definition of subjective culture also provides a base for defining "diversity" in a way that includes both international and domestic cultures at different levels of abstraction. National groups such as Japanese, Mexican, and U.S. American and pan-national ethnic groups such as Arab and Zulu are cultures at a high level of abstraction—the qualities that adhere to most (but not all) members of the culture are very general, and the group includes a lot of diversity. At this level of abstraction we can only point to general differences in patterns of thinking and behaving between cultures. For instance, we might observe that U.S. American culture is more characterized by individualism than is Japanese culture, which is more collectivist.

While cultural difference at a high level of abstraction provides a rich base for analyzing national cultural behavior, there are significant group and individual differences within each national group that are concealed at this level. These differences provide a diversifying force that balances the unifying force of national culture.

At a lower level of abstraction, more specific groups such as ethnicities can be described in cultural terms. In the United States, some of these groups are African American, Asian American, American Indian, Hispanic/Latino American, and European American. People in these groups may share many of the broad national culture patterns while differing significantly in the more specific patterns of their respective ethnicities. It should be noted that in terms of subjective culture, ethnicity is a cultural rather than a genetic heritage; dark skin and other Negroid features may make one "black," but that person has not necessarily experienced African American enculturation. Most black people in the world are not American in any sense. Similarly, "whites" are not necessarily European American, although in the United States it is difficult for them to escape being socialized in the patterns that are currently dominant in U.S. American society.

Other categories of subjective cultural diversity usually include gender, regionality, socioeconomic class, physical ability, sexual orientation, religion, organization, and vocation. The concept can embrace other long-term groupings such as single parents or avid sports fans, as long as the groups maintain the clear patterns of behavior and thinking of an "identity group." By definition, individuals do not have different cultures; the term for patterns of individual behavior is "personality."

Stereotypes and Generalizations

Whenever the topic of cultural difference is discussed, the allegation of stereotyping usually is not far behind. For instance, if cultural patterns of men and women are being compared, someone may well offer that she is a woman and doesn't act that way at all.

Stereotypes arise when we act as if all members of a culture or group share the same characteristics. Stereotypes can be attached to any assumed indicator of group membership, such as race, religion, ethnicity, age, or gender, as well as national culture. The characteristics that

are assumedly shared by members of the group may be respected by the observer, in which case it is a positive stereotype. In the more likely case that the characteristics are disrespected, it is a negative stereotype. Stereotypes of both kinds are problematic in intercultural communication for several obvious reasons. One is that they may give us a false sense of understanding our communication partners. Whether the stereotype is positive or negative, it is usually only partially correct. Additionally, stereotypes may become self-fulfilling prophecies, where we observe others in selective ways that confirm our prejudice.

Despite the problems with stereotypes, it is necessary in intercultural communication to make cultural generalizations. Without any kind of supposition or hypothesis about the cultural differences we may encounter in an intercultural situation, we may fall prey to naive individualism, where we assume that every person is acting in some completely unique way. Or we may rely inordinately on "common sense" to direct our communication behavior. Common sense is, of course, common only to a particular culture. Its application outside of one's own culture is usually ethnocentric.

Cultural generalizations can be made while avoiding stereotypes by maintaining the idea of preponderance of belief. Nearly all possible beliefs are represented in all cultures at all times, but each different culture has a preference for some beliefs over others. The description of this preference, derived from large-group research, is a cultural generalization. Of course, individuals can be found in any culture who hold beliefs similar to people in a different culture. There just aren't so many of them—they don't represent the preponderance of people who hold beliefs closer to the norm or "central tendency" of the group.

Deductive stereotypes occur when we assume that abstract cultural generalizations apply to every single individual in the culture. While it is appropriate to generalize that U.S. Americans as a group are more individualistic than Japanese, it is stereotyping to assume that every American is strongly individualistic; the person with whom you are communicating may be a deviant. Cultural generalizations should be used tentatively as working hypotheses that need to be tested in each case; sometimes they work very well, sometimes they need to be modified, and sometimes they don't apply to the particular case at all. The idea is to derive the benefit of recognizing cultural patterns without experiencing too much "hardening of the categories."

Generalizing from too small a sample may generate an inductive stereotype. For example, we may inappropriately assume some general knowledge about Mexican culture based on having met one or a few Mexicans. This assumption is particularly troublesome, since initial cross-cultural contacts may often be conducted by people who are deviant in their own cultures. ("Typical" members of the culture would more likely associate only with their cultural compatriots—how they stay typical.) So generalizing cultural patterns from any one person's behavior (including your own) in cross-cultural contact is likely to be both stereotypical and inaccurate.[4]"

In a paper presented at the Diversity Symposium in Boston, Massachusetts, in June 2001, Janet and Milton Bennett offered useful definitions for terms associated with culture, ethnicity, and race. Again, the extensive quotation below aids the reader in framing the context for working with the DMIS.

"Like other authors preceding us, we have a disciplinary perspective which informs our work in diversity and which, in our case, emerges from the social science field of intercultural communication, the study of face-to-face interactions between people who are culturally different. Since intercultural communication draws heavily on psychology, anthropology, and sociology, it is inherently interdisciplinary. While none of us has a panacea for all the complexities of diversity, intercultural communication brings a particularly useful emphasis on the development of intercultural competence. In general terms, intercultural competence is the ability to communicate effectively in cross-cultural situations and to relate appropriately in a variety of cultural contexts. Developing this kind of competence is usually a primary goal of diversity initiatives in organizations, where it is assumed to contribute to effective recruitment and retention of members of underrepresented groups, management of a diverse workforce, productivity of multicultural teams, marketing across cultures, and to the development of a climate of respect for diversity in the organization.

Based on this subjective culture perspective, diversity is defined as cultural differences in values, beliefs, and behaviors learned and shared by groups of interacting people defined by nationality, ethnicity, gender, age, physical characteristics, sexual orientation, economic status, education, profession, religion, organizational affiliation, and any other grouping that generates identifiable patterns.

While the definition of subjective culture is fairly standard among diversity professionals, it does stimulate a variety of other questions about the meaning of culture. The first of these questions immediately arises from reading the above list: Where's race in this configuration? Two of the most challenging issues in diversity work are overcoming the idea that race is culture and overcoming racism itself. The latter issue will be examined later in this paper, but the definitional foundation of culture must be clarified, and the distinction between culture and race must be established.

The outdated view that biological characteristics somehow define the way people behave, think, and interact has now been thoroughly discredited by the recent genome studies. People do not behave the way they do primarily because of race, but rather because of cultural factors.

While this brief foundation cannot begin to address the power and complexity of race issues, it is vital for the diversity professional to recognize the distinction between self-identification and that designated by others. This self-identification may be entirely different from the designation given to the individual by observers. Diversity professionals must consistently attend to both the individual's self-perception and worldview on racial (and cultural) matters and to those likely designations assigned by others. Confusing the two is not wise.

Finally, just because race is not culture does not mean that the impact of color and white privilege can somehow be left out of diversity training. Our worldviews are heavily structured by our experience of culture, but they are also formed by our experience of color. The distinction between these two kinds of experience does not elevate one above the other; in fact, it is a necessary first step in the difficult task of minimizing the incidence of racism and privilege while simultaneously maximizing the appreciation of diversity.[5]"

A DEVELOPMENTAL MODEL OF INTERCULTURAL SENSITIVITY
Milton J. Bennett, Ph.D.

Denial	Defense	Minimization	Acceptance	Adaptation	Integration

ETHNOCENTRIC STAGES | ETHNORELATIVE STAGES

Milton Bennett first published his model of intercultural sensitivity in an article appearing in *Education for the Intercultural Experience* edited by Michael Paige.[6] This model is the core of intercultural competency assessment. The reader is encouraged to examine the model in its entirety in the original article. The reader will be well served in finding practical definitions, implications, and suggestions for development steps. As an additional step, I would encourage a representative from your institution to participate in the Intercultural Communication Institute Intercultural Development Inventory (IDI) Seminar to become certified to administer the IDI to students and faculty at your institution. This instrument is an ideal way to aid individuals in understanding their personal status and issues related to intercultural competency. The inventory is an excellent tool to use as a before-and-after measure for students prior to and following their participation in an off-campus program.

In 2003-2004, D. Christopher Brooks, assistant professor of political science at St. Olaf College, conducted a study using the Bennett/Hammer model of Intercultural Sensitivity and the IDI instrument. Brooks administered the IDI to an on-campus, full semester [14 weeks] course (Central European Politics) and an off-campus, interim semester [4 weeks] course (Post-Communist Democracy in the Czech Republic). The inventory was administered to all students in each of the courses prior to the beginning of the course and again at the end of the course. The analysis of the results of the study conducted by the professor confirmed that comparative politics courses "tend to increase students' levels of intercultural sensitivity" in both domestic and international contexts.

Professor Brooks found there was no difference between the on- and off-campus students' changes to their levels of intercultural sensitivity while there were significant differences in students' pre- and post-test scores for BOTH classes. In other words, while both courses generated significant improvements in levels of intercultural sensitivity, there was not a significant difference between the courses.

Speculation suggests that because the off-campus course was able to achieve the same levels of change with 10 fewer weeks of class time, a full semester off-campus course would probably exceed the levels of change of a full semester on-campus course. However, lacking data, we cannot say this with any degree of certainty. More field tests using the IDI are needed to fully use this valuable instrument and development assessment for students engaged in off-campus study.[7]

Logistics
The third dimension is the logistics. The earlier chapters in this book provide models and examples for the planning and implementation of the myriad of details necessary to support short-term programs abroad. Assessment models for this dimension are abundant, as most institutions already use an instrument that solicits information from the student regarding the nonacademic aspects of the off-campus study program. It is understood that although these elements are technically "nonacademic," they do play a crucial role in the overall success of the program. The reader is referred to the "International and Off-Campus Studies Returning Student Evaluation" and the "Returning Student Questionnaire" found at the end of this chapter. Each of these instruments gets at slightly different aspects of an off-campus program.

Assessment of Program Quality
The final dimension in designing an assessment strategy for off-campus study is program review. The reader is encouraged to take advantage of existing documents that assist in program review from sources such as NAFSA: Association of International Educators and the Council on International Educational Exchange (CIEE). The reader is also referred to The Institute for the International Education of Students (IES) Model Assessment Practice. The Off-Campus Study Program Evaluation/Review in this chapter may also prove to be helpful.

OFF CAMPUS STUDY PROGRAM EVALUATION/REVIEW

The criteria used to evaluate and review off-campus programs is based on information provided by (1) student feedback using formal evaluation instruments and oral debriefing sessions following the program, (2) faculty member written report and oral debriefing on faculty-led programs, and when appropriate, (3) the host evaluation and summary report.

Items that are included from the various information providers are:

1. The specific objectives of the course
2. The academic character of the course
   a. academic viability of host institution (accreditation status), when appropriate
   b. full course description, syllabus
   c. student course evaluations
   d. description of nature of instruction and types of learning experiences (lecture, seminar, field trips, experiential learning components, associated cultural events—theater, museum, etc.)
   e. curriculum vitae of instructor(s) in course
   f. how the course relates to general education, graduation, and major requirements
   g. how the course integrates with the on-campus curriculum (prior to and following the program).
   h. the role of language learning in the program
3. Program staffing on site
   a. qualifications of administrators, staff members, tour agents, and guides
   b. method of selection of home-stay families (if appropriate)
   c. opportunities for cultural immersion
   d. how are students prepared to understand and engage the culture and what opportunities are there to reflect on that cultural understanding
4. Health and safety issues
   a. specific health concerns, access to English-speaking medical care
   b. insurance statements of coverage for any transportation carriers
   c. specific safety concerns of program site and methods used to manage risk
5. Enrollment patterns over past three years.
6. Program cost
7. How the course fits into geographic distribution compared with all other programs
8. Academic discipline(s) represented in the program
9. Student recruitment, selection, orientation, and reentry issues

Documentation of all details of course including examples of student work

[Source: Adapted from St. Olaf College]

REPORTING OF CONCLUSIONS

From these various sources, the individual or individuals charged with the responsibility for assessing short-term programs abroad must formulate a case for the value of the program and develop the necessary documentation to validate the analysis of the information and data. This information should then be made available to a campus-based off-campus policy committee or the individuals and/or groups having the capacity for making necessary changes for the improvement of study abroad opportunities.

We should also remember that the long-term effects of study abroad represent an important dimension that has not been addressed in this chapter. The implications of the study abroad program for a student five, 10, and more years after the experience can be substantial.

And finally, the ultimate value of implementing this strategy is to provide substantive assessment for students, faculty, and the institution and provide legitimate supporting data affirming the student's statement that the short-term off-campus study program did indeed, "CHANGE MY LIFE!"

Endnotes:

[1] Williams, Tennessee (1944). "The Glass Menagerie," in *Six Modern American Plays* (Act I). New York: Random House.

[2] Rubin, Donald L. and Richard Sutton (Spring 2001-Volume X, Number 2). "Assessing Student Learning Outcomes from Study Abroad," *International Educator*, NAFSA: Association of International Educators, Washington, D.C., 31-32. Used by permission.

[3] Angelo, T. A. and Cross, K. P. (1993). *Classroom Assessment Techniques: A Handbook for College Teachers*. San Francisco: Jossey-Bass. Used by permission.

[4] Bennett, Milton J. (1998) "Intercultural Communication: A Current Perspective," in *Basic Concepts of Intercultural Communication*. Selected Readings, edited by Milton J. Bennett. Yarmouth, ME, Intercultural Press, Inc., 3-8.

[5] Bennett, Janet M. and Bennett, Milton J. "Developing Intercultural Sensitivity: An Integrative Approach to Global and Domestic Diversity." Paper presented at the Diversity Symposium, June 28-29, 2001, Boston, MA, 5–10.

[6] Bennett, Milton J. (1993) "Towards Ethnorelativism: The Developmental Model of Intercultural Sensitivity" in *Education for the Intercultural Experience*, edited by R. Michael Paige. 2nd edition. Yarmouth, ME, Intercultural Press, Inc.

[7] D. Christopher Brooks, "Learning Tolerance: The Impact of Comparative Politics Courses on Levels of Cultural Sensitivity," *The Journal of Political Science Education*, 1:2, (May-August 2005): 221-232.

Purpose: The Teaching/Learning Goals Inventory is an assessment of instructional goals. Its purpose is threefold: (1) to help teachers become more aware of what they want students to accomplish on off-campus study programs; (2) to help determine assessment techniques to assess how well students are achieving their learning goals; and (3) to provide a starting point for discussions of teaching and learning goals among colleagues.

Directions: Please select one short-term course in which you are currently involved. Respond to each item on the inventory in relation to that particular course. (Your responses might be quite different if you were asked about your overall teaching and learning goals, for example, or the appropriate instructional goals for your discipline.)

Title of the specific course you are focusing on:

Rate the importance of each of the 51 goals listed below to the specific course you have selected. Assess each goal's importance to what you deliberately aim to have students accomplish, rather than the goal's general worthiness or overall importance to your institution's mission. There are no "right" or "wrong" answers; only personally more or less accurate ones.

For each goal, circle only one response on the 1-to-5 rating scale. You may want to read quickly through all 51 goals before rating their relative importance.

In relation to the program or course you are focusing on, indicate whether each goal you rate is:

(5)	*Essential*	A goal you always/nearly always try to achieve
(4)	*Very important*	A goal you often try to achieve
(3)	*Important*	A goal you sometimes try to achieve
(2)	*Unimportant*	A goal you rarely try to achieve
(1)	*Not applicable*	A goal you never try to achieve

PART I

Rate the importance of each goal to what you aim to have students accomplish in the course.
(Note: Only 5 items out of the 51 items can have a "5" [essential] rank.)

1. Develop ability to apply principles and generalizations already learned to new problems and situations	5	4	3	2	1
2. Develop analytic skills	5	4	3	2	1
3. Develop problem-solving skills	5	4	3	2	1
4. Develop ability to draw reasonable inferences	5	4	3	2	1
5. Develop ability to synthesize and integrate	5	4	3	2	1
6. Develop ability to think holistically: to see the whole as well as the parts	5	4	3	2	1
7. Develop ability to think creatively	5	4	3	2	1
8. Develop ability to distinguish between fact and opinion	5	4	3	2	1
9. Improve skill at paying attention	5	4	3	2	1
10. Develop ability to concentrate	5	4	3	2	1
11. Improve memory skills	5	4	3	2	1
12. Improve listening skills	5	4	3	2	1

13. Improve speaking skills	5	4	3	2	1
14. Improve reading skills	5	4	3	2	1
15. Improve writing skills	5	4	3	2	1
16. Develop appropriate study skills, strategies, and habits	5	4	3	2	1
17. Improve mathematical skills	5	4	3	2	1
18. Learn terms and facts of this subject	5	4	3	2	1
19. Learn concepts and theories in this subject	5	4	3	2	1
20. Develop skill in using materials, tools, and/or technology central to this subject	5	4	3	2	1
21. Learn to understand perspectives and values of subject	5	4	3	2	1
22. Prepare for transfer or graduate study	5	4	3	2	1
23. Learn techniques and methods used to gain new knowledge in this subject	5	4	3	2	1
24. Learn to evaluate methods and materials in this subject	5	4	3	2	1
25. Learn to appreciate important contributions to this subject	5	4	3	2	1
26. Develop an appreciation of the liberal arts and sciences	5	4	3	2	1
27. Develop an openness to new ideas	5	4	3	2	1
28. Develop an informed concern about contemporary social issues	5	4	3	2	1
29. Develop a commitment to exercise the rights and responsibilities of citizenship	5	4	3	2	1
30. Develop a lifelong love of learning	5	4	3	2	1
31. Develop aesthetic appreciation	5	4	3	2	1
32. Develop an informed historical perspective	5	4	3	2	1
33. Develop an informed understanding of the role of science and technology	5	4	3	2	1
34. Develop an informed appreciation of other cultures	5	4	3	2	1
35. Develop capacity to make informed ethical choices	5	4	3	2	1
36. Develop ability to work productively with others	5	4	3	2	1
37. Develop management skills	5	4	3	2	1
38. Develop leadership skills	5	4	3	2	1
39. Develop a commitment to accurate work	5	4	3	2	1
40. Improve ability to follow directions, instructions, and plans	5	4	3	2	1
41. Improve ability to organize and use time effectively	5	4	3	2	1
42. Develop a commitment to personal achievement	5	4	3	2	1
43. Develop ability to perform skillfully	5	4	3	2	1
44. Cultivate a sense of responsibility for one's own behavior	5	4	3	2	1
45. Improve self-esteem/self-confidence	5	4	3	2	1
46. Develop a commitment to one's own values	5	4	3	2	1
47. Develop respect for others	5	4	3	2	1

48. Cultivate emotional health and well-being	5	4	3	2	1
49. Cultivate an active commitment to honesty	5	4	3	2	1
50. Develop capacity to think for one's self	5	4	3	2	1
51. Develop capacity to make wise decisions	5	4	3	2	1

In general, how do you see your primary role as a facilitator of short-term programs abroad?

(Although more than one statement may apply, please circle only one.)

1. Teaching students facts and principles of the subject matter

2. Providing a role model for students

3. Helping students develop higher-order thinking skills

4. Preparing students for jobs/careers

5. Fostering student development and personal growth

6. Helping students develop basic learning skills

PART II

	Cluster Number and Name	Goals Included in Cluster	Total number of "Essential" goals in each cluster	Clusters Ranked–from 1st to 6th by number of "Essential" goals
I	Higher-order thinking skills	1-8		
II	Basic academic success skills	9-17		
III	Discipline-specific knowledge and skills	18-25		
IV	Liberal arts and academic values	26-35		
V	Work and career preparation	36-43		
VI	Personal development	44-51		

PART III Compute your cluster scores (average item ratings by cluster) using the following worksheet.

	Cluster Number and Name	Goals Included	Sum of Ratings Given to Goals in that Cluster	Divided C by this Number	Your Cluster Scores
I	Higher-order thinking skills	1-8		8	
II	Basic academic success skills	9-17		8	
III	Discipline-specific knowledge and skills	18-25		8	
IV	Liberal arts and academic values	26-35		10	
V	Work and career preparation	36-43		8	
VI	Personal development	44-51		8	

[Source: Adapted, with permission, from Angelo, T.A. and Cross, K.P. (1993). *Classroom Assessment Techniques.* San Francisco: Jossey-Bass.]

INTERNATIONAL AND OFF-CAMPUS STUDIES RETURNING STUDENT EVALUATION

We are asking you to assist in the planning of future programs by completing this questionnaire. Please let us know any positive or negative aspects of the interim and how we can improve our assistance to you.

Thank you very much for your help.

Name of Short-Term Study Program

Department and Course Number   **Instructor's Name**

A. PERSONAL INFORMATION

1. What is your sex?	2. What is your age?	3. What is your class?
a. Female	a. 19	a. Sophomore
b. Male	b. 20	b. Junior
	c. 21	c. Senior
	d. 22	d. Special
	e. Other:	

4. What is your race: (optional)   **5. Major:**

B. TRAVEL ARRANGEMENTS

1. Travel arrangements were generally:	Excellent	Good	Fair	Poor
a. Air	1	2	3	4
b. Train	1	2	3	4
c. Bus	1	2	3	4
d. Van	1	2	3	4

Comments:

2. Accommodations were:	Excellent	Good	Fair	Poor
a.	1	2	3	4
b.	1	2	3	4
c.	1	2	3	4
d.	1	2	3	4
e.	1	2	3	4
f.	1	2	3	4
g.	1	2	3	4
h.	1	2	3	4
i.	1	2	3	4

3. Program Itinerary:	Excellent	Good	Fair	Poor
a. Places visited	1	2	3	4
b. Time spent in each place	1	2	3	4

Please list places you wish to comment on separately:	Adequate	Too Short	Too Long
a.	1	2	3
b.	1	2	3
c.	1	2	3
d.	1	2	3
e.	1	2	3

4. Were there any problems with visas? (If applicable)

5. Do you plan to take another off-campus program?	International	Domestic
a. Interim	1	2
b. Semester or year program	1	2

C. GENERAL INFORMATION

1. There are many reasons why people study off-campus. We would like to know how important each of the following reasons was in influencing your decision.	Extremely Important	Somewhat Important	Not Important
a. To support academic goals	1	2	3
b. To explore career options	1	2	3
c. To heighten interest in community service	1	2	3
d. To broaden knowledge of specific geographical and cultural areas	1	2	3
e. To gain another perspective on the United States	1	2	3
f. To become acquainted with students from other places	1	2	3

2. Which of the above really happened on the interim? (Circle all that apply)	a	b	c	d	e	f
3. Which one of the above reasons (a-f) was the most important influence in your decision to study off-campus?	a	b	c	d	e	f

	Exceptionally Well	Reasonably Well	Poorly
4. How well did this form of learning (experiential/academic) suit you?	1	2	3
5. How well did the experience contribute to your understanding of the cultures involved?	1	2	3
6. How well did the academic and cultural experiences complement one another?	1	2	3

	Enough	Too Much	Too Little
7. Opportunities for activities outside the curriculum (independent sight-seeing, local contacts, cultural functions):	1	2	3
8. Did study off-campus offer you resources which would not have been available if you had remained on campus during interim?	1	2	3

9. Would you recommend this course to a friend? Why or why not?

D. PREDEPARTURE INFORMATION AND ORIENTATION	Excellent	Good	Fair	Poor	Did Not Attend
1. The orientation meetings with the interim instructor were:	1	2	3	4	5
2. Interim evening orientation:	1	2	3	4	5
3. Application assistance from the office of international and off-campus studies:	1	2	3	4	5
4. Availability of information concerning travel arrangements and accommodations	1	2	3	4	5

Comments:

5. Orientation materials (if provided):	1	2	3	4	5

a. If orientation materials were not provided, what should have been provided?

E. Miscellaneous

Is there anything necessary for your interim which was not provided?	○ Yes	○ No

Comments:

2. If you went on a domestic interim, did you do so because an international interim was too expensive	○ Yes	○ No

3. How much did you spend in addition to the required program costs?	○ Less than $500	○ $500-$1,000
	○ $1,000-$1,500	○ More than $1,5000

4. Was the interim worth the cost?	○ Yes	○ No

Comments:

RETURNING STUDENT QUESTIONNAIRE

We are interested in maintaining high-quality international studies programs and in finding ways to improve them. An important way of doing this is to learn how the program affected individual student participants. Your responses to this questionnaire will allow you to reflect on the impact your study abroad experience had on you as well as provide insights that will help ensure that those who follow you will have as positive an experience as possible. Your responses will remain confidential. Your student number is included for research purposes only.

Thank you.

International Program:

Major:

Sex:			Class:		
	○	1. Male		○	1. Sophomore
	○	2. Female		○	2. Junior
				○	3. Senior
				○	4. Special

Student Number (Used for Research Purposes Only)

1. There are many reasons why students study abroad. We would like to know how important each of the following reasons was in influencing your decision to study abroad.	Extremely Important	Very Important	Somewhat Important	Not Important
1) To support academic goals in your major.	1	2	3	4
2) To add diversity to your academic program.	1	2	3	4
3) To explore options for your future.	1	2	3	4
5) To gain another perspective on the United States.	1	2	3	4
6) To gain a sense of self-confidence/independence.	1	2	3	4
7) To take advantage of an opportunity to travel and see new places.	1	2	3	4

2.) Which of the above (1-7) really happened on the program? (Circle ALL that apply)	1	2	3	4	5	6	7
3. Which one of the above (1-7) was most important influence in your decision to study abroad? (Circle ONE)	1	2	3	4	5	6	7

Has your experience abroad:	Very Much	Somewhat	Little or Not at All
4. Enhanced your foreign language skills?	1	2	3
5. Influenced your future plans?	1	2	3
6. Influenced a change in your lifestyle?	1	2	3
7. Altered your world view?	1	2	3
8. Increased your understanding of the United States?	1	2	3
9. Increased your feelings of self-confidence?	1	2	3
10. Increased your world political awareness?	1	2	3
11. Caused you to seriously consider living and/or working in another country?	1	2	3
12. Increased your desire to travel abroad?	1	2	3
13. Increased your understanding of your self?	1	2	3
14. Increased your ability to cope with and adapt to new and different situations?	1	2	3
15. Altered your values, priorities, and goals?	1	2	3
16. Heightened your interest in community service?	1	2	3
17. Increased your knowledge of the country(ies) in which you studied?	1	2	3
18. Increased your sensitivity to and understanding of news reports in the United States from countries you visited?	1	2	3
19. Increased your appreciation for the study of foreign languages?	1	2	3
20. Altered your academic direction?	1	2	3

	Exceptionally Well	Reasonably Well	Not Very Well	Poorly
21. How well did the study abroad program contribute to your understanding of the culture(s) involved?	1	2	3	4
22. How well did the academic components of your program and your own cultural interactions complement one another?	1	2	3	4
23. How well did the program structure (e.g., organization, schedule, and activities) contribute to enhancing your experience?	1	2	3	4
24. In retrospect, how well prepared were you for your study abroad experience?	1	2	3	4

25. PROGRAM ASSISTANCE. Please evaluate the following:	Excellent	Good	Fair	Poor
1) International and Off-Campus Studies catalog and other written information about programs	1	2	3	4
2) Advising from International/Off-Campus Studies prior to application	1	2	3	4
3) Applications and application process	1	2	3	4
4) Selection process/interview	1	2	3	4
5) Financial information	1	2	3	4
6) Predeparture assistance from International/Off-Campus Studies	1	2	3	4
7) Orientation	1	2	3	4

26. FINANCES.

1) How much did you spend in addition to the required program costs?	○ Less than $500	○ $500-$1,000	○ $1,000-$1,500
	○ $1,500-$2,000	○ More than $2,000	

2) How much spending money would you recommend participants on this program take?

27. Would you recommend your program to other students?	○ Yes	○ Maybe	○ No

Why or why not?

28. What is the most important thing you have learned from this experience?

29. What should we do to incorporate a greater international perspective in on-campus courses?

COURSE/FACULTY EVALUATION FORM

THE STUDENT

1. Class:	○ First Year	2. Gender	○ a) Male	3. How does this course fit into your academic program?
	○ Sophomore		○ b) Female	○ a) General or distribution requirements
	○ Junior			○ b) Major/concentration requirement or elective
	○ Senior			○ c) Elective (not in major or concentration)
	○ Special			○ d) Unsure
				○ e) Other (specify:)

4. How much interest did you have in the subject matter before taking this course?	5. Compared to other courses you have taken on-campus, the amount of effort you put in was:	6. Compared to other courses you have taken on-campus, the amount you learned was:
○ a) Almost none	○ a) Much less in this course	○ a) Much less in this course
○ b) Little	○ b) Somewhat less	○ b) Somewhat less
○ c) A fair amount	○ c) About the same	○ c) About the same
○ d) Much	○ d) Somewhat more	○ d) Somewhat more
○ e) An exceptional amount	○ e) Much more in this course	○ e) Much more in this course

THE COURSE

	SD	D	DS	AS	A	SA	DK/DA
7. The course had clear objectives.	1	2	3	4	5	6	
8. The assigned reading material was helpful in meeting course objectives.	1	2	3	4	5	6	
9. The classroom sessions (lectures, discussions, etc.) and reading material worked well to complement one another.	1	2	3	4	5	6	
10. The assignments or papers made a significant contribution to learning in this course.	1	2	3	4	5	6	
11. The examinations reflected the important aspects in the course.	1	2	3	4	5	6	
12. The evaluation of students' work was fair and impartial.	1	2	3	4	5	6	
13. Students felt free to ask questions, disagree, and express their ideas in this course.	1	2	3	4	5	6	
14. The course provided a stimulating atmosphere for critical and independent thinking.	1	2	3	4	5	6	
15. The course stimulated my interest in the subject.	1	2	3	4	5	6	
16. The course material was well organized.	1	2	3	4	5	6	

THE INSTRUCTOR

17. Was skillful in helping students understand difficult topics.	1	2	3	4	5	6	
18. Showed a genuine interest in students.	1	2	3	4	5	6	
19. Provided helpful feedback on written work, when assigned.	1	2	3	4	5	6	
20. Was sufficiently available for office hours and appointments.	1	2	3	4	5	6	
21. Kept students adequately informed of their progress.	1	2	3	4	5	6	
22. Returned written work with reasonable promptness.	1	2	3	4	5	6	
23. Related the subject to other disciplines when appropriate.	1	2	3	4	5	6	
24. Was effective in eliciting good classroom discussions.	1	2	3	4	5	6	
25. Treated students with respect.	1	2	3	4	5	6	
26. Provided an equitable learning environment for men and women.	1	2	3	4	5	6	

OVERALL	Poor	Fair	Good	Very Good	Excellent
27. How would you rate this instructor's teaching effectiveness?	1	2	3	4	5
28. How would you rate this course overall?	1	2	3	4	5

ADDITIONAL QUESTIONS

(Response options provided for up to 28 additional questions supplied by the course instructor.)

OPEN-ENDED ITEMS

What were the strengths of this instructor or course?

What suggestions do you have for improvements? (You may wish to discuss those items for which you darkened a disagree response on the reverse side.)

[Source: Adapted from St. Olaf College]

Pleased to meet you.
It's a pleasure.
How was your trip?
How are things in (London)?

...aying in (Lon...

Part IV

PREPARING TO TRAVEL

ROLES AND PREPARATION OF PROGRAM DIRECTORS

13

Susan MacNally & Sarah E. Spencer

As short-term program models continue to expand in discipline, locations, and pedagogy, so have the professionals who direct such programs. Once the responsibility of a single faculty member, more institutions are requiring two adults to travel with all programs, unless strong on-site support is available.

Today, leadership teams may consist of:
- Pairs of faculty directors – veteran and novice;
- Faculty director and staff/administrator, especially professionals who offer student development and advising experience;
- Faculty director and a graduate teaching assistant;
- Faculty director and his/her partner, especially those who have host country and/or language knowledge.

Roles and responsibilities of the leadership team must be articulated and defined—to each other, students, international office staff, and on-site providers. It is also important for faculty and other leaders to be adequately prepared for these responsibilities. This chapter will examine such issues. For simplicity, the faculty director, whose role is paramount in a credit-granting program, will be the focus. If faculty are partners with others, do not forget to expand these concepts to all involved.

WEARING MORE THAN ONE HAT

Classroom teaching does not in itself prepare a faculty member for successfully directing a study abroad program. In addition to the role of instructor, a director dons several hats, as William Hoffa discusses in "Teaching Short-Term Off-Campus Courses: An Overview" at the end of this chapter. As the title "director" implies, there are administrative duties such as logistics, enrollment, and financial matters. The director is likely to encounter difficult and ambiguous situations requiring skills of leadership, interpretation, decisionmaking, and diplomacy that are rarely if ever faced in the classroom. He or she is literally removed from familiar campus support systems, including colleagues and home culture. On top of all this, the faculty director is working with students who are adjusting physically and emotionally to the new site, their group, and the culture they have come to learn about.

Preparing faculty directors includes advising them of the job duties and providing resources to help them think outside the literal classroom and to consider course material in relation to the variables of time, activities, cultural learning, and student goals. Preparation encompasses training faculty in administrative procedures such as enrollment changes, bookkeeping, and protocol for student conduct. It is about helping faculty understand their role as intercultural guide and to recognize patterns of cultural adjustment in students. A faculty director must be able to uphold and implement institutional policies and positions on issues of conduct, alcohol, student privacy, and student health. Preparation involves coaching faculty to maintain a role of authority, establish a positive relationship with students, recognize potential problems, and resolve behavioral issues effectively. Finally, preparation is about ensuring that faculty directors understand and rely on the support systems on site and at the home campus that will help distribute the burden of all of these responsibilities.

The responsibilities are awesome, but the faculty director does not have to shoulder them all alone. Safety, responsibility, and liability concerns prompt us to advocate a model where the faculty director and the program are firmly connected to institutional and on-site support. Common sense tells us that the more responsibilities piled on one person, the greater the chances are for something to go wrong. Faculty preparation is as much about defining the institutional role as it is about defining the additional responsibilities the director must assume.

A good faculty preparation program will consist of establishing the director's responsibilities to the students and to the institution, grounding these responsibilities to support structures at the home institution and on site, and offering opportunities for faculty to develop skills to meet the challenges of directorship effectively.

DEFINING RESPONSIBILITIES

Job Descriptions

Every program, depending on its design, will have different responsibilities in the job description. Every faculty member approaches directing a study abroad program with slightly different expectations of what such a task entails. A written job description will help to avoid the confusion and frustration bound to erupt when a program provider or an institution and faculty director find that their expectations do not match. Although every program may have a different set of specific tasks for the director, institutions can develop a document written in general terms that addresses the institutional expectations of all faculty directors. Ongoing programs, especially those which change directors, should have a detailed job description. If the program collaborates with other offices or onsite partners, job descriptions should include each constituency's role.

Keep It Simple. A director's general job description should focus on broad areas of responsibility not encountered in the classroom or of heightened importance while leading a group abroad. Grouping responsibilities under different "hats" will help faculty (and administrators) develop a clear, organized picture of the job. Several key roles are outlined in the Sample Faculty Director Job Description at the end of this chapter. In addition, the administrative responsibility lists in Chapter 3, Administrative Processes, will provide fodder for defining the job.

Get Approval. Since the faculty director's responsibilities cross academic, administrative, and student life branches of the institution, these offices should be consulted. A bonus of involving various offices is that it raises consciousness about the complexity of the job. The resulting official job description can be an effective tool with which to advocate for additional compensation and recognition.

Faculty Contracts

Home institutions continue to move toward requiring faculty to sign agreements or contracts for a specific short-term program. These agreements articulate the unique role and responsibilities and also may require participation in promotional events, as well as faculty and student orientations, and completion of financial paperwork and a report by the

due date. Policies for faculty directors should also be included, and should be designed to support the job description. Consider who should send such agreements, such as the chief academic officer, dean, or appropriate person. See the "Faculty Director Agreement" and "Policies for Faculty Director" examples at the end of the chapter.

Key Roles

Most short-term programs require the following roles as part of a director's responsibility:

The <u>developer</u> role requires an investment of time and energy before the program begins. As a developer, the faculty director addresses the academic side of programming, integrating site and curriculum as well as logistics and financial planning. The director must be involved in the planning stages to be able to take on administrative and financial responsibilities on site.

Faculty involvement in <u>recruiting</u> is essential. There is no more effective recruiter than a faculty director who is excited about his or her program. Not only does the faculty director represent the fundamental value of the program, academic credit, he or she is the guide to a new experience. Students need to have the opportunity to interact with the person who will lead them in this venture.

The roles of <u>administrator</u> and <u>financial</u> manager are perhaps the most clear-cut. On site, the director may have to confirm logistical arrangements, make payments, manage discretionary funds, keep financial records, and handle enrollment changes. There may be specific state or institutional rules to follow that have dire consequences if broken.

The director acts as the <u>institutional representative</u> to the students and to the host culture. She or he establishes and maintains institutional relationships with the counterparts, hosts, and providers that make the program happen. In addition, she or he governs how participants behave. The faculty director must facilitate administrative processes, uphold institutional policies, and be willing to implement disciplinary sanctions. Finally, the director is the communication link back to the home institution.

The role of <u>adviser/facilitator</u> to students involves establishing a leadership role and positive group dynamic, preparing students before departure, providing assistance and referrals when a student is in need, and intervening when appropriate. Skillful advisers/facilitators are often able to prevent issues from becoming problems. Whether or not culture is an academic focus of the program, the faculty director is also the intercultural facilitator; she or he is the liaison between home and host cultures.

Faculty preparation is all about avoiding as many crises as possible, but faculty directors may still find themselves in the role of <u>crisis manager.</u> Some crises cannot be prevented, and at that point the institution and the students rely heavily on the director for strength, level-headedness, direction, communication, and good judgment.

PREPARING DIRECTORS: TIMELINES AND TOOLS

Preparing program directors is not unlike preparing students for studying abroad. Students have different questions and need different types of information at various stages of their journey: program selection, application, orientation (critical and colloquial), on site, and upon return to the home campus. The faculty director's journey is analogous: program idea and development, recruitment/admission/selection of participants, faculty and student orientation, on-site management, and reporting and debriefing on return.

When to Start Preparation

The old adage—it's never too early—applies here. Institutions should consider the following options:

☐ **Recruitment Phase:** nuts and bolts information sessions on benefits in directing a program, responsibilities and policies, funding options for site visits, experiences of veteran directors, and an overview of the proposal process.

☐ **Proposal Process:** a session focused specifically on designing the academic/intercultural program, including learning objectives, teaching techniques, etc.

☐ **Program Development & Administrative Phase:** a session for new directors covering logistics, marketing and enrollment, as well as the roles of other offices who support program.

☐ **Predeparture:** bring together novice and experienced faculty to review best practices: orientation, intercultural facilitation, crisis management, student life issues, and case studies.

Extra sessions may be scheduled to bring in new topics, such as intercultural growth, global and local issues, or dealing with the unexpected.

SAMPLE FACULTY DIRECTOR JOB DESCRIPTION
UNIVERSITY OF UTAH INTERNATIONAL CENTER DIRECTORS MANUAL

I. RESPONSIBILITIES
Academic Counseling
It is the director's role to provide academic advice to participants, ensuring that the academic experience is appropriate to a university-level study and learning experience. The director's assistance to students should be continuous throughout the program.

Personal Assistance
The director will act as a resource to participants who may need assistance with personal, emotional, financial, and health problems that may arise during the program. The director acts as the liaison among participants and the appropriate local agencies that provide assistance in these areas.

Activities
The director is expected to organize (as appropriate) activities that will enhance participants' learning experience. Excursions, field trips, and cultural events are examples of activities that may be organized.

Institutional Liaison
The director serves as the liaison between the participants and the university. It is the director's primary responsibility to inform the international center of any emergency situation that may arise during the program, including participant behavior problems. Discretionary judgment is assumed on the part of the director in these matters.

II. BUDGET AND FINANCES
The director is responsible for the management of the group's funds during the program. The director will meet with the international center's finance officer prior to departure to review the program budget, including expense allowances, payments abroad, and institutional accounting requirements. A complete budget report will be required from the director at the end of the program.

III. LIABILITY AND INDEMNIFICATION
The director and all program assistants approved by the university are considered the legal representatives of the university. As such, they are entitled to the same liability protection given to all university representatives. Legal representation will be provided for the director and assistant(s) in all matters related to the program if required.

IV. CRISIS MANAGEMENT AND EMERGENCY RESPONSE
It is the responsibility of the director to be prepared to respond appropriately to any emergency situation that might arise during the program. The director's first responsibility will be to attend to the safety of participants and to determine whether or not there is a threat. If it is determined that there is potential risk to the participants, the director will notify the international center at the university as soon as possible, informing the office about any action taken to minimize or eliminate that risk.

[Source: Adapted, with permission, from University of Utah]

TOOLS FOR PREPARATION

We all have different learning styles, and directors are no exception. Consider the following diverse preparation tools:

Handbooks

A well-designed handbook should be distributed to cover policies and procedures (e.g., budget guidelines, meeting minimums, acceptance procedures, confirming student participation, deadlines, and enrollment).

Printed handbooks can have limitations, including becoming quickly outdated, requiring updates for faculty who have already received one, and coming with no guarantee that they will be thoroughly read. Organizations increasingly are moving to Web sites, where the same information is documented, but can be easily updated. Directed e-mails to faculty notifying them of updates will help keep up with new information.

Other Written Resources

The international education field provides numerous articles and publications, including this book. If director feedback notes are available, make sure that future directors are included in distribution.

Orientation Sessions

Scheduling orientation sessions and—ideally—making them mandatory, is essential to a quality training program. You may consider having more than one, as shown on the Agenda Examples for Faculty Directors' Meeting at the end of this chapter. This informational need is very difficult to meet by text alone. Opportunity for discussion and consultation with administrative representatives from general counsel, counseling services, the offices of academic deans, and student life is important to answer questions as well as to demonstrate institutional support. In addition to covering concepts such as "in loco parentis," sessions should explore examples of the kind of decisions faculty directors face.

Guidelines and Ideas for Faculty Orientations

- ☐ Include representatives from other campus offices.
- ☐ Require attendance.
- ☐ Support from the administration and deans is necessary.
- ☐ Seasoned pros come as mentors.
- ☐ Invite the study abroad or international committee, deans, and chairs.
- ☐ Administrators who attend show their support of faculty and will better understand the value of the directors' work.
- ☐ Keep it short; faculty are busy.
- ☐ Focus on topics that can't easily be covered another way, such as in print or during a one-on-one appointment.

- ☐ Schedule time for questions at the end.
- ☐ Provide real-life examples and case studies
- ☐ Include examples of behavioral, academic, mental health, and alcohol problems.
- ☐ Provide reference material.

OTHER OPPORTUNITIES TO BUILD SKILLS

Likewise, each faculty director has his or her own strengths and weaknesses. Each program has the need for different levels of involvement in the key roles listed above. For instance, there are charismatic faculty members who have to do little more than walk into a classroom to get a full slate of applicants. Others may have trouble conveying their excitement about the program to students, or perhaps they are addressing a much smaller pool of students. Faculty who are great teachers and directors but who are not detail oriented might be better off using a program provider to reduce logistical and financial duties on site. Be realistic when laying out the job in relation to the program design. It is worth spending time with a prospective director in the early stages to draw out his or her strengths and to anticipate areas where a bit more training and support is needed.

Written materials such as a handbook and related forms and documents provide critical information. Skills that directors rely on are not, however, best acquired by simply reading about them. Providing opportunities to build leadership skills is a key part of your preparation program. This is more fully covered in Chapter 14, If You Cross Over the Sea...Program Leadership for Intercultural Development. Some ideas for skill-building opportunities include:

- ☐ Pairing new directors with experienced mentors during development and planning;
- ☐ Round table discussions with representatives of counseling, general counsel, or student life;
- ☐ Best practices sessions with experienced faculty;
- ☐ Leadership training through the human resources department;
- ☐ Site-integrative teaching methods workshops with the curriculum development center or education faculty; and
- ☐ E-mail listservs, especially those that offer a forum for discussion.

It is extra work to organize and promote these added opportunities, but there are bonuses. Offering such programming for faculty underscores institutional support, recognizes the complexity of the director's job, enhances the confidence directors have in the organizing office, and most importantly, builds a cadre of faculty director colleagues who can support one another in their journeys on the path of directing study abroad programs.

Linking Director Responsibilities to Support

This section looks at possible forms of support for the various roles directors play, in terms of (1) informational tools, (2) training, and (3) on-site assistance. Note that the roles of developer/recruiter and administrator/financial manager are detailed in written form (handbook) whereas institutional representative, adviser/facilitator, and crisis manager rely on interactive training (faculty orientation) for effective preparation.

If faculty are working by themselves, it is still critical that institutional support be defined before departure. Know what offices you can rely on for assistance and know what liability coverage is provided (see Chapter 3, Internal Support Systems). Faculty members working without much support from the home institution, in particular, should consider using a program provider.

Developer/Recruiter

Tools:
- ☐ Samples of program plans, itineraries, syllabi.
- ☐ Resources for development—overseas institutions, providers, contacts, environmental information.
- ☐ Promotional materials and events.
- ☐ Marketing plan.
- ☐ Cheat sheet of points to cover in class visits.

Training:
- ☐ Work with experienced faculty mentors.
- ☐ Hold a program development workshop.

Assistance:
- ☐ Faculty colleagues can help spread the word and offer further contacts for program development.
- ☐ Department can offer development and recruitment assistance.

Administrator/Financial Manager

Tools:
- ☐ The faculty handbook or Web site is one of the most effective tools to inform directors about procedural responsibilities.
- ☐ Clear rules and simple forms for financial management and enrollment procedures; guidelines should be concise enough to take overseas.
- ☐ Timeline for critical due dates.
- ☐ Records of correspondence with on-site providers.
- ☐ Coded budget to take overseas, showing what is to be paid on site and what has been prepaid.

Training:
- ☐ Lectures about administrative procedures are ineffective; use other means to disseminate the information.
- ☐ Try e-mail reminders that refer to the handbook or Web site documents.

Assistance:
- ☐ Make prepayments to reduce financial burden on site.
- ☐ Use on-site providers to handle arrangements and payments.

For more detailed information about financial forms and systems, refer to Chapter 9, Financial Matters.

Institutional Representative

Tools:
- ☐ Copies of important policies, particularly the student code of conduct available via Web site or in print, to take along;
- ☐ Scenarios and case studies to use as discussion start points to illustrate the type of situations that crop up, the type of decisions that must be made, how policies are implemented, how sanctions might be imposed, and when it is appropriate to dismiss a participant.

Training:
- ☐ Orientation session with representatives from general counsel, student life, offices of the academic deans.
- ☐ Explanation of institutional policies as they relate to study abroad, including the student code of conduct (academic and nonacademic), additional rules for study abroad participants, alcohol and drug abuse, sexual harassment, crime reporting, etc.
- ☐ Discussion of the institutional interpretation of concepts such as "in loco parentis," due process, and legislation such as the Family Educational Rights and Privacy Act and the Americans with Disabilities Act.
- ☐ Discussion of faculty scenarios and case studies, especially with respect to behavioral/academic grounds for dismissal.

Assistance:
- ☐ Easy access to consultation with home offices while abroad, either directly or through the international office.

Adviser/Facilitator

Tools:
- ☐ Tips and topics for holding a program orientation and assembling orientation materials.
- ☐ Concise counseling guidelines for recognizing signs of trouble, knowing when to assist, how to intervene.
- ☐ Ice-breaker suggestions for building group cohesion.

Training:
- ☐ Involve the counseling center.
- ☐ Cover leadership topics such as developing a positive group dynamic, encouraging students to set individual goals, managing behavioral problems, maintaining authority while being friendly, preserving participant confidentiality, and overseeing program time and free time.

- ☐ Discuss providing assistance to students in need: recognizing signs of emotional or mental health problems, when and how to assist or, if necessary, intervene.
- ☐ Intercultural session (facilitators from the multicultural center, communications department, international center) to discuss cultural passage of students, physical and emotional ranges and fluctuations, how to guide participants in cross-cultural learning.
- ☐ Best practices sessions with experienced faculty.

Assistance:
- ☐ Control ratio of students to staff.
- ☐ Send a new director as an understudy to an experienced director.
- ☐ Identify on-site counseling resources.
- ☐ Identify an on-site intercultural facilitator.
- ☐ Ensure easy access to home institution offices for consultation.

Crisis Manager

(For more detailed information, see Chapter 16: Safeguards for Short-Term Programs.)
Tools:
- ☐ Local emergency numbers: medical, emergency evacuation services, legal, police, consulate, housing.
- ☐ Concise emergency procedures on site, including when to call home.
- ☐ Emergency documentation form.

- ☐ Emergency numbers to home institution: key offices and contacts.
- ☐ Tips sheet for emergencies.
- ☐ Student emergency contact information.

Training:
- ☐ Discuss types of emergencies: student, personal, program, natural disaster, political/social.
- ☐ Discuss locating on-site resources: contacts, agencies, facilities.
- ☐ Discuss when to notify the home institution.

Assistance:
- ☐ Ensure easy access to home institution offices for consultation.
- ☐ Contact available resources on site: people, agencies, facilities.

Group Dynamics and Student Expectations

1. Establish these at orientation with students.
2. The director sets a tone—put a positive spin on the program rules.
3. Establish concern for individual student experience by checking in occasionally with students and being available for private consultation.
4. The director sets student expectations. Identify the goals and objectives of program and motivate students to be adult learners.

TEACHING SHORT-TERM OFF-CAMPUS: AN OVERVIEW
William Hoffa

Teaching a diverse group of students in a foreign setting represents a huge challenge that you will likely find at times to be both time consuming and frustrating. No one should enter this work with the anticipation of accomplishing much scholarly research overseas—which, except in the rarest of circumstances, must be subordinated to prescribed teaching and administrative duties. Many personal and professional satisfactions, however, will come with the successful implementation of the program and the knowledge that the lives of U.S. students have been significantly enriched through the experience. In sum, although you will have to balance a wide variety of responsibilities and roles—teacher, intermediary, adviser, program administrator, and advocate for students—this enlarged faculty role brings with it ample additional rewards and gratifications from students, family, your faculty counterparts, and your home institution. Faculty members who have directed past programs are almost universal in commenting on the unique professional development and personal rewards of living, traveling, and learning with students far from home, as well as the enhancement of their teaching on campus.

In his article "It's Like Wearing All the Hats,"[1] John C. O'Neal, professor of French and director of the Hamilton College Junior Year in France, provides an insightful account of the demands of directing an overseas program. Professor O'Neal, serving his fourth year as director of the Hamilton program, likens the overseas experience to being college president and dean and academic adviser and lecturer and psychological counselor and accountant and even, in some cases, repairman. This perceptive article describes these multiple roles as a series of constantly shifting responsibilities for which adequate prior training is likely to be minimal and on-the-spot problem-solving ability, critical. Although some of what O'Neal says applies only to year-long, branch-campus programs, in point of fact, no matter how long or short the overseas experience, leadership demands remain surprisingly congruent whatever the length, location, or curricular focus.

As faculty director, you are the curricular architect of the program. Beyond this, you serve as liaison, coordinator, and facilitator among the many different constituencies and components of the program: home campus, students, on-site facilities, host families, the local and national government overseas, and last but not least, the host culture. What any given faculty member does obviously depends largely on the nature and purpose, the design and structure of the particular program she or he is directing.

Once overseas, you assume full administrative and academic responsibility for the integrity of the program, as well as personal responsibility for the well being of all students. You are the legal representative of your home institution for the period of the program. You may be asked to contact your home campus at intervals—by whatever means (e-mail, fax, phone)—with program updates, though many on-site decisions are inevitably left to your own judgment. As an administrator, you are responsible for the overall direction of the on-site program. Your on-site administrative responsibilities necessarily begin well before arrival. Housing assignments, special dietary arrangements, health issues, special needs accommodations—all must be dealt with well in advance of arrival.

Above all, you are responsible for the academic quality of the program and must be willing to assure those who need to know that the expectations of both participants and your home campus are being met. Your on-site supervision assures that academic quality comparable with home institution standards is being maintained. This may require extensive and structured student contact. You might schedule frequent one-on-one sessions with students, offer optional times for consultation, or set up optional or mandatory group discussions to process what has been read or seen. The daily schedule of teaching, student advising, and making logistical contacts with host organizations and individuals is likely to be rigorous and demanding.

Directing a study abroad program for participants who most likely have limited experience in a new culture provides a range of challenges that go far beyond what might be required at home. Participants will see you as a resource person who can alleviate the initial confusion and disorientation that confronts them and then guide them along the paths of new knowledge and cultural integration. It is very important to understand the variety of motivations that encourage students to study overseas; not all will be as purely academic as faculty would prefer. Indeed, the desire to "get away" from the academic pressures of the home campus may be as fundamental as a student's desire to test him- or herself in a new and "foreign" environment. Successful teaching and advising must acknowledge this complexity of student hopes and desires, providing counsel that balances the twin academic and experiential bases of international education.

You will need to be skilled in diplomacy, logistics, and group dynamics. You will invariably be asked to be a cultural interpreter and analyst, helping students understand what is going on and how it relates (or doesn't relate) to things back home. Unless there is someone else on the local scene who really knows the host country's social, cultural, and academic fabric, you must be prepared to take on the role of explaining it to students. Above all, you must be prepared to be a cheerful and supportive friend-in-need to students, not simply an authority figure. Whatever is prescribed and expected, chance and circumstance often rise up to demand yet additional imperatives and responsibilities.

Experience shows that the most successful faculty directors are those with the physical stamina to manage long hours and a high level of interaction with students and local contacts, the patience and good humor to deal with frequent frustrations, and the knowledge and independence to function well in a culture not their own. Fundamental to all of the above, you need to be an eager and committed teacher who knows how what you are teaching relates both to the home campus and to the culture of the host country. In sum, you are responsible for providing reasonable access to opportunities for both successful academic and personal experiences.

Due to the sensitive nature in acting as both advocate for the students and liaison among the distinct program components, you must exercise caution in personal matters concerning individual students. This is especially true during periods of emotional stress that some students may experience as they undergo cultural shock and learn strategies for adapting to a new cultural setting. Conversations with individual students must be regarded as confidential. Matters of particular concern are the violation of trust or privacy of students through the unauthorized sharing or disclosure of information; any act that can be interpreted as sexual harassment; or any discriminatory act reflecting prejudice based on sex, age, race, sexual orientation, or religious belief.

As faculty director, you are expected to behave as a trustworthy representative of your home institution, and be conscious of what this implies. Dignity, decorum, tact, and discretion must be the rule in both public behavior and private handling of individual problems. Few faculty would consciously cause problems through careless words or acts, by a misplaced sense of humor, or by a cross remark in pressured situations, but this can sometimes happen under the pressures of the moment.

You must work to develop and maintain rapport with the group, but a certain social distance should be maintained as well. The ideal combination is "a heart of gold and a will of iron," as one past director said, in the face of unreasonable complaints and attempts by students to ignore program regulations. You should work to avoid the perception that you have favorites with the group; do not reveal a personal dislike for any participant or on-site staff member. Be professional.

Your role in the face of any student problems is to work with the student to find a solution, no matter how long it takes. In addressing physical and mental health issues, a rule of thumb is not to assume that problems that persist for more than three days will eventually go away by themselves. Keep on top of the situation from the beginning to prevent escalation and a potential crisis. Finally, if a student expresses a wish to return home, listen carefully and empathetically, offering coping strategies and other suggestions. If the student persists, despite your efforts to help in the adaptation process, let the student make travel plans to leave. Often this serves as enough of an outlet for the student's frustration and she or he may decide to reconsider things.

We hope the preceding paragraphs have not frightened you away from teaching abroad, but have given you a realistic picture of what may happen while abroad. In sum, your home campus provides faculty with an opportunity to work with students from otherinstitutions, and to get to know this generation of students beyond the classroom.

Endnotes:
[1] John C. O'Neal, "It's Like Wearing All the Hats," ACADEME, Sept./Oct. 1995

POLICIES FOR FACULTY DIRECTORS

1. **Faculty Eligibility.** Any faculty member, with approval of her/his department chair and dean, may propose an international or off-campus short-term program.

2. **Experience in the proposed location:** Faculty must have on-site experience before proposing a short-term program. If two faculty members intend to co-direct a program, at least one faculty member must have on-site experience. Sufficient on-site experience means that the faculty member must have visited the majority of the proposed sites in such a way as to understand and be able to communicate their contributions to the program, as well as their limitations.

3. **Program Approval and Deadlines.** All short-term, off-campus programs are administered by International Education and thus under the purview of the Academic Review Committee for International Education (ARCIE). For UST-sponsored programs, the final deadlines for short-term proposals are mid-October for fall and January term proposals, and late April for spring and summer proposals.

    All proposed programs — new or previously offered — must be submitted to ARCIE using the UST Proposal for Short-term Off-campus Programs form. For ARCIE approved programs for 'On-going Status', a Letter of Intent for Short-term Off-campus Programs must be submitted by the final deadlines listed above.

4. **Addition of Second/Substitute Directors.** The department chair, dean, as well as ARCIE, must approve the addition of a second or substitute director, by using the Request for Second/Substitute Faculty Director form.

5. **January and Summer Term.** Both January and Summer Terms are discrete units of study. Faculty directors may not require preparatory work prior to the end of the preceding term or summary work after the beginning of the following term. Required reading for the program will be listed on specific course descriptions so that students may begin reading after the end of the preceding semester.

6. **Faculty Directors/Departments*** are responsible for the following: **may include schools/colleges or programs*

    a. **Academic Content** of the program including the syllabus, book orders and printing, course materials, classrooms, and lectures.

    b. **Travel and Logistical Arrangements:** If no program provider or on-site coordinator is utilized to arrange program logistics (housing, in-country and local transportation, meals and excursions), it is the faculty director/department's responsibility to make these arrangements. In this case, where no program provider or on-site coordinator is used, International Education will arrange flights unless students are instructed to make their own flight arrangements.

        For group flights, one faculty director must accompany the group from the point of origin and be with the group for the duration of the course. Any exception to this policy would require International Education approval.

    c. **Budget:** Faculty must provide budget figures for all academic and travel expenses. International Education will establish the tentative and approve final program fees.

    d. **Course Descriptions:** Faculty/Department must develop a program description, incorporating brief narratives of the academic course, program structure, eligibility requirements, faculty biography, as well as prerequisites, degree requirements fulfilled, housing and meals, and any physical demands students must meet to participate in the program.

    e. **Marketing and Recruitment:** *Program-specific marketing and the recruitment of students is one of the faculty director/department's primary responsibilities.* International Education will only publish brief descriptions of the program and carry out general marketing for the off-campus curriculum for that term. Faculty/departments should expect to promote their program to students and peers, to visit classes and create printed and e-publications as needed.

    f. **Enrollment:** International Education coordinates the student enrollment process. All students are required to submit an application dossier by the dates specified by International Education. Faculty directors will select students, based on the application dossier and other resources, including interviews and additional paperwork, and use eligibility requirements published on the course description and in Policies & Procedures, Any program that does not meet its minimum enrollment by the application deadline will be cancelled.

        Non-UST students and non-student applicants are accepted on a space available basis subject to the faculty director's approval.

    g. **General Supervision of Students:** Faculty directors will supervise and direct students in the academic and intercultural goals of the program both while in this country and while on the program. Faculty are the primary person responsible for the supervision and welfare of the students participating in the program, and are, among other things, responsible for supervising and monitoring each student's conformance to University and other applicable policies, rules, regulations, and standards of conduct. Directors should be familiar with the Disciplinary Rights and Procedures for Study Abroad Programs-Academic and Non-Academic that are contained in the Student Policy Handbook.

7. **Compensation.** Faculty Director's compensation is approved by her/his Dean and includes pre-approved academic and program required travel expenses. The faculty director's department is responsible for arranging for the payment of salary. All stipends will be arranged by International Education and will be disbursed during and after the conclusion of the Program.

Teaching Load Guidelines

a. Undergraduate - January Term Abroad

1. If a faculty member teaches a course for St. Thomas credit and three (3) or more St. Thomas students enroll, it counts as part of the six-course load.

2. If two faculty co-direct a short-term program, they each get credit for a full course if enrollment reaches 20 with a minimum of three (3) St. Thomas students. If enrollment is less than 20, the amount of credit towards load will be negotiated on a case-by-case basis with their Dean.

3. If a faculty member directs a program and students receive instruction through another institution or program, the experience will not count as part of the course load. However, the faculty member's expenses will be paid and they will receive a stipend to be determined by the dean.
Undergraduate – Summer

a. For summer programs, on-campus salary policies are followed.

b. Graduate Teaching Load Guidelines will be approved on a program-specific basis by the faculty director's department chair and dean.

8. **Cancellation.** The University of St. Thomas reserves the right to discontinue short-term programs at any time before or after departure, at its sole discretion. Among the reasons for discontinuation and cancellation of programs is insufficient enrollment.

9. **Withdrawal.** It is expected that faculty directors will not withdraw except in an emergency. If it is impossible to serve as faculty director, International Education must be notified immediately. Depending on the withdrawal date, the program may be cancelled or a replacement faculty director obtained.

10. **Collaboration with International Education.** Faculty directors must work in collaboration with the International Education staff to deliver the highest quality program. Because there are individual as well as shared responsibilities, program directors and International Education staff must plan to communicate and meet regularly.

11. **Student Orientations.** Because these programs are intense group experiences, whose success depends on good group dynamics and clear expectations, faculty directors are required to schedule at least one pre-departure orientation session with student participants. Additional pre-departure meetings and return activities, as well as correspondence are highly encouraged.

   Programs must have an on-site orientation, conducted during the first two days after arrival, and faculty are expected to plan frequent times during the Program for students to process and reflect on their intercultural experience.

12. **Faculty Director Preparation.** Throughout the year, faculty should take advantage of sessions made available by International Education and Center for Faculty Development to gain expertise as an off-campus faculty director.

13. **Financial Reporting.**
   The University of St. Thomas requires complete financial reporting for all expenses incurred by the program. Meetings will be arranged prior to departure to review the program budget and the requirements for reporting expenditures according to the University's accounting procedures. Faculty are required to submit all receipts and documentation for expenses incurred, including cash advance and credit card, within 30 days of return.

   See the Accounts Payable web site www.stthomas.edu/accountspayable for complete University Policies and Procedures regarding cash management. Below is information that relates directly to short-term program finances, taken from these policies:

   a. **Expenses not covered by St. Thomas:**
      □ Passport, photos, related expenses.
      □ Personal expenses, such as laundry, clothing, medicine; vaccinations, inoculations, etc.
      □ Personal entertainment and incidental expenses.
      □ Non-approved customs duty on items mailed to destination.
      □ Non-approved overweight baggage charges.
      □ Telephone charges unrelated to program.
      □ Penalties for changes in travel itinerary once your tickets are issued.

[Source: Adapted from the University of St. Thomas]

b. University of St. Thomas Employee Reimbursement Policy

This policy has been established to provide guidelines on university reimbursement for those expenses incurred by university employees on business. It is university policy to reimburse employees for all expenses that are reasonable, necessary, and actually incurred for authorized university business.

Employees are expected to:

- ☐ Exercise good judgment with respect to expenses, determining the most economical means of obtaining lodging, meals, transportation, supplies, etc.
- ☐ Spend university money carefully and judiciously.
- ☐ Claim reimbursement only for necessary and reasonable expenses (i.e., employees are expected neither to lose nor gain financially).

c. Cash Advance

Cash advances are given to employees involved with Foreign Travel, Group/Team Travel, and Student Travel. A cash advance is a personal liability to the employee until he or she has provided the appropriate documentation and returned any excess funds.

All cash advances are to be settled within thirty (30) days after return from the program by completing an Employee Expense Report and submitting it to International Education with appropriate substantiation. Original receipts must be submitted. Amounts owed to the employee will be processed in the normal course of business. Per IRS guide-lines, employees are not to retain unused portions of advance funds for future trips. The unused portion must be returned by attaching a check to the reimbursement form.

Taxation - If the unused portion of the cash advance is not returned or the expenses are not substantiated within forty-five (45) days from the return of travel, those amounts will be taxable income to the employee and included in his or her Form W-2.

d. International Education Direct-Pay Credit Card

Depending on the type of on-site expenditures necessary for the program, faculty may be issued a credit card. The charges made on the credit card, issued through International Education, are posted directly against the program budget. Prior to departure, faculty will be notified of the program budget, spending, and credit card limit amounts. The credit card should be used for administrative expenses, transportation, group-related events, meals, etc as dis-cussed with International Education prior to departure.

e. Refund Policy for Program Fees

If there is a remaining balance in the budget upon the return of the program, it will be returned to the university at fiscal year end.

14. **Families Accompanying Programs.** St. Thomas is willing to consider allowing families to accompany a program, with the understanding that any additional expenses must be paid separately. It should also be understood that the faculty directors' demanding role is not likely to allow much free time of private social or recreational activities. An adult who is fully responsible for child care must accompany any children under 18 years old.

15. **Liability coverage.** Faculty directors are covered by St. Thomas for Bodily Injury and Property Damage insurance to others for which they are legally liable. She or he must make themselves and St. Thomas aware of any and all unusual or difficult legal requirements in foreign countries, especially regarding vehicles, alcohol use and property damage laws, and make sure current legal information is obtained prior to departure. Accompanying persons (non-St. Thomas employees) are not covered by this insurance, and will be asked to sign documents indemnifying the University of St. Thomas before departure.

St. Thomas insurance does not cover the damage or loss of the personal possessions of either faculty or students — electronics, computers, cameras, baggage, etc. Faculty need to make their own insurance arrangements for replacing such items if they are damaged, lost, or stolen and should check their homeowners or renters insurance policies.

16. **Medical Coverage/Off-Campus Assistance**

a. Blue Cross/Blue Shield Coverage. The Blue Cross/Blue Shield of Minnesota coverage through St. Thomas remains effective abroad. As with most U.S. policies, faculty should be prepared to pay on-site and then file a claim to seek reimbursement. For cash-less access to care, see http://www.bluecross.com/healthtravel/index.html. Cash-less care may be easier in some countries than others (and may be impossible in some places). Blue Cross members may call COLLECT any time of the day or night from any domestic or international destination for advice on how to proceed in obtaining care abroad at: 804.673.1177.

    b. **International Teacher ID Card**. Faculty traveling to international sites will receive an International Teacher Identity Card (ITIC). Faculty are required to submit an ID-sized photo and birth date. The ITIC provides numerous discounts on entry fees to museums and monuments, depending on the country, and overseas insurance coverage, including medical evacuation and repatriation.

    c. **Assist America.** All St. Thomas employees have access to this service. It is not insurance, but rather a worldwide emergency medical assistance service that can provide help accessing 24-hour multilingual service, obtaining a prescription abroad, lost luggage assistance, etc. It is very similar to the TRAVEL GUARD coverage provided by the ITIC (see above). Faculty must carry an Assist America card with the phone number and St. Thomas reference number on it to use this service.

17. **Health, Safety and Communication.**

    a. In the interest of the health and safety of participants in off-campus courses, these conditions will be observed:

    b. UST-sponsored programs will only be offered in countries with which the United States has official relations. (Cuba is the exception.)

    c. Directors will arrange for means to contact the St. Thomas campus either at or near the site(s) of the program, and will have a clear communication link to the campus. Regardless of the location(s), directors should be prepared to respond to health and safety problems, whether emergency or routine in nature.

    d. All short-term programs must comply with the University of St. Thomas policies about rental and use of motor vehicles.

    e. All private carriers hired to provide required group transportation scheduled must provide certification of appropriate insurance coverage.

18. **Final Report & Evaluation.** A final financial report will be submitted to International Education by the January or Summer grade due date, or earlier. Follow up meetings with International Education must be scheduled and should discuss detailed information about the academics and logistics or the program and should discuss problems, successes and make recommendations for future programs.

19. **Student Assessment.** Student and program evaluation forms are provided to faculty before departure. Students should complete these forms as soon as possible following the conclusion of the program. Individual student academic performance will be assessed in accordance with announced criteria by the University Registrar.

[Source: Adapted from the University of St. Thomas]

EXAMPLE OF FACULTY CONTRACT LETTER OF APPOINTMENT

Dear _____:

I am pleased to offer you an appointment, in collaboration with International Education, as Faculty Director of the following short-term off-campus program:

Program name, Term/Year

Responsibility for this position begins immediately, and will continue through the semester subsequent to your return. On behalf of [the College/School of _____], I appreciate your willingness to provide the academic, intercultural and administrative leadership that will enable this Program to succeed.

Duties and Responsibilities
Your duties and responsibilities as Faculty Director include:
1. Academic Content: You are responsible for the academic content of the Program, including the syllabus, book orders and printing, classrooms and lectures.
2. Travel and Logistical Arrangements: If no program provider or on-site coordinator is utilized to arrange program logistics (housing, in-country and local transportation, meals and excursions), it is your responsibility to make these arrangements. In this case, where no program provider or on-site coordinator is used, International Education will arrange flights.
3. Budget: You must provide budget figures for all academic and travel expenses. International Education will establish the tentative and final program fees.
4. Course Descriptions: You are responsible for developing a course description, which should incorporate brief narratives of the academic course, program structure, faculty biography, as well as prerequisites, degree requirements fulfilled, housing and meals, and any physical demands students must meet to participate in the Program.
5. Marketing and Recruitment: Program-specific marketing and the recruitment of students is one of your primary responsibilities. International Education itself will only publish brief descriptions of the Program and carry out general marketing for the off-campus curriculum for that term. You should expect to promote your Program to students and your peers, to visit classes and create printed and e-publications as needed.
6. Enrollment: International Education coordinates the student enrollment process. All students are required to submit an application dossier by the dates specified by International Education. You will select students, based on eligibility requirements, the dossier and other resources, including interviews and additional paperwork.
7. General Supervision of Students: You will supervise and direct students in the academic and intercultural goals of the Program both while in this country and while on the Program. You are the primary adult responsible for the supervision and welfare of the students participating in the Program. Among other things, you are responsible for supervising and monitoring each student's conformance to University and other applicable policies, rules, regulations and standards of conduct. You should be familiar with the Disciplinary Rights and Procedures for Study Abroad Programs-Academic and Non-Academic that are contained in the Student Policy Handbook.

After approval by the Academic Review Committee for International Education, you must develop the Program by March 1, for Fall/January programs and September 1 for Spring/Summer programs. The tasks described in paragraph numbers 1 through 5 must be completed by this deadline.

Compensation
Your compensation for serving as Faculty Director will be _____ plus your pre-approved academic and program required travel expenses. Your department is responsible for arranging for the payment of your salary while you are participating in the Program. All stipends will be arranged by International Education and will be disbursed during and after the conclusion of the Program.

Cancellation
The University of St. Thomas reserves the right to discontinue this Program at any time before or after departure, at its sole discretion. Among the reasons for discontinuation and cancellation of this Program are travel warnings and advisories from the US Department of State and insufficient enrollment. If this Program does not reach minimum enrollment by the final application deadline, it will be cancelled.

Withdrawal

It is expected that you will not withdraw from the position of Faculty Director for the Program except in an emergency. If it is impossible for you to serve as Faculty Director, you must immediately notify International Education. Depending on the withdrawal date, the Program may be cancelled or a replacement Faculty Director obtained.

Collaboration with International Education

You must work in collaboration with the International Education staff to deliver the highest quality Program. Because there are individual as well as shared responsibilities, you and International Education staff must plan to communicate and meet regularly. If this is your first experience serving as a Faculty Director, you will receive The Guide to Successful Short Term Programs Abroad that will assist you in preparation to direct this Program.

Student Orientations

Because the Program is an intense group experience, whose success depends on good group dynamics and clear expectations, you are required to schedule at least one pre-departure orientation session with your student participants. International Education will provide each student a pre-departure handbook and Culturegram, which should be used as a tool to discuss your Program's specific location, climate and culture.

All January Term 2008 orientations are scheduled for Friday, November 16, 2007 from 3:00-6:00 p.m. International Education will work with you to schedule Spring/Summer sessions. Additional pre-departure meetings and correspondence are highly encouraged.

Your Program must have an on-site orientation, conducted during the first two days after arrival, and you are expected to plan frequent times during the Program for students to process and reflect on their intercultural experience.

Faculty Director Preparation

Throughout the year, sessions will be available to you to support your development as an off-campus Faculty Director. As this role is both challenging and complex, you are encouraged you to take advantage of these opportunities.

Financial Reporting

The University of St. Thomas requires complete financial reporting for all expenses incurred by the Program. Meetings will be arranged prior to departure to review the Program budget and the requirements for reporting expenditures according to the University's accounting procedures. You are required to submit all receipts and documentation for expenses incurred within 30 days of your return.

The staff of International Education looks forward to working with you over the next several months. Your commitment to international and off-campus education is highly valued.

Best regards,

_____

Dean, College of

I accept this offer of appointment as Faculty Director. I have read, understand and agree to the above described expectations and responsibilities and have been provided a copy of the Policies for Directing a St. Thomas Short-Term Off-Campus Program. I understand that my role as Faculty Director is critical to the success of the Program.

Date:_____

_____
Faculty Name

cc: International Education

[Source: Adapted from the University of St. Thomas]

AGENDA EXAMPLES FOR FACULTY DIRECTORS' MEETING

MEETING #1: BEFORE ENROLLMENT MEETING

WELCOME!

New Interims:

Discuss Timeline

Second Person/Backup Policy

Application & Selection Procedures

Open House Information Student Orientation
- Large Group Orientations
- Group specific meetings
- Student reentry

Preview of Faculty Orientation Meetings in the Fall
- Selected Articles
- Student Expectations
- Academic expectations
- Instructor departs with students
- Group Dynamics
- College Policies and how they travel
- Liability Issues

Who does what – Instructor/Liaison
- Transportation/Accommodation-Excursions/Guides
- Academic Contacts/Museum visits
- Safety/Security Concerns

MEETING #2: THREE MONTHS PRIOR TO DEPARTURE

WELCOME

Support Personnel for 2007:

Packet Contents:
- Orientation Schedules/Orientation Handbooks (ID's)
- Health & Medical Disclosure form
- Emergency Response Plan
- Emergency Check List
- Statement on Safety on Off-Campus Programs
- Crisis Management Plan
- Alcohol Policy
- Student Conditions of Participation
- Parent/Guardian Conditions of Participation
- Authorization for Medical Treatment
- Student Agreement Form
- Philosophy, Policy and Procedures
- Flight & Ticket Contingency Plans for January, 2007
- Listing of the Interim Instructor Packet Contents for
- December meeting
- Sample Parent Letter
- Guidelines for Faculty Narrative Report (new IDOCS document)
- IDOCS Suggested Orientation Activities
- Completing the Circle (Re-entry)
- Maximizing Study Abroad

Academic focus of programs

Evaluation Forms

Policies: Departure with students, free time, religious services opportunities, long-distance calls

[Souce: Adapted from St. Olaf College]

MEETING #3: MONTH BEFORE DEPARTURE

3:30   Welcome and Christmas Cheer

3:35   QUICK Review of packet materials:

   ☐ *Health and Medical Information Forms* (Be sure to discuss issues raised by students
     PRIOR TO DEPARTURE! Consult Director or Liaison if you wish.

   ☐ *International IDs* – review of benefits. Remind students to get them before they leave campus.

   ☐ *Communication with parents* – remind students that it is IOS policy to contact parents in the event
     of group or personal emergency. If a student has an objection to this policy, please discuss the
     issue with the student and report the outcome to IOS.

   ☐ *Crisis Management, Emergency Response, Emergency Checklist, Incident Report* – any questions?
     Advice: Bring these with you.

3:45   MISCELLANEOUS

   ☐ ***REMIND STUDENTS TO REPORT CONCERNS TO YOU, FIRST, PRIOR TO CALLING PARENTS!!***

   ☐ *Remind students of past problems with Long Distance Telephone Charges.*

   ☐ *Reminder of Important Dates:*
     February 6: Ice Cream Social, 3:30-4:30, Ballroom
     February 8: Interim Grades due at noon.
     February 8: Return Interim Instructors Meeting, 3:30-5:00, Black ballroom
     February 15: Financial Report Due
     February 15: Narrative reports due for New Interims if being offered again in 2008
     March 1: All narrative reports due

3:50   Gifts, Flight Updates (including deviations), Final Meetings with liaisons, Bag Tags, review of
        Contingency Plans

4:00   College Travel Expense Policy and Group Travel

4:15   Harassment Officer: Issues related to unwelcome behavior

4:25   Photo/Literary Contest
        Reentry information
        Electronic evaluations/gold forms

4:35   College Counselor: Psychological Issues

[Souce: Adapted from St. Olaf College]

SAMPLE 1: DIRECTOR'S HANDBOOK TABLE OF CONTENTS

TABLE OF CONTENTS

[Source: Adapted from University of Utah]

[Source: Adapted from University of St. Thomas]

SAMPLE FACULTY ORIENTATION AGENDA- 2 HOURS

Set up - Chairs in a circle, a newsprint/makers/easel, and enough room to get up and walk around.

5 min	Introductions - ask a question such as "What is your favorite place in the world? Why?" Be sure to let them know each person has only #_____ seconds. Everyone in the room should participate in this, including you and other presenters. This sets a tone for collective learning and sharing.
2 min	Review of agenda
10 min	Icebreaker/Teambuilder activity - my favorite is Travel Bingo since it gets everyone walking around
10 min	Fears and Expectations
30 min	Health, Safety and Travel info - often their fears are about how to handle emergencies, etc
20 min	Teaching on the Road - see sections in Sarah and Kathy's book about academics, assignments, and handling difficult students
30 min	Diversity - within each faculty leader, in the group they will be leading, and/or in the country they are going to.
5 min	Reentry - how to prepare the group (while still away) for returning to the United States.
5 min	Closure - go around the circle and ask a question, for example "What is one thing from today's workshop that you think will be especially useful to you?"

Notes:
If time and enough people, add 30 minutes for the Great Expectations Exercise, then discuss the challenges and rewards for leading these programs. It is an excellent activity that puts everything in perspective.

Even if everyone in the group knows each other, it is a good idea to start the workshop by going around the circle and have each person answer a simple question. This gets their voices warmed up, sets a tone for active participation, and helps each person get focused on the issues at hand (instead of thinking about the meeting they just came from).

A closing question at the end of the workshop gives everyone a chance to share a parting thought, and most importantly it functions as a review and reminder of the learning that occurred.

Sample Faculty Directors Dinner
University of St. Thomas
5:30 pm – 7:30 pm

I. WELCOME – SES

    a. 5th Annual Faculty Directors Dinner

    b. January Term both UMAIE and UST, Spring semester faculty directors

    c. This time gives us not only a chance to gather together, but for IEC to thank you

    d. Also, opportunity to think about upcoming orientations

    e. In future, we plan to have more opportunities that focus on teaching off-campus, including collaborating with Faculty Development.

** Friday, December 5, Eve Stoddard and Grant Cornwell will be on campus. Over the lunch hour, they will be holding a session for faculty directors and the UMAIE Board of Directors on teaching global citizenship through debriefing. That afternoon, they will facilitate a workshop on Teaching for Global Citizenship.

II. TONIGHT'S AGENDA - SES

    a. While you snack on starters and wine, spend a bit of time talking about "**Teaching Here-Teaching There**" with the help of Britain Scott, Steve Hoffman, and Rob Riley. All opinions and questions are welcome!

    b. Second hour - **Dinner** – continue the conversation.
        2 vegetarian meals have been requested.
        Dining on Chicken Chardonnay.

    c. First, **INTRODUCTIONS** since you may not know each other

    a. Name, department, name of program, term,

    d. But first, Last May I presented in a 4-hour workshop on "Preparing Faculty to Direct Programs Abroad."

    e. 60 attendees, ½ faculty/ ½ education abroad professionals

III. GREAT EXPECTATIONS

- Most successful thing we did – **GREAT EXPECTATIONS**
- Demonstrates not only the various roles that are thrust upon you – as faculty directors – when you take students abroad, but the various expectations by assorted constituencies.
- So much fun – we thought we'd do it here.
- Each table is a different constituency – **HAND OUT GOLDENRODS**!
- List your expectations of the faculty directors from THEIR point of view.
- About 7 minutes. I will ask for one faculty director to VOLUNTEER of have these expectations read to them by each table.

[Source: Adapted from the University of St. Thomas]

Sample Faculty Director's Dinner Continued

V. TEACHING HERE – TEACHING THERE
      a. First day on campus versus first contact with students.
      b. Personal and professional boundaries
      c. Processing and debriefing – different than on-campus

V. WRAP UP
      a. Should have *The Guide to Successful Short-Term Programs Abroad* **(SHOW BOOK)**
      b. For January Term faculty directors – orientation information is forthcoming **(SHOW BOOKS)**
      c. Individual meetings are scheduled to cover budgets and financial management and everything else.
      d. In the workshop, the least successful topic – the most resistant – was Icebreakers and Teambuilders. **(HAND OUT GREEN SHEETS!)**

Great Expectations of STUDENTS
As a student participating in an off-campus program, what are your expectations of the faculty director(s)? List below and identify one person at your table who is willing to share with the group.

Great Expectations of PARENTS
As a parent of a student participating in an off-campus program, what are your expectations of the faculty director(s)? List below and identify one person at your table who is willing to share with the group.

Great Expectations of UST ADMINISTRATION
As a member of the UST Administration, what are your expectations of these faculty director(s)? List below and identify one person at your table who is willing to share with the group.

Great Expectations of HOST INSTITUTION or ORGANZATION or TOUR OPERATOR (onsite)
You are hosting or providing services to a St. Thomas off-campus program. What are your expectations of the faculty director(s) who are responsible for the group? List below and identify one person at your table who is willing to share with the group

[Souce: Adapted from the University of St. Thomas]

SAMPLE AGENDA FOR A CONSORTIUM

Faculty Orientation
10:00 am – 12:45 pm

WELCOME

INTERESTING FACTS FOR JANUARY 2004
- ☐ 13 Jennifers, 12 Megans
- ☐ 72% female this year
- ☐ 28% male
- ☐ Over 100+ business & econ majors, 60 math/bio/chem majors; 38 psych/sociology
- ☐ Over 40 years, 12,000 students

FACULTY INTRODUCTIONS (VERY VERY BRIEF!)
- ☐ Name/school
- ☐ Nickname
- ☐ How many times have you directed programs?
- ☐ One sentence – why you are directing

TODAY'S IMMEDIATE BUSINESS
- ☐ Faculty Info sheets
- ☐ Name badges for student orientation
- ☐ Confirm contact information for students (pass sheet)
- ☐ Passport numbers
- ☐ Encourage correspondence
- ☐ Phone cards
- ☐ Meal Allowances/group funds

TRAVEL ARRANGEMENTS BOOK
- ☐ Itinerary
- ☐ Grade reports
- ☐ Evaluations
- ☐ Participant lists
- ☐ Airline information
- ☐ General suggestions, e.g.tipping
- ☐ Expense forms
- ☐ Embassy information
- ☐ In Case of Emergency
- ☐ Operations itinerary and vouchers
- ☐ Student medical forms & passport photos
- ☐ Roommates

THREE FACULTY DIRECTORS SHARED
- ☐ One director had directed only once – discuss fears and what she did to deal with fears
- ☐ Experienced director – Yes, it's possible to flunk Europe
- ☐ Director to discuss leadership expectations (from the three Trusted Faculty Advice)

EDUCATION
Abroad

By James L. Citron

Dr. Jim's Tips for Directors of U.S. Students Abroad

(As told by students…all learned the hard way.)

A KEY TO MAKING INTERNATIONAL STUDY NOT JUST AN EXPERIENCE BUT an experiential education, is for us students to come up with realistic learning goals that we continuously monitor and work toward under your guidance. Goals should stretch us out of our comfort zones, but not into our panic zones, and should be compatible with our larger educational and life goals.

We U.S. students might often feel more comfortable when we are in control our environments. The discomfort we may feel in unfamiliar environments can be exacerbated when we're living in cultures where a more fatalistic orientation toward life prevails. During the earliest moments of orientation, it can help to openly acknowledge this cultural tendency and how it may interfere with cultural immersion. Encourage us to let go, trust the process, and expect the unexpected. Some languages use the same word for "crisis" and "opportunity." Before events even occur, encourage us to decide in advance to let go of our "inner control freaks" and reframe those inevitable last-minute schedule changes, unpredictable com-

mutes, or unexpected living conditions as learning experiences. Groups that adopt "It's All Good" as the group motto have so much more fun.

Getting Us Ready, Keeping Us (and You) Aware

Orientation is an ongoing process. Teach for the moment. We learn much better when there's a need to know. We won't remember a subway map of a strange new city if you show it to us, out of context, a week before we go on the excursion. Please go over it with us again when we get there.

Be our "culture coach." If we tell you how rude a shopkeeper just was, how aggressive we find old la-

> One or two well-timed group or individual meetings during the program
> can serve as a great reality check, rekindling the group energy,
> and redirecting us all toward the goals we've set for ourselves.
> If we're not reaching our goals, it may be time to ask why.

dies on the metro, or how nosey one of our host parents is, seize this teachable moment. Encourage us to explore both the reasons for our reactions and alternative explanations for the other person's behavior. (Warning: This is going to be easier to do when our complaints aren't about *you* or the program.)

As the director, you don't have to know all the answers. If in doubt about the bus routes, where the best cell phone deals or Internet cafés are, or where to eat in a new city, assign us students to figure out the answers as a team and bring them back to share with the rest of the group (in the form of maps, schedules, price lists, etc.). It actively engages us in the host language and culture and it takes the burden off you.

If there are two leaders, share the visibility, convey to us that you trust each other, and settle any disagreements you may have with each other behind closed doors.

Document expenses every day. You may think you'll remember them all later, but you won't.

You're not going crazy.

Eat, Drink, and Be Merry?

Pizza Hut bad; local cuisine good. We all know we've come here to experience something different, but sometimes we forget. Whenever you can, structure our experience in a way that encourages us to get out of our U.S. bubble and interact with the host culture on its own terms.

If we're under the age of 21, we can't legally buy alcohol or drink it at home. Many of us do so anyway, but we usually have to do it behind closed doors. When we travel to countries where we're "legal," it's often such a novelty that we might need a little help making the transition away from thinking of alcohol as something to get away with, to something to be done with respect for local culture, customs, and traditions, our peers, our bodies, and our hosts. Don't assume it will be easy. But don't assume we can't do it either—especially if you teach us the cultural significance of alcohol in the host country and any customs around its use that we might not know, treat us with respect, convey that you are putting your trust in us to be responsible, and ask for our support and help in the process.

Sometimes it can help to remind us gently that we can always come back some day on our own at much less expense, but that right now, we're on a study abroad program earning academic credit (and, in many cases, financial aid), and representing the United States, our home institutions, and our study abroad program, with all the rights, benefits, and responsibilities that this entails. In other words, it's bigger than us.

Try to foster in us a respect for the host culture's ways of doing

things—from meal hours to health care. A goal can be for us to meet each of Maslow's needs (physiological, safety, belongingness and love, esteem, and self-actualization) on the host culture's terms. When we get home, we can always decide which we want to hold on to and which we don't.

Don't waste energy on the uncontrollable.

You're not going crazy.

Communication 411

Remember our group goals and my individual goals? Pull them out from time to time, look at them with us, and ask "How are we doing on this?" One or two well-timed group or individual meetings during the program can serve as a great reality check, rekindling the group energy, and redirecting us all toward the goals we've set for ourselves. If we're not reaching our goals, it may be time to ask why. We may need to either redouble our efforts before it's too late or reassess and rewrite our goals.

Telephone bad; journal good. Phone conversations are transient. Journal entries are free and last forever. You may need to remind us from time to time. But don't nag!

It may also help to remind us at times that, although e-mail can be an invaluable tool to facilitate communication, excessive use of it to communicate with our friends at home can disengage us from the very culture we came abroad to experience—and that's *not* good!

The U.S. orientation toward authority and power is complex: We don't want to feel we've been manipulated and controlled, but we do want to know we're in a safe environment to explore and grow. So share the decisions when you can, encourage participation and growth, explain to us why we're doing what we're doing, and involve us in the process so we feel ownership of decisions that affect us. But when the bus breaks down on a deserted highway at midnight, take charge.

The above paradox applies to physical travel as well: We need you to provide direction and convey that you know where you're leading us, but it's also important to bring up the rear: Always have us board public transportation and go through points of no return, like security and immigration checkpoints, ahead of you. You don't want to already be in your seat when one of us discovers we've lost a passport and security personnel won't let us on the plane.

The U.S. orientation toward time is unique, too, and this orientation is reflected in our language. We spend it, we invest it, we manage it, we buy it, we borrow it, we save it; in fact, we treat time like a commodity. One of the worst ways to offend someone from the United States is to make us feel that our time is being wasted. Another way to quickly lose our good will is to tell us we're going to have free time and then take it away from us. Exploring this issue when it arises can provide great cultural learning opportunities, but unless you seize this teachable moment, we might never realize that the whole world wouldn't have the same reaction, and we're more likely to simply label you or the program "unorganized."

You're not going crazy.

Culture Shock Solutions

What the literature calls "culture shock"—that feeling of being out of control and having the props knocked out from underneath us—hits us all in different ways at different times, sometimes weeks or months after we arrive abroad. Even if we've lived abroad before! And even if we're in an English-speaking country! And especially when we are convinced that what we're experiencing is *not* culture shock. That's because we hardly ever recognize culture shock when it's happening to us and the last thing we want anyone to tell us is that we're just going through culture shock because that sounds demeaning.

When we get together to complain about the culture or about the program, our professors, our housing, the length of our daily commutes, or the like, it's a pretty safe bet that we're going through culture shock. The best way to inoculate us against this is to discuss this very phenomenon (i.e., what the signs of culture shock are and how we won't usually recognize it in ourselves and that everyone will need a little support from time to time) during the earliest moments of orientation, while it's all still hypothetical and not yet personalized. Then be there for us to help us recognize it when it happens to us. If you don't, as soon as the complaints become real-and especially when they are about the organization of the program or other things in which you have more ego invested—you will have lost the battle.

Making Sense of It All

Debrief, debrief, debrief! Discussion time is important throughout the program. A final meeting (or two or three) to identify what we've learned, how our attitudes or understandings have changed, and what we're going to do with it all when we go back home, is absolutely essential.

We may not recognize a lot of what you've done for us until it's too late to thank you, but don't think it's not worth it. And, okay, maybe you were going just a little crazy there in the middle, but in our hearts we know you were doing it for us. But it's all good, right?!   **IE**

JAMES L. CITRON is dean of overseas studies at Lexia International.

Editor's note: This article, while cast in the voice of students, was written by an experienced study abroad program director.

[Source: *International Educator* magazine. Published by NAFSA: Association of International Educato

If You Cross Over the Sea ...
PROGRAM LEADERSHIP FOR INTERCULTURAL DEVELOPMENT

14

John Sunnygard

A s discussed at the beginning of this book, not all short-term programs abroad enjoy the best reputation among campus faculty or with some "seasoned" education abroad professionals. Some faculty members perceive these programs as quasi-academic Bacchanalian tourist excursions. Many education abroad professionals consider them diminutive siblings of the "junior year abroad" ideal. Poorly organized programs may encourage these stereotypes. As demonstrated, on the other hand, short-term programs can be an effective means of increasing student participation in off-campus opportunities, offering rewarding faculty development opportunities, and meeting core elements of institutional "internationalization." Properly researched, planned, and directed short-term programs can very effectively fulfill many objectives. Although it uses academic programs as the primary model, this chapter seeks to provide a development-based foundation for any "international educator" leader.

For many U.S. undergraduates, a study abroad experience will be limited to three to eight weeks, usually during the summer.[1] Generally, students will be directed by a faculty member from their U.S. institution whose program was carefully scrutinized to conform to a structured set of academic guidelines. Slightly less than half of faculty directors who direct short-term programs have had some preparation for teaching off-campus programs. Faculty training is often focused on institutional policy, program recruitment, the director's responsibilities, handling university funds overseas, appropriate means of travel and accommodation, and other logistical issues.[2] A great deal of legitimate concern will be expressed for student health and safety issues, but less attention may be given to the course curriculum and the intercultural learning experience. Unfortunately in some quarters, intercultural interaction is only described as "culture shock," which, fortunately, can be overcome. Why is the program going overseas?

To design, recruit, and implement short-term programs abroad focused on cognitive and intercultural development, a three-sided model, the "Triad of Inter-

cultural Leadership in Short-Term Programs," has been created. The triad consists of a base in intercultural development theory, with rising sides of motivation factors and program design. Experience indicates that programs that use the triad model lead to more effective long-term learning experiences.

TRIAD OF INTERCULTURAL LEADERSHIP IN SHORT-TERM PROGRAMS

Whether a faculty member has elected to teach a short-term program for pedagogical or more personal reasons, the impact on the students and the faculty director will be profound and enduring. However, sheer physical presence in another culture or country does not guarantee intercultural learning. One can, for example, teach the same Shakespeare course in Stratford, Connecticut, or Stratford, Ontario, Canada, or Stratford-upon-Avon, England, with the same cognitive effect. Indeed, many English departments would demand that the material covered in a United Kingdom "study tour" be the Connecticut equivalent but with the addition of a few visits and a lecture or two by a local expert. Both courses will creatively teach objective "Culture"[3] in the high literary sense, and provide the education that the department expects. However, guided and critical observation of the British and U.S. cultures would not only enhance understanding of the essence of the Bard's work and the proximate opportunity of Stratford-upon-Avon; it would lead to students' more complete understanding of themselves and their British counterparts. Understanding subjective "culture"[4] is more likely to lead to intercultural competence. By incorporating the new environment, its culture, and the impact both have on student development and identity, the faculty director has become an effective international educator.

Successful short-term program directors understand how they themselves function within foreign cultures. Furthermore, they are aware of the interpersonal qualities that are affected by intercultural transitions and the dimensions of cultural difference. Faculty directors who have made the transition from educators to international educators teach not only for cognitive growth, but for affective intercultural development as well. By bringing a realistic understanding of potential participants' motivations and assumptions, they can more effectively recruit students and create the proper learning environment.

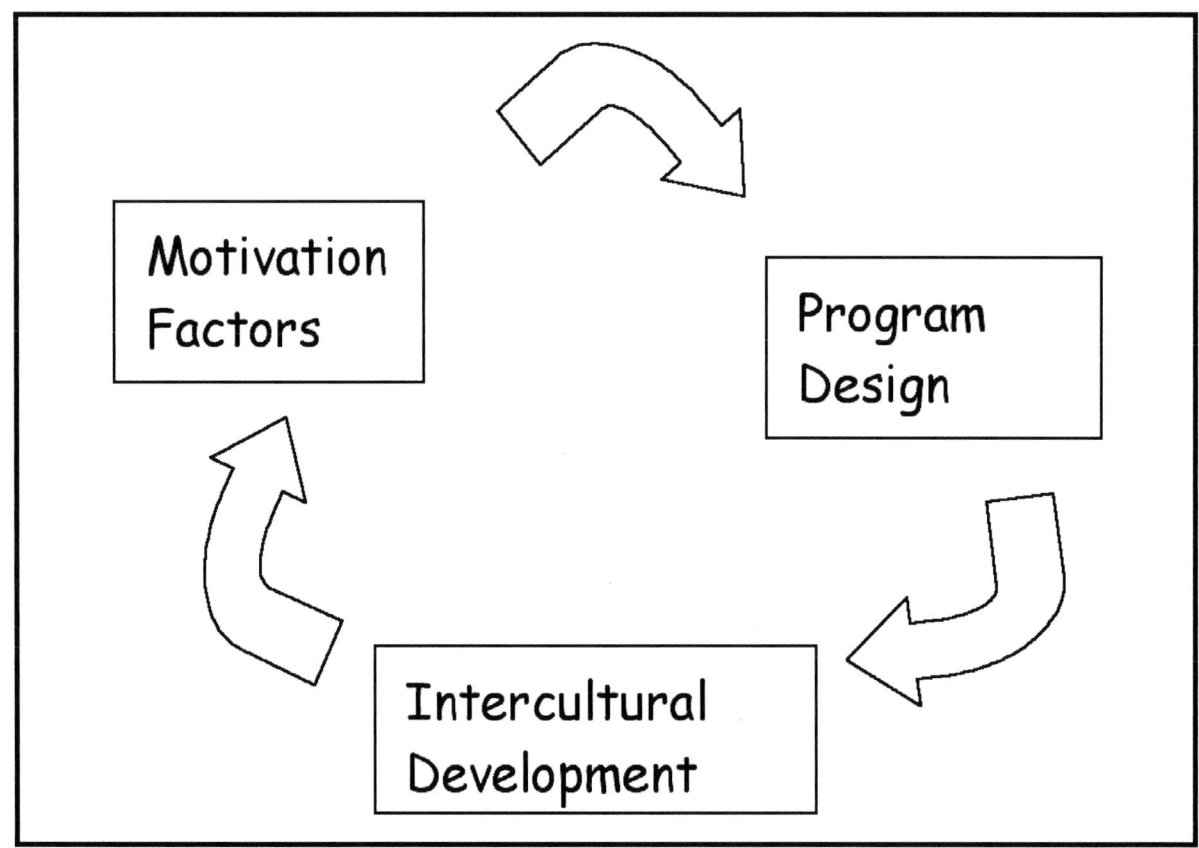

INTERCULTURAL DEVELOPMENT THEORIES

Intercultural development theories draw from several disciplines. Three seminal theory groups have been selected that derive from research in psychology, international business, and intercultural communications. This does not represent a comprehensive survey of the growing body of intercultural theory. However, based on experience, even a cursory understanding of the key points of the ideas represented here can help explain interactions and experiences, and inform planning and curricular decisions. Furthermore, presenting students with the basic ideas of intercultural interactions

and development can lead students to a more rewarding experience.

The discussion of theory will begin at a personal level, by considering four factors of how people respond in cross-cultural situations. I will then consider how a dynamic, six-dimensional model of cultural diversity informs people engaged in intercultural dealings. I will conclude by discussing Milton Bennett's "Development Model of Intercultural Sensitivity" as benchmark criteria for intercultural growth.

Each theoretical model can be viewed and applied at three levels: cognitive, interpersonal, and intrapersonal. The cognitive level—for example, the academic program—is the one most commonly approached in short-term programming. The academic program is usually the primary justification for a program, and as such warrants considerable attention. At the interpersonal level, we are concerned with relationships between people. The theories presented can help take us beyond simplistic and often misleading stereotypes of people from different cultures to informed tools for understanding and action. Students (and most faculty) returning from a successful study abroad program often declare how the experience in another culture has changed their lives and the way they view the world. Intrapersonal growth is enhanced by thoughtful planning and leadership.

When discussing a program and interpersonal interactions, examples frequently include stereotypes and generalizations with presentations of "how to." Orientation sessions may include sections on "how to get along with Moroccans," and so on. Of course, getting along with Moroccans is very important, but presenting and reinforcing cultural stereotypes does not contribute to intercultural development. Indeed, cultural stereotypes can inhibit intercultural growth.

"Know thyself." The intrapersonal dimension, or self-understanding and knowledge, is a critical part of intercultural understanding. By understanding one's own responses to uncertainty, difference, and risk, the intercultural actor can make more informed choices of behavior. The baseline, therefore, for each of these theories is self-understanding. After self-understanding, it is helpful for the faculty director to know the general and, as well as possible, the specific baselines of program participants to intercultural situations. By understanding the starting point—the baseline—the director can target areas for improvement and anticipate potential areas of difficulty. Areas for student improvement can also be creatively addressed during the planning stages.

RESPONSES TO INTERCULTURAL INTERACTIONS

Psychologists Colleen Kelley and Judith Meyers developed the "Cross-Cultural Adaptability Inventory" (CCAI) to help an individual assess her or his potential effectiveness in cross-cultural situations. "Culture shock" is a term often used to express the feelings of loneliness, frustration, alienation, and anxiety encountered after prolonged exposure to another culture. After extensive research, Kelly and Meyers identified four components of cross-cultural adaptability.

Emotional Resilience

"Emotionally resilient people like new experiences and have confidence in their ability to cope with ambiguity."[5] People often have negative emotional responses of loneliness, confusion, or frustration when they are unable to identify or understand basic cues in intercultural interactions.

Flexibility/Openness

"Open, flexible people enjoy interacting with people who think differently from themselves."[6] Open, flexible people tend to be less judgmental, more tolerant, and comfortable with those who are different from them. People who are inflexible can become distraught or disoriented by the inconsistent cues given by people different from themselves.

Perceptual Acuity

"People who are perceptually acute are attentive to verbal and nonverbal behavior, to the context of communication, and to interpersonal relations."[7] Intercultural communication involves both verbal and nonverbal communication cues that may differ significantly among cultures and lead to miscommunication or misunderstanding.

Personal Autonomy

"Personally autonomous people are not overly dependent upon cues from the environment for their sense of identity."[8] People who are highly dependent on other people and their environment for their own identity can have difficulty adjusting to new environments or people who do not issue the same comforting cues. On the other hand, people who feel alienated from their own culture's environment may feel a sense of personal exhilaration when they encounter new cues.

The CCAI offers a means of self-assessing one's response to cultural interactions based on these components. A good, honest understanding of one's own responses in the face of intercultural interactions can help one prepare for dealing with cultural situations. As students experience frustration when interacting with a new culture, these items can help the faculty director to understand and respond to the student and help provide better counseling. All involved in program development and the administrator and leadership team should be encouraged to first understand their own responses to intercultural interactions and, second, to present the components to participants. As the program progresses, one can do a status check to see how she or he is holding up.

Journal writing, or keeping an "analytical notebook" as recommended by Magistrale and Wagner[9] is an excellent vehicle for exploring one's responses to a new culture. Writing is contemplative. Writing the day's activities and one's responses and emotions to new encounters in a journal is an intellectually stimulating, emotionally soothing activity that leaves an enduring record. As discussed in Chapter 5, Designing the Academic Course: Principles and Practicalities, there is an analytical difference between an academic journal used in the evaluation process and a journal kept as a record.

DIMENSIONS OF INTERCULTURAL INTERACTIONS

Effective intercultural understanding, communication, and interaction are essential to the modern global corporation. Charles Hampden-Turner and Fons Trompenaars' recent work, *Building Cross-Cultural Competence: How to Create*

Wealth from Conflicting Values, uses the dilemma theory to explore the tension between opposing values from a group of six "universal dilemmas." The universal dilemmas, outlined below, are represented by opposing values across a continuum. Hampden-Turner and Trompenaars believe that value (or wealth) is created when an organization successfully uses the strengths of each value system to reconcile values-in-tension. In the study abroad context, educational value is created when the international educator and students recognize and reconcile the different cultural values they encounter while abroad. Hampden-Turner and Trompenaars conducted exhaustive research that identified six value-tension pairs:

For one example, most Americans subscribe to the concept of sequential time, where time is linear and a schedule is a point on the line. It is commonly accepted (except perhaps with some college students) that one adheres to the schedule or one misses the point, forever. For members

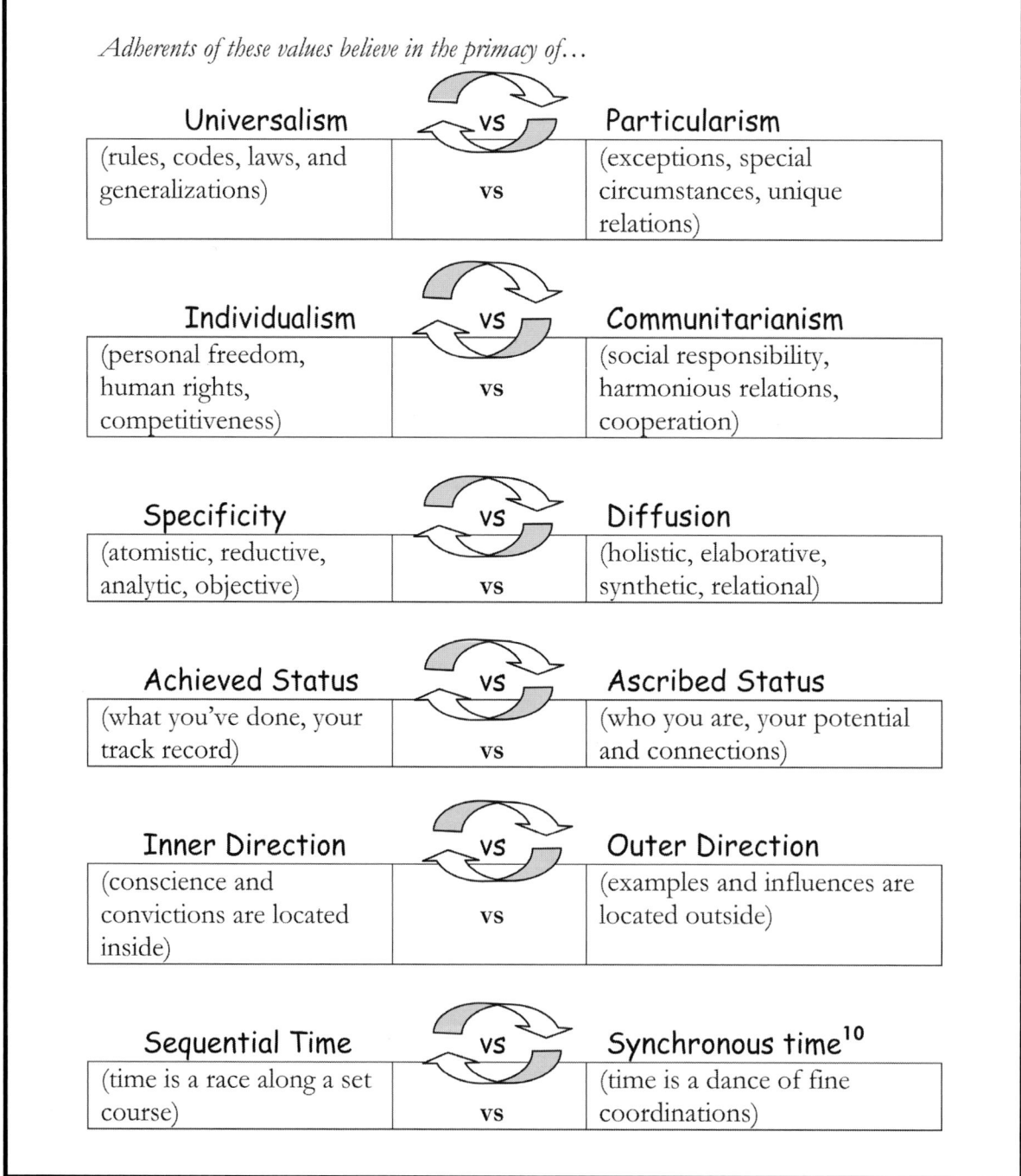

Adherents of these values believe in the primacy of...

Universalism	vs	Particularism
(rules, codes, laws, and generalizations)	vs	(exceptions, special circumstances, unique relations)

Individualism	vs	Communitarianism
(personal freedom, human rights, competitiveness)	vs	(social responsibility, harmonious relations, cooperation)

Specificity	vs	Diffusion
(atomistic, reductive, analytic, objective)	vs	(holistic, elaborative, synthetic, relational)

Achieved Status	vs	Ascribed Status
(what you've done, your track record)	vs	(who you are, your potential and connections)

Inner Direction	vs	Outer Direction
(conscience and convictions are located inside)	vs	(examples and influences are located outside)

Sequential Time	vs	Synchronous time[10]
(time is a race along a set course)	vs	(time is a dance of fine coordinations)

of other cultures time is circular; schedules are flexible because one cannot do everything at once and opportunities may arise again. To look at it another way, Americans are in a time joust. The "sequential" knight rides in a straight line and has one opportunity to hit the target, or the knight has to turn around and start again. The "synchronous" knight is on a merry-go-round, thrusting a sword at the dangling ring as he goes round. If the knight misses the ring, he may get another chance the next time around. For both knights, the actual moment of contact is critical, and it is hit or miss; how the knights arrive at the decisive moment is completely different.

For short-term programming, this model is instructive in at least two ways. First, the primary, universal sources of cultural differences and one's relationship to them are clarified. Second, by accepting that value arises from reconciling a dilemma, directors and students can see growth through experiencing a cross-cultural dilemma. When a student returns home from a program and demonstrates an increased sense of self-confidence, a greater understanding of the world, and increased tolerance for difference, it is an indication that he or she has reconciled some value dilemmas.

THE DMIS, A MODEL OF INTERCULTURAL DEVELOPMENT

Milton Bennett's "Development Model of Intercultural Sensitivity" (DMIS) provides a set of developmental benchmarks of intercultural development. The DMIS has been successfully quantified by a psychometric instrument, the Intercultural Development Inventory (IDI). Both the model and instrument have been described in detail in Chapter 12, It Changed My Life: Strategies for Assessing Student Learning. Review that chapter for further details of the model.

The DMIS has proven to be a versatile and effective means of explaining intercultural development. For the purposes of this chapter, the essential strength of the DMIS is identifying the categorical differences between ethnocentric and ethnorelative stages of intercultural development.[11] Rudyard Kipling's poem, We and They, is a beautiful illustration of some stages appropriate to this goal.

Father, Mother, and Me,
    Sister and Auntie say
All the people like us are We,
    And everyone else is They.
And They live over the sea
    While we live over the way,
But – would you believe it? – They look upon We
    As only a sort of They!
We eat pork and beef
    With cow-horn handled knives.
They who gobble Their rice off a leaf
    Are horrified out of Their lives;
While They who live up a tree,
    Feast on grubs and clay,

(Isn't it scandalous?) look upon We
    As a simply disgusting They!
We eat kitcheny food.
    We have doors that latch.
They drink milk and blood
    Under an open thatch. We have doctors to fee.
    They have wizards to pay.
And (impudent heathen!) They look upon We
    As a quite impossible They!
All good people agree,
    And all good people say,
All nice people, like us, are We
    And everyone else is They:
But if you cross over the sea,
    Instead of over the way,
You may end by (think of it) looking on We
    As only a sort of They!
        —Rudyard Kipling 1926[12]

Kipling's exploration of perceptions and interpretations of different cultures almost follows the first two stages of the DMIS: denial and defense. In the first stanza, Kipling reveals the petty suspicions between family members or neighbors with his first definition of "we" and "they." Intercultural differences are denied by simply being relegated to geography and gross characterization, "everyone else is They." The next two stanzas perfectly illustrate defense, where one culture denigrates another and also declares its cultural superiority. Kipling's challenging conclusion urges us to venture over the sea, to experience cultural difference, and suggests that as a result of this experience we can move into a culturally relativistic worldview.

Awareness of cultural differences is a laudable and realistic goal of a short-term program abroad. Acceptance of cultural difference in an ethnorelativistic sense would be an ideal. With careful program structure, and by providing guided critical analysis of cultural difference, the international educator can at least help students open the door to intercultural development. If students can begin to "look [sic] on We as only a sort of They," the program could arguably be declared an intercultural success. Students will have not only mastered the cognitive elements of the program but also gained significant intrapersonal insights.

MOTIVATION FACTORS

Why go "over the sea," instead of "over the way?" Some reasons are blatantly obvious. Paris is a beautiful city overflowing with art. London has a vibrant theater community. People speak Japanese in Kyoto. The Humboldt University has an immense library. Tanzania has bones. Australia has Bondi beach. Of course, there are many other reasons for going abroad as well. Understanding the motivating factors to study abroad can help faculty plan a more effective program. Students and faculty often have differing assumptions, expectations, and goals of a study abroad program. Refer to "Twenty Questions for Students and Faculty" at the end of this chapter to help assess student and faculty motivation factors for study abroad.

Assumptions and Expectations

There are four players in the academic study abroad chain: the teacher, the student, the university administration, and the parent. Each has its own collection of assumptions and expectations of a study abroad program. To express basic assumptions simply: the teacher assumes that the student wants to learn; the student assumes that the program will be fun; the parent assumes that the child will be cared for; the administration assumes the teacher will be responsible (and likely that the student will not).

Similarly, each player has expectations of the study abroad program. Students expect travel, but may not expect homework. Faculty expect to teach, but may not expect to referee roommate disputes. All parties may have hidden expectations not readily expressed in planning or discussion. Bring all of the expectations and assumptions to the table to avoid misrepresentation, misunderstanding, and disappointment.

MANAGING EXPECTATIONS

Before planning a program, take an inventory of the assumptions and expectations of all of the characters. Seek out common expectations. Carefully consider the differences. Which expectations will contribute to the program? Which expectations do you want to dispel? Students' expectations will be set by the information they receive prior to enrolling in the program. Expectations will be solidified during the orientations.

Carefully consider how the program is being presented by study abroad administrators, faculty directors, and past participants. For example, a European Union (EU) program that visits three cities will likely include frequent visits to EU institutions, lectures by local professors and governmental and nongovernmental officials, and research assignments. Students will also want to explore the cities and the nightlife, and other points in Europe. Which parts of the program will be used to describe the program? Which elements will be discussed to recruit students? Which elements will the program alumni present with the most enthusiasm?

A short-term program abroad is a holistic experience, not an isolated classroom experience. A successful program will achieve equilibrium among academic content, travel, and fun. A program should have a balance between classroom time and free time. Clearly, one cannot misrepresent or deny aspects of the program. Clubs and pubs are important venues for both students and faculty, and if dealt with maturely and proportionately, the right tone can be set. De-

nying the existence of nightlife, travel, and so on creates a taboo to be broken. On the other hand, placing too much emphasis on travel from a tourist's perspective or partying from an undergraduate perspective will skew student motivations in the wrong direction. Once assumptions and expectations have been established, it is extremely difficult to modify them, particularly in a short-term program abroad.

GOALS

Like assumptions and expectations, each party has different goals and objectives for the program. Faculty directors and the international office should have a clear set of goals and objectives in mind for the program. The goals should be based on practical realities, academic requirements and opportunities, faculty strengths, student interest, and most importantly, the attributes of the local environment.

Goals should be made clear to students during recruiting and with promotional materials. Program and student goals and objectives should be discussed as a part of orientations. Longer-term goals should also be discussed at orientation; for example, "What do you want to bring back from this experience that you can incorporate into your academic or professional life?" or "What do you want to bring into your personal life?"

Discussing student goals begins the learning process. Often student expectations and goals are unclear and unrefined. Many students have never had this kind of learning experience before and don't know what is possible or what to expect. By learning student goals and objectives, the program and curriculum can be better informed and incorporated for immediate program relevance.

Finally, assessing assumptions, expectations, and goals can have a significant impact on the health, safety, and security of all members. Nightclubs, mountains, urban explorations, and rural wanderings all pose their own unique risks. It is always helpful to know who wants to scale the Materhorn, who wants to party, and who plans to stay in the room. When the faculty director is aware of the student's other ambitions, she or he can help the students manage their goals with the risks involved. The director can help the students determine locally appropriate means of achieving their goals.

Program Design

Program design is discussed in great detail throughout this volume, with different nuance. This chapter is focused on incorporating intercultural learning and development into the equation. The three theories discussed present frameworks and approaches to intercultural learning. Taking stock of the different assumptions, expectations, and goals of all of the players gives a clearer picture of what needs to be satisfied by the program. Careful consideration of the assumptions, expectations, and goals informs realistic objectives for planning, recruitment, program implementation, and program follow-up.

Academic and Intercultural Learning

You are planning a short-term program abroad. You are not a travel agent. The first objective must include clear learning objectives. A balance should be drawn between academic and intercultural learning objectives. Being realistic cannot be overemphasized in program planning. Most study abroad destinations offer a lifetime of learning opportunities; a three-week program cannot possibly encounter even a fraction of the opportunities in a meaningful way.

Academic objectives should include any departmental requirements. Creativity should be used to find the right combination of classroom and nonclassroom approaches to learning. Sites provide valuable experiences for students who need to touch and feel otherwise abstract connections to the subject. However, physical sites are not the only means of connecting to a writer, scientist, or philosopher.

Invite local professors and students to lecture on the subject matter, but also to discuss the ways in which they approach the subject matter. At large, prestigious city universities that frequently receive Americans (e.g., the University of London), students are frequently too "busy" to spend time with Americans visiting for a few hours. At less renowned institutions (e.g., the University of East London), students are academically accomplished but also eager to make outside connections. Discussions with students can lead to the satisfaction of both academic and intercultural goals.

Analytical notebooks, previously mentioned, are very useful assignments. These writing assignments should be started before departure to include goals, expectations, and assumptions. Begin by asking students to look at their own cultural identities. What values do they hold? What do they enjoy doing at home? What do they expect to be different? The same? See the Authoethnography Exercise at the end of in Chapter 15.

Structure and Flexibility

Clear program goals presume a structure. However, even the most structured programs in the most structured countries will require latitude and flexibility. Showing up regularly at a classroom or a lab on the home campus is very easy. Changing classrooms, locations, relying on other lecturers, and so on, increases the level of complexity and risk for delay or error. Plan to leave and arrive early at all sites. Allow open afternoons or mornings to make up for missed time or to take advantage of unforeseen opportunities.

Faculty directors and students may encounter frustrations and anxiety from being in another culture. Plan relief opportunities, breaks, and free time. Exploration of new places and people is an invaluable part of the program.

However, students often do not know how to cope with new experiences and prefer to stay with what is comfortable and familiar. Let them know of possible opportunities and encourage them to explore. Again, write such opportunities down in the analytical notebook.

Twenty Questions for Faculty and Students

Faculty	
1.	Can you describe the top five goals for your study abroad program?
2.	How familiar are you with your destination? e.g., a map, travel book, literature, history, newspapers/magazines, values, etc....
3.	What is your worst fear about this program?
4.	Why do your students want to go on this program?
5.	Why do you want to direct this program?
6.	What is your plan for accessing emergency funds and evacuating your students?
7.	Who is responsible for helping you plan each segment of this program and carry it through?
8.	What do you think will offer the greatest challenge and what are you doing to prepare yourself for it?
9.	What has been your previous cross-cultural experience (U.S. or abroad) and how do you think it will apply to this experience?
10.	How can you keep the study abroad experience alive for students following your return?
Students	
1.	Can you describe the top five goals for you studying abroad?
2.	How does study abroad fit in with your study plans? Your long-term career objectives? Your personal objectives?
3.	What has been your previous cross-cultural experience (U.S. or abroad) and how do you think it will apply to this experience?
4.	How familiar are you with your destination? (e.g., a map, travel book, literature, history, newspapers/magazines, values, etc....
5.	Name five benefits that you expect to experience in this program?
6.	What in your life experience do you think has helped you to prepare for this program?
7.	How would you rate yourself as an international person open to diverse cultural experiences?
8.	What are your fears, if any, about studying abroad?
9.	What do you want to bring home from this program?
10.	What will you do to make the most of this opportunity abroad?

Short-Term Programs Abroad That Lead to Long-Term Development

A framework, not specific answers or prescriptions, has been presented for off-campus learning. Motivated, creative, dedicated international educators develop rewarding programs for their students and institutions. There is no prescription for intercultural learning, but exposure to new and different people and places combined with critical analysis and opportunity for reflection can lead to long-term rewards.

Endnotes

1 *Open Doors: Statistics on International Student Mobility, 2000.* Institute of International Education.

2 Unpublished research by IES, the Institute for the International Education of Students, Chicago, Illinois. August 2001.

3 Culture (uppercase), or high culture for our purposes, refers to objective culture, the objects and institutions of culture (i.e., art, literature, dance; social, economic, political, andlinguistic systems). See Patrick Quade's Chapter 12, "It Changed My Life": Strategies for Assessing Student Learning, for additional details and references.

4 culture (lowercase), or low culture for our purposes, refers to subjective culture, the learned and shared patterns of beliefs, behaviors, and values held by a group of people.

5 Kelley, Colleen and Meyers, Judith (1995). *CCAI Cross-Cultural Adaptability Inventory Manual.* Minneapolis, MN, National Computer Systems, Inc., 13.

6 Ibid. p. 14.

7 Ibid. p. 15.

8 Ibid. pp. 16–17.

9 Magistrale, Tony and Wagner, Kenneth (1995). *Writing Across Culture: An Introduction to Study Abroad and the Writing Process.* New York, Peter Lang Publishing.

10 Hampden-Turner, Charles and Trompenaars, Fons (2000). *Building Cross-Cultural Competence: How to Create Wealth from Conflicting Values.* New Haven, CT and London, UK, Yale University Press, 11.

11 Bennett, Milton J. (1993) "Towards a Developmental Model of Intercultural Sensitivity" in R. Michael Paige, ed. *Education for the Intercultural Experience.* Yarmouth, ME, Intercultural Press, Inc.

12 Kipling, Rudyard (1926) "We and They" in Storti, Craig (1990) *The Art of Crossing Cultures.* Yarmouth, ME, Intercultural Press, Inc., 91.

15

ORIENTATION AND REENTRY

Joe Kinsella, Melissa Smith-Simonet, and Kathy Tuma

PREDEPARTURE AND REENTRY SEMINARS: FRAMING A SOJOURN ABROAD FOR ACADEMIC CREDIT

Integrating Experience and Ideas

For all study abroad programs in general, but particularly for short-term study abroad programs, predeparture and reentry orientations play a critical role in making a visit to another society a valuable learning experience. Without such orientations, academic travel abroad has the potential to become superficial tourism, rather than transformative learning. As institutions develop and implement educational programs that involve students directly experiencing people and places in the world, educators need to concentrate at least as much effort on the learning that takes place on the home campus as they do on the program abroad. Limited budgets and administrative time notwithstanding, if short-term programs are to retain academic credibility, students must be able to articulate what they have learned abroad with their lives at home. Operating quality programs abroad involves operating quality programs on the home campus that support and supplement the students' experience overseas and provide them with the tools of analysis that help them turn those experiences into learning.

The notion that students can learn anything by traveling to another place is grounded in the pedagogy of experiential learning. These concepts are described in Chapter 5: Designing the Academic Course: Principles and Practicalities. Structured around this experiential pedagogy, the orientation and reentry program described here is designed to help students integrate cognitive or "book" learning (i.e., "facts," ideas, and the reasoning involved in understanding them) and affective ("common sense" and value-laden feelings that shape behavior) aspects of learning. As a part of learning that is both cognitive and affective, this approach attempts to frame an experience abroad with ideas and concepts that students can actively engage with local people and places abroad. Using guided reflections about those experiences before and during travel abroad as well as after returning to the home

campus empowers students to not only grasp firsthand empirical knowledge about their hosts, but helps them transform that knowledge into transformative learning. By integrating a program abroad with predeparture and reentry seminars that highlight the interaction between cognitive and affective learning, we have found that students have more enriching learning experiences in which they are able to connect what they learn in the classroom with what they observe directly in the field. In addition, faculty are more satisfied with their students' interaction and the learning they demonstrate as a result.

The short-term challenge

Short-term programs (as has been said in earlier chapters) have often been regarded by study abroad practitioners as at best an easy way out of a term-long commitment on the part of students, and at worst a kind of superficial academic tourism that reinforces stereotypes and misunderstandings of "the Other." This is why it is critical that international educators carefully consider their academic and programmatic goals as they develop these types of international programs. [1,2]

A great deal of research on the effects of study abroad indicates that there is a strong correlation between the length of time actually spent abroad and the degree of impact on students' cross-cultural competence and understanding.[3] Although some recent research challenges this premise, almost any international educator will agree that there is no substitute for a term (or longer) immersion experience for broadening students' worldviews and their perceptions of themselves as transnational actors on "global" stages.

But as students of our institutions become more diverse, with the "typical" student as likely to have a full-time job, a child, and family commitments as she is to be 18 years old and single, international educators must explore alternatives to the traditional term or year abroad to facilitate an intellectually and personally transformative international experience for a more inclusive array of students. For a student who must support a family or work to stay in school, a short-term program is often the only option available. Therefore, it is in the interest of a diverse student body and educational access to explore how we can make short-term experiences abroad meaningful educational experiences that are intellectually and curricularly valued.

Sikkema and Niyekawa have presented a useful model for engaging students on campus before and after traveling abroad in order to "become a cross-culturally flexible person."[4] Their approach emphasizes the development of particular skills and behaviors that are necessary in cross-cultural communication and adaptation and is useful in structuring the affective aspects of learning that I propose here. But their design for cross-cultural learning assumes that while in the field students will be doing something that will engage them with local people and institutions. While providing an excellent conceptual outline for defining and teaching cross-cultural skills and understanding, their model glosses over cultural specificity in favor of an approach that treats "culture" as a generic entity. This nonspecific approach to societies leaves out any indication of what students would actually encounter on a day-to-day basis while visiting another place; on short-term programs in particular this cannot be left to chance.

What, then, is to be done with short-term programs? Is it possible to learn something about society, self, or "culture" during a brief visit to another place? Building short-term programs around central ideas and issues in the host society as a course that focuses on a single topic, and provides students with the tools necessary to explore that topic, lends a sense of purpose to the broader goals of nurturing cross-cultural skills of adaptation and communication.

International educators must pay careful attention to the wide range of personal and intellectual needs of their students throughout the three phases of the program—preparation, field experience, and reentry—from the moment a student considers the possibility of participating in a study abroad program through the in-field learning abroad, and long after their return to their home institution. A well-planned and executed predeparture and reentry program ultimately makes short-term experiences abroad more meaningful personally and intellectually to the students who take part in them.

The approach we use at DePaul University in Chicago is straightforward: we start by focusing on a particular academic theme or disciplinary perspective during a predeparture seminar. These seminars introduce students to a concept, issue, or cultural phenomenon that is of interest to the faculty and pertinent in the host society. These predeparture lectures and discussions expose students to relevant research methods or modes of critical thinking (visual sociology to explore urban geography, or theatre criticism and reader-response theory as an entrée into understanding cultural diversity, for example) that facilitate and foster ideas about the overall program theme. This can be done through either a series of meetings, and/or assigned readings with a single reflection paper or, minimally, guided discussions. If time is tight, utilizing Web technologies such as Blackboard or other online instructional tools can help routinize these discussions while you encourage students to explore ideas on their own. At DePaul, in addition to these discussions and readings students are required to maintain a daily journal from the day they are admitted to the program. This predeparture journal gets students to focus their preparation on questions they have about the host society and helps them formulate early observations and intellectual questions related to the program's academic content. This journal also provides a space for students to reflect on their individual goals (personal and academic) while they practice reflective writing that will prepare them to record their thoughts and experiences while abroad.

Students are then taken abroad where they continue their exploration of these ideas and concepts while meeting and interacting with local people. Throughout their time in the field students are required to maintain their journals, in which they are asked to reflect on their daily activities and integrate their reflections with the program theme and content. In several programs at DePaul, a series of journal prompts are used to evoke reflection and social action as part of a service project. Students are lectured to by both local guests and the accompanying faculty, and provided with group discussion time to process their feelings, thoughts, and experiences in the field. Time in the field on a short-term program is critical and must be efficiently used. However, faculty should be mindful not to over-program their students during travel, and make sure to leave time for individual reflection and exploration.

After returning home, a series of structured group discussions and presentations provides students the chance to process and digest what they have seen and done abroad, and serves as a kind of capstone for students' international learning experiences. After a short-term program, this reentry seminar is particularly useful for faculty to help students integrate their new knowledge and cross-cultural awareness with their lives at home and to assess their students' learning through sustained post-travel contact.

These predeparture and reentry seminars should be part of the academic credit granted for a short-term program, and students' grades should be contingent on successful participation and completion of assignments before, during, and after the time spent abroad.

Creating the Frame

The remainder of this chapter will detail a "best practices" approach for designing predeparture and reentry classroom seminars to frame in-field experiences during short-term programs abroad. These recommendations are based on 18 years of experience working in the study abroad profession, running programs at DePaul University in Chicago in which the in-field component lasts between two weeks to three months (a single quarter). In addition, my anthropological work around ethnographic methodology and phenomenology and development of my own ethnographic research projects in Zimbabwe and Uganda have reinforced my conviction that field-based methodological training is a powerful tool in preparing students to be astute observers while engaging people in another society. Examples will be drawn from a number of short-term programs operated at DePaul, in particular "Amsterdam, Rotterdam, Brussels and Prague: Comparative Perspectives in Urban Development" and "Modern British Theatre: Text, Performance, Gender, and Criticism." These two programs typify the best of short-term programs at DePaul. With an institutional commitment to providing economic access to education and serving nontraditional student populations, DePaul has been an excellent environment in which to develop these types of programs.

What follows is neither a comprehensive nor exhaustive list, but highlights what I believe to be the potential strengths of short-term programs. Predeparture and reentry seminars are an important mechanism to assuage the inadequacies of the short-term program format vis-à-vis term- and yearlong programs. At the root of this argument is the supposition that short-term study programs cannot and should not have the same learning goals and objectives as longer programs, with broad objectives to build cross-cultural awareness and skills. Rather, short-term programs must be conceived of as focused learning experiences that are facilitated and orchestrated by faculty dealing with limited topics within the target society.

This is not to suggest that general cross-cultural skills of adaptation, and/or culture-specific skills (such as language learning, personal flexibility, appreciation for differences, etc.) are not learnable in a short-term program format. To be academically honest to our students, however, educators involved with short-term programs must acknowledge that the same depth and kind of learning possible in a term- or year-long program is less possible through a short visit to another society. The strength of any short-term program, therefore, lies in the ability of educators to effectively link doing and reflecting, experiencing and comprehending within a short timeframe. This is the foundation of experiential learning.

The learning that takes place in any study abroad program should be considered a process that extends from predeparture preparations to readjustment processes back home. The time actually spent abroad is only a part of the whole learning experience. In *NAFSA's Guide to Education Abroad for Advisers and Administrators*, *Second Edition*, Hoffa, Pearson, et al. speak of a "three-phase, inclusive learning process" that prepares students personally and practically for a term or longer immersion experience abroad while motivating them to "learn more about the host culture … and become familiar with the process of cross-cultural adaptation."[5] Their "culture-general" approach is an excellent way to help students understand cross-cultural perspectives, and develop skills of cross-cultural adaptation and flexibility.

By definition, however, short-term programs do not enjoy the luxury of time for students to really experience cross-cultural adaptation in a profoundly personal way. Therefore, short-term programs must have a clear focus on culture-specific preparation and training. Again, the broad goals of cross-cultural adaptation must be modified on a short-term program and give way to more focused study about the host society and particular issues within that society. While a student living abroad for a year, for example, can eventually learn about interpersonal relationships and particular cultural practices through sustained and repeated interaction, these skills of cross-cultural communication and understanding take time to develop. In a short-term format, therefore, it is necessary for faculty to actively focus the attention of their students on a particular set of ideas that are pertinent to the host society, and help them develop a set of tools by which they can systematically explore those ideas in the field. Ideally, this will take place during predeparture seminars, run as regular on-campus class meetings for an abbreviated period of time prior to departure (at DePaul we recommend that predeparture and reentry contact total five to eight hours for each course unit offered for credit). The key is to communicate to students the same expectations regarding attendance and participation in these on-campus meetings as would be demanded in a "regular" on-campus course.

A Word on Experiential Learning and Anthropology

The concept of experiential learning is often employed to describe and legitimate study abroad programs. Working from another perspective, however, it is useful to examine the components of what is considered to be the process of learning from experience in order to structure an entire study abroad program, from predeparture through reentry. David Kolb's circular process of experiential learning that involves a dialectical relationship between concrete experiences and abstract concepts, reflection and experimentation, is an excellent conceptual model around which to structure program activities and goals (see Figure 1). According to Kolb, "experiential learning can be described as a four-stage cycle involving four adaptive learning modes - concrete experience, reflective observation, abstract conceptualization, and active experimentation."[6]

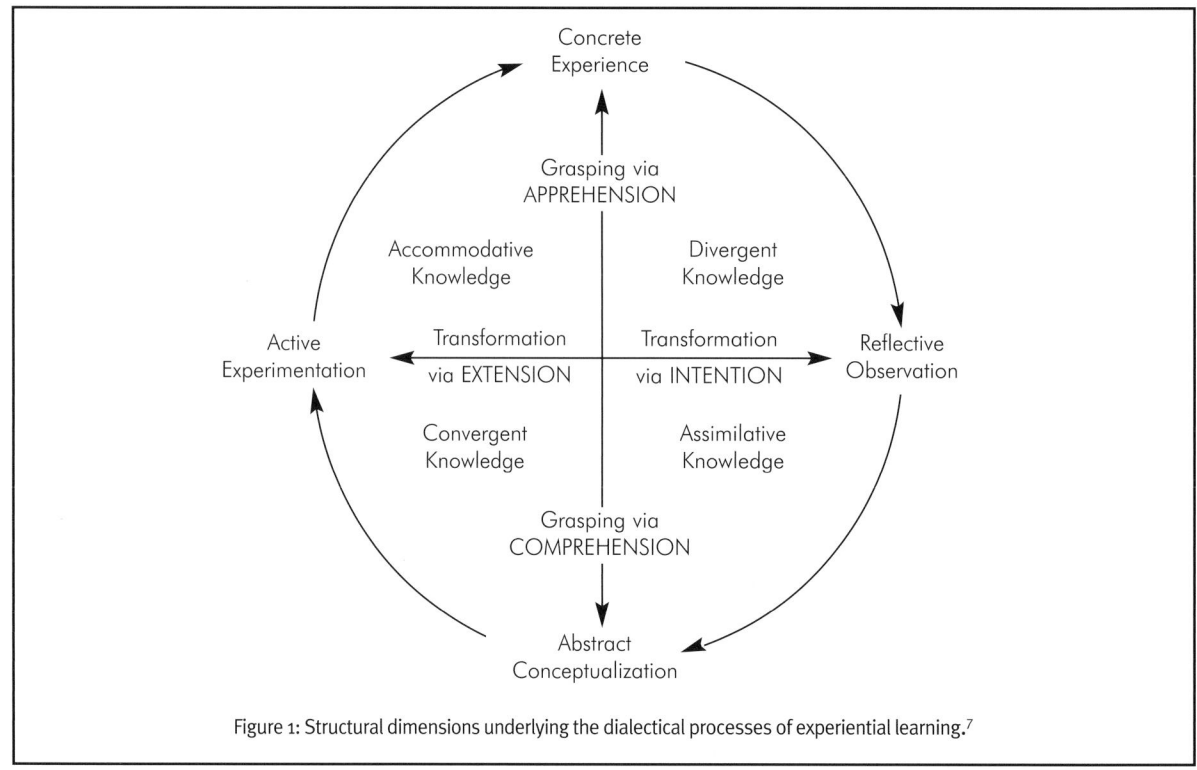

Figure 1: Structural dimensions underlying the dialectical processes of experiential learning.[7]

In short-term programs, students must be taken through this cycle repeatedly in a guided manner so that they will be able to apprehend the differences they encounter, and transform those brief encounters into concepts against which they can compare the concepts presented by faculty in readings and lectures.

From an anthropological perspective, this cyclical process can be compared to the ethnographic methodology known as participant-observation, in which the researcher establishes routine interactions with local people around some task or project (concrete experiences) in order to participate in the daily lives of a group of people. Engaged in these ongoing activities while continually reflecting on experiences and interactions with people in the form of field notes, participant-observation is a holistic approach to understanding abstract concepts about a particular group, which then shapes further interaction and inquiry. This grounded approach to research has been found to provide researchers with both intuitive and intellectual grasps of the cultural practices of groups of people, and is the cornerstone of ethnographic knowledge. As an anthropologist, therefore, it is tempting to suggest that we should create apprentice ethnographers of all study abroad students as a way to prepare them for living abroad (see Autoenthography assignment at end of this chapter). In the case of short-term programs, however, close faculty participation in the theoretical and methodological preparation of students is critically important to assist them in managing the cognitive aspects of learning in such a condensed format while apprehending the new (and emerging) world around them.

Kolb's model of experiential learning is made up of a "four-stage cycle involving four adaptive learning modes... learning is the result of the interaction, conflict, and resolution of these different learning modes."[8] In Kolb's model, which is grounded in the work of Jean Piaget, learning necessitates the apprehension and comprehension of particular experiences to be transformed through some sort of action, either mental or physical, on the part of the learner.

The key to understanding Kolb's model of experiential learning, therefore, is in the relationship and tensions between what he identifies as the "prehension" and "transformation" dimensions of these learning modes, represented by the cross axes in Figure 1. These two dimensions of learning, that each have dialectically opposed adaptive tendencies toward the world, are best understood as the ways in which we "grasp" at understanding (prehension consisting of experiences and ideas) and what we subsequently do once we have grasped the meanings of those experiences and ideas (transformation consisting of reflection and experimentation). This model is particularly helpful when organizing predeparture and reentry seminars as a way to structure the relationships between the experiences students have and the ideas they evoke, and how those experiences and ideas are transformed into knowledge through reflection and experimentation.

As role models of cross-cultural adaptation, faculty directors must also understand how their own skills and appreciation for diversity are a significant part of affective aspects of an international learning experience. While directing students' attention to the opportunities for intense cross-cultural learning during a sojourn abroad, faculty directors should be aware of how their own behavior is perceived and modeled by their students. In this way the faculty directors of short-term programs must be prepared to serve not only as sources of factual information and theoretical orientation for students, but must also be able to model the skills necessary to function in a foreign milieu—they must be good examples of cross-cultural adaptability and sensitivity. It is the job of the study abroad professional, therefore, to ensure that faculty understand their expanded educational role in undertaking programs of this sort and to help them explore pedagogical means through which to integrate the cognitive and affective aspects of learning.

Seminar Format

The ideal format for a short-term program abroad involves a series of weekly seminars that run three to five weeks during the term immediately before, and three to five weeks immediately after travel. Whether the travel portion of the program is developed and administered by home institution faculty or the international office, or is a predesigned course working with a program provider with local faculty abroad serving as instructors, the bottom line is that students participating in a short-term program must be given time to clarify academic and personal goals prior to departure. This can be done by focusing their attention on a narrow set of concepts related to the site. If you are a lone administrator sending students on programs without faculty from your institution you should consider having students sign up for independent study courses with appropriate faculty who can orient them to specific ideas and facts relevant to the

host society prior to departure. Developing a list of courses relevant to study abroad programs being offered is a great way to help faculty fill their courses and help students make connections with faculty working in their areas of interest. The absolute minimum recommended is to give students an ongoing journal assignment that requires them to set intellectual and personal goals and engage in an ongoing process of reflecting on those goals while abroad (see Study Abroad Program In-field Journal Reflection Assignment at the end of this chapter).

Ideally, predeparture and reentry meetings are structured as seminars. The content of these meetings should be a blend of lecture and discussion about assigned readings, and delivery of factual "practical" information. Reading assignments should introduce students to an aspect of the place to be visited, as well as a methodological approach that is to be employed while abroad.

As part of their methodological preparation students should also be required to maintain a journal throughout the entire period. Reflection on discussions and personal insights should be recorded in this journal that students use to generate journal summaries for class each week. These summaries are based on guiding questions or prompts offered by the instructor, designed to get students into communities and places abroad while thinking about the course focus (see Study Abroad Program In-field Journal Reflection Assignment at the end of this chapter).

In designing predeparture and reentry seminars, you should also consider utilizing experiential techniques to acquaint students with the affective aspects of cross-cultural learning. Information-based techniques should be balanced with an experiential approach in order to reinforce for students the holistic nature of the educational experience abroad, and to acquaint them with the ongoing process of reflection about their experiences. Excellent ideas for in-class experiential techniques can be found in publications from Intercultural Press.

Seminar Design: Focus, Prepare, Integrate

Because the time spent abroad on a short-term program is brief, and therefore contact with local people and social institutions can be fairly cursory, the integration of a particular disciplinary exploration of the places and people to be visited (such as urban growth, poverty, or artistic expression, for example), along with "practical" information about travel, safety, and program logistics before departure is absolutely necessary. This section will give you some guidelines for developing predeparture and reentry seminars and materials.

Clearly there can be as many models for these activities as there are educators who design them, but there are important issues that should be addressed during some sort of on-campus programming that is to complement a brief experience abroad. First and foremost of these issues is the need for faculty involved to focus student attention on the concepts and ideas to be explored before they depart. As topical explorations of specific issues in specific locations, predeparture and reentry seminars provide conceptual orientation for students throughout the three phases of a study abroad program. Teaching students about appropriate methodological approaches gives them tools needed to systematically explore these concepts. By integrating theoretical and methodological concepts, the predeparture and reentry seminars are designed to give students focused trajectories on which to briefly explore the cultural practices and social issues of people from another place while simultaneously giving them some activity or routine through which to apprehend themselves as socially and culturally positioned actors.

As a frame for their experience abroad, pre- and post-travel meetings should:

1. Focus students' attention on a particular set of ideas or concepts related to the places to be visited, and academic and personal expectations on obtainable goals in light of the particular program. This preparation should in some way build students' awareness of themselves as part of particular cultural traditions and used as a springboard toward deeper cross-cultural understanding or global comprehension; toward cultural relativism.

2. Prepare them logistically for their program abroad by providing "practical" information (packing, money, safety, etc.).

3. Help them to integrate their international experience into their personal and academic lives back on campus after their return. In terms of personal internalization, the reentry seminar should provide a forum in which students are encouraged to reflect on observations, interactions, and personal changes since returning home. Academic integration suggests a conceptual value of study abroad toward institutional learning goals and curricula. Students should also be afforded the opportunity to demonstrate knowledge they have gained and helped to articulate how they see this knowledge beneficial to their academic, professional, and personal life.

If institutional structures and resources permit, encouraging faculty to develop short-term programs in pairs allows for the possibility of a theoretical/methodological approach in which one faculty focuses on a theoretical topic (urban growth in Europe or identity in British theatre, for example) and the other offers a disciplinary approach to field methodologies (visual sociology or literary critique, for example). For revenue-conscious deans, it is important to emphasize that this model generates two courses worth of tuition revenue, and that having two faculty members participating in a single program goes a long way in limiting liability and ensuring safety in the event of a crisis.

Seminar: Theoretical Focus, Methodological Practice, and Cultural Awareness

Most short-term programs cannot give students the same kind of immersion experience that term- or year-long programs can. Students need to be told this up front. From this frank discussion should come an outline of the academic and cross-cultural goals of the program, and students should be required to articulate reasonable personal and academic expectations that are in tune with their interests and skills and match the broad goals of the courses.

Theoretical Focus

Academic goals must be precise examinations of particular topics related to the area of travel. As I suggested earlier, "exploring culture" is not an appropriate academic goal, as it provides little to no focus on academic content (what, after all is culture, and how does one go about exploring it?). Faculty developing short-term programs should be encouraged to utilize the field site as a "text" through which they will explore a particular research problem or sociocultural, physical, or historical phenomenon (whatever their discipline). This is the aspect of the seminar that most resembles a "typical" course. This theoretical or topical exploration should be broad enough to help students develop their specific interests within the same conceptual paradigm.

Methodological Practice

Predeparture meetings should also focus on developing field research projects that deal with the topic(s) at hand while encouraging students to meet people and explore the places visited. Again, it is important to be clear with students that their short-term experience abroad necessitates a very focused and intensive sojourn that pretty much has them following the lead of their faculty director(s). Helping students understand methodology will support this. It will also help them develop mechanisms through which they can potentially have meaningful interaction with their hosts.

In a number of short-term programs operated at DePaul, paired teams of faculty offer theoretical and methodological foci around which students are encouraged to build their specific research/program project. In the program "Amsterdam, Rotterdam, Brussels and Prague: Comparative Perspectives in Urban Development," for example, students are asked to explore "the particular urban forms exemplified by the cities of Amsterdam, Rotterdam, Brussels, and Prague, and the social and economic forces that have shaped these European cities over time..." Through the lens of a camera, students are guided through an exploration of the history and urban development of these cities while they continually reflect on their own position within social urban geographies and class structures. Two professors whose areas of interest are in human geography and urban planning and renewal oversee the in-field portion of the program. As a method for exploring various aspects of the urban spaces to be visited they have their students focus on "visual/visible signs and symbols of contemporary issues of urban development" in order to explore "comparative central city redevelopment, gentrification, changing social and cultural urban geography...through photography and other methods and forms of fieldwork..." As an easily understood method for "capturing experiences" (or collecting data), photography provides an outstanding memory stimulus through which students can continually reflect on their experiences at different points in time.

Journals are also maintained as a mechanism to hone students' skills at reflective observation and abstract conceptualization in relation to the ideas and theories being explored. In addition, the journal can facilitate reflection about students' personal and academic goals, cultural values, and the emerging global society as they engage in a cross-cultural immersion experience abroad. The journal is a way to help students "discover" their own emerging cultural identity in relation to, and as part of crisscrossing networks of global media, social organizations, and human movement. This discovery of self-knowledge will come about through guided and continuous reflective observation and journaling within the context of students' preparation for, participation in, and return from a study abroad experience. During the London Theatre program, in which students spend three weeks in London viewing plays and reflecting on how cultural identity is enacted both on stage and in the audience, students are required to maintain a particularly interesting group journal online. This group journal is the basis upon which further discussions and lectures are grounded. These group journals are also a good way to capture data and ideas for further group work after returning to the United States.

Cultural Awareness: Toward Cultural Relativism

To maintain focus on the place to be visited, a "culture-specific" approach should be employed to expose students to some of the cross-cultural issues and challenges they might face in a particular location. As stated earlier, broader cross-cultural goals of a study abroad program are certainly appropriate goals of short-term programs, but because of the brevity of the visit, educators must pay careful attention to 1) the deconstruction (and/or inadvertent perpetuation) of sociocultural and nationalistic stereotypes within the context of the course and travel, and 2) the modeling of skills necessary to successfully operate in diverse cultural and social environments. An understanding of the anthropological concept of cultural relativism will assist in breaking down these stereotypes, but faculty directors must also serve as models for students, sharing their expertise and experiences of functioning in the target society and helping students understand through real-life situations—at restaurants, hotels, etc.—what it means to work in an international milieu. This is an aspect of the short-term program that must be attended to with thought and careful consideration. Faculty

must be able and willing to model skills in cross-cultural adaptation and should speak openly with students about how they can nurture these skills within themselves.

Opposed to "culture" conceived of as a normative set of rules, cultural relativism is a conceptual stance employed by anthropologists in the field that demands them, when observing any sort of behavior or cultural practice, to try to understand those practices from the point of view of the people doing them. When observing new or unusual practices of people outside our own societies, cultural relativism requires us to suspend any kind of judgment about those practices until we can better understand the motivations and cultural assumptions of the actors. The concept of cultural relativism is rooted in Franz Boas' heavily empirical research into the production of language in Baffinland and British Columbia. Boas, who worked at the turn of the twentieth century with Native North Americans, argued that cultural phenomena are "historically conditioned and transmitted by the learning process." He pointed out that these cultural phenomena are themselves, "determinants of our very perceptions of the external world."[9] In other words, as they began to grapple with the developing concept of "culture," anthropologists in the late nineteenth and twentieth centuries came face-to-face with human variability through reports of diverse human practices and belief systems they were collecting from around the world.

This variability, as turn-of-the-century anthropological theory suggested, was supposedly the result of different stages of cultural evolution that groups of people had or had not apparently achieved; European culture, from this perspective, was imagined to be the highest form of culture. Boas and his students encountered cultural practices that challenged this ethnocentric view. Their "comparative perspective" disrupted the "grand scheme" of cultural evolution and eventually replaced anthropological theories based on "cultural stages of savagery, barbarism, and civilization" with an understanding of the "multiplicity of cultures" that operated through different histories, beliefs, and cultural practices. The ethnocentrism of sociocultural evolution, which conflated the ways in which biology and society work, was mitigated in anthropological thinking through an engagement with cultural relativism that required investigators to consciously suspend their culturally based (and biased) judgments about a particular practice in order to first attempt to understand the practice from the point of the participants.

This position of cultural relativism is critical to apprehending the belief systems and cultural practices of people anywhere. While I am careful to insist that as an academic position, it does not suggest a neutrality on ethical judgments, or some sort of imagined objectivity when it comes to human injustice or suffering. Rather I insist that cultural relativity needs to be understood as a temporary suspension of the students' moral judgments long enough to ask the question and seriously seek an answer to the question "why would a group of people think a particular practice is a good thing to do?"

Reentry Seminar: Internalization, Integration, and Demonstration of Knowledge

The post-field program enables the students to re-interpret, integrate, and formulate their learning into a whole experience. It enables them to stand back and see the structure or connectedness of things. It also helps them avoid closure at a time when they are still uncertain about the new concepts and consciousness they have been exploring within themselves. It is important for the students to keep the learning alive and moving; they cannot, as happens too frequently with a course, finish and say, "Well, that was an interesting experience." Learning has just begun and should not be filed away and regarded as complete. [10]

The reentry seminar is probably the most important phase in a study abroad program for sustained learning to be established, it is also the phase that is most often neglected. This may have to do with a persistent concept of learning in the United States that envisions learning as a one-way process, in which data is simply transmitted to an individual for storage. Paulo Freire refers to this one-way notion of education as the "banking account concept" in which information is simply deposited into the head of the learner by a putatively knowledgeable teacher.[11] According to experiential pedagogy, however, learning is ongoing dialectic exchanges between experiences and concepts and observation and experimentation in which the experimentation with newfound knowledge is just as important for the learner as are the "factual" concepts presented by the teachers and texts. The reentry seminar, therefore, is an excellent time for faculty and students to collaboratively reflect on the experiences they have shared abroad, and to come up with new insights about themselves and the societies in which they have been given the opportunity to operate.

The reentry seminar should also help students recognize the personal growth they have undergone as a result of the program abroad. While still in the field, students should be encouraged to begin reflecting on the changes that have taken place within their own concepts of themselves and prepare for the potential of "reverse culture shock" in which they could feel alienated from family and friends. While reverse culture shock is not as major an issue with short-term programs, students often indicate that they have formed new friendships with students on their program and feel a sense of loss when they realize that they have experienced

an important, life-changing event without their friends and family from before. The phenomenon of being asked "How it was," followed by glossy stares as they begin to tell a story from abroad is a common one, and one that puts strains on relationships at home. Students should be prepared for the personal challenges their experience abroad can cause.

For the success of a learning experience to be fully realized, from an experiential perspective, there must be a structured means through which students bring the experience "home" and apply what they have learned to their everyday lives. Like a collection of photos placed in a picture book and left on the shelf to collect dust, the collection of experiences from abroad must not be allowed to collect dust in the minds of learners. On the contrary, for learning to occur, the emotional and cognitive growth must be internalized personally and integrated intellectually. To do this, some sort of outlet for creative intellectual development and expression must be provided.

At DePaul a number of models are emerging for this reentry seminar. One involves several follow-up meetings of the group during the term immediately after their return. Like the seminars, these are regular course meetings in which students are guided through some form of analysis of their experiences and the "data" they collected while in the field. Another has students preparing presentations of their work abroad for symposia, conferences, and in the case of graduate programs, sometimes for publication. A third emerging model provides support for students to follow an experience abroad with a service project in a local community connected in some way to their study abroad hosts. For example, many students who participate in our programs to El Salvador or Nogales, Mexico, will begin working with El Salvadorian communities in Chicago or organizations focused on immigrant issues.

Personal Internalization

The process of reentry is significantly more acute after a term-long stay abroad; this should not suggest, however, that attention to the personal transformation on a short-term program can be omitted because the visit to another society has been shorter. Students on any length program should be encouraged to reflect on the changes they have gone through, and the "new" person they now imagine themselves to be. Very often the learning, if everything goes well, on a short-term program can be just as transformative as on term-long programs. A key to ensuring this is a sustained and structured series of interactions after returning to the home campus.

This post-travel process of internalization "enables the students to re-interpret, integrate and formulate their learning into a whole experience" within the context of their home culture.[12] During the reentry phase, the faculty directors at DePaul are encouraged to minimally engage in a process of reflection and dialogue with their students for at least the term following their return. "Behavior that is not sustained by peers, by society, or by a respected authority seldom becomes permanent in a human life."[13] This sustained contact and reflection will both strengthen the personal and intellectual bonds established abroad, and will be an active demonstration—another experience, if you will—of the learning that they have engaged. In this sense, the role of the faculty director truly does become that of a role model.

All students participating in programs at DePaul are required to complete a journal summary (see Study Abroad Program In-field Journal Reflection Assignment at the end of this chapter) in which cross-cultural learning goals are evaluated against Kelly and Meyers' *Cross-Cultural Adaptability Inventory* (1995). I have found this inventory to be a useful tool that helps measure critical skills of adaptation and observation. Students are not given a grade for this journal summary, but are invited to discuss (either in person or as part of regular returnee group meetings) their reflections and continued goals in the area of cross-cultural communication. Faculty leading short-term programs abroad are encouraged to adapt this journal assignment to their courses, and integrate it with their content-based courses.

Academic Integration and the Demonstration of Knowledge

Academic integration is another area of reentry that is often given short attention by teachers and administrators of study abroad programs. Students returning from any experience abroad seek out ways to make their newly found international identity and ideas meaningful within the context of their academic degree. It is important for educators involved to help students develop an integrated understanding of their international experiences as a part of their academic career. Part of this simply involves students discussing their experiences in other classes and venues on campus.

The desire to demonstrate what one has learned abroad is a natural, but very often frustrating part of returning from a study abroad experience. This is the point at which students are compelled to engage in a level of conversation in which they had not previously been accustomed to participate. Students returning from an experience abroad are constantly asked to summarize their experiences in one or two sentences by friends, family, and academics alike. The unprepared students are always taken by surprise when, on reflection, they are unable to perform this sort of summary. If they attempt to enter into a more substantive explanation of their experiences, they are often met with blank stares or simply cut off by an impatient audience. What quickly becomes apparent to the returned study abroad student is that their experience is to a great extent somewhat incomprehensible to people who have not shared similar experiences.

In order for overseas learning to be an experience of growth, learners must be able to use their experiences abroad to enhance future experiences in their lives. First, however, they must develop skills at articulating their experience. A final research project or other creative expression of what they have learned serves as a means through which students can focus their life-altering experience toward a specific area of interest. The research project also serves as a means through which students can potentially develop their experience into further research, or simply gain a more in-depth understanding of a particular aspect of the people and places visited.

In addition to writing, students should be given the opportunity to talk to other students about their experience. Hiring students as assistants and/or inviting them to speak at recruitment and predeparture seminars are excellent means through which the student can feel a tangible sense of accomplishment, as well as assist the study abroad office in the task of encouraging other students to apply. Follow-up activities, such as academic presentations, group projects, and service learning provide outstanding opportunities for students to develop deeper meanings for their experiences abroad. By providing opportunities for students to engage their communities in an ongoing dialogue, we help our students continue learning, bringing it home to engage their society and their minds in ongoing dialogues. This reentry seminar, therefore, is a powerful tool in perpetuating the learning that began long before the plane left the runway.

As educators committed to promoting and developing quality programs abroad, we must be extraordinarily conscious of the ways in which students are able to build their international learning into their lives as emerging actors on global stages. Hopefully the suggestions found here will promote an ongoing conversation as to how best to do this.

GENERAL ORIENTATION

Short-term programs abroad do not afford students the luxury of time to understand the lay of the land in their host countries. To enable students to make the most of the on-site time they do have, they need to have as much advance preparation as possible.

Of course, much of what students learn in the predeparture orientation meetings and handbooks will not mean much to them until they are on site. But if you have provided sufficient academic, logistical, and cultural information, it will make sense to them once they have landed.

In addition to the expected benefit of increased student preparedness, a solid orientation program can also help to reduce institutional liability. If it can be documented that Student A was advised against Behavior B, your institution will be in a better position in any legal situation.

Orientation Meetings

Make every effort to have at least one orientation meeting with the students. If you are administering a number of programs, it makes the best use of time to have a single general information meeting for participants in all programs, facilitated by the international office. Individual group meetings led by the faculty director can follow this general meeting. In fact, having the small group meetings immediately following the general session can help to ensure that students will attend. Students may not be missed in a meeting of 300 participants, but it will certainly be obvious if they do not attend the meeting of their group of 15.

SAMPLE AGENDA FOR A GENERAL STUDENT ORIENTATION MEETING	
7:00	Welcome by director of international office
7:05	Comments from former student participant: what to expect
7:15	General safety presentation by campus security director
7:30	Group dynamics presentation by experienced faculty
7:45	Psychological issues presentation by counseling center staff
8:00	College policies abroad presentation by dean of students
8:15	Cross-cultural issues presentation by experienced faculty leader
8:30	Health issues presentation by college physician
8:45	International studies office staff: reminders and Q&A
9:00	Small group meetings: faculty director and students

Orientation Handbooks

Written information needs to be given to students, too, usually in the form of a predeparture handbook. Students may receive their handbooks before or after the general meeting—there are advantages to each. What is most important is that the relevant details need to be given to students in writing, because they will only recall brief bits of what they hear at the orientation meeting. When a question comes up, students should refer to the printed materials for answers.

Required Information

In all cases, be careful not to assume advance knowledge on the part of the students. They may not have any idea how to go about obtaining a passport; the only visa they know is a credit card; and they may not know that it is not safe to drink the water in some areas (and yes, that includes ice.)

Information that should be given both at orientation meetings and in writing includes the following.

Logistical

- ☐ The need for a passport, visas, and other essential documents should be explained. Explain the process for getting a passport. If students already have passports, ask them to check the expiration date. If a visa is needed, give students the necessary forms and instructions to obtain one.
- ☐ International travel arrangements should be spelled out clearly in writing by the travel agent or other service provider, and shared with the students in writing, with extra copies for family and friends. Tell students what time to arrive at the airport and where to meet

the group. Talk to them about security measures they are likely to experience in airports.
- ☐ What is and is not included in the program fee (e.g., housing, home stays, and meals) should be clearly spelled out in the course description. If there is to be a home stay, students should be given as much information as possible about the host family, including family members' names and ages, and if available, the address and phone number. Students should be encouraged to bring hospitality gifts.
- ☐ Students should be advised about how much additional cash will be required to cover meals not included, recommended amounts for personal spending, additional travel, and so on. They should be given advice on how to carry the funds (e.g., will a credit card work or do they need travelers' checks, cash, or local currency?).
- ☐ Packing recommendations and airline luggage restrictions: include a list of suggestions about appropriate clothing to bring, how many formal outfits should be taken, and so on. Encourage the students to pack what they think they need and then walk at least four blocks with their fully loaded suitcase. If they cannot do it, they need to lighten the load.
- ☐ Phone and e-mail services abroad: tell students that access to these services may be more limited than in the United States. If students buy phone cards, make sure that they know how to use the cards correctly. Students have been surprised to receive large phone bills from hotels despite the fact that they were using a prepaid card. It is fine to visit an Internet café occasionally to touch base with home. But encourage students to spend their precious time exploring the culture— better to take in one more museum than to spend an afternoon sending e-mails to friends.
- ☐ Use of cell phones: In this day and age, it does little good to try to ban students from bringing cell phones on programs. Be sure that they are aware that their U.S. phones may or may not work in another country and that it is up to them to research this. Under no circumstances should the faculty leader be expected to solve cell phone crises of the students. While banning cell phones isn't an option, coming up with a plan for the courteous and responsible use of them is. This plan can be determined by the group as a whole before leaving the United States. It is a good way for the students to begin to think as a group.
- ☐ Parental contact. Advise students NOT to promise to call their parents the minute they arrive at their program site. Airline delays, problems with phone systems and just plain jetlag can interfere with a student's well-intentioned plan to phone home. This results in nervous parents and anxious calls to the study abroad office.

Academic Policies

- ☐ Faculty directors should provide syllabi and class expectations, a schedule of class meetings (before, during, and after travel), and in-field activities.
- ☐ Grading and assessment policy: like any course, expectations must be spelled out clearly. See Chapter 5, Designing the Academic Course.
- ☐ Policy to add/drop courses after program has begun (e.g., if a student wishes to withdraw from a course after the program has begun, what are the academic and financial penalties?).
- ☐ Academic policies about plagiarism and disciplinary procedures should be clearly articulated.

Health, Safety, and Legal Issues

(Chapter 16, Safeguards for Short-Term Programs, provides extensive information on the items listed here.)

- ☐ Inoculations (if necessary) and requirements for medical examinations before departure.
- ☐ Precautions and recommended procedures for transporting prescription and over-the-counter medicines.
- ☐ Explanation of how medical emergencies will be handled, and the general availability of medical facilities in the host country.
- ☐ Advice on how to keep oneself healthy before, during, and after travel; include information about "jet lag" and "traveler's flu."
- ☐ Caution about depression and eating disorders; ask students to be frank in sharing medical information with you about such issues.
- ☐ Risks of being sexually active with other group members or local people during program.
- ☐ The policy on alcohol and drug use abroad should be discussed and should also be distributed separately in writing.
- ☐ Health insurance coverage: explain the institutional policy. If health insurance is the responsibility of the student, make that clear.
- ☐ The list of emergency contacts and telephone numbers can be printed on wallet-size cards to ensure that students always know how to call for help.
- ☐ Encourage students to access the U.S. State Department Web site (http://travel.state.gov). The U.S. State Department publishes a number of pamphlets that include both country-specific recommendations, as well as general travel advice for Americans traveling abroad.

Group Building

Short-term programs abroad are intense experiences that require group cohesion and cooperation. During orientation, discuss issues around "group travel" and the attendant stress this may put on students and their intergroup relationships. Make sure students understand that there are times when the wishes of the individual must be sacrificed for the good of the group.

In discussions about academic/theoretical aspects of class, get group members to talk openly about their personal reactions, ideas, and ideologies, and discuss differences of opinion among group members fairly and openly. This not only builds trust among students, but also provides for great discussions about relative perspectives and respect for different opinions.

Build learning communities. Each person in the group should be familiar with the academic and personal goals of other members, and the faculty director should foster an environment of trust and mutual support.

Country/Culture Awareness Exercises

There are a number of exercises that the faculty director can do with the students to get them thinking about where they are going and how it might differ from their own environment. The Autoethnography Exercise at the end of this chapter is a good tool for promoting cultural awareness.

General Reentry

The intense "togetherness" of the short-term program abroad will create a strong bond among the students. Once the program has ended, they will feel somewhat bereft without their traveling companions. The international office, the faculty director, or both should create times to bring the groups back together to talk about their shared experiences.

Program-specific debriefings. If possible, international office staff should schedule a one- to two-hour meeting with each group to discuss all aspects of the program—academic, logistical, and social. Give students the opportunity to let you know what worked well and to give suggestions for improvement. This can also be a time for students to discuss any readjustment problems they may have and to find out that their group-mates share those issues.

Welcome back events. Schedule an event (e.g., dinner or an ice cream party) and invite all students returning from short-term programs. This gives students a chance to talk with participants in other programs and to share experiences.

Written evaluations. Because of the nature of these programs, students may be loathe to discuss any negatives at the group meetings. Using a written evaluation allows the students to criticize and make suggestions in an anonymous way. (See Chapter 12, "It Changed My Life": Strategies for Assessing Student Learning.)

ON-SITE ORIENTATION

The on-site student orientation is one of the most important moments of your study abroad program. Your orientation meeting will set the tone for the overseas experience the students are about to commence. A good orientation should address the practical issues as well as the cultural challenges the students are about to face. Your meeting makes everything real because the students are now (at last) in the host country and your task at hand is to facilitate their transition to the new environment.

While preparing your meeting agenda, remember that certain practical issues should be addressed regardless of the home institution, the field of study, or the length of the program. However, each orientation should be tailored to the specific type of student, the length of the program, and the nature of the material being studied.

Important goals to keep in mind throughout the orientation preparation and process are to give the program a solid beginning, to provide a strong foundation for the program, and to establish trust and respect among the students and yourself. Finally, and most importantly, your on-site orientation is meant to prepare and inform the students for the weeks ahead.

Ideally, on-site orientation should be broken down into layers: the arrival-and-survival orientation, the general orientation, the academic orientation, and the accommodation orientation. By breaking down your orientation, the students have time to focus on the subject at hand and are less overwhelmed than when they hear and try to process everything at once. Remember, students need time to get settled, as well as time to sleep and to get over jet lag, before they can to absorb information in an appropriate and timely fashion.

Arrival and Survival

It is extremely useful to have a welcome letter ready and waiting for each student upon the group's arrival in the host country. Students receive the letter when they check in. It should be brief, yet it must contain pertinent and important information including:

- ☐ Program obligations such as times and places of important first program meetings;
- ☐ A map of the area where they will be living (with pharmacy, ATM, police station, subway stop, and food shops clearly marked);
- ☐ Directions to and from the housing location to the site of your general orientation meeting; and
- ☐ Information on how to call home.

It is a good idea to check in the group all together. A group check-in facilitates tasks such as handing out items such as keys and linens, and explaining rules, regulations, curfews, and security. It makes pointing out important facilities, such as kitchens, cafeterias, bathrooms and showers, laundry, and Internet access much easier, too.

A walking tour of the neighborhood is always useful and appreciated by the students. Be sure to point out:

- ☐ Public transportation stops

- ☐ ATM machines
- ☐ The supermarket
- ☐ The post office
- ☐ The pharmacy
- ☐ The police station
- ☐ Historical sites
- ☐ Parks

A walking tour is also a good time to give students a few important safety tips for the host city or country. Stick to basic and simple things to remember such as not walking home alone late at night. Keep in mind that your students are generally extremely tired and that your more in-depth safety talk will be at your general orientation meeting the following day.

General Orientation

General orientation should be held as close to the arrival of the students as possible, though it is better not to have it on the actual day of arrival in the host country. Experience has shown that covering important topics on arrival day is ineffective because students are too tired to absorb or learn anything of importance.

Tips on running a successful orientation meeting include the following:

- ☐ Have a specific agenda of subjects to cover.
- ☐ Try to be brief yet complete in your explanation of the subjects discussed.
- ☐ Have more than one person present the information, to keep student attention.
- ☐ If available, use visual aids such as slides, posters, transparencies, handouts and copies, and Microsoft ® PowerPoint presentations.
- ☐ Allow some time for questions and answers after each topic is covered, but keep the meeting moving.

Each participant should receive a packet of information and a program calendar. Your orientation packet should include written material about the topics covered at the meeting for later reference. Your packets should also include maps, timely periodicals or articles about the host city or country, any in-house publications you may have, as well as information on local happenings, concerts, exhibits, and events occurring during the program's duration.

Topics to be covered at your general orientation meeting should include the following:

- ☐ The program calendar and introduction
- ☐ Money and banking
- ☐ Telephone and post office
- ☐ Transportation
- ☐ Health and safety

Program Calendar

When reviewing the program calendar with your group, make sure the students understand the dates when classes begin; when exams will be held (to be discussed further and in greater detail during your academic orientation); departure points and times for any museum visits, trips, or excursions; and the end date of the program, which is obviously important for planning the group's departure from the program accommodations and host city.

Money and Banking

During the money and banking segment of your orientation, it is useful to have some of the local currency on hand for students to refer to while you explain the notes and coins used in the host country. Be sure to explain how and where to change currency in the host city, as well as local banking hours. Assume that most of your students have never traveled abroad before and supply them with reliable and convenient addresses for banks and exchange bureaus.

When discussing money and banking, explain sales tax in the host country as well as local tipping practices. Because student budgets are personal and can vary enormously, it is generally not useful to discuss budgeting at length, though reiterating that planning ahead will help students' budgets. It is also a good idea to point out items or services that are particularly expensive in the host city.

Communications

Communication is an important part of any orientation and is best presented by discussing it in terms of telephoning, post office services, and e-mail access.

Telephones. Explain to students how telephones work in the host country: are pay phones coin operated or do they take cards? If phone cards are needed, tell students how and where to purchase the cards. Be sure to have up-to-date prices.

Inform students of the calling rates within the host country and internationally. Cover all possibilities, including direct dial, collect calling, and U.S. phone credit card calling; provide students with the necessary dialing codes. Explain how students can call home and how people from home can call students. Many parents will be dialing overseas for the first time and will not know how to place the call; if you inform the students, they can tell their folks. Suggest to students the least expensive way to call and remind them of the time differences!

Cell phones have taken off around the world and more and more students are purchasing cell phones during the first days after they arrive in the host country. You may want to try to find the best deal available to students or work out a deal with a local company especially for your students. Although it is impossible to know everything about cell phones because the choices are vast and beyond what most

of us ever imagined available, try to at least inform yourself of the general way cellular calling works in the host country so that you can point students in the right direction.

Things to note regarding cell phones: Will the phone have international calling access? Will it have voicemail? Do students pay to receive calls? Are the phones available with a prepaid card system, to avoid unpaid bills? Will students need a bank account to establish a contract with a local phone company? Have a reliable address or two ready for phone stores should your students decide to buy or rent cell phones.

Cell phones are a great help in that they allow parents and friends to contact students directly without waiting to be passed through a receptionist in a dormitory or having to learn the local language to leave a message. Cell phones have also lightened the stress and tension related to telephone use in home-stay situations.

Post Office. Local post office information should be made available to the students. Inform them of the post office's hours and the rates for sending postcards and letters via airmail. Give students an idea of how long they can expect to wait for a letter or a package. You should warn students of possible customs taxes on large packages, and of things that will not clear customs easily. Be sure to mention any other relevant services available to them at the post office. For example, in France, La Poste is a bank and a money exchange, and it has Western Union facilities.

E-mail. Regarding e-mail, most students have no intention of living without it, no matter where in the world they are! If your program facilities do not have a computer, be sure to identify Internet cafés with flexible hours and good rates, or tell students how to find one themselves.

Transportation

An important section of your orientation will cover transportation in the host city or country. Many students will have never taken public transportation in their lives. Try to plan an activity in the first day or so where students can take public transportation with you the first time. That way their transportation orientation is "live and in person."

Give a clear, basic explanation of the subway and/or bus system in the host city. Include the hours the system operates and anything pertinent or special to the system that students will need to know. Make sure each student has a map, and during your meeting run through a couple of sample trips to places in town they might visit. Mention areas that are better off avoided in the evenings or parts of town that are undesirable. Be sure to give students the correct vocabulary for purchasing tickets or passes and have current prices available.

A short discussion of using taxis is also helpful. Provide students with approximate costs and hailing procedures, again always keeping in mind that your students may have never taken a taxi before. Wherever possible, supply students with a phone number to call a taxi should they need to get home late at night. Make sure the company you suggest is legitimate and reliable.

Health and Safety

Certainly one of the most crucial parts of your general orientation meeting is the discussion of health and safety. It is useful to provide the students with a list of doctors they can contact should they become ill. Ideally, these doctors would speak English so that the students could communicate more comfortably. Information on local hospitals and pharmacies is useful as well. Be sure to explain to students how health care is paid for in the host country: are students expected to pay first and be reimbursed by insurance later? Inform them of how much a typical visit to the doctor will cost as well as what mode of payment is accepted. If the program provides insurance for the students, make sure you have a copy of the policy and that you have read it over and understand it as you will no doubt at some point during your program be asked to give a sick student an explanation of it.

Students should be given the phone number to call for ambulance, fire, and police—the host-culture equivalent of 911 in the United States.

Because student safety is always a top priority, the topic should be addressed formally at general orientation. However, staying safe is an ongoing process for your group, so you should be available to discuss safety issues at any time during the program. Sometimes the best safety discussions with students happen in more casual settings and situations, such as during a group meal or on a long train ride.

Students need to think about their safety at all times and should be instructed, reminded, and encouraged to make good decisions for themselves throughout their time abroad.

The safety section of your orientation is a good time to review the rules and regulations of student conduct. This includes discussion of use of alcohol and drugs. Know your program's policy on alcohol use as well as the legal drinking age in the host country. When discussing alcohol, be clear about what may be tolerated (e.g., a glass of wine at dinner with their host family) versus what will be considered grounds for expulsion from the program. Remind students that one of the keys in staying safe in a foreign environment is keeping their wits about them to recognize anything that doesn't feel right and to make good decisions. If student thinking is clouded by alcohol or drug use, their chances of making the best choices and decisions are not as good, hence putting them at a higher security and safety risk.

U.S. student safety abroad since the events of September 11 is a crucial part of any on-site general orientation. Now, more than ever, we need to provide open communication and plans should the unthinkable happen.

Prepare an emergency card to give to each student showing simple steps to take in case of emergency. Keep it simple and to the point. The card should have emergency contact numbers, including the U.S. consulate in the host city.

Encourage communication within your group. For example, always provide information about how students can contact you during travel weekends and breaks. Ask students to provide you with information about their destinations as well. Should you need to account for everyone at short notice you at least have an idea of where the students are and when they are expected back. Students understand the need for the information they are providing and are typically very cooperative.

It is important to get the tone of this section of orientation just right. You need students to understand the seriousness of what you are discussing, as well as the importance of having a "what if" plan of action, but you do not want to cause confusion or panic or have students dwelling on the topic unreasonably. Think about your presentation carefully beforehand to ensure projection of the right feeling.

Accommodations Orientation

Accommodations are an extremely important part of the short-term experience. Students who are comfortable and happy with their program housing acclimate to their new environment more easily than those who are unhappy with their lodgings. Therefore, preprogram preparation and selection of student housing is vital to the overall success of your program.

During your housing meeting with the students, be clear about general rules and regulations. Be extra clear on program rules about excessive noise, parties, curfews, and overnight guests. Students should receive clear instructions on telephoning from their place of residence, as well as information and instructions about kitchen, cafeteria, and laundry facilities.

The type of housing your program offers may influence how you present the accommodations section of orientation. Below are some tried and true ways to orient students to various standard housing options.

Residence Halls

Present rules and regulations of the residence hall to the students clearly. It is always better to tell students exactly what they are responsible for before the program begins than to try to backtrack later should anything go wrong.

Providing house rules in the form of a contract that the students read and sign is an effective way to get them to heed regulations. In this contract you should be clear on the following issues:

☐ Obligations and procedures regarding students' keys and lockouts of their rooms.

☐ Responsibility for damage to the residence and the need to replace anything broken or damaged.

☐ Obligations and procedures regarding guests and visitors.

☐ Rules and regulations regarding noise, parties, making curfew, etc.

☐ Obligations and procedures regarding housekeeping. Will custodial staff clean students' rooms, or are the students responsible for cleaning their rooms themselves? What about trash? What are students responsible for regarding cleaning linens and towels?

☐ How does the telephone system in the residence work? Are phones automatically connected and able to call anywhere? Are the phones prepaid or will students have phone bills to pay?

Home Stays

Students in home stays tend to be much more nervous than other students about their housing. And why not? After all, for the most part they have moved out of their parents' house and been on their own for a couple of years and now they are moving into somebody else's parents' house with a new set of rules and procedures. Students in home stays are always worried about language barriers, whether they will like their host family, whether the host family will like them, and whether or not it will all work out between them. They need to feel confident in your choice of their home stay situation and of your understanding of what they are looking for in their home stay selection.

Students will want to know how the program selects its host families. Briefly explain the procedure: is there a person on the staff who is in charge of family stays or does the program work through an agency? In the latter case, be sure that the agency is reputable and that it understands the type of student on your program. Be clear regarding meals, kitchen privileges, and academic schedules that may interfere with family meal times. Clarity on prices and rents is obviously important, as well as whether or not laundry facilities and telephone access will be available to your students.

On the day of arrival, meet with the students as a group to talk about their home stay situations; go over the general rules and regulations that apply to every family. Field general questions and remain positive! Reassure students that in most cases, the extra anxiety they may be feeling and the extra effort they will be making is well worth it. Experience has shown time and again that students in home stays improve their language abilities far beyond those living in a student residence or student apartment and that the experience of living with the local people is one they will carry with them throughout their lives.

Review with the students some guidelines on having a successful family stay. Reiterate what they are responsible for regarding rent, phone bills, and meals. Of course

students will have already heard all of this back in their pre-departure orientation in the United States, but generally students listen a lot more closely once they are on site.

After you have met with the students as a group, each student should have a short individual meeting with whoever has organized their housing for them. At the individual meeting details about the family can be discussed. Have an information card prepared for each student with the name, address, and phone number of their host family as well as directions to and from the home to the site of your general orientation meeting. Prepare a list of family-specific living guidelines for students to have and to read before they move in.

If it is not possible for the host family to pick up the student from your office or arrival site, try to send students via taxi to their new homes. Finally, arrange for students to have a welcome lunch or dinner with their hosts on the day of arrival.

Apartments

Students staying in apartments will need much of the same information as students in home stays. On the day of arrival have the apartment address and phone numbers ready for each student, as well as information about the students' floors, codes, and keys. Try to send students to their apartments via taxi, and as with the home stays, provide directions from each individual apartment back to the site of the general orientation. As with students living in a residence hall, provide a map of the neighborhood with the post office, subway station, ATM, police station, pharmacy, and grocery store clearly marked.

To help the students feel at home and to make sure the apartment is being treated properly, it is important to have someone who knows the apartment do a short orientation once the students have moved in. This person could be the apartment owner, a staff housing coordinator, or a person from the real estate agency. Make time to explain and show the students how different appliances work, how to get the heat and water on, or simply how to jiggle a tricky lock. Doing so will save everyone time, money, and headaches down the road.

Orientation is a good time to review apartment contracts. Be as specific as possible on rules and regulations as well as any utilities the students are responsible for paying. Go over security deposits, including what could possibly be deducted from the students' deposits at the end of the program. Be clear on the "do's and don'ts" of apartment living in the host country. Do not assume students know; often, student apartments in the United States are located together, and the only neighbors are other students. In the experience abroad, this will most likely not be the case and students should be told what they can expect as well as what is expected of them as neighbors.

Food in the Host Culture

At some point during your on-site orientation, the subject of food in the host culture should be addressed. Topics include the importance of food in the host culture and the rituals of meals in the host culture. It is useful to explain to students the different options they have for eating out, such as restaurants, cafés, bistros, and so on. Briefly discuss what kinds of foods students can expect to find in the host culture, what things cost, and general cultural differences regarding food.

If food shopping is greatly different in the host country than it is in the United States, it is worthwhile to chat with students about appropriate procedures at the local market and review with them communication and interaction with small shopkeepers. Depending on how fluent students are in the local language, you may want to provide them with an easy reference list of food terms. Often, U.S. students are surprised to learn of the culinary delights the rest of the world enjoys that are not readily available at home.

Finally, a talk about vegetarianism outside the United States may be useful. More and more U.S. students describe themselves as vegetarians, yet they may not be prepared for the reception of vegetarianism in their host families or local restaurants. This part of your food talk may or may not be necessary for your students depending on the host culture.

Academic Orientation

One of the most important aspects of your on-site orientation is the segment pertaining to student academics because, after all, that is the very reason students are abroad in the first place.

Students will have been given information about classes offered and credits earned before they leave the United States. It is important to review this information with them once they are on site. Again, as with every other aspect of your orientation, students tend to listen better once they are on site.

Begin with a review of classes offered by the program. Give information and background on any local institutions in which your students may be enrolled. The best way for students to be familiarized with their new school is to organize another, separate orientation meeting with someone from the school. Ideally, this meeting should take place before classes begin.

Have a general talk with your group about procedures for registration, dropping and adding classes, and general academic administration. Students need to know who will be acting as their academic coordinator while they are abroad. If there is no one on site to fulfill this role for them, then students need to know whom they should contact at the sponsoring U.S. institution.

Go over the students' class schedules. Be clear about where they need to be and when. Students abroad often need more support from their faculty director since local educational institutions outside the United States operate very differently than the ones at home. Furthermore, students abroad are generally expected to be much more independent and self-starting than they needed to be back home since U.S. academic institutions tend to do much more hand holding than do overseas institutions.

Review the attendance policies in effect on your program because attendance may not be a factor/requirement at the students' home schools. Make sure students know what they are responsible for should they be absent, what constitutes an excused absence, and what is required in terms of make-up work.

Provide information on where to purchase textbooks. If any books are to be purchased before leaving the United States, students obviously would bring these texts with them. However, often there are books and workbooks to be purchased on site. It is useful for participants to know when and where to get the books and to have an idea about their cost.

Set up individual academic registration and confirmation meetings with each student during the first week abroad. That way, there is no confusion about exactly which courses students are signed up for, the number of credits they will be receiving, and what their academic obligations and requirements are.

Prepare the necessary paperwork to be completed and signed to facilitate the meeting. This will help keep meetings moving along and will provide you with an accurate academic record for each participant on your program.

Conclusion

Remember, orientation is an ongoing process throughout the entire program. After all your meetings, presentations, walking tours, and cultural lectures are done, the process continues. For the cultural learning and understanding of the host culture to continue, you and your team need to be available throughout the time abroad to act as a sounding board, to give guidance, to help, or sometimes just to lend a sympathetic ear. The more prepared the students are for their study abroad experience, the better, deeper, and more enriching the experience will be for all concerned.

CONGRATULATIONS ON BEING ACCEPTED TO THE LIBERAL ARTS AND SCIENCES STUDY ABROAD PROGRAM!

As you prepare for this experience (one that many returning students claim to have changed their lives) you have been asked to maintain a personal journal in which you will record your thoughts, feelings, and observations about yourself and the place to which you are planning to travel. During this process of preparation you should use your journal to reflect on three areas of learning, which are explained in more detail in the three "Learning Threads" below. Briefly, your journal should help you to:

1. Learn about your own cultural practices, values and "common sense." In so doing, I would also encourage you to think about how your society and cultural background have prepared you to communicate and live in another cultural environment (i.e., how do you deal with stress and ambiguity?).

2. Learn about your program and your expectations for the program. What do you hope to accomplish during your study abroad experience? What role(s) do you expect to take on as a participant in this program? What precisely do you plan to do in order to achieve those goals and objectives? Do you think your role(s) will inhibit or further those goals?

Where are you going? You should be reading as much as you can about the place you're going. Talk to others who have been there; check the Web for interesting details about the city; read, read, read!!!

This journal will be the primary tool through you will learn about your study abroad experience as a whole, and in turn share with me your reflections on this learning. You should reflect on your personal experiences in your journal on a regular, ongoing basis, writing in it no less than three times per week.

I will also ask you to bring your journals to orientation meetings so that you can include spontaneous thoughts and observations evoked through these meetings in your ongoing reflections. I will never ask you to surrender your journal to me, nor will I ever ask you to share specific pages with me. I WILL ask you to summarize your observations at periodic moments during the next six months, and I may also ask you to share those observations with your fellow students. Please be prepared with examples of what you've written for our first orientation meeting.

In the end, this journal is for you. You should consider your journal as essential to the success of your program as finding a place to live, or getting the airplane ticket. Your journal, along with your photos, will constitute your memory of your experience abroad. You owe it to yourself to make a sincere effort at maintaining this dialogue with yourself. At the end of your program I will collect a 4- to 5-page summary from each of you as a condition of my submitting your grades to the registrar's office. In other words, you will not be graded for your journal or summary, but you will receive your grades in exchange for the summary. I wish you luck in your preparation, and success as you explore and engage the emerging world of the transnational!

Three Learning Threads

I. Who are you?

Throughout your preparation you should be learning about yourself and your cultural values, "world-views," and how those values inform your identity. Who are you and what makes you you? To get you going on this task, I have included a "Value statements exercise" that you should read and reflect on in your journal. Please complete and bring this exercise with you to your first orientation meeting.

During the cross-cultural workshops you will also be asked to reflect on common stereotypes of Americans that are often held by foreigners. How do you think encountering these potentially conflicting attitudes and stereotypes will affect your experience abroad? What strategies can you come up with that will help you deal with the stress of encountering these attitudes. This stress is often associated with a phenomenon known as "culture shock." Have you ever experienced culture shock before? If so, write about some of your feelings about those experiences. If not, what do you imagine culture shock to be like. Please note that I did NOT ask you if you think you will encounter culture shock—you will. My intention here is to get you to come up with strategies for dealing with culture shock in a healthy, productive way.

II. What are your goals and objectives for participating in this program?

Your decision to participate in this challenging cross-cultural experience is a significant commitment. What do you hope to "get out of" the program? You should come up with at least one objective each month of preparation, and in your journal think about how you plan to accomplish these objectives through specific goals. Do you anticipate any difficulties in accomplishing your goals? What specifically do you think you will need from those of us administering the program in order to succeed? For example, one objective you might set is to become more fluent in the target language. A goal that will help you meet this objective would be regular attendance at your language classes. Can you think of any other goals that would help you achieve your objective of fluency?

What does it mean to "immerse" oneself in a culture? What is culture? What do you know about the program that you feel will help you gain greater insight into the lives and practices of the people you will be meeting?

III. Where are you going?

During your interviews I asked each of you to try to imagine (or remember) what your destination city smells and tastes like. Hopefully you have been indulging yourself in dreaming about your destination.

In asking you to maintain this ongoing dialogue with yourself, I hope that you will begin to create the program in your head (and your journal). Include in your journal your excitement, anticipations, hopes, dreams, fears and anxieties about going abroad. In other words, I am asking you, in a focused manner, to seriously think about what you are getting yourself into. In the end this is your program, and the degree of success you achieve is ultimately your own. Good luck with your task.

[Source: Adapted from DePaul University]

GUIDED REFLECTIONS

As you begin your new adventure, learning and living abroad, please use the following weekly questions and "prompts" to guide your journal reflections. These are not meant to dictate what you write in your journal, but should be used as a way to focus your thoughts and reflections about your experience abroad as it is happening. Remember, this is your journal and I provide these questions as a way to keep your journal focused on what you are learning and experiencing.

These guided questions will be critical as you begin to put together your final Journal Reflection at the end of your program. If you have any questions regarding this ongoing assignment, please feel free to write to me at jkinsell@depaul.edu. As a reminder, a journal summary must be turned in at the completion of your program in order to receive credit for your courses.

Have a safe and wonderful time abroad! Explore, experience and learn!

In-Field Journal Reflection #1

Now that you have arrived, you should begin to observe your reactions to, and feelings about your living situation, your classes, the school you are attending and your classmates (both other DePaul students and other students and host family members). In this first in-field journal summary assignment, write about one thing that surprised you and one thing that you expected about your:

1. Living situation

2. Classes

3. Host city

4. Classmates

What other things about your new environment have been particularly confusing, frustrating or otherwise uncomfortable? Explain in detail and using as many examples as possible.

In-Field Journal Reflection #2

By the second week you should have some sort of daily routine established. What are you doing every day? Have you noticed any times that you feel the need to be alone? What do you do during these times? Are you spending time with other North American students on a regular basis? If so, explain the context. Have you made any local friends?

What nonprogram trips have you gone on? Have you visited (or made plans to visit) any places of interest to you? If so, describe your experiences there. What other activities are you doing to achieve your personal learning goals? Do you feel that you are adapting to your new environment well? What makes you feel this?

In-Field Journal Reflection #3

Write in your journal about your classes. How are they contributing to your overall experience? Explain. Describe any confusing or different ways that courses are handled in your host society that you have encountered. If you are finding your classes difficult, consider how they are a manifestation of a particular aspect of society. Find a local student who can help you understand your teachers. Describe your conversations with this person.

In-Field Journal Reflection #4

Go to a typical "tourist" attraction or event in your host city. Describe where you went, what you saw, and how you felt during your visit. How was the event or the site presented to you as a tourist? Take pictures and incorporate them into your journal.

Try to imagine what the people who designed the site think this event will communicate about this place. Who do they think you—as a tourist/member of an audience—are?

In-Field Journal Reflection #5

Write one paragraph about each of your classes. Each description should include a) a list of the books/articles you're reading, b) the main ideas or concepts the course is examining, and c) your reflections about the readings and the concepts.

In-Field Journal Reflection #6

Describe the three closest contacts you have made to date with people from the host society. These might include members of your home-stay family, teachers, other students, or members of your own family who live abroad. Describe one or two situations in which you spent significant time with these people, how you felt about the interaction and (if appropriate) what you discussed. What other activities, classes or events help you understand how these people act and think?

In-Field Journal Reflection #7

At this point in your time abroad you should have made significant contact with local people. Describe three interactions that you have had in which "American culture" was discussed. What did your contacts say about Americans? What did you say/how did you react? How did these conversations make you feel? What are you learning in your classes that helps you understand the perception of Americans by local people?

In-Field Journal Reflection #8

Describe something totally new or unexpected that you have learned about your host society. How did you learn about this? Is there anything that you could have done prior to departure that might have prepared you for this? Does anything you've learned in class discussions or through reading explain these differences?

In-Field Journal Reflection #9

Reflect on the learning goals you set prior to your departure (remember those learning goals?). Are these goals appropriate for your experience to date? What have you been doing to achieve these goals? Are there any goals that you wish to modify, add, or remove? Are your classes helping you achieve your goals?

In-Field Journal Reflection #10

Describe the first time you left your host city for more than two nights. Where did you go? What did you do? How did you feel when you returned? What did these feelings teach you about your sense of security and feelings of "home"?

IIn-Field Journal Reflection #11

What has changed most significantly about your perception and attitudes toward the host society since your arrival? Look back at your journal entries you wrote prior to your departure. What has surprised you? What did you anticipate? Explain. Do you feel that you are being accepted by your hosts (at school, at home, and on the street)? What make you feel this way?

In-Field Journal Reflection #12

By now you should be familiar with local issues and events (political, social issues, natural disasters and concerns, etc.) that have become important during your stay. Using newspaper articles, magazine stories and other information sources, write in your journal about these issues, and how understanding it helps you better understand your hosts and their values, beliefs, etc.

In-Field Journal Reflection #13

As you prepare to return to the United States, what kinds of feelings are you experiencing? Is there anything that you did not do that you wish you could have done earlier (place to visit, people to see)? What is your proudest accomplishment? What do you wish you had done better?

[Source: Adapted from DePaul University]

STUDY ABROAD PROGRAM: FINAL JOURNAL SUMMARY ASSIGNMENT

Winter/Spring 2006
Due dates:
Athens, Dublin, Leuven, Osaka & Paris-IES: 16 June 2006
Sheffield, Hong Kong, Mérida & Paris-AF: 14 July 2006
Bonn: 25 August 2006

Spend a day or two rereading your journal from the beginning. Remember the day you interviewed with me, and first heard of this journal assignment. Do you recall the way you felt, the excitement of starting your journey abroad? Were you anxious about anything? What goals did you set for yourself? Who were you then?

As you read your journal, consider how you have changed over the last term. Have you been able to achieve the personal and academic goals that you set for yourself in the months prior to departing? What do you wish you had done differently? About which accomplishments are you particularly proud?

After reading your journal and reflecting on your experience abroad, write a page or two on each of the four broad questions below. Please be specific and precise when you recall experiences or events. I am not looking for large amounts of prose here, and would appreciate concise and clear answers to these questions. Try to avoid overly vague references, and focus on the experiences you had abroad, and how they made you feel (i.e., "I remember when I finally felt comfortable speaking Spanish with my host family. It was during supper the second week in Mérida when I..."). Please include stories and short narratives about your time abroad that will help me better understand you, your goals, and your accomplishments.

If you have specific complaints with the program, the administration of DePaul or your host institution, your field director or some "logistical" aspect of the program, please do not focus on them here. While these negative feelings certainly would play a part in formulating your answers, and certainly may be presented here, this is not a program evaluation, per se. I am trying to better understand what you learned about yourself and your hosts while you negotiated the program—and your life—abroad.

Your paper will be due on 25 August. I strongly encourage you to begin writing it as soon as possible, however. If you have any questions, please feel free to contact me before your paper is due at jkinsell@depaul.edu. If at all possible, I would like to receive your papers in electronic format only. Please e-mail them to me as Word document attachments.

Good Luck!

Joe Kinsella

Please write in clear, concise language using correct grammar. All summaries must be typewritten, and will be accepted as MS Word-compatible e-mail attachments (but not as e-mail text).

Question #1
Stereotypes are common ways that we (as humans) begin to understand other people. As our understanding of other people deepens, those stereotypes should give way to a more specific, complex and sophisticated understanding. Tell me a story about the most surprising, confusing or strange difference that you noticed about a person from your host society (a habit, a phrase, a way of doing—or not doing—something, etc). Be specific. Do not talk about "Parisians" or "most people." Give me a real story about particular people. Did you classes and/or contact with others in the host society help you understand this difference? Why/why not? Looking back at that difference now, explain if and how understanding this difference helps you understand your hosts better. (FO)

Question #2
Write about one thing that you learned in one of your courses or from outside readings that helped you understand your hosts' society or a particular cultural practice. Be specific. Describe the cultural practices, and then discuss your observations of them in the field. Did anything you read or learned in your classes help you better understand these practices/activities or stereotypes (refer to question #1) in this society? Explain. (PAC)

Question #3
Write the key values, beliefs, or identities that you used to describe yourself in the journal entries you made before you left. Please be specific and use direct quotes from your journal to tell me about your values and beliefs before you left. Then compare those beliefs with the parallel beliefs and values of your host society. Tell me a story about your time abroad that will illuminate the similarities and differences that you perceived between yourself and your hosts. (ER)

Question #4
Tell me about a current issue or problem that was important in your host society during your stay. Use newspaper quotes to describe the issue, and then reflect on how by better understanding this issue you are able to gain important insight about your hosts. How did you learn about this issue? What do you think about this issue? Why? (PA)

SAMPLE TABLE OF CONTENTS FOR A PREDEPARTURE ORIENTATION HANDBOOK

[Source: Adapted from University of Kansas]

Autoethnography is your view of your own cultural background and the values and interests that come from it. It is important to what we will call "positioning" in terms of the country-specific culture we experience in a short-term course abroad. Positioning refers to the perspective, or lens, that each of us brings to our observations and interpretation of another culture. From knowing our position vis-à-vis another culture, we can better be aware of how our views and backgrounds might affect what we see and the way we interpret what we see.

Please write on the front and back of this page about your own cultural background, using the following areas as a guide:

☐ Your religious background; how important it is to you; values from that background.

☐ Your cultural/ethnic background; how important it is to you; values from that background.

☐ Rituals or traditions that you celebrate as part of your culture or your family. Describe what is important to you about this tradition or custom, and why?

☐ Do you belong to some cultural or social group that you strongly identify with?

☐ Political leanings: do you have strong feelings about certain political issues?

☐ What values do you have that you think are part of U.S. history and culture? How strongly do you feel about these values? What do you do when these values are attacked?

☐ Your lifestyle: in what ways do you think your lifestyle is "typically American?"

☐ Interests and hobbies: course-specific ideas, such as have you ever studied art, dance, theater or film, or performed in a play or dance or attended performances?

☐ Brainstorm words and phrases that would describe your likes and dislikes, your identity, or your values.

☐ Have you ever experienced prejudice against who you are, or against a group to which you belong?

☐ What are your favorite American stories?

Course- and Country-Specific Example: Egypt

☐ Without thinking too much, write down all the words and phrases you have associated with the Middle East, Egypt, Arabs, and/or Muslims. These may be from media, movies, books, or your own personal experience.

☐ What background do you have in Middle Eastern history or culture?

[Source: Pamela Nice, University of St. Thomas]

What Do You Need to Know and Do Before You Go?

This exercise is intended to spur you to think about all of the things that you need to do to prepare yourself for your study abroad program. It is not a comprehensive checklist or to-do list, but it might give you some ideas for making your own list. Have fun!

Check yes if a statement is true, no if it is not...yet. Count up your yes responses.

How many yes responses did you get?

20 or more	You are a regular Marco Polo! Have a great adventure studying abroad!
15–19	Almost ready! You just need to polish a few globes before you go.
10–14	You have more than just packing to do before departure…
less than 10	Are you sure you know where you are going? Use the time before you go wisely!

Is this true of you?	YES, of course!	Uh...NO, not yet
I have a passport and have made copies to leave at home and take with me.		
I know how to say "thank-you" in my host country language.		
I know the entry requirements to my host country for persons of my nationality.		
I have spoken with a native of my host country.		
I know what electrical current is standard in my host country.		
I have read a magazine, newspaper, or book from my host country in the last 3 to 6 months.		
I can locate my host country and study site on the map.		
I have had physical, dental, and eye checkups in preparation for going abroad.		
I have gotten written prescriptions to take with me for glasses and any medications I take regularly, and plan to take a supply for my entire stay.		
I have searched the Web, viewed television, or listened to a radio broadcast from my host country in the last 3 months.		
I am familiar with any predeparture health recommendations for the region I will visit.		
I know the type of government in my host country.		
I have checked the exchange rate for my host country in the past month and have practiced converting amounts in my head.		
I know how I'm going to take money overseas, and know how I will get emergency funds if necessary.		
I can sing the national anthem of my host country.		
I have copied all credit cards and other important documents to leave at home in case of loss or theft.		
I know the predominant religion of my host country.		
I can draw freehand a reasonable map of my host country and surrounding countries.		
I know the time difference between my home town and my study site.		
I know the country telephone codes for the United States that I will need to call home from overseas.		
I know the name of the head of government of my host country.		
I know how much a meal will cost in my host country.		
I am receiving financial aid and I have seen an office of study abroad financial adviser to make sure arrangements are in place.		
All my payments and forms for study abroad are in and up to date.		

[Source: Adapted from University of Kansas]

Study Abroad Orientation Quiz

Complete this open book quiz and turn it in at orientation by **9:45am** to get a complimentary gift. Page numbers refer to the yellow student handbook. Several questions have more than one correct answer.

1. What is a safe way to carry valuables such as money and documents? (pp. 26-27)

2. What are three things that you should leave behind when going abroad? (p. 24)

   a)_____

   b)_____

   c)_____

3. Does the U.S. Constitution protect you when you are outside the United States? (p. 28)

4. What information will you find on the U.S. State Department Consular Information sheet for the country you will visit? (pp. 24-25)

   a) Unusual health conditions
   b) Where you can find other Americans
   c) Crime and security situation
   d) The phone numbers of area hospitals
   e) Drug penalties
   f) Political disturbances and areas of instability

5. The overseas U.S. embassy can: (p. 28)

   a) Get you out of jail.
   b) Provide a list of English-speaking lawyers.
   c) Provide temporary payment of medical bills.
   d) Provide a loan if you run out of money.
   e) Help your family track you down, if you have registered your presence.
   f) Replace your passport, if lost or stolen.

6. Why should all international travelers be concerned about AIDS? (p. 13-14)

   a) Standards for screening blood transfusions and sterilizing needles are not the same worldwide.
   b) Travelers are exposed to more public toilets, so will be at greater risk of contracting the virus.
   c) Availability, quality, and social acceptability of condoms is not the same worldwide.

7. List the precautions you will take for packing (12, 23-24):

   Eye glasses _____
   Prescription drugs_____
   Luggage ID _____
   Personal ID _____

8. Describe three strategies you, personally, will employ to ensure that your health remains good while you are abroad. (pp. 11-12)

   a)_____
   b)_____
   c)_____

9. Describe three common pick-pocket techniques (p. 26)

   a)_____
   b)_____
   c)_____

10. If you lose or are robbed of your passport, credit cards, plane ticket, and money, what will you do? What precautions can you take to make replacement easier? (pp. 24, 27)

11. You have a long weekend coming up and you would like to go traveling. What do you do? (pp. 38-39)

    a) Ask natives or your on-site director for suggestions
    b) Leave your itinerary with a friend or the director
    c) Travel with a friend for safety and companionship

12. Name three coping strategies you can use when faced with feelings of culture "shock" or cultural fatigue (pp. 20-21).

    a)_____
    b)_____
    c)_____

True or False?

____ ATMs are now universal. It is no longer advisable to take some money in travelers' checks. (p. 31-32)

____ Federal Express will not ship prescription medications overseas. I should take all I need with me. (p. 12, 34)

____ In most cases, the best defense against unwanted male attention is a severe glare and an angry retort.

____ Foreign hospitals will, in most cases, not take a U.S. health insurance card for payment; the individual must pay the bill and be reimbursed by her/his health insurance company. (p. 9)

____ It is best to exchange MOST of the money you will take abroad BEFORE you depart. (p. 31)

[Source: Adapted from University of Kansas]

Self-Test: Safety Scenarios

Answers to most questions will be found in the student handbook for short-term and summer programs. If you are in doubt about safe solutions to any of the scenarios, however, do not hesitate to consult the office of study abroad.

1. **This is your first experience** in the country you are visiting and initial adjustment is a bit tougher than you thought. You haven't slept in 5 days, you're not hungry, you're beginning to get a cold. All you want to do is curl up in your bed and ignore everything. Classes are the last thing on your mind.

   - What are some coping strategies that might help you out?
   - Should you seek help? If so, from whom?

2. **You and three friends** take an overnight train back to your host city after a weekend excursion on your own. You four are the only people in the train compartment, so you've piled your luggage in the middle toward the window. It's not a restful journey and you don't think you really got to sleep at all. However, when you arrive at your destination, your bag/purse is missing!

   - What happened?
   - What valuables could be missing?
   - What is your next step?
   - What can you do to prevent this?

3. **You are traveling on a break.** On arrival in your destination, you find that the well-known, inexpensive hostel where you had planned to stay is full. In fact, you were so sure you'd be able to stay at this place, you gave the address and phone number to your (seemingly) overprotective mother and told her you'd call her when you arrived.

   - What do you do?
   - What are your resources?
   - What would you do differently next time?

4. **Two men on a train befriend you**, an older fellow and one closer to your age. They are friendly and seem harmless. After about 45 minutes of conversation, they offer you some of the beverage they are drinking.

   - Should you accept?
   - Why or why not?
   - What are the risks?

5. **You were warned**, but you thought, "what's the harm in bringing *one* little joint?" The following week, however, you get caught smoking it in your dorm room.

   - What are the consequences?
   - Who can help you out?

6. **You are 20—not of age to drink** in the United States, but legal in the country in which you are studying. You take advantage of this with gusto. You find that you can purchase alcohol at any time of the day, and begin to do so, sometimes before class. Things seem to be getting a little out of control, but you don't seem to be able to stop.

   - What are some of the negative consequences of continuing like this?
   - Consider health, safety, academics.
   - Are the consequences just personal or are they more far-reaching?
   - What can you do?

7. **You are in the kitchen** preparing dinner and you are alone. You cut yourself with a knife and you know you'll need stitches. Before you pass out from loss of blood

   - What precautions have you taken for this sort of emergency?
   - What emergency contact numbers should you have?
   - What questions should you ask at the on-site orientation about obtaining medical care?

8. **You're on a bus alone at night.** You start talking to the people next to you. You get up to get out of the bus, and you notice the people next to you are also going to exit. You are uncomfortable with the situation.

   - What do you do?
   - How would you avoid this situation?

9. **You notice a political demonstration.** It looks interesting! What do you do? (choose one)

   - Be a passive observer rather than an active participant.
   - Join in and "do as the Romans do!"
   - Assess the situation. What are clues that you should leave the area immediately?

10. **You arrived 2 weeks ago**, and you've noticed that you attract more sexually-oriented attention than you are comfortable with. You feel a bit threatened.

    - What can you do to reduce the likelihood of attracting attention?
    - Should you consult someone? If so, who? What questions will you ask?

[Source: Adapted from University of Kansas]

Endnotes

1. Gochenour, Theodore (1993). *Beyond Experience: The Experiential Approach to Cross-Cultural Education* (2nd edition). Yarmouth, ME: Intercultural Press.

2. Kauffmann, Norman L., Judith N. Martin, and Henry D. Weaver (1992). *Students Abroad: Strangers at Home: Education for a Global Society.* Yarmouth, ME: Intercultural Press, Inc.

3. Koester, J. (1985). "A Profile of the U.S. Student Abroad". New York: Council on International Educational Exchange.

4. Sikkema, Mildred, and Agnes Niyekawa (1987). *Design for Cross-Cultural Learning.* Yarmouth, ME: Intercultural Press.

5. Hoffa, William, and John Pearson (eds.) (1997) *NAFSA's Guide to Education Abroad for Advisers and Administrators, 2nd Edition.* Washington, DC: NAFSA: Association of International Educators, 233-234.

6. Kolb, David A. (1984). *Experiential Learning: Experience as the Source of Learning and Development.* Englewood Cliffs, NJ: Prentice Hall, 40.

7. Kolb, David A. (1984). *Experiential Learning: Experience as the Source of Learning and Development.* Englewood Cliffs, NJ: Prentice Hall, 42. © Reprinted by permission of Pearson Education, Inc., Upper Saddle River, NJ.

8. Kolb, David A. (1984). *Experiential Learning: Experience as the Source of Learning and Development.* Englewood Cliffs, NJ: Prentice Hall, 40-41.

9. Stocking, George W., Jr. (1968). *Race, Culture, and Evolution: Essays in the History of Anthropology.* New York: The Free Press, 156-160.

10. Sikkema, Mildred, and Agnes Niyekawa (1987). *Design for Cross-Cultural Learning.* Yarmouth, ME: Intercultural Press, 50.

11. Freire, Paulo (1970). *Pedagogy of the Oppressed.* New York: Herder and Herder.

12. Steinaker, Norman W., and M. Robert Bell (1979). *The Experiential Taxonomy: A New Approach to Teaching and Learning.* New York: Academic Press.

13. Kelley, Colleen, and Judith Meyers (1995). CCAI *Cross-Cultural Adaptability Inventory Manual.* Minneapolis, MN: National Computer Systems, Inc.

SAFEGUARDS FOR SHORT-TERM PROGRAMS

16

Mickey Slind and Sarah E. Spencer

Designing, directing, and administering study abroad programs, especially if they are short-term, presents a special challenge for faculty and administrators. It is assumed that students and faculty directors should be encouraged to take responsibility for their own health and wellness. However, there is the additional responsibility of informing students and directors of unusual hazards, such as specific health, safety, and liability concerns that may await them off campus, and of coordinating an appropriate and effective support system.

Liability issues are becoming increasingly complex on campuses. Every effort should be made to implement institutional policies, sound operating procedures, and responsible programming. However, convincing students and faculty to concentrate on good preventive care and to be in tune with wellness practices is the key to success.

In summary, everyone must be proactive. This section will highlight what areas to focus on in safety and security, health, insurance, liability, and crisis management.

Short-Term Considerations

Whereas semester- or year-long programs allow the luxury of time to solve many problems that may occur overseas, the critical short-term issue is lack of time. Whereas questions of health and safety, risk, and liability are the same in all programs, the impact on the program, its program directors, and its students can be profound when encapsulated into the limited time period of a short-term program. The questions are not only related to health and safety, but to academics as well. If a student becomes ill at the beginning of a three- or four-week program, and is unable to attend class for a week or two, how will credit be earned when so much time has been lost?

If a student has an accident while on a program that travels extensively, as many short-term programs do, who stays behind to attend to the student's medical needs while the group moves on to the next site? What kind of local health care is available and how can your faculty director access it should the occasion arise? Have you warned your students of any aspect of your program that may carry a higher risk of injury or danger? These are just some of the important issues that face administrators of all programs, but particularly those that are considered short-term.

Special Precautions

If the program involves research in the field or physically rigorous activities, local conditions need to be confirmed and students need to be advised of any necessary precautions that should be taken ahead of time—ideally, before they apply for the program, and minimally, well before departure. If there are unusual activities or high risks involved, you should proactively inform participants. Examples include sports or physical activities, political instability, environmental concerns, and health issues. Environmental concerns include anything from poisonous snakes and insects, to air or water pollution, to extreme traffic hazards.

Preparation

As covered in Chapters 13 and 15, thorough preparation of students and directors is essential. As you develop orientation programming and written materials, health and safety issues such as immunizations and on-site risks, insurance, and basic host country medical systems must be included.

The following topics should be considered:

- ☐ Basic hygiene
- ☐ Medical insurance
- ☐ Medical kit
- ☐ Immunizations
- ☐ Disease prevention
- ☐ Eye care
- ☐ Alcohol (responsible use of) and drugs (prescription and controlled substance)
- ☐ Personal security
- ☐ Road safety and car rental concerns
- ☐ Accident and injury prevention
- ☐ Altitude sickness
- ☐ Jet lag
- ☐ Emergency situations
- ☐ Mental health issues
- ☐ Emotional problems
- ☐ Anxiety and stress
- ☐ Nutrition
- ☐ Eating disorders
- ☐ Environmental health issues
- ☐ Preexisting conditions
- ☐ Health care delivery overseas
- ☐ Sexuality and relationships
- ☐ Principles of safe sex
- ☐ Information on sexually transmitted disease, including HIV/AIDS
- ☐ Contraceptive needs

It is important that all students and their faculty directors receive the same information and that the appropriate person reinforces the importance of these concerns during the program. Students, faculty directors, and administrators should understand how to respond to health emergencies.

SECURITY AND SAFETY ISSUES

While always an important leading factor in any program off-campus, current world events have brought age-old wisdom from many an administrator to the attention of more constituents, including organization's executives, parents, and even the media. A country or region's stability should be one of the first feasibility factors considered. Administrators and directors must keep on top of global issues, and how situations may affect a program.

Security

Security situations can change momentarily, hence resources should be identified and available for consultation. The U.S. Department of State is the first step for most international educators. It offers the following:

Consular Information Sheets are available for every country of the world. They describe entry requirements, cur-

rency regulations, unusual health conditions, the crime and security situation, political disturbances, areas of instability, special information about driving and road conditions, and drug penalties. The information sheets also provide addresses and emergency telephone numbers for U.S. embassies and consulates. In general, these documents do not give advice but describe conditions so that travelers can make informed decisions.

Public Announcements are another means by which the U.S. State Department disseminates information about terrorist threats and other relatively short-term and/or transnational conditions posing significant risks to the security of U.S. travelers. Announcements are issued when there is a perceived threat usually involving Americans as a particular target group. In the past, public announcements have been issued to deal with short-term coups, preelection disturbances, violence by terrorists, and anniversary dates of specific terrorist events.

Travel Warnings - In some situations, however, the U.S. State Department recommends that U.S. citizens defer travel to a country. In such a case, a travel warning is issued for the country for a limited time period.

Some institutions may have policies that determine if students are allowed to study where a travel warning has been issued. This policy may determine if a program should be relocated, cancelled, or if other specific action is required.

Other Resources

If a situation warrants specific attention, be sure to look beyond the State Department, including onsite program providers, U.S.-based study abroad program administrators, local informants, as well as media Web sites.

Wardens

Consider registering the group with the U.S. embassy in the country or countries to be visited, and identify a warden if possible. Wardens are designated contacts that the U.S. embassy or consulate will reach in case of an emergency. Embassy information can be found at www.embassyworld.com.

The Bureau of Consular Affairs' Web site address is http://travel.state.gov. It includes Consular Information Sheets, Travel Warnings, and Public Announcements; passport and visa information; travel publications; background on international adoption and international child abduction services; and international legal assistance. It also links to the U.S. State Department's main Web site at http://www.state.gov, which contains current foreign affairs information.

Safety

Safety of all group participants must be considered at all times during program development, predeparture, and, of course, while onsite. The good news is that most safety problems can be drastically reduced with excellent predeparture information, planning, and action.

What to Bring

☐ Safety begins while packing. Travelers should dress conservatively to avoid being a target; as much as possible, avoid the appearance of affluence.

☐ Travel light.

☐ The minimum number of important documents necessary should be carried. Plan a place or places to conceal them. Passport, cash, and credit cards are most secure when locked in a hotel safe. When carried on the person, conceal them in several places rather than putting them all in one wallet or pouch. Avoid handbags, fanny packs, and outside pockets, which are easy targets for thieves.

☐ An extra set of passport photos.

☐ A copy of birth certificate.

☐ Travelers should label their luggage and put name, address, and telephone number inside and outside of each piece of luggage. They should use covered luggage tags to avoid casual observation of identity or nationality.

☐ Note credit card and ATM information and spending limits, including the phone number if the card is lost or stolen. Because of fraud protection systems, call the credit card company before departure to document which countries the card will be used in.

☐ Two photocopies of the passport identification page, airline tickets information, and driver's license. One photocopy should be left with family or friends at home, the other packed in a place separate from where valuables are carried.

☐ If carrying traveler's checks, a copy of the check's serial numbers should be left with a friend or relative at home. Travelers should carry their copy in a separate place and cross their numbers off the list as checks are cashed.

What to Leave at Home

☐ Valuable or expensive-looking jewelry.

☐ Irreplaceable family objects.

☐ All unnecessary credit cards.

☐ A copy of the itinerary with family or friends.

☐ Copies of passport, credit card numbers, and itineraries.

Precautions to Take While Traveling

Safety on the Street

All participants should use the same common sense traveling overseas that they would at home, and they should be especially cautious in or avoid areas where they are likely to be victimized. These include crowded subways, train stations, elevators, tourist sites, market places, festivals, and marginal areas of cities.[1]

Specifically, travelers should be warned:

☐ Do not travel alone, especially at night.

☐ Do not use shortcuts, narrow alleys, or poorly lit streets.

☐ Avoid public demonstrations and other civil disturbances.

☐ Keep a low profile and avoid loud conversations or arguments. Do not discuss travel plans or other personal matters with strangers.

☐ Avoid scam artists. Beware of strangers who approach offering bargains or to be a guide.

☐ Beware of pickpockets. They often have an accomplice who will jostle, ask for directions or the time, point to something spilled on clothing, or create a disturbance to distract the traveler. A child or even a woman carrying a baby can be a pickpocket. Beware of groups of vagrant children who create a distraction while picking pockets.

☐ Wear the shoulder strap of a bag across the chest and walk with the bag away from the curb to avoid drive-by purse snatchers.

☐ Try to seem purposeful when moving about. Even if lost, the traveler should act as if they know where they are going. When possible, ask directions only from individuals in authority.

☐ Know how to use a pay telephone and have the proper change or token on hand.

☐ Learn a few phrases in the local language to signal a need for help, the police, or a doctor. Make note of emergency telephone numbers that may be needed: police, fire, your hotel, and the nearest U.S. embassy or consulate.

☐ If confronted, do not fight back. Travelers should give up their valuables since their money and passport, unlike themselves, are replaceable.

☐ Carry the hotel name, address, and telephone number in the local language and in English.

Safety in Hotels

☐ Keep hotel doors locked at all times. Meet visitors only in the lobby.

☐ Do not leave money and other valuables in the hotel room while out. Use the hotel safe.

☐ Let someone know when to expect your return.

- ☐ If out late at night alone, do not get on an elevator if there is a suspicious-looking person inside.
- ☐ Read the fire safety instructions in the hotel room. Know how to report a fire. Know where the nearest fire exit and alternate exits are located. Count the doors between the room and the nearest exit. This could be a lifesaver if required to crawl through a smoke-filled corridor.

Safety on Public Transportation

If a country has a pattern of tourists being targeted by criminals on public transport, such information is mentioned in the Consular Information Sheet under the "Crime Information" section.

- ☐ Only take taxis clearly identified with official markings. Beware of unmarked cabs. Ask for, and where appropriate, negotiate the fare before entering cab.
- ☐ If the way is being blocked by a stranger and another person is very close behind, move away. This can happen in the corridor of a train or on the platform or station.
- ☐ Do not accept food or drink from strangers. Criminals have been known to drug food or drink offered to passengers. Criminals may also spray sleeping gas in train compartments.
- ☐ Do not be afraid to alert authorities if feeling threatened in any way. Extra police are often assigned to ride trains on routes where crime is a serious problem.

How to Handle Money Safely

- ☐ Be careful when using an ATM machine. Keep the four-digit code secure.
- ☐ Do not flash large amounts of money when paying a bill.
- ☐ Make sure credit cards are returned after each transaction.
- ☐ Deal only with authorized agents when exchanging money. Do not change money on the street or black market.
- ☐ If using travelers' checks, change only as currency is needed to avoid carrying large amounts of cash. Countersign travelers' checks only in front of the person who will cash them.
- ☐ If possessions are lost or stolen, report the loss immediately to the local police. Keep a copy of the police report for insurance claims and as an explanation of the situation. After reporting missing items to the police, report the loss or theft of:
  - o credit cards to the issuing company;
  - o passport to the nearest U.S. embassy or consulate.
  - o If printed, airline tickets to the airline or travel agent; and
  - o travelers' checks to the nearest agent of the issuing company;

How to Avoid Legal Difficulties

Travelers can be arrested overseas for actions that may be either legal or considered minor infractions in the United States. They should be aware of what is considered criminal in the country visited. Consular Information Sheets include information on unusual patterns of arrests in various countries when appropriate.

Drug violations. More than one third of U.S. citizens incarcerated abroad are held on drug charges. Some countries do not distinguish between possession and trafficking. Many countries have mandatory sentences—even for possession of a small amount of marijuana or cocaine. A number of Americans have been arrested for possessing prescription drugs, particularly tranquilizers and amphetamines, that they purchased legally in certain Asian countries and then brought to some countries in the Middle East where they are illegal. Other U.S. citizens have been arrested for purchasing prescription drugs abroad in quantities that local authorities suspected were for commercial use. If in doubt about foreign drug laws, ask local authorities or the nearest U.S. embassy or consulate.

Photography. In many countries, travelers can be harassed or detained for photographing such things as police and military installations, government buildings, border areas, and transportation facilities. If in doubt, ask permission before taking photographs.

Protection Against Terrorism

Terrorist acts occur at random and are unpredictable, making it impossible to protect participants absolutely. The first and best protection is to avoid travel to areas with a persistent record of terrorist attacks or kidnapping. The vast majority of foreign states have good records of maintaining public order and protecting residents and visitors within their borders from terrorism.

Most terrorist attacks are the result of long and careful planning. Just as a car thief will first be attracted to an unlocked car with the key in the ignition, terrorists are looking for defenseless, easily accessible targets who follow predictable patterns. The chance that a traveler with an unpublished program or itinerary would be the victim of terrorism is extremely slight.

Nevertheless, the following pointers may help participants to avoid becoming a target of opportunity. They should be considered as adjuncts to the tips listed in the previous sections on how to protect travelers against the far greater likelihood of being a victim of crime. These precautions may provide some degree of protection and can serve as practical and psychological deterrents to would-be terrorists.

- ☐ Be aware of what is discussed with strangers and watch out for anyone who may be eavesdropping.
- ☐ Try to minimize the time spent in the public area of an airport, which is less protected. Move quickly from the check-in counter to the secured areas.

- ☐ As much as possible, avoid dress and behavior (e.g., baseball hats, college sweatshirts, fanny packs, loud voices) that may identify you as an American.
- ☐ Keep an eye out for suspicious abandoned packages or briefcases. Report them to airport security or other authorities and leave the area promptly.
- ☐ Avoid places where Americans and Westerners are known to congregate, such as McDonalds and other fast food restaurants, and U.S.-owned companies, such as The Gap.

Contingency Plans

Don't forget to set up a contingency contact plan, if a situation should occur while on site. Include primary and secondary meeting places, and a list with numbers of whom to call, such as the onsite program provider or hotel, plus a quick call to home. Consider buying calling cards for such emergencies.

Alcohol and Drug Use or Abuse

Rule number one: use of illegal substances is absolutely prohibited. It should be made clear to students that anyone caught using illegal substances will be immediately removed from the program. It should also be made clear that penalties for use of illegal substances in other countries can be much stronger than in the United States and there is nothing the faculty director or the U.S. embassy can do to assist someone caught breaking the laws of the host country.

Use of alcohol in off-campus programs can be a problem, especially for those students who have suddenly achieved legal drinking age. First, check to see whether your institution has a policy prohibiting the use of alcohol at college-sponsored functions. If so, you need an interpretation from your risk manager or legal counsel about how that policy should be applied on an off-campus program.

In any case, the issue of alcohol use should be addressed with students. You may wish to consider a policy such as the one that follows:

Responsible Use of Alcohol is When:

1. A student abides by the laws of the country or state in which he or she is living.
2. A student does not miss any scheduled event because of the effects of alcohol consumption.
3. A student does not become ill due to the effects of alcohol consumption.
4. A student does not engage in inappropriate behavior toward other individuals as a result of alcohol consumption.
5. A student does not engage in destructive behavior toward property as a result of alcohol consumption.
6. A student does not engage in behavior that causes embarrassment to the other members of the group, the faculty member(s) or the in-country host(s) as a result of alcohol consumption.
7. Students in a group do not facilitate/encourage or ignore a fellow student who is abusing alcohol. Providing alcohol to persons under the legal drinking age is illegal and against policy. Transporting quantities of alcohol to program sites with the intent of sharing the alcohol with members of the group is considered to be irresponsible use of alcohol.

[Source: Adapted from St. Olaf College]

Students are encouraged to use good judgment if consuming alcohol at private homes or other accommodations during nonprogram hours. Student groups are encouraged to discuss issues related to alcohol abuse by other members of their group with the program supervisor/instructor.

If a student becomes incapacitated due to alcohol overuse, or if he or she is in need of medical attention, others are strongly encouraged to contact the faculty member or program site supervisor immediately, to protect the health and well being of the affected student.

Other Safety Concerns

High-Risk Activities

Certain activities carry a high risk. Institutions that sponsor programs that include activities such as horseback riding, surfing, scuba diving, skiing, mountain climbing, or swimming as a part of the program-related excursions or activities should consider carrying a rider on their insurance policy to cover the increased risk and exposure. Weigh the risks to the group of the proposed activity, and pay special attention to safety issues when providing predeparture orientation. Inform students of any dangerous situations that may occur. Obviously, risks in a backcountry archaeology program or a jungle trek may be quite different from those in Paris or Hong Kong.

Traffic and Vehicles

Advise students to be aware of traffic patterns. It is easy to become confused in countries where drivers use the opposite side of the road. Consequences for drinking and driving are very severe in most countries.

Warn students to be sure that any equipment they rent or use (bicycles, mopeds, motorcycles, cars) is operationally safe. If the faculty director or any member of the group plans to rent a car anywhere, inquire about driving regulations, learn traffic signals, and make sure they can legally drive in the country. Some programs may prohibit students from renting vehicles.

Swimming

Swimming carries a high level of risk unless you are in a well-chlorinated pool. However, even pools can be a health hazard. Of special concern is the risk of disease from contaminated lakes and rivers that can cause a variety of skin, eye, ear, and intestinal infections. Ocean swimming is usually the cleanest, but it is always good practice to check with the local authorities before venturing into unknown bodies of water. Tides and undertows can be deadly to the uninformed swimmer. Beaches and coastlines that are marked with the international code for "no swimming allowed" are to be avoided.

HEALTH ISSUES

Students, and some program directors, may assume that since they are participating in a short-term program, health issues do not need to be addressed. Nothing could be further from reality, whether malaria, diarrhea, or sunburn. As you prepare students to study abroad, take into account the following specific considerations.

The Medical Report

As demonstrated in Chapter 11, Student Selection and Enrollment, clear procedures and policies must be defined as programs develop, especially with regard to refund policies if a student withdraws or a program is canceled.

Although the administrator or faculty director cannot ask for medical information before a student is selected to participate, many programs do request that students complete a medical report or health information form after acceptance (see Short-Term Study Abroad Off-Campus Medical Report" at the end of this chapter).

There is some debate over requesting health information at all or whether a physician's signature should be required. However, by having students self-disclose any illness such as asthma or diabetes, or required medication, assistance can be anticipated and provided. The collected information is strictly confidential, and faculty directors should have copies to review and take abroad.

Before moving forward, always check with your organization and legal counsel for appropriate language and whether a form such as the "Medical Report" can be used.

Immunizations

If your program visits a country where immunizations are recommended or required, you may wish to work with a local health clinic (either institutionally or community-based, depending on your circumstances) to provide information, support, and the immunizations. Many clinics have a health education component and often are very supportive of efforts toward ensuring students' good health overseas. Health educators, on campus and in the community, can form a partnership with administrators to deliver appropriate predeparture information to students and faculty directors. They will also advise on immunizations that are recommended or required, based on information from the Centers for Disease Control and the World Health Organization.

Students must be informed of recommended immunizations or medicines well before departure to follow the appropriate steps. A country- or program-specific information sheet, such as the Peru Interim Immunization Recommendations/General Precautions at the end of this chapter, is highly recommended. If student access to travel clinics is difficult, you may wish to set up travel clinics at a time when participants can receive appropriate inoculations as a group.

Region-Specific Health Issues

Extra precautions are necessary when short-term programs travel to areas with particular health risks, and there are many excellent resources to use, such as the Centers for Disease Control and Prevention and the International Association for Medical Assistance to Travelers (IAMAT). Areas of concern and advice to participants include the following:

Diarrhea
☐ Do not drink the local water or ice unless it is 100 percent safe (and still, question the source of information).

- ☐ Travelers should avoid salads, thin-skinned fruits (such as grapes), milk and milk products, and seafood that is far from where it was originally caught.
- ☐ Cooked foods should be thoroughly cooked.

Malaria
- ☐ Found mainly in rural areas and areas with night-biting mosquitoes.
- ☐ If going to an area where malaria is prevalent, a physician should be consulted for the best type of preventative medicine.
- ☐ Travelers may not donate blood for three years after leaving a country where malaria is found.

Hepatitis A
- ☐ Common in countries where sanitation is poor.
- ☐ Infection comes from person-to-person contact or through contaminated food and water.
- ☐ Since the incidence of hepatitis A is growing worldwide, it is recommended that all travelers be immunized.

Hepatitis B
- ☐ Widespread in many developing countries. Spread in the same way as AIDS.
- ☐ Travelers spending more than six months in an infected area or engaging in at-risk behavior should receive vaccination.

Typhoid
- ☐ Transmitted from person-to-person contact or through contaminated food and water.
- ☐ Vaccination recommended for travelers to risk areas.

Yellow Fever
- ☐ Viral disease carried by mosquitoes in some areas of Central and South America and tropical regions of Africa.
- ☐ Travelers to disease areas, or those transiting through a disease area and entering another country, may be required to show a certificate of vaccination against yellow fever for legal entry.

Diphtheria/Tetanus
- ☐ Tetanus is particularly prevalent in rural areas.
- ☐ Diphtheria and tetanus are easily prevented with a DPT or DT inoculation; this inoculation is recommended every five years.

Tuberculosis (TB)
- ☐ Greater number of incidences in many region-specific areas.
- ☐ Student may have a TB test upon return.

HIV/AIDS
- ☐ 80 percent of HIV-infected people acquire the infection through sexual contact.
- ☐ May also be contracted through blood transfusions or injections with contaminated needles that have not been properly sterilized.
- ☐ Sexual contact should be avoided or a latex condom used correctly for every sexual contact.
- ☐ If regular injections are needed, bring your own supply of needles and syringes.
- ☐ If regular blood treatment is needed, bring your own supply of blood products if possible.

Cholera
- ☐ Transmitted through contaminated food and water.
- ☐ Immunization needed if traveler will have close contact with local population in areas with a high incidence of cholera.

Polio
- ☐ Disease that occurs in the developing world outside North and South America.
- ☐ Most U.S. citizens have had their primary immunization series.
- ☐ Booster required every 10 years if traveling to areas where disease is prevalent.

Rabies
- ☐ Infection from a bite, scratch, or, less commonly, lick from an infected animal.
- ☐ Travelers who will have frequent animal contact would benefit from a rabies preexposure vaccine series before departure.

How To Treat Diarrhea

Symptoms of diarrhea can range from mild to very severe and can occur with little warning. Here are some recommendations to participants for treating diarrhea:

- ☐ Replace fluids. Dehydration is one of the problems associated with diarrhea. The goal of treatment is not to suppress the symptoms of diarrhea, but to correct the body's fluid imbalances.
- ☐ Add salt to diet.
- ☐ Avoid dairy products (they inhibit the body's absorption of salt).
- ☐ After one to two days, use medications such as Imodium, Lomotile, Pepto-Bismol, or Paregoric to relieve abdominal cramps. These medications should be used only for two to three days to give symptomatic relief.
- ☐ If symptoms persist longer than a few days, consult a physician.
- ☐ If diarrhea is accompanied by a high fever, shaking chills, and/or blood in the stool, consult a physician immediately.

□ Anyone potentially exposed to rabies must seek prompt medical attention.

Prescription Drugs

Most of us at some point take two different kinds of medications—prescription and over-the-counter drugs. Before leaving, students and faculty directors must plan for what medications they will need while abroad.

Suggestions for Prescription Medications

□ Take a minimum supply of one and a half, if not a full double supply.

□ Be very careful to keep medications in a place where they cannot be lost or stolen. Keep all medications in carry-on luggage.

□ Keep medications in their original containers to avoid problems in customs.

□ Upon arrival at the destination, keep medications in two separate places.

□ Prescription medicines are not always the same abroad as in the United States. Do not plan on having U.S. prescriptions filled while abroad. If carrying a prescription, have the physician write the drug's generic name, instructions, dosage, and reason for prescribing the drug.

□ Check with the physician before departure for advice on how to adjust when to take medication, and how to reduce the risk of over- or underdosing from the time difference between home and destination.

Suggestions for Over-the-Counter Medications

□ Over-the-counter drugs may not be the same as in the United States.

□ Travelers should consider bringing their preferred over-the-counter brands of:

o headache and fever medicine

o vitamins

o diarrhea and constipation medicine

o antacid

o antihistamine

o motion-sickness tablets

o decongestant

o hydrocortisone cream

Glasses and Contact Lens Wearers

Suggest that participants take along an extra pair of glasses or contact lenses, as well as a lens prescription.

Medic Alert

If a participant has any serious condition not easily recognized, such as allergies, diabetes, or epilepsy, he or she may want to acquire a Medic Alert emblem.

For more information, contact:
http://www.medicalert.com
Medic Alert Foundation International
P.O. Box 1009, Turlock, CA 95380
800.633.4260

Adjusting to the Heat

If students will be traveling to a country with a year-round warm climate, they need to think about how they will adjust to the weather, especially if their home environment has the opposite climate. Extreme changes in climate and temperature variations will affect both the comfort and health of those who are not prepared. For the most enjoyable time in the heat, suggest that students:

□ minimize the amount of time they are in direct sunlight;

□ drink plenty of fluids, especially water;

□ wear loose-fitting clothing that is made of cotton or another material capable of absorbing perspiration;

□ wear light colors, especially white, which will reflect sunlight;

□ wear a wide-brimmed hat of a light material; and

□ use sun block.

Sexually Transmitted Diseases, Including HIV/AIDS

Sexually transmitted diseases, such as gonorrhea, syphilis, and herpes continue to pose health risks in almost every country. The HIV virus, which causes AIDS, is not only transmitted sexually, but also through contaminated needles and blood supplies, and thus presents a general health risk abroad. If a student should require surgery, medical evacuation should be carefully considered. Invasive medical procedures such as transfusions and injections may be high risk because the instruments and blood may not be safe or screened. Needles and syringes should be single-use, disposable, and prepackaged in a sealed container. Travelers to high-risk areas of the world may consider carrying these items along in their travel medical kit for use in case of emergency.

Overseas Medical Care

Should a student or faculty director require medical care while overseas, they should recognize that there are cultural and medical differences in health care. In some countries, physicians are far less likely to prescribe drugs than doctors in the United States, and in others, patients' families provide food and feed the patient. Prepare students for the unexpected, both in occurrence and in practice. There may be a severe shortage of medicine or an unavailability of technology. On the other hand, students may be surprised at the efficient care they will receive in many countries as compared to the United States, and at a much lower cost.

To prepare, check with the health officer or nurse at the U.S. embassy or consulate in the host country, who can identify local health care resources should they become necessary. Names and addresses of several embassy-recommended physicians can be obtained before participants become ill or need medical attention, saving precious time in an emergency.

International Association for Medical Assistance to Travelers

Consider becoming a member of the International Association for Medical Assistance to Travelers (IAMAT), a nonprofit organization that provides medical information for countries around the world. For more information, visit http://www.iamat.org.

Overseas Decisions

Most travelers' complaints are colds, intestinal upsets, and minor aches and pains—conditions that require no professional medical assistance. Food- and waterborne diseases are the number one cause of illness to travelers. It is only when these complaints escalate or when other emergency situations arise that require further treatment that decisions for local care or evacuation should be made. Confirm that all participants have insurance for medical evacuation.

If a member of the group requires emergency assistance overseas, ask the program provider, on-site coordinator, or the hotel for assistance. Taking a taxi to a hospital or emergency room is another easy, quick solution. If language is a problem, try to obtain the services of someone who can translate for you. Even an experienced faculty director with good command of the language may have difficulty obtaining information without a vocabulary that covers basic medical terms.

INSURANCE MATTERS

Any student participating in a short-term program abroad should be required to produce evidence, prior to departure, of adequate health and accident insurance. Your organization should set the terms of what is determined to be adequate for specific circumstances and programs. You may wish to require mandatory insurance, which can be built into the program fee or purchased separately. A point in favor of mandatory insurance is that the organization has prescribed the basic coverage, and you can be assured that each participant has satisfied the requirements.

Contracting for Study Abroad Insurance Coverage

Before requiring a certain type of insurance for participants in your program, check with your institution's legal counsel or risk management office to clarify the liability situation for university- or college-sponsored programs. If your organization has its own comprehensive policies, does the coverage extend overseas? Who is included? Is there an age limit? Does the student have to be enrolled full time to qualify? Are faculty directors covered as well? These are some of the questions that should be discussed before selecting an insurance provider.

The policy should cover the participant for the entire period of the program, and should include medical expenses related to sickness or injury, medical evacuation at a limit for the program's site, and repatriation in case of death. Does it include medical evacuation back to a student's home or to a health care delivery site overseas? What exclusions are there for medical evacuation? Who will make this decision and under what conditions? When establishing an insurance plan for a program, other things to consider are supplementary lost baggage, stolen property, or trip cancellation/interruption insurance.

Preexisting Conditions

Preexisting conditions have been a very complex area of insurance coverage. How is a preexisting condition determined and by whom? What is excluded? Is the student fully informed of the exclusion? There is nothing worse than telling a parent, partner, or guardian that the student's health insurance does not cover significant medical costs overseas.

Claims Process

Carefully review the insurance policy for its claims process.

☐ Are payments made directly to the hospital and/or physician overseas, or do they require the student to pay and then file for reimbursement?

☐ If the latter is true, students must be informed of the importance of retaining receipts for payment for medical treatment. Without a receipt for services rendered, the student may never be able to collect on the claim.

☐ Has the claims process been made clear to students and faculty directors?

☐ If the student is required to pay in full at time of treatment, he or she will need to produce a credit card with an adequate credit line to allow for payment. If credit cards cannot be used and faculty directors have to pay out of group funds, students should agree to repayment by signing a document written by the faculty director.

Student Options for Insurance

International Student Identification Card

Many educational institutions require the International Student Identification Card for all study abroad participants. The card covers basic health and accident insurance coverage, as well as medical evacuation and repatriation of remains, but it only covers a small portion of expenses for major accidents or illness. It should be viewed as supplemental and not primary insurance coverage.

Insurance Through Parents, Spouse, School, or Other Insurance

Participants should talk with their family and insurance agent to find out exactly what coverage includes.

Participants may want to consider the following:

☐ Does the plan include hospitalization coverage for accidents and illnesses while abroad?

☐ What is the maximum amount of coverage provided?

☐ Are there deductibles? If so, what are they?

☐ Will the plan include emergency room expenses?

☐ What is the coverage for medical evacuation (i.e., returning to the United States to be given the appropriate medical treatment for injury or illness; sometimes includes returning on an airplane with a medical unit)?

☐ In the event of death, what is the coverage for repatriation (i.e., return of bodily remains after death to country of origin)?

☐ What should the student do under the plan if he or she has to pay cash up front and has no money?

☐ Does the plan cover visits to the doctor or medication prescribed while abroad?

☐ What are the procedures for filing a claim, and how long does it take to get reimbursed after filing?

☐ If it is a trip cancellation plan, what are the guidelines regarding preexisting conditions?

☐ When does the plan begin and end?

☐ Does the plan enable the student to have continuous coverage before, during, and after he or she goes abroad?

☐ Is the plan the primary or secondary carrier? If secondary, when does the coverage begin?

☐ Is there a booklet explaining coverage in detail?

Trip Cancellation Insurance

Trip cancellation insurance protects students financially if they have to cancel or interrupt their study abroad program for medical reasons. If cancellation from the study abroad program occurs after the final deadline for any reason, students usually forfeit not only the deposit but also the entire program fee. For more information on trip cancellation insurance, see the Web Resources section at the end of this book.

Disclosure of Insurance Information

More organizations are requesting proof of insurance from the companies that provide services for study abroad programs. Ask your risk manager or legal counsel if this is necessary. See the "Proof of Insurance" example at the end of this chapter.

Faculty Directors Options for Insurance

Don't overlook the program directors' needs for insurance. The organization's health insurance and benefit plan should be reviewed for overseas travel, and employees with that coverage should understand the claims process.

Faculty should consider the International Teacher Identification Card, which mirrors the student coverage.

LIABILITY ISSUES

Liability issues will never go away, and no organization can eliminate all liable situations, on campus or overseas. The key with any off-campus program is to reduce your liability whenever and wherever possible. For short-term programs, take the following steps to reduce your liability:

☐ Make sure that all administrators and faculty directors understand what defines "appropriate and inappropriate personal and professional behavior" on campus and overseas.

☐ Review your program with an eye to eliminate potential threats.

☐ Conduct a legal audit—by your legal counsel or attorney hired to coordinate with the international office—to review the program's policies and procedures.

☐ Be sure your legal counsel has reviewed all of your program documents that are contractual in nature for validity, duration, enforceability, exceptions, and/or conflicts. Promotional materials should be reviewed annually to ensure that the program is accurately represented.

☐ Add a disclaimer to publicity and promotional materials to protect the administrator against unforeseen changes in program arrangement, including such things as currency fluctuations or increased airfares.

☐ If your program involves unusual or high risks, inform the participants of the potential risks, and be sure your publicity and promotional materials state the risks clearly. In addition, never promise what you cannot deliver.

For detailed information on legal issues and education abroad, see *NAFSA's Guide to Education Abroad for Administrators and Advisers (3rd edition)*, pp. 511–533.

Liability Waivers/Release

The most important thing you can do to reduce your liability is to require participants to read and sign a release, disclaimer, agreement, or liability waiver. When students who are legal minors are allowed to participate, require their parents or guardians to also sign and receive copies of relevant forms and materials.

Included at the end of this chapter are examples of liability waivers and study abroad agreements from a variety of schools:

The University of Delaware (public university)

☐ Student/Parent Liability Release

☐ Provider's Proof of Insurance

☐ Medical Report Form

☐ Conditions of Participation

St. Olaf College (small, private, liberal arts college)

☐ Parent Conditions of Participation

☐ Student Conditions of Participation

☐ Off-Campus Interim Agreement Form
☐ Medical Authorization

University of St. Thomas (large, private university)
☐ Short-Term Off-Campus Agreement

CRISIS MANAGEMENT

While it has always been important for an institution to have a well-developed crisis management plan, recent events have made such a plan even more important. Your credibility with students, parents, and even your own administration is enhanced by an effective crisis management plan.

Disaster can hit a program with sweeping effects: a debilitating health problem might require a student to withdraw; the faculty director might suffer a stroke or heart attack; one of the group may be lost or abducted; a group member abusing alcohol can manifest behavior that is destructive to himself or herself and the program. As an administrator or faculty director, you must be aware of the many types of problems that may endanger your students and the program. They may never happen, but to be aware is to be prepared.

Considerations

1. Does your organization have an existing crisis management plan to deal with a domestic crisis, such as the death of a student on campus?
2. Is there a 24-hour number in place for faculty or students to call?
3. If a program provider is retained, is he or she available 24 hours a day?
4. Has your crisis management plan been approved by senior administration and leadership?

At the end of this chapter, you will find examples of plans for crisis management, suspension, or cancellation and evacuation of study abroad programs, and preventative actions for faculty directors overseas.

Sending Students Home

There are many reasons why a student may need to return home during a short-term program abroad. Some returns will be voluntary, such as for medical reasons or a death in the family. Other returns will be disciplinary, prompted by the action (or inaction) of the student. A policy should be developed for when and how to send students home. This policy should be well understood by your office as well as your faculty director or on-site director.

In any situation, facts and details must be thoroughly documented by those involved on-site as well as by staff at the home institution. Some campuses and programs develop forms to guide this documentation, such as the Incident Report sample at the end of this chapter.

Medical or Psychological Reasons

When a student needs to return home for a medical or emotional/psychological reason, you should have a plan to determine whether the student needs to be accompanied. This can be very problematic, especially if you are managing shorter programs. Students are adults, and cannot be forced to return against their will. Professional advice must be sought on the student's condition, and the best procedure should be determined. Since emotional problems and mental illness are usually excluded by medical insurance policies, your program should be prepared to assist the student and the student's family. A ticket may have to be arranged for whoever would accompany the student home under these circumstances.

Disciplinary Cases

Unfortunately, there may be circumstances that necessitate sending a student home, especially if the student breaks published rules of the organization or the code of conduct. Again, it is vital to have published expectations of behavior in all written materials, such as a student policy handbook. See Sample Disciplinary Rights and Procedures for Study Abroad Programs, Academic and Nonacademic, at the end of this chapter.

Each faculty director will have different thresholds for student behavior and it is important to articulate these expectations to students at the orientation, in the syllabus, and again after arrival on-site.

Behavior Contracts

If a student breaks a rule for the first time, the faculty director may write a "behavior contract," a document that lists the infraction and asks for the student's signature. See the sample Behavior Contract at the end of this chapter.

Expelling a Student from the Program

If a student violates the rules of conduct a second time, or the student's first violation (such as drug use) warrants expulsion from the program, you may be required to expel the student. See the Sample Expulsion Form at the end of this chapter.

If a student does need to be sent home, consider the following helpful hints from others who have been faced with the difficult decision to expel a student:

☐ Faculty directors do not need to make these decisions on their own. A network should be in place to support the faculty director, the group, and the situation.

☐ An extreme case may call for a student to be expelled from the home institution as well as from the study abroad program. In such cases, working with your dean of students and legal counsel is imperative.

☐ The logistical issues, such as the group's location far away from the departure city, may be the most challenging. Work with your program provider or travel agent to limit the cost of the expulsion to the other students on the program.

o   Check to see whether a student is a minor or legal audit (21 years or younger) and make sure that all study abroad students waive their FERPA rights as discussed in Chapter 11, Student Selection and Enrollment.

Conclusion

With all of the precautions and warnings, and the listing of health issues and hazards, administrators, faculty directors, or short-term providers should not give in to the temptation of seeing a problem or lawsuit lurking behind every administrative decision or indecision. U.S. institutions send thousands of students overseas every year, with very little incidence of health emergency or catastrophe.

Endnotes

[1]   "A Safe Trip Abroad." Department of State Publication 10399, Bureau of Consular Affairs, revised 1996.

Study Abroad/Domestic Study-Travel Programs

Agreement and General Release

WHEREAS, the University of Delaware (hereinafter UD) offers a travel study program in _____ ("Host Country") from _____(Program Start Date) to _____(Program End Date), to qualified students of UD and of other selected colleges and of other selected universities ("the Program"); and

WHEREAS, _____(Participant's Name), voluntarily desires to participate in the Program:

IT IS HEREBY AGREED by and between the Participant, the Participant's parent or legal Guardian if Participant is under the age of 18, (collectively "the Undersigned"[1]) and UD, as follows:

1.0 Participation in the Academic Program: The Undersigned have been informed by UD of the scope and focus of the Program, eligibility requirements, costs, registration procedures, travel, itinerary, logistics, terms of cancellation, academic contact, and credit. By signing this Agreement and General Release, the Undersigned acknowledge that they have fully educated themselves as to the details of this program and agree to abide by its terms. It is expressly acknowledged that Participant is not required to participate in the Program. In consideration of the Undersigned's execution of this Agreement and General Release and their agreement to be legally bound by its terms, UD will permit the Participant to enter into the Program subject to the provisions set forth herein.

2.0 Waiver of UD's Liability for Risks and Dangers: The Undersigned understand that there are certain dangers, hazards, and risks inherent in international and domestic travel and the activities included in the Program, including but not limited to risks of injury, permanent disability or death, property damage and severe social or economic loss, which may result from the actions, inactions, or negligence of the Participant or others, weather conditions, conditions of equipment used, language barriers, differing social cultures, national and local laws, sickness, strikes, natural disasters, civil unrest or hostilities, terrorist activities or acts of war, and that UD, its trustees, employees, and agents (collectively hereinafter UD) cannot assume responsibility for any such personal injury, property damage or other loss. The Undersigned further understand that the above risks are also associated with any activities undertaken by the Participant which are not activities included in the Program. Such activities include, but are not limited to, individual travel by the Participant during vacation periods, or periods of time extending beyond the termination of the Program, or during other periods in which the Participant is not undertaking program activities. UD cannot and does not assume responsibility for any such personal injury, property damage, or other loss suffered by Participant during such times.

3.0 Participant Responsibility for Medical Needs

3.1 The Undersigned understand that healthcare facilities may be minimal/absent in rural/remote areas and that all types of health care, including for emergencies, may be difficult to find. The Undersigned further understands that the Participant should not expect the same type of health care as would be available in the Participant's home country. Having read and understood the information UD provided on healthcare precautions, the Participant has fully informed UD of any condition of his/her mental/physical health that might affect the Undersigned participation in the program.

3.2 The Undersigned assure UD that the Participant has consulted with a medical doctor with regard to the Participant's personal medical needs such that the Undersigned can and do further state that there are no health-related reasons or problems which preclude or restrict the Participant's participation in the Program.

3.3 The Undersigned are aware of all applicable personal medical needs, as well as having arranged for adequate hospitalization insurance to meet any and all needs for payment of hospital costs while the Participant is undertaking the Program. The Undersigned agree that UD cannot be and is not responsible for attending to any of the Participant's medical or medication needs, that the Undersigned assume all risk and responsibility therefore, and that if the Participant is required to be hospitalized while in a foreign country or in the United States during the Program, UD cannot and does not assume any legal responsibility for payment of such costs.

4.0 Participant's Life, Health, and Property Insurance: The Undersigned are aware that there are other potential risks in which the Participant may be placed or in which the Participant may place himself or herself during the Program which neither the Undersigned nor UD are able to foresee at this time. The Undersigned are aware that life, health, and property insurance is sold by American companies in order to reduce the financial consequences of such risk.

5.0 UD's Rights and Powers: The University reserves the following rights and powers:

5.1 The right to cancel the Program without penalty;

5.2 The right to alter or withdraw any part of the Program and to make any alterations, deletions or modifications in the itinerary and/or academic program as deemed necessary by UD or by the course instructors as agents of UD.

5.3 The Undersigned have made themselves aware of the rules and regulations as contained in the UD *Student Guide to University Policies* and all relevant UD travel study documents. The Participant agrees to uphold individual and group standards appropriate to the cultural setting of the program. If the Participant's actions violate local or national laws and/or UD or host institution regulations, or are judged to be injurious to the program and/or seriously offensive to the host cultures, and/or damaging to the reputation of UD, the Participant acknowledges that the faculty director(s) has the right, after consultation with a representative of UD, to terminate the Participant's enrollment in the program without refund of tuition nor fees and to return the Participant to the United States at his own expense.

5.4 The Undersigned understand that military actions, terrorist threats, labor strikes, civil unrest, and natural disasters, as well as other situations which are disruptive to the learning environment and/or the life of and safety of the Program group, may result in an alteration in the Program itinerary. The Undersigned agree to accept financial responsibility for the Participant which may result from such a change in the program itinerary and agree to follow the leadership and direction of UD in the decision to change travel plans.

6.0 Potential Travel and Accommodation Problems

6.1 The Undersigned acknowledge and agree to accept all responsibility for loss or additional expenses due to delays or other changes in transportation due to sickness, weather, strikes, or other unforeseen causes. The Undersigned acknowledge and understand that UD assumes no liability whatsoever for any loss, damage, destruction, theft or the like to the Participant's luggage or personal belongings, and that the Participant has retained adequate insurance or has sufficient funds to replace such belongings and will hold UD harmless therefrom.

6.2 The Undersigned acknowledge and understand that in the event the Participant becomes detached from the Program group, fails to meet a departure bus, airplane, train, or other conveyance, or becomes sick or injured, the Participant will bear all responsibility to seek out,

---

[1] The term, Undersigned, is used in this Agreement and General Release as pertaining to more than one person. If the participant is of majority age, it refers only to the Participant. If the Participant is not of majority age, Undersigned refers to the Participant and the Participant's Parent or Guardian, signatory, hereto.

contact, and reach the Program group at its next available destination; and that the Participant shall bear all costs attendant to contacting and reaching the field trip group at its next available destination.

6.3 The Undersigned acknowledge and understand that there are risks associated with operating a motor vehicle while participating in the Program and that UD assumes no liability whatever for any death, injury, damage, loss, accident or delay resulting from the Participant's operating a motor vehicle while participating in the Program

6.4 All services and accommodations are subject to the laws of the country in which they are provided.

6.5 The Undersigned understand that UD in no way represents, or acts as agent for, the transportation carriers, hotels, and other suppliers of services connected with the Program. The Undersigned further understand and agree that UD, its governing board, employees and agents are:

6.5.1 Not responsible or liable for any injury, damage, loss, accident, delay, or other irregularity which may be caused by the defect of any vehicle or the negligence or default by any company or person engaged in providing or performing any of the services involved in the Program;

6.5.2 Not responsible for any disruption of travel arrangements, or any consequent additional expenses that may be incurred therefrom.

7.0 Legal Problems: The Undersigned acknowledge and understand that should the Participant have or develop legal problems with any foreign nationals or with any government while participating in the Program the Participant will attend to the matter personally with the Participant's own personal funds. UD is not responsible for providing any assistance under such circumstances.

8.0 Conduct of the Participant: The Undersigned are aware of the means by which sexually transmitted diseases are contracted and recognize the inherent risks of unprotected sexual activity and intravenous drug use. The Undersigned are aware of the health, safety, and legal implications associated with the use of alcohol and drugs and will educate themselves, prior to departure, as to the local or national laws of the host country. The Undersigned acknowledge and understand that UD assumes no liability whatsoever for any death, injury, loss, damage, harm, accident or delay resulting from the Participant's conduct as described in this paragraph 8.0.

9.0 Governing Law: The Undersigned agree that this Agreement and General Release shall be construed in accordance with the laws of the State of Delaware, which shall be the forum for any lawsuits filed under or incident to the Agreement and General Release or the Program. The terms and provisions of this Agreement and General Release shall be severable, such that if a court of competent jurisdiction holds any term to be illegal, unenforceable, or in conflict with any law governing this Agreement and General Release, the validity of the remaining portions shall not be affected thereby.

10.0 Assumption of the Risks Involved

10.1 Knowing the dangers, hazards, and risks described herein, or otherwise associated with participation in the Program whether foreseen or unforeseen, and in consideration of being permitted to participate in the Program, the Undersigned, on behalf of the Participant's family, heirs, and personal representative(s), agree to assume all risks and responsibilities surrounding Participant's participation in the Program including transit to, during and from the Program, and to forever discharge, release and waive any claims against UD for any and all liability related to any harm, injury, damage, claims, demands, actions, causes of action, costs, and expenses of any nature whatsoever which the Participant may have or which may hereafter accrue to the Undersigned, arising out of or related to any loss, damage, or injury, including but not limited to suffering and death, that may be sustained by the Participant or by any property belonging to the Participant, except for loss or injury arising out of the sole negligence or willful misconduct of UD.

10.2 The Undersigned understand and agree that UD does not have medical personnel available at the location of the Program or during transportation or anywhere in the Host Country. The Undersigned understand and agree that the UD is granted permission to authorize emergency medical treatment, if necessary, and that such action by UD shall be subject to the terms of this Agreement and General Release. The Undersigned understand that UD assumes no responsibility for any injury or damage which might arise out of or in connection with such authorized emergency medical treatment.

10.3 The Undersigned acknowledges having read and understood all Consular Information sheets, travel warnings, and other announcements posted on the Web site of the U.S. State Department and relating to the country or countries visited during the Program.

11.0 Other Claims: It is the Undersigned's express intent that this Agreement and General Release shall bind the members of the Undersigned's family and spouse, if Participant is alive, and Participant's family, estate, heirs, administrators, personal representatives, or assigns, if Participant is deceased, and shall be deemed as a Release, Waiver, Discharge, and Covenant not to Sue UD. The Undersigned agree to save and hold harmless, indemnify, and defend UD from any claim by the Undersigned or Participant's family, arising out of the Participant's participation in the Program.

12.0 Age of Participant: The Undersigned state that Participant _____ at least eighteen (18) years of age and fully competent   to sign this Agreement.   *"is or is NOT"*

13.0 Entire Agreement: In signing this Release, the Undersigned acknowledge and represent that the Undersigned have become fully informed of the content of this Agreement and General Release by reading it before signing it and that no oral representations, statements, or inducements, apart from the foregoing written statement, have been made.

THIS IS A RELEASE OF LEGAL RIGHTS
READ AND UNDERSTAND BEFORE SIGNING

SIGNED_____   _____DATE: _____
            (Signed in the presence of notary)   **(printed last name)**

_____DATE: _____
(Co-Signature of Parent or Guardian if Participant is under 18 years of age)

SECTION FOR NOTARY PUBLIC USE:

Sworn and subscribed before me this _____ day of _____, 200_____.

Signature of Notary Public: _____**Seal of Notary Public.**

Rev. 12/02/03

PERU INTERIM
IMMUNIZATION RECOMMENDATIONS/GENERAL PRECAUTIONS

Following are immunization recommendations made by the Center for Disease Control and the St. Olaf Health Service to protect you while traveling abroad. Talk with your parents to see if these immunizations/medications are covered by your hospitalization insurance. If so, make arrangements with your local clinic or a travel clinic.

If they are not covered by your hospitalization insurance, it will likely be less expensive to obtain the immunizations/medications from the St. Olaf Health Service.

** If you plan to take the immunizations from the St. Olaf Health Service, let them know as soon as possible so that sufficient supplies can be ordered.

- -

IMMUNIZATIONS/MEDICATIONS:
Tetanus-Diphtheria-Pertussis - Need Tdap booster every 5 years when traveling. ($40)
Measles/Mumps/Rubella - Must have had two doses after 1 year of age. ($40.00)
Hepatitis A - First dose prior to departure, second dose 6 months-1 year later. ($65 per injection)
Hepatitis B - Series of three injections. First dose when possible, second dose 1 month later, third dose six months to one year after first injection ($18 per injection if 19; $36 per injection if 20 and over)
OR:
Twin Rix – if you haven't been immunized against either Hepatitis A or Hepatitis B, you can get this immunization which protects against both. Three injections total - $95 each.
Typhoid - One injection at least two weeks, or longer, before   departure ($45)
Varicella - Indicated for all persons born outside the U.S. or born in the U.S. after 1965, except not indicated for persons with an adequate vaccination history (1 dose before age 13 years or 2 doses after age 13 years), reliable evidence of previous infection, or laboratory confirmation of immunity. (Not available at St. Olaf Health Service).
Flu Vaccine – one injection ($25)

GENERAL PRECAUTIONS:
Dengue Fever – Risk in urban and rural areas in southern provinces. Daytime insect precautions recommended.

NOTE: It is recommended that you have a Tuberculosis screening prior to departure and 6 weeks after your return. ($3)

NOTE: You may experience trouble with altitude sickness. Consider getting a prescription for Acetozolamide.

NOTE: Because some of the above recommendations require sequential dosing, and because there may be issues of interaction, you should contact the Health Service or your Health Care provider early to plan a course of action.

- -
UNLESS NOTED, ALL OF YOUR IMMUNIZATION RECORDS ARE AVAILABLE AT THE ON-CAMPUS HEALTH SERVICE. CHECK WITH THEM TO SEE WHICH OF THE ABOVE YOU NEED.

** FOLLOW THE ADVICE OF YOUR PERSONAL PHYSICIAN OR HEALTH CLINIC PROFESSIONAL IF IT DIFFERS FROM THE ABOVE.

These are the immunizations currently recommended for the scheduled itinerary for your program. Since these can change without notice, it would be good for you and/or your health care professional to check the web site for the Center for Disease Control to see if there are changes before you begin your regimen of immunizations. The CDC website is: www.cdc.gov. Also, if you intend to visit other countries or regions during free time or at the end of your program, you should check the CDC web site   to see if there are additional recommendations for the areas you plan to visit.

[Source: Adapted from St. Olaf College]

UNIVERSITY
of ST.THOMAS
MINNESOTA

Short-Term Off-Campus Programs Medical Report
International Education

The purpose of this form is to determine your health history and any special medical needs you may have when you study abroad. Information provided will be treated confidentially. Any information considered important and essential will be forwarded to your faculty director for the purpose of serving you as promptly and correctly as possible, should you require medical or counseling services during your time off-campus.

To Be Completed By Applicant

Name (please print)		Height	Weight	Gender ☐ F ☐ M

Course Name/Program

Are you generally in good physical condition? ☐ Yes ☐ No	If no, please explain.
Are you currently being treated for any physical condition? ☐ Yes ☐ No	If so, please explain.

Are you a diabetiic? ☐ Yes ☐ No	Have you ever had epilepsy or other seizure disorders? ☐ Yes ☐ No	Do you have asthma? ☐ Yes ☐ No

Do you have a heart condition? ☐ Yes ☐ No	Do you have or have you had any eating disorders? ☐ Yes ☐ No

What diseases have you had in the past five years (if any)?

Have you ever been treated for an emotional disorder? ☐ Yes ☐ No	If so, please describe.* * Please explain to the extent that this information should be known by the staff concerned with your well-being during the period abroad.
Do you have any allergies to foods, medications, enviornmental factors, insects, etc? ☐ Yes ☐ No	If so, what happens when you come into contact with the allergen?
Are you taking any medication? ☐ Yes ☐ No	If so, please describe.
Are you on a restricted diet (vegetarian)? ☐ Yes ☐ No	If so, please describe.
Do you anticipate needing any health care or counseling while abroad? ☐ Yes ☐ No	If so, please describe.

If there is any additional health information that would be helpful for the faculty director to be aware of during the off-campus program, please describe below.

Medical Insurance

All students are required to be covered by a medical insurance policy while they are off-campus. Please check with your insurance company to see if your benefits extend to another state or country.

I am insured for any medical expenses which may incur while I participate in the Program. This policy is with:

Insurance Company	Policy Number

I certify that all responses made on this Medical Report form are true and accurate, and I will notify International Education hereafter of any relevant changes in my health that occur prior to the start of the Program. I understand that this form is for information purposes only and in no way implies that the University of St. Thomas takes responsibility for my health.

Student Signature	Date

INTE 1492 3/03 Short-Term

[Source: University of St. Thomas]

OFF-CAMPUS INTERIM AGREEMENT FORM
INTERNATIONAL AND OFF-CAMPUS STUDY
ST. OLAF COLLEGE

Name of Program_____

My signature below indicates that I,_____:
                                        (PLEASE PRINT NAME)

1. agree to adhere to the payment schedule as outlined in the Off-Campus Interims Brochure;

2. agree to inform the International & Off-Campus Study Office in writing should I need to cancel participation in the program to which I have been accepted;

3. understand that cancellation fees for my program are payable as outlined in the Off-Campus Interims brochure;

4. have read and understand all of the general information in the Off-Campus Interims Brochure and on the Off-Campus Interims Application

5. understand that St. Olaf College and its International and Off-Campus Study program cannot guarantee a risk free environment or accept responsibility for accidents or illnesses on an off-campus study program.

6. recognize the need for the following rules, agree to abide by them, and realize that I could be sent home for violating them and know that a decision to terminate my participation in the program is final, unappeal-able and at my own expense:

    a. I will not buy, sell, or use drugs at any time (except for prescription drugs used according to prescription).

    b. I will not engage in abusive use of alcohol.

    c. I will not engage in disruptive behavior.

    d. I will participate in all classes and scheduled activities unless I am ill.

    e. I will abide by dress and cultural codes suitable in the cultures visited.

    f. I will avoid demonstrations, especially in politically volatile countries.

    g. I will obey the laws of the location of my off-campus program.

7. have read, understand, and will abide by the "Philosophy, Policies and Procedures" material;

8. agree to participate in any orientation meetings, and/or retreats for my program;

9. agree to complete and return to the International & Off-Campus Study Office all documents required by them to make arrangements for my program.

_____   _____ _____
Student's Signature   Student Number   Date

I understand that my son or daughter has read and agreed to the above.

_____   _____
Parent's Signature   Date

4/3/03

PARENT/GUARDIAN CONDITIONS OF PARTICIPATION
INTERNATIONAL AND OFF-CAMPUS TRAVEL PROGRAMS
ST. OLAF COLLEGE

I, _____, am the parent/guardian of _____
___ (name of student). I consent to the participation of my son/daughter/ward in _____
_____ ("Travel Program"), an International or Domestic Off Campus Travel Program offered by St. Olaf College (the "College"), which I understand will necessitate travel away from the College's campus. In consideration for my son/daughter/ward's participation in the Travel Program, I agree to the following:

1. Risks of Study Abroad.
I understand that participation in the College's Travel Program involves risks not found in study at the College. These risks include but are not limited to traveling to and within, and returning from, one or more foreign countries; foreign, political, legal, social and economic conditions; different standards of design, safety and maintenance of buildings, public places and conveyances; local medical practices and conditions; natural hazards; disease, illness and injury; and crime. I understand that these and other risks are further described in the U.S. Department of State Consular Information Sheet and Travel Warning for the country or countries to which my son/daughter/ward will be traveling. I have accessed the applicable Information Sheet(s) and Travel Warning(s) at http://travel.state.gov/travel/, or have been provided with a copy of each by the College. I have reviewed the Information Sheet(s) and Travel Warning(s) and understand that all warnings contained therein are incorporated by reference in these Conditions of Participation. I further understand that domestic travel also involves risks that in some circumstances are similar to those presented by travel abroad. I acknowledge that I am aware of these risks, that the College has no control over these risks, and that it is my son/daughter/ward's responsibility alone to take precautions to minimize such risks.

2. Release of Claims.
With full knowledge of these risks I, on behalf of myself and my legal representatives, heirs, successors and assigns, hereby RELEASE the College, and its regents, officers, employees, agents, successors and assigns, from any and all claims (including but not limited to claims for negligence), causes of action, liabilities and costs which I or any of my legal representatives, heirs, successors and assigns may have or claim to have relating to or arising out of my son/daughter/ward's participation in the Travel Program, including, without limitation, any and all claims and causes of action for property damage, bodily injury, illness and death, caused by, related to or arising out of any action or inaction of the College, its regents, officers, employees or agents, except for such damages or injury as may be caused by the gross negligence or willful misconduct of the College, its regents, officers, employees or agents.

3. Indemnification.
I agree to indemnify, defend and hold harmless the College, and its regents, officers, employees, agents, successors and assigns, from any and all claims, liabilities and costs asserted by or on behalf of my son/daughter/ward or any of my son/daughter/ward's legal representatives, heirs, successors and assigns, or by or on behalf of me or any of my legal representatives, heirs, successors and assigns, within the scope of the release in Paragraph 2 above.

4. Independent Travel.
I give permission for my son/daughter/ward to travel independently on weekends and academic holidays at his/her own expense during the period covered by the Travel Program and after the conclusion of the Travel Program. The College is not responsible for my son/daughter/ward while he/she is traveling independently.

5. Health and Safety.
A. I represent that my son/daughter/ward has no health-related problems or concerns that would preclude or restrict his/her participation in the Travel Program.

B. I understand that if the Travel Program in which my son/daughter/ward is participating is scheduled to last longer than one month, my son/daughter/ward is required to have a physician complete the Report of Medical History form to be provided by the Office of International & Off-Campus Studies, and return it to the Office of International and Off-Campus Studies at least 60 days prior to departure.

C.   My son/daughter/ward has sufficient health, accident, disability, hospitalization and personal property insurance to cover any injuries, illnesses or property damage that my son/daughter/ward may sustain or experience during his/her participation in the Travel Program. The College is not responsible for providing health or accident insurance benefits for my son/daughter/ward in connection with the Travel Program.

D.   I authorize any representative of the College to secure dental and medical treatment for my son/daughter/ward if he/she is injured or becomes ill while participating in the Travel Program, including without limitation anesthetic and surgical treatment, and to sign authorization forms necessary to obtain the treatment. I assume full responsibility for all costs relating to or arising out of the treatment.

6. Standards of Conduct.

I understand that the College has the authority to establish rules for the operation of the Travel Program, and that my son/daughter/ward is expected to comply with those rules. I further understand that the Travel Program Supervisor may terminate my son/daughter/ward's participation in the Travel Program for violating the rules or for behavior which is disruptive or which could affect adversely the reputation of the Travel Program. If my son/daughter/ward's participation in the Travel Program is terminated, he/she will receive no academic credit and will return home at his/her own expense with no refund of fees.

7. Governing Law.

I agree that these Conditions of Participation will be governed by the laws of the State of Minnesota and that the venue for any legal proceedings relating to these Conditions of Participation shall be in the state of Minnesota. I have carefully read this Parent/Guardian Conditions of Participation and the Student Conditions of Participation that my son/daughter/ward, with my permission, has signed. I understand that, by signing these Conditions of Participation, I am giving up legal rights and remedies that might otherwise be available to me. I acknowledge that I have the right and the opportunity to consult with an attorney or other advisor of my choice prior to signing this document. I understand these Conditions of Participation and voluntarily agree to be bound by them and the provisions of the Student Conditions of Participation.

Date:_____

_____
Signature of Parent/Guardian

_____
Printed Name

Home Address _____

_____ Phone #_____

Health Insurance Provider _____ Policy #_____

Keep one copy for your records.

3/17/06
GP:1711646 v4

[Source: Adapted from St. Olaf College]

STUDENT CONDITIONS OF PARTICIPATION
INTERNATIONAL AND OFF-CAMPUS TRAVEL PROGRAMS
ST. OLAF COLLEGE

I, _____

_____ ("Student"), wish to participate in

_____ ("Travel Program"),
an International or Domestic Off-Campus Travel Program
offered by St. Olaf College (the "College"). I understand
that I have the opportunity to gain academic credit
through enrollment in the Travel Program. I realize that if
I do not sign this document, and comply with all its terms,
I will not be permitted to participate in the Travel Program.
In consideration for my participation in the Travel Program, I agree to the following:

1. Risks of International and Off-Campus Study.
I understand that participation in the College's Travel
Program involves risks not found in study at the College.
These risks include but are not limited to traveling to and
within, and returning from, one or more foreign countries;
foreign, political, legal, social and economic conditions;
different standards of design, safety and maintenance of
buildings, public places and conveyances; local medical practices and conditions; natural hazards; disease,
illness and injury; and crime. I understand that these and
other risks are further described in the U.S. Department
of State Consular Information Sheet and Travel Warning
for the country or countries to which I will be traveling. I
have accessed the applicable Information Sheet(s) and
Travel Warning(s) at http://travel.state.gov/travel/, or have
been provided with a copy of each by the College. I have
reviewed the Information Sheet(s) and Travel Warning(s),
and understand that all warnings contained therein are
incorporated by reference in these Conditions of Participation. I further understand that domestic travel also
involves risks that in some circumstances are similar to
those presented by travel abroad. I acknowledge that I am
aware of these risks, that the College has no control over
these risks, and that it is my responsibility alone to take
precautions to minimize such risks.

2. Standards of Conduct.
A.   If I am traveling abroad, I understand that each
      foreign country has its own laws and standards
      of acceptable conduct, including but not limited
      to those relating to religion, dress, manners,
      morals, politics, drug use and general conduct. I
      recognize that conduct contrary to those laws or
      standards could jeopardize my own health and
      safety, as well as the College's relationships with
      the country and its institutions. I will become
      informed of, and abide by, all applicable laws and
      standards for each country to or through which I
      will travel during the Travel Program.

B.   I will also comply with the College's rules,
      standards and instructions for student behavior.
      I agree that the College has the right to enforce
      these rules, standards and instructions and that it
      may impose restrictions, up to and including my
      removal from the Travel Program, for any violation
      of these rules, standards and instructions, or for
      any behavior that it, in its sole judgment, deems
      detrimental to or incompatible with the interest,
      harmony and welfare of the College, the Travel
      Program or other participants. I understand
      that if my participation in the Travel Program is
      terminated, I will receive no academic credit, and
      I consent to returning home at my own expense,
      with no refund of fees.

3. Release of Claims._____ (Applicant's Initials)
I understand that there are unavoidable risks in overseas
and domestic travel. I agree, on behalf of myself and
my legal representatives, heirs, successors and assigns,
to assume all the risks and responsibilities surrounding
my participation in the Travel Program. I, on behalf of
myself and my legal representatives, heirs, successors and
assigns, hereby RELEASE the College, and its regents,
officers, employees, agents, successors and assigns, from
any and all claims (including but not limited to claims for
negligence), causes of action, liabilities and costs which
I or any of my legal representatives, heirs, successors and
assigns may have or claim to have relating to or arising
out of my participation in the Travel Program, including, without limitation, any and all claims and causes of
action for property damage or bodily injury, illness and
death, caused by, related to or arising out of any action
or inaction of the College, its regents, officers, employees
or agents, except for such damages or injury as may be
caused by the gross negligence or willful misconduct of
the College, its regents, officers, employees or agents.

4. Indemnification.
I agree to indemnify, defend and hold harmless the College, and its regents, officers, employees, agents, successors and assigns, from any and all claims, liabilities and
costs asserted by or on behalf of me or any of my legal
representatives, heirs, successors and assigns within the
scope of the release in Paragraph 3 above.

5. Independent Travel.

Any independent traveling I do on weekends and academic holidays during the period covered by the Travel Program and after the conclusion of the Travel Program will be at my expense. The College is not responsible for me while I am traveling independently.

6. Health and Safety.

A. I represent that I have no health-related problems or concerns that would preclude or restrict my participation in the Travel Program.

B. I understand that if the Travel Program in which I am participating is scheduled to last longer than one month, I am required to have a physician complete the Report of Medical History form to be provided by the Office of International & Off-Campus Studies, and return it to the Office of International and Off-Campus Studies at least 60 days prior to departure.

C. I have sufficient health, accident, disability, hospitalization and personal property insurance to cover any injuries, illnesses or property damage that I may sustain or experience during my participation in the Travel Program. The College is not responsible for providing health or accident insurance benefits for me in connection with the Travel Program.

D. I authorize any representative of the College to secure dental and medical treatment for me if I am injured or become ill while participating in the Travel Program, including without limitation anesthetic and surgical treatment, and to sign authorization forms necessary to obtain the treatment. I assume full responsibility for all costs relating to or arising out of the treatment.

E. I understand that state and federal law (including but not limited to the Family Educational Rights & Privacy Act) obligates the College to keep certain information about me confidential. I also understand that certain people may want to know about my whereabouts and condition when I am participating in the Travel Program. For that reason, as to the following persons, I hereby waive my confidentiality rights as they relate to my whereabouts and condition when I am participating in the Travel Program, and authorize the College to disclose such information to (check as appropriate):

_____ My parents _____
_____ My spouse _____
_____ Other(s) _____

7. Miscellaneous.

A. Representations. I have secured or will secure the signature of my parent(s) or guardian(s) on the College's Parent/Guardian Conditions of Participation form. I further acknowledge that participation in this Travel Program is not required by the College and that while I may not participate in the Travel Program without signing this Agreement, my agreement to the provisions contained in these Conditions of Participation is otherwise wholly voluntary.

B. Governing Law. I agree that these Conditions of Participation will be governed by the laws of the State of Minnesota and that the venue for any legal proceedings relating to these Conditions of Participation shall be in the state of Minnesota.

I have carefully read these Conditions of Participation in their entirety and fully understand that by signing this document, I am giving up legal rights and remedies that may otherwise be available to me. I acknowledge that I have the right and opportunity to consult with an attorney or other advisor of my choice prior to signing these Conditions of Participation.

Note: The Student's parent/guardian must complete the Parent/Guardian Conditions of Participation

_____
DATE

_____
PRINTED NAME

_____
SIGNATURE

_____
HOME ADDRESS

_____
CITY, STATE, ZIP

_____
TELEPHONE NUMBER

Keep one copy for your records.
03/17/06

[Source: Adapted from St. Olaf College]

AUTHORIZATION FOR MEDICAL TREATMENT

I, _____ hereby authorize any represen-

tative of St. Olaf College (the "College") to secure dental and medical treatment for me if i am injured

or become ill while participation in a domestic or international travel program sponsored by the College,

including without limitation, anesthetic and surgical treatment. I agree that is such case, the College

representative may sign all authorization forms necessary to obtain the treatment. I assume full respon-

sibility for all costs relating to or arising out of the treatment.

_____
Student Name

_____
Signature   Date

I, _____, the parent/guardian of _____

(Name of Student, hereby authorize any representative of St. Olaf College (the "College") to secure den-

tal and medical treatment for my on/daughter/ward if he/she is injured or becomes ill while participating

in a domestic or international travel program sponsored by the College, including without limitation,

anesthetic and surgical treatment. I agree that in such case, the College representative may sign all

authorization forms necessary to obtain the treatment. I assume full responsibility for all costs relating to

or arising out of the treatment.

_____
Parent/Guardian Name

_____
Signature   Date

Keep one copy for your records

3/17/2006

[Source: Adapted from St. Olaf College]

CRISIS MANAGEMENT PLAN
INTERNATIONAL & OFF-CAMPUS STUDIES (IOS)
ST. OLAF COLLEGE

Orientation information, both printed and oral, contains information for faculty and students about health and safety issues related to International & Off-Campus travel. Adherence to this information, along with appropriate behavior, caution, and common sense, can prevent many crisis situations.

Decisions regarding program itineraries are made based on information from the US State Department, and on-site coordinators. IOS is prepared to make changes on short notice should a situation arise in-country that causes serious concern.

IOS will not allow students to begin a program at a site which is designated by the US State Department as existing under a travel warning.

1. CONDITIONS REQUIRING CRISIS MANAGEMENT
The staff of the International & Off-Campus Studies Office shall be contacted under the following circumstances:
- A. Serious illness, injury or death.
- B. Emotional or psychological stress that appears to require removal from the situation or professional attention.
- C. Being the victim of a crime - theft, assault, rape, harassment, etc. or being accused of committing a crime.
- D. A situation in-country arises that causes serious concern, i.e., a political uprising or a natural disaster.

2. COURSE OF ACTION:
St. Olaf faculty member or on-site coordinator or student (in case of incapacity of the faculty member or on-site coordinator) contacts the appropriate local authorities (i.e., police, US Embassy, medical personnel) to begin the local action necessary to handle the situation.

St. Olaf faculty member, on-site coordinator or student (in case of incapacity of the faculty member or on-site coordinator) contacts the appropriate person from the St. Olaf Emergency Contact Card. In most cases, that will be the Director or Assistant Director of International & Off-Campus Studies. There may be situations when it is also appropriate to contact other persons, i.e., the College Counseling Center or the Dean of Students.

Director of International & Off-Campus Studies is the official spokesperson to parents/officials/on-site coordinators. Director of International & Off-Campus Studies and/or Senior Director of College Communications will act as official spokesperson to media sources.

3. IOS ACTION
The staff of the International & Off-Campus Studies Office will initiate appropriate procedures. IOS will inform the Campus Program Adviser of any situation which involves on-campus intervention in an off-campus program.

A. Ill or Injured Student:
1. IOS will contact Travel Guard International to get them involved in evaluating the situation. Telephone: 877-370-4742.
2. IOS will contact parents of student to apprise them of the situation.
3. IOS will contact the Dean of Students.
4. IOS will contact Senior Director of College Communications.
5. Necessary action will be taken - provision for necessary medical care in-country, emergency evacuation, etc.
6. St. Olaf College will, if necessary, make funds available to cover emergency costs. Such expenses are the responsibility of student/parents, but St. Olaf will advance funds as needed to assure a timely solution of

1. Such expenses are the responsibility of student/parents, but St. Olaf will advance funds as needed to assure a timely solution of the situation.

B. Ill or Injured Faculty Member:

1. IOS will contact Travel Guard International to get them involved in evaluating the situation. Telephone: 877-370-4742.
2. IOS will contact family of the faculty member to apprise them of the situation.
3. IOS will contact the Dean of the College.
4. IOS will contact Senior Director of College Communications.
5. Necessary action will be taken - provision for necessary medical care in-country, emergency evacuation, etc.
6. St. Olaf College will, if necessary, make funds available to cover emergency costs. Such expenses are the responsibility of the faculty member, but St. Olaf will advance funds as needed to assure a timely solution of the situation.
7. If necessary, St. Olaf will make funds and staff available to insure adequate group supervision and continuation of program.

C. Death of Student or Faculty Member:

1. IOS will contact Travel Guard International to get them involved in repatriation efforts. Telephone: 877-370-4742.
2. IOS will contact parents of student or family of faculty member.
3. IOS will contact the Dean of Students or the Dean of the College who will, in turn, contact the St. Olaf Legal Counsel.
4. IOS will contact College Pastor.
5. IOS will contact Counseling Center to begin appropriate counseling for other members of the group.
6. IOS will contact Senior Director of College Communications.

D. Student or St. Olaf Faculty Member with emotional or psychological problems.

1. 1. IOS will contact the College Counselors. College Counselors will be in touch with student, faculty or on-site coordinator to evaluate the situation and make necessary recommendations.
2. 2. IOS will contact parents of student or family of faculty member.
3. 3. IOS will contact the Dean of Students or the Dean of the College.

E. Student or St. Olaf faculty member is the victim of a crime - theft, assault, rape, harassment, etc. or has been accused of committing a crime.

1. IOS will contact the Director of Human Resources & Affirmative Action Officer.
2. IOS will contact the Dean of Students and/or the Dean of the College.
3. IOS will contact Senior Director of College Communications.
4. If the incident is between two student members of the group, the Dean of Students has primary responsibility and College policy will apply.
5. f the incident is between a student member of the group and a St. Olaf faculty member, the Dean of the College has primary responsibility and College policy will apply.
6. If the incident is between a member of the group and an outside party, action taken will depend on legal requirements of the host country and the wishes of the group member.
7. College Legal Counsel will be contacted through the Dean of Students or Dean of the College, if necessary, for appropriate advice
8. IOS will contact local on-site authorities if necessary, for appropriate action.
9. IOS will contact parents of student and/or emergency contact as designated by student.

F. A situation in-country arises that causes serious concern, i.e., a political uprising or a natural disaster.

1. IOS will contact local program coordinators for a preliminary assessment.
2. IOS will contact the US State Department (see telephone numbers listed below) to receive the latest public announcements or travel warnings.
3. IOS will take necessary action based on advice from US State Department and local program coordinators. That could be evacuation, move to Embassy compound, remaining on-site and maintaining low profile, or quarantine.
4. When the status of the group has been accurately determined, IOS, in cooperation with the on-site coordinator or faculty member and with senior college administrators, will disseminate the information to appropriate parties.

5. IOS will contact Senior Director of College Communications.

4. CONTACTS

State Department Telephone Numbers:	
State Department Switchboard: (Call this number and ask for the country desk)	202-647-4000
Overseas Emergency:	202-647-5225
Consular Affairs	202-647-3600
After Hours Duty Officer	202-647-1512
Travel Warnings & Consular Information Sheets: http://travel.state.gov/travel_warnings.html	

LIST CAMPUS CONTACTS WITH EMAIL, OFFICE PHONE, HOME PHONE

Distribution List:

IOS Staff, Including Student Workers
Program Advisers
Participating Faculty
Dean of Students
Dean of the College
Director of Human Resources
Director of Counseling Center

Senior Director of College Communications
On-site Coordinators
College Legal Counsel
Director of Health Service

[Source: Adapted from St. Olaf College]

DISCIPLINARY RIGHTS AND PROCEDURES FOR INTERNATIONAL AND OFF-CAMPUS PROGRAMS-ACADEMIC AND NON ACADEMIC

In all international and off-campus courses and programs, students are subject to the University of St. Thomas Rules of Conduct as stated in this Student Policy Book.

In these cases the faculty or staff person who is in charge of supervising the course or program will have the full authority of the Dean of Students (for non-academic violations) and the appropriate academic dean (for academic violations) to adjudicate disciplinary violations of the Rules of Conduct.

When feasible, the faculty or staff person in charge should make every effort to informally resolve problems that arise. However, if a formal process is required, the following procedures for adjudicating violations of the Rules of Conduct will be followed. (The internal disciplinary processes and procedures described in the Student Policy Book do not apply to the international or off-campus program).

1. The staff or faculty member who administers the program onsite will notify students of alleged violations in writing.

2. A meeting will be held between the student accused and the faculty or staff member after the student receives the violation letter to determine if the student violated the Rules of Conduct.

3. After the meeting, the faculty or staff member will determine whether or not the Rules of Conduct have been violated and, in consultation with the International Education staff and the Dean of Students or the appropriate academic dean, determine sanctions, if applicable.

4. The student will receive a decision letter stating whether it has been determined that the student violated the Rules of Conduct and the appropriate sanction, if any. A copy of the decision letter will be forwarded to the appropriate academic dean for inclusion in the student's disciplinary file.

5. There is no appeal of discipline occurring in connection with an international or off-campus program. Faculty or staff in charge of the administration of the program have full authority for imposing sanctions, including sending the student home prior to the completion of the class or program.

6. In extreme cases, the faculty or staff member who oversees the class or program may, in consultation with International Education staff and the Dean of Students or appropriate academic dean, immediately suspend a student from the program and send the student home at the student's expense. The decision of the faculty or staff member is final.

Due to the unique nature of international or off-campus programs, disciplinary decisions made by faculty or staff during these programs are not subject to review by the Dean of Students. However, nothing precludes the dean from taking further disciplinary action if circumstances warrant.

[Source: Adapted from the University of St. Thomas]

PROVIDER'S PROOF OF INSURANCE

DISCLOSURE OF INSURANCE INFORMATION
(Name of Home Institution here [hereinafter "Home"])

Name of your institution _____

    A. Please provide Home with information about insurance for transportation services (e.g., buses, automobiles, vans, etc.) that your institution provides to Home students. Please include a copy of the proof of insurance.

        Name of insurance company: _____

        Insurance policy number: _____

    B. Please provide Home with information about property (e.g., fire, theft, etc.) insurance for the buildings and property at your institution where Home students live and study. Please include a copy of the proof of insurance.

        Name of insurance company: _____

        Insurance policy number: _____

    C. Please provide Home with information about liability insurance against accidental death or injury of Home students at your institution. Please include a copy of the proof of insurance.

        Name of insurance company: _____

        Insurance policy number: _____

Note: If you contract with other agencies to provide transportation, accommodations, or other services to Home students, please provide us with their insurance information as well.

Please return this completed form, with attachements to Host in the envelope provied.

Thank You.

[Source: Adapted from St. Olaf College]

PREVENTATIVE ACTIONS FOR FACULTY DIRECTORS OVERSEAS

Before Departure

☐ Leave a copy of your passport (first two pages) with the international office or department in case of replacement.

☐ Confirm that your emergency contact is updated with human resources.

☐ Confirm that the international office and department has received the latest itinerary, with all phone, fax, and e-mail numbers.

On-Site

☐ Make sure that all students and faculty have been listed with the U.S. embassy.

☐ Keep emergency contact numbers for each student. Establish a procedure for reaching the contacts in case of an emergency.

☐ Make sure students know how to reach you 24 hours a day in case of an emergency.

☐ Caution students about speculative communication and advise them to wait until clear information is available before contacting home.

☐ If students plan to travel independently, they should notify faculty directors of:

✗ their planned itinerary, giving as much information as possible about location (city/country), hotel/hostel, or other addresses and phone numbers and any other contact information;

✗ their mode of transportation, that is, all scheduled plane and train information, including fromto, departure, and arrival dates and times and plane or train numbers;

✗ their cell phone number if they have one (list the full number, including access and country codes).

[Source: Adapted from the University of St. Thomas]

BEHAVIOR CONTRACT

I, [student name], failed to [list infraction]. I understand that this requirement is meant to benefit the group, and that my behavior is a disruption to the successful functioning of thisacademic experience.

I understand that my actions impact the group, and that I must keep the group interests inmind when making decisions about my behavior.

I understand that if a similar infraction of course requirements occurs, I will be sent home atmy expense, in accordance with policy.

Student signature _____

[Source: Adapted from the University of St. Thomas]

SAMPLE EXPULSION FORM

[Student name], you have repeatedly violated the behavioral expectations set up in the study abroad agreement that you signed before departing for this course. In that agreement, you stated that you would comply with all rules and regulations issued by the organization, the faculty director, or any coordinating organization, and that you would:

a) not buy, sell, or use drugs at any time;

b) not engage in abusive use of alcohol;

c) not engage in disruptive behavior;

d) participate in all classes and scheduled activities unless ill; and

e) abide by dress and cultural codes suitable in the countries visited.

You were clearly reminded of [list infraction] during the predeparture meeting with the facultydirector on [list orientation date], and in the contract you signed on the day after your firstinfraction [list date of behavior contract].

Minimally, you have violated the conditions of the study abroad agreement by:
[List specific incidents.]_____

As stated on page X of the student policy book, "In all study abroad programs, students are subject to the rules of conduct…" and, "There is no appeal of discipline occurring in connection with a study abroad program." At the faculty director's discretion, you will not face further disciplinary action when you return.

Your behavior has not only been a clear violation of your contractual obligations, but also has been disruptive and disrespectful to your classmates and to your faculty director. At the orientation, and repeatedly thereafter, your faculty director has emphasized that this is first,and foremost an academic experience. Through your behavior you have demonstrated a lack,of commitment to that priority.

Arrangements have been made for your early departure. [List travel specifics.] Your parents or guardians will be notified by [administrator] to expect your early return.

Statement authored by faculty director.

I have read and understand this statement.

_____
Student signature
(not required)

[Source: Adapted from the University of St. Thomas]

INCIDENT REPORT

Please fill out this form as completely as possible. In the event of any legal action this form will serve as the basic official college record of what transpired and what actions were taken by, responsible college officials at the scene of the incident. Attach extra sheets as necessary and any documentary evidence. Fax a copy of your report to _____ _____ as soon as possible. Submit the complete original report and all supporting materials to_____ upon your return to the United States.

Date of incident_____ Location of incident _____

Time of incident_____ Were you present?_____

Name of student involved (please use a separate form for each student): _____

Names of other students involved: _____ _____

Brief description of what happened: _____ _____

Who provided this description if you were not a witness (please list all names):_____

_____

If you were not present, when were you informed? _____

What actions did you take? _____

If the student was transported to a hospital or clinic, please provide complete name of the

facility, its phone and fax numbers, and address _____

Names and phone numbers of all physicians who examined or treated the student

Dr. _____ Phone: _____

Dr. _____ Phone: _____

(turn over)

Exact names of any medications prescribed to the student *(please keep all packaging/inserts):*

Rx: _____

Rx:_____

Rx:_____

Rx:_____

Was the student conscious and capable of making informed judgments about his or her medical treatment?____ _____

_____

If the student was not capable of making medical decisions, who made any decisions? _____

What if any follow-up care was recommended? _____

Were the police or legal authorities notified of the incident or present at the scene?_____

Names and phone numbers of responsible legal authorities in charge of the case: _____

_____ Case#: _____

Was the U.S. or relevant embassy notified: Name and number of responsible consular officials involved in this

incident: _____

_____

Dates/times of contact with international student office and/or parents: _____

_____

_____

_____

— — — — —

Signature Date Time

[Source: Adapted from St. Olaf College]

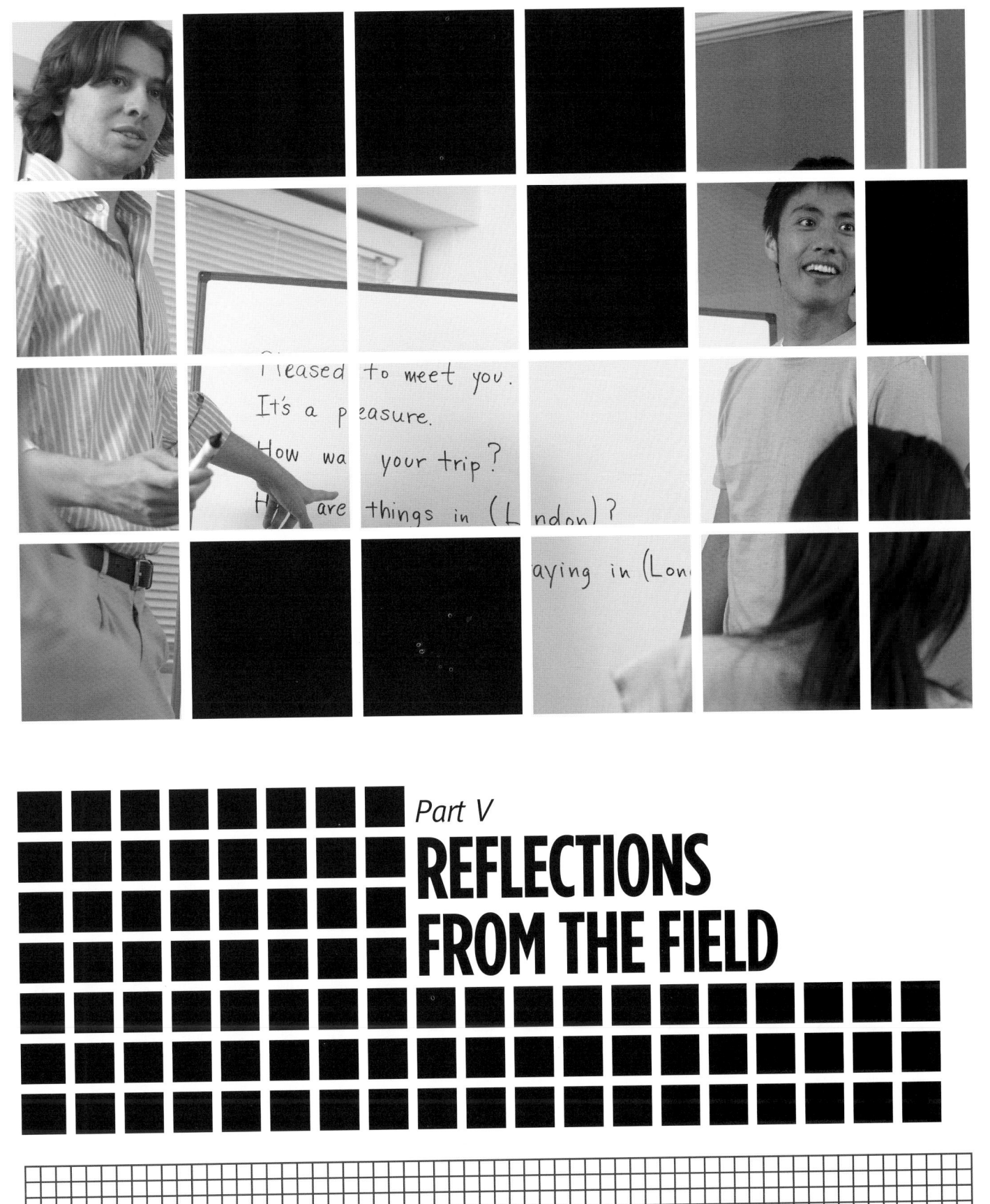

Part V

REFLECTIONS
FROM THE FIELD

REFLECTIONS FROM THE FIELD

Jonathan Hill

"Professor Hill, can we climb the mountain?"

How much freedom should you give students on overseas travel programs? Is one the professor? The parent? The pal? The fellow traveler? What happens when all the normal formalities of campus and the classroom are absent, when the usual protectiveness of office hours, and the fail-safe escape route of leaving campus are no longer there? How can one continue to maintain some measure of academic dignity and authority when the whole class, on a trip to the beach, has seen you knocked over by a wave and stagger back with a swimsuit full of sand? When your karaoke rendering of "Who Let the Dogs Out?" has caused the group to bow their heads and quietly leave the restaurant? These are the kinds of questions, keen and merciless, that confront the leader of overseas study programs.

The mountain my students referred to is one of the most spectacular in the Caribbean, the Petit Piton on the southwestern coast of Saint Lucia. It bursts out of the water like an arrow, a 2,400-foot volcanic spike, a shaft of tropical vegetation. Next to it is the Gros Piton, wider at the base, more blunted in shape, but still a fearsome climb, as I had discovered some years previously when I had been led up by Desir, a local fisherman and guide. Desir, lithe and spring-heeled, danced up. I spent most of the ascent on my belly, all of the descent on my backside. He delivered me back to my wife an assortment of trembling muscles and wobbly legs.

By the time I came to tell the story to my students — we were in Saint Lucia, the last stop in a month-long, January interim course, Literatures of the Eastern Caribbean — I had forgotten the toil and remembered only the achievement. As their eyes lit up, my account became more expansive, more vivid, even a little smug. I was playing to my audience. I provoked their question: "Professor, can we climb the mountain?"

There is nothing like overseas travel to shake students out of their familiar habits of thinking, feeling and judging. Nothing like travel stretches and exercises their sense of wonder, empathy and discovery. College is mainly about intellectual training and challenge. It is about catching young people at their most receptive, among like-minded peers, and pushing their cognitive powers to the limit. We academics privilege ideas and the intellect, but, at the end of the day, we know we do not live in an abstract world of ideas. However far we may travel in our minds, we must always return to the real world of our fellow humans — numerous, varied, baffling, inspiring, annoying. Overseas travel enforces that lesson. It is living through the senses. Felt experience, the evidence of one's eyes and ears, of tongue, touch and nose, re-root one in the physical world we all inhabit. It is a paradox that to most fully know those around us, we must leave them for a while. Only when we step away, or outside, can we see our own surroundings and society with freshness of perception.

In the West Indies my students lived for a month in African-Caribbean societies. They were the highly visible minority. They found, however, that they were not the target of hostility. West Indians are far better informed about the world than my students, and quite used to strangers. True, the women could be harassed, but that can happen anywhere—which does not make it any less reprehensible. My students had to retune their hearing to three different versions of their own language—solid Bajun, singsong Trinidadian, and percussive Saint Lucian. They discovered foods they had never heard of—breadfruit, cassava, christophine, dasheen, soursop; traveled on crowded min-buses; saw, side-by-side, lavish hotels and simple huts, and watched the evening sun drop, a ball of molten lead, into the Caribbean. They became aware of what it is like for tiny, fragile island nations to live in the shadow of the giant to the north, the giant that was them. They learned how these same nations had risen above the tragedy of their founding and achieved pride and endurance. What they had always taken for granted in their own culture, had never questioned about their American way of life, they now had to defend and justify. In seeing the West Indies, they saw their own country for the first time.

We speak of college as a time of opportunity. Overseas travel is hyper-opportunity. In the Middle Ages of legend knights errant went out and fought battles, traveled through dark forests, slew dragons, and defended the defenseless. Today, students errant accomplish deeds equally bold to earn their spurs of maturity—making it through passport control, walking along unknown streets, clubbing in foreign cities, exchanging curious glances with strangers, encountering exotic insects in their bedrooms, and living without coke or e-mail. Overseas study is adventure, of body and mind. For each student it is adventure as vivid and as dramatic as any tale ever told. That is why leading overseas programs is so gratifying. The education of the whole person takes place right in front of us. Each day we witness self-consciousness evolve into self-confidence. We become re-energized by our students, and glimpse through their enthusiasm and daring the limitlessness of human possibility. We have the urge to urge them on.

"Professor, can we climb the mountain?"

I said, "Yes." And to encourage them, I added, "It's just a steep walk."

I contacted my former guide, Desir. He decided, however, that they should climb not the Gros Piton, but the Petit Piton. "Professor, Petit much faster!" And since he was getting too old for this kind of thing, he arranged for three local youths to guide the group. The three young guides went barefoot, and every so often stopped for a little ganja.

For my students, the steep walk quickly turned into a terrifying climb. Sheer rock faces, knife narrow ledges, over-hanging boulders, precipitous fissures, and everyone hanging onto each other. I read later that the climb was not recommended for anyone who did not have mountaineering experience. My students had no such experience. All they had was their youth and one another. Somehow they got to the top—on the summit they even mooned a tourist helicopter—and somehow they got down. They arrived back wilted, tearful, and covered in scratches and grime. The ride back in the bus to their lodgings was silent, the mood resentful. "And you said it was just a steep walk."

But by the next day the climb had become one of the most thrilling experiences of their lives. The tale began to take shape, the moments of danger recalled first with amazement, then with laughter, then with pride. They had tested and proven their courage. They had overcome fear. They had slain a dragon in a strange land. In the zest of their youth and newfound self-belief, they were ready, yet again, for another challenge.

"Professor, can we walk on water?"

Jonathan Hill

Saint Olaf College

CONTRIBUTORS

Elise Amel is an associate professor of psychology at the University of St. Thomas in St. Paul, Minnesota. She has taught many courses abroad ranging from decisionmaking and workplace behavior to the intersection of psychoanalysis and feminism. She is currently working on a program focusing on conservation psychology in Western and Central Europe. Elise has served as chair of St. Thomas' Academic Review Committee for International Education. She and her husband have two young daughters who, thankfully, are very eager travelers.

Lisa Chieffo taught German and Italian in the University of Delaware's Department of Foreign Languages and Literatures before becoming study abroad coordinator there in 1993. As an undergraduate she studied in Vienna, Austria. As a graduate student, she spent a year in Tübingen, Germany, on a Fulbright scholarship and taught English for one semester in Bayreuth. Soon after receiving her Ed.D. degree in Educational Leadership in 2000, she became associate director for student programs in Delaware's Center for International Studies. Lisa has presented research findings related to short-term education abroad programs at several NAFSA annual conference sessions and has participated in the annual preconference workshop on short-term programs since 2003.

Jonathan Hill, born and raised in England, has taught in the St. Olaf College Department of English for the past 37 years. He has led many overseas study programs, including "Literatures of the Eastern Caribbean."

Peter Hovde is the former director of international education at Concordia College in Moorhead, Minnesota, serving from 1990 to 2003. His publication and presentation record mainly focuses on program design and impact, and he was instrumental in obtaining and directing three large grants aimed at getting faculty overseas to prepare

them to lead study abroad programs. The return to full-time teaching as professor of political science has allowed Peter to pursue his life-long passion—protection of the environment. From activist organizing to documentary film-making, environmental protection has enabled Peter to practice the activism Concordia's mission expects from its students. In what little remains of his leisure time, he enjoys golf and lake life with his wife Charlie.

Sue Jackson is director of off-campus programs at Whitworth College in Spokane, Washington. She holds a master's degree from Indiana University, is on the trainer corps of NAFSA: Association of International Educators, and has led NAFSA Professional Practice Workshops on "Developing and Administering Quality Short-Term Education Abroad Programs," and "Foundations of International Education: Education Abroad Advising." She has also presented on various topics at NAFSA regional conferences.

Julie Johnson is the former associate director of campus relations for the American InterContinental University. Her previous positions include associate director of study abroad at the University of Illinois at Urbana-Champaign and coordinator of study abroad at Ohio University. She has been active in NAFSA since 1995 and has been a member of the SECUSSA trainer corps since 1998. She has been a frequent presenter at regional and national conferences and has contributed to foundations and professional practice workshops, including "Developing and Administering Quality Short-Term Programs." She holds a B.A. in French and Psychology from Central Washington University and an M.A. in International Affairs from Ohio University. Her overseas experiences include teaching English in Japan and Chad and studying at the Université de Savoie, France, as a participant in the International Student Exchange Program.

Allison Keith is the director of U.S. operations for ACCENT International Consortium for Academic Programs Abroad, a program provider specializing in Western Europe, specifically France, Italy, Spain, and the United Kingdom. She has worked with ACCENT since the opening of its San Francisco headquarters in 1991. The San Francisco Center of ACCENT currently oversees the developmental, contractual, and predeparture phases of close to 100 programs annually, of which roughly half are short-term programs. Allison was a panel member for the NAFSA Professional Practice Workshop "Developing and Administering Quality Short-Term Education Abroad Programs" from 1997 through 2004.

Joe Kinsella has worked for 17 years in international education, focusing his energies on cross-cultural training, pedagogy, and assessment. Prior to becoming the associate vice president for international programs in 2006, Kinsella served as the director of study abroad at DePaul University from 2000 to 2006, and as the assistant director of study abroad from 1989 to 1996. His research in anthropology focuses on transnational and postcolonial identity formation and aesthetics. As an interpretive anthropologist, Kinsella's areas of specialization are in ethnographic and visual methodology exploring the production of material culture within global social and economic structures. He is particularly interested in nation-state formations and processes of globalization that shape nationalist and transnationalist social movements and identities. He has carried out field-work in Zimbabwe, Morocco, Uganda, Nicaragua, and Italy, and speaks Italian, limited French, and basic Shona. He has designed and orchestrated short-term faculty programs abroad for Academic Affairs and the Quality of Instruction Council, DePaul University, and has accompanied students and negotiated program details with local coordinators and program administrators on behalf of the Study Abroad Program at DePaul University.

Mark Lund is the director of international education at Luther College in Decorah, Iowa. He has been directing Luther's study abroad program since 1990. After receiving his Ph.D. in economics in 1975 from Iowa State University, he taught courses in introductory economics, international economics, and development economics at the undergraduate level. He has been involved in development work in Peru with USAID and in Zimbabwe and Tanzania with Lutheran World Federation/World Service. He continued teaching economics full time until 2000, when he added the directorship (administration and teaching) of Luther's International Studies Program to his study abroad duties. As a faculty leader he has led students on semester programs in Norway and Mexico and on January Term courses to Peru, Tanzania, Kenya, Zimbabwe, Turkey, Russia, and Nepal. Since 1990 he

has worked with over 120 Luther College faculty members as they developed study abroad programs or courses in 60 countries.

Susan MacNally, former assistant director at the University of Kansas Office of Study Abroad (KU OSA), worked at KU OSA for nine years in a variety of positions, including student data development, publications and outreach, and administering and developing short-term programs. At KU, she oversaw the administration of all KU short-term programs and developed approximately 25 new short-term programs. Susan was a panel member of the NAFSA Professional Practice Workshop "Developing Quality Short-Term Education Abroad Programs" from 1997 through 2002, and has been a member of the NAFSA trainer corps since 1998. She also served as Region II SECUSSA representative from 2000-2002.

Tim Pauly, in his role as the associate director of U.S. Operations at ACCENT, works with all partner schools to develop new programs—from initial idea to final contract. He has served on the NAFSA workshop panel "Developing and Administering Quality Short-Term Education Abroad Programs" for three years. Tim's international experience includes a semester in Rennes, France, a year in Brussels, and a year in Aix-en-Provence as a Rotary Club scholarship recipient. Personal travel to places such as the Caribbean, Canada, Australia, Africa, and Japan continues to fuel Tim's passion for international education. Originally from Georgia, Tim has found his home in San Francisco.

Patrick Quade served as the director of international and off-campus studies at St. Olaf College from 1997 until 2004. He currently serves as the interim director of International Education at Gustavus Adolphus College. He holds the rank of emeritus professor at St. Olaf. He is a graduate of St. Olaf College (1965), the University of Wisconsin (M.A. in 1968), and the University of Minnesota (M.F.A. in 1972). In 2005-2006 he was a visiting professor and international education consultant at California Lutheran University in Thousand Oaks, California. He has led many student and adult-learner groups on programs to various parts of the world. In 1993 and again in 1996 he led the St. Olaf College Global Semester Program, a five-month-long study program with 28 students in Switzerland, Egypt, Israel, India, Nepal, Hong Kong, Japan, and Korea. In 2004 he led the student five-month Term in the Middle East program to Turkey, Morocco, Egypt, and Greece. He is a veteran of 13 Theater in London January short-term study programs. In 1976 and 1980 he served as the resident director of the Associate Colleges of the Midwest Arts of London and Florence Program.

Mickey Slind has spent more than 25 years in international education. During her career, she worked as a study abroad adviser, program administrator, resident director, and program representative. She served in various international education positions at Hamline University in St. Paul, Minnesota, the University of Minnesota in Minneapolis, the American Institute For Foreign Study in Stamford, Connecticut, and the Institute for Study Abroad at Butler University in Indianapolis, Indiana. From 1993 to 1996, Slind was a member of NAFSA's Insurance Advisory Committee. In 1993, she organized and chaired the first NAFSA conference workshop on short-term programs, "Designing and Administering the Short-Term Study Abroad Program." Over the years, Slind has been a frequent presenter and contributor on issues related to short-term programs and health and safety issues in education abroad. In 1995, SECUSSA presented Slind with its Lily von Klemperer Award for service and commitment to the field of study abroad, and in 2004, she received the Education Abroad Leadership Award. Slind has held various leadership positions within NAFSA and is a past chair of SECUSSA. Upon her retirement in 2004, NAFSA presented its Life Member Award to Mickey Slind.

Melissa Smith-Simonet is originally from New York and a graduate of the State University of New York-Albany. She has been living in Paris since 1987 and has worked with ACCENT since 1989, first as administrative assistant, then Paris program and housing coordinator, and since 1998 as ACCENT Paris director. Melissa is the director of an international team of 11 administrative staff and 15 faculty and is responsible for the management and administration of more than 50 study abroad programs per year in Paris.

Sarah E. Spencer directs the short-term off-campus program at the University of St. Thomas. She has overseen the growth of the institution's short-term programs, which have increased dramatically from three to 32 since her arrival in 1993. She holds a B.A. from St. Olaf College and an M.A. in English from the University of St. Thomas. She has studied and worked in England as well as traveling extensively. Sarah cochaired the NAFSA Professional Practice Workshop "Developing and Administrating Quality Short-Term Education Abroad Programs" from 1997-2003, frequently presents at regional and national conferences, and is a member of NAFSA's trainer corps. She also served as the Region IV SECUSSA representative and the SECUSSA representative to education and training. Recently, she has taught NAFSA's "Preparing Faculty to Direct Programs" workshop at the annual conference.

John Sunnygard is the director of the Center for Global Educational Opportunities (C-GEO) at the University of Texas at Austin. C-GEO is one of the nation's largest study abroad

programs. John has been instrumental in establishing a successful "Maymester Abroad" program on campus; developing summer programs in Argentina, Brazil, France, India, Mexico, Spain, and the Czech Republic. He serves on the provost's International Education Task Force, the Engineering Study Abroad Committee, the Student Deans Advisory Group, and the European Studies Center Faculty Advisory Board. Off-campus, John serves on CIEE's ACB, IES' Academic Council, Arcadia University's NAB, and the School for Field Studies Board of Trustees. John has presented at several professional conferences including SIETAR Europa, SEITAR Japan, AIESA, NAFSA, and CIEE. He has also worked for IES in Chicago and London. John has taught in the UK, Japan, and Morocco. John is a returned Peace Corps volunteer. He holds a B.A. from the University of Nebraska-Lincoln and an MIM from Thunderbird, the American Graduate School of International Management.

Kathy Tuma is the associate director of the International and Off-Campus Studies Office at St. Olaf College in Northfield, Minnesota. She has worked with St. Olaf's short-term programs for all of her 32 years at the college (yes, they had airplanes that could fly across the oceans that long ago). St. Olaf continually ranks as one of the nation's top private, liberal arts institutions in sending students abroad. In 1995, Kathy had the privilege of participating in and learning from the Fulbright Program for Administrators in Germany. She first presented a session on short-term programs at NAFSA's Region IV conference in 1995. In 1996, she presented the first short-term study abroad workshop at NAFSA's annual conference and has done so every year since. In addition, she is a member of NAFSA's trainer corps. Beyond working to help promote the cause of quality short-term programs, Kathy has presented other professional practice workshops, including "Foundations of International Education: Education Abroad Advising and Administration of Education Abroad Programs." She has also participated in a number of other workshops and sessions related to health, safety, and liability issues.

Anders Uhrskov has been associated with Denmark's International Study Program (DIS), which is affiliated with the University of Copenhagen, since 1978. He has been director for DIS since 1987. He holds a Cand.mag. degree in political science from the University of Copenhagen (1977), and has held various academic positions, including associate professor at Statens Kursus (1977–1978) and visiting scholar at the University of California-Berkeley (1985). He has also been a member of the NAFSA Board of Directors (1988–1991 and 2006-2008); the Board, Denmark-America Foundation (since 1992); Academic Selection Committee; and Crown Prince Frederik's Fund (since 1993). He holds an honorary doctoral degree from Whittier College (1999) and has presented with the NAFSA Professional Practice Workshop "Developing and Administering Quality Short-Term Education Abroad Programs" since 1999.

Dawn White is director of international faculty services at Portland State University (PSU). In a career at PSU spanning nearly three decades, she has also served as director of international education services, which encompassed education abroad and services to international students and scholars. A regular presenter of sessions and workshops at NAFSA's annual conferences and in Region I, Dawn cowrote (with John Pearson and Nancy Stubbs) the "NAFSA/AT&T Travel Tips" booklet published in 1998 and the revised "Basic Facts on Study Abroad," published in 1997 by NAFSA, CIEE, and IIE. She served Region I as chair in 1996-1997 and has held other leadership positions in her region.

WEB RESOURCES

R

Culturegrams
http://www.culturegrams.com
- ☐ Individual country descriptions

U.S. State Department
http://travel.state.gov
- ☐ How to apply for a U.S. passport
- ☐ Entry requirements to foreign countries for U.S. citizens (includes visa requirements)
- ☐ U.S. State Department Travel Warnings
- ☐ Tips for travelers for different world regions from the U.S. State Department

Centers for Disease Control
http://www.cdc.gov
- ☐ Health Information by country

Embassies
http://www.embassyworld.com
- ☐ U.S. embassies and national embassies in the United States

Mobility International
http://www.miusa.org
- ☐ Information on traveling abroad for people with disabilities

Lesbigay Links
http://www.indiana.edu/~overseas/lesbigay
- ☐ Links to sites dealing with issues involving the lesbigay community and international travel

Insurance
http://www.insuremytrip.com
- ☐ Offers information on 28 different plans and allows you to compare each plan online.
- ☐ This site does not include information on every travel insurance plan available.

http://www.studyabroadinsurance.com
- ☐ Travel insurance offered by a local travelcompany specializing in student travel

http://www.travelguard.com
- ☐ Offers trip cancellation insurance

International Student Identity Card
https://www.myisic.com/MyISIC/

IAMAT: International Association for Medical Assistance to Travelers
http://www.iamat.org
- ☐ Nonprofit organization that provides medication information around the world.

U.S. Postal Service
http://www.uspsglobal.com
- ☐ International shipping rules, regulations, and rates. Good links, too.

Currency Conversions
http://www.xe.net/ucc/

MapQuest
http://www.mapquest.com/
- ☐ Maps of various cities around the world

Tourism
http://www.hostels.com/hostel.menu.html
- ☐ Hostels by country

http://www.iyhf.org/
- ☐ International Youth Hostels

http://www.travelocity.com
- ☐ Travelocity

http://www.railpass.com/

http://www.raileurope.com
- ☐ European and British rail passes

Travel Guides
http://www.lonelyplanet.com
- ☐ Lonely Planet homepage

http://www.roughguides.com
- ☐ Rough Guides

http://www.letsgo.com
- ☐ Let's Go

http://www.fodors.com
- ☐ Fodor's

INDEX